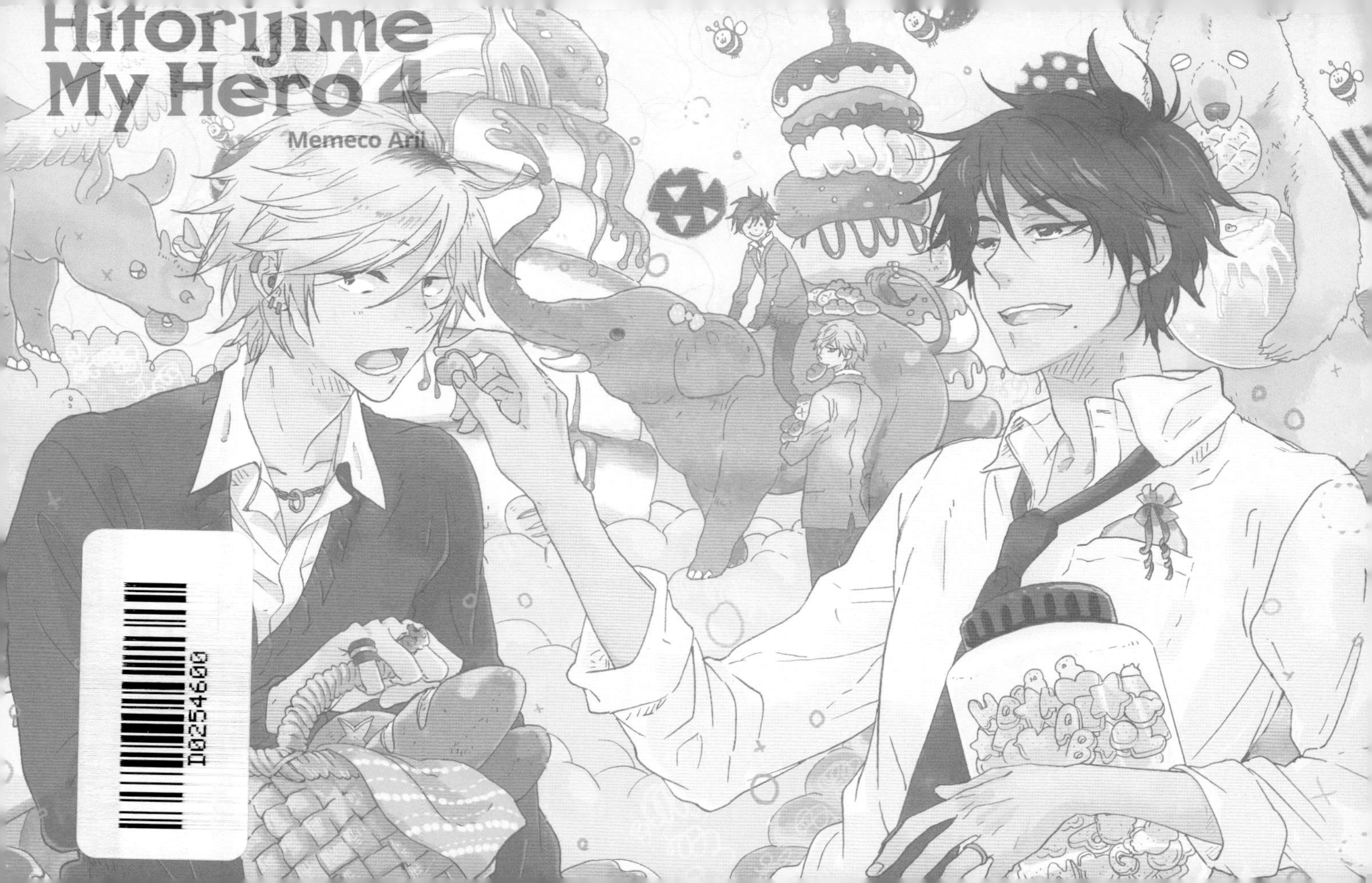
Hitorijime
My Hero 4
Memeco Arii

Hitorijime My Hero CONTENTS

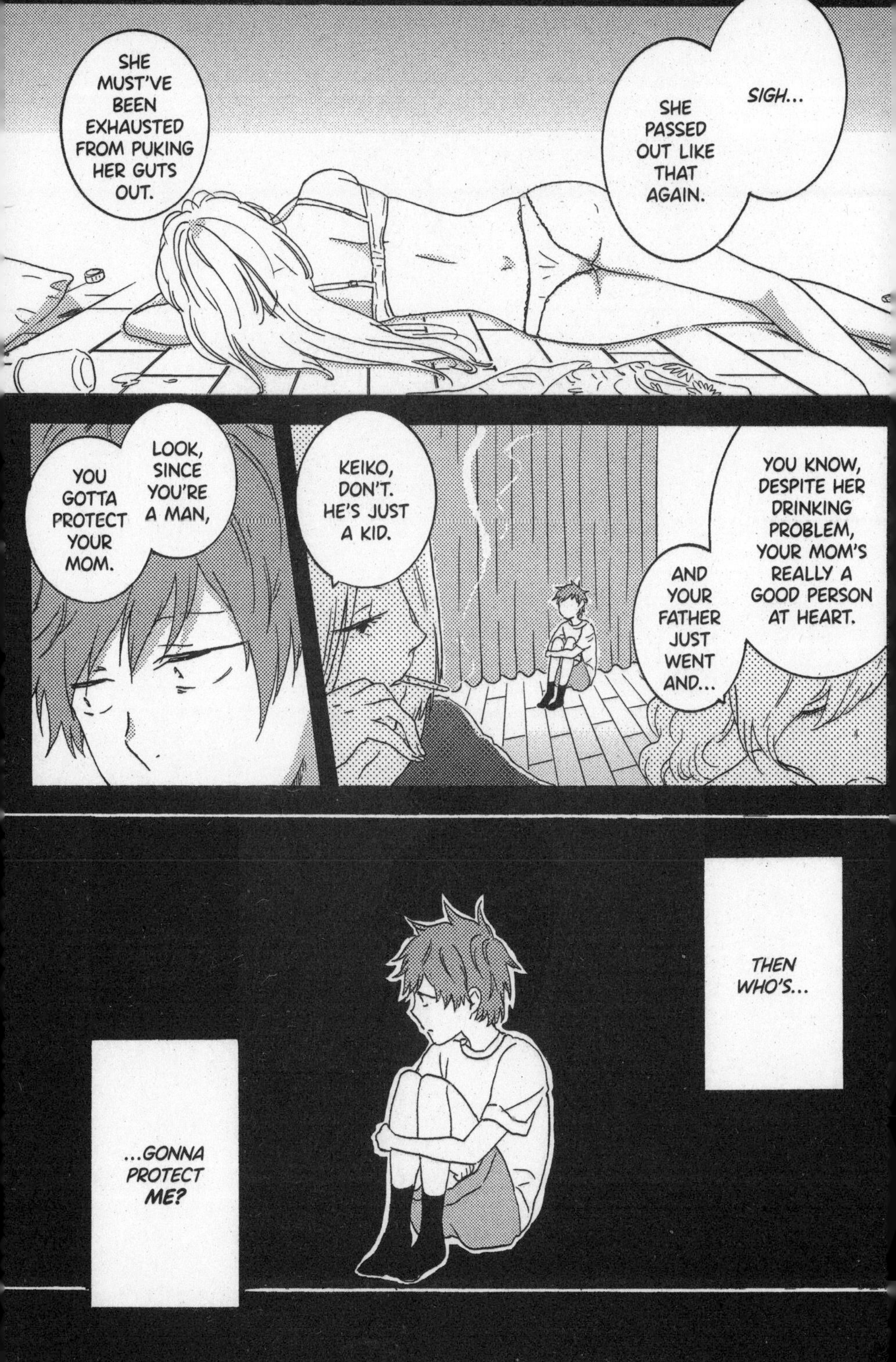
SIGH...
SHE PASSED OUT LIKE THAT AGAIN.
SHE MUST'VE BEEN EXHAUSTED FROM PUKING HER GUTS OUT.
YOU KNOW, DESPITE HER DRINKING PROBLEM, YOUR MOM'S REALLY A GOOD PERSON AT HEART.
AND YOUR FATHER JUST WENT AND...
KEIKO, DON'T. HE'S JUST A KID.
LOOK, SINCE YOU'RE A MAN,
YOU GOTTA PROTECT YOUR MOM.
THEN WHO'S...
...GONNA PROTECT ME?

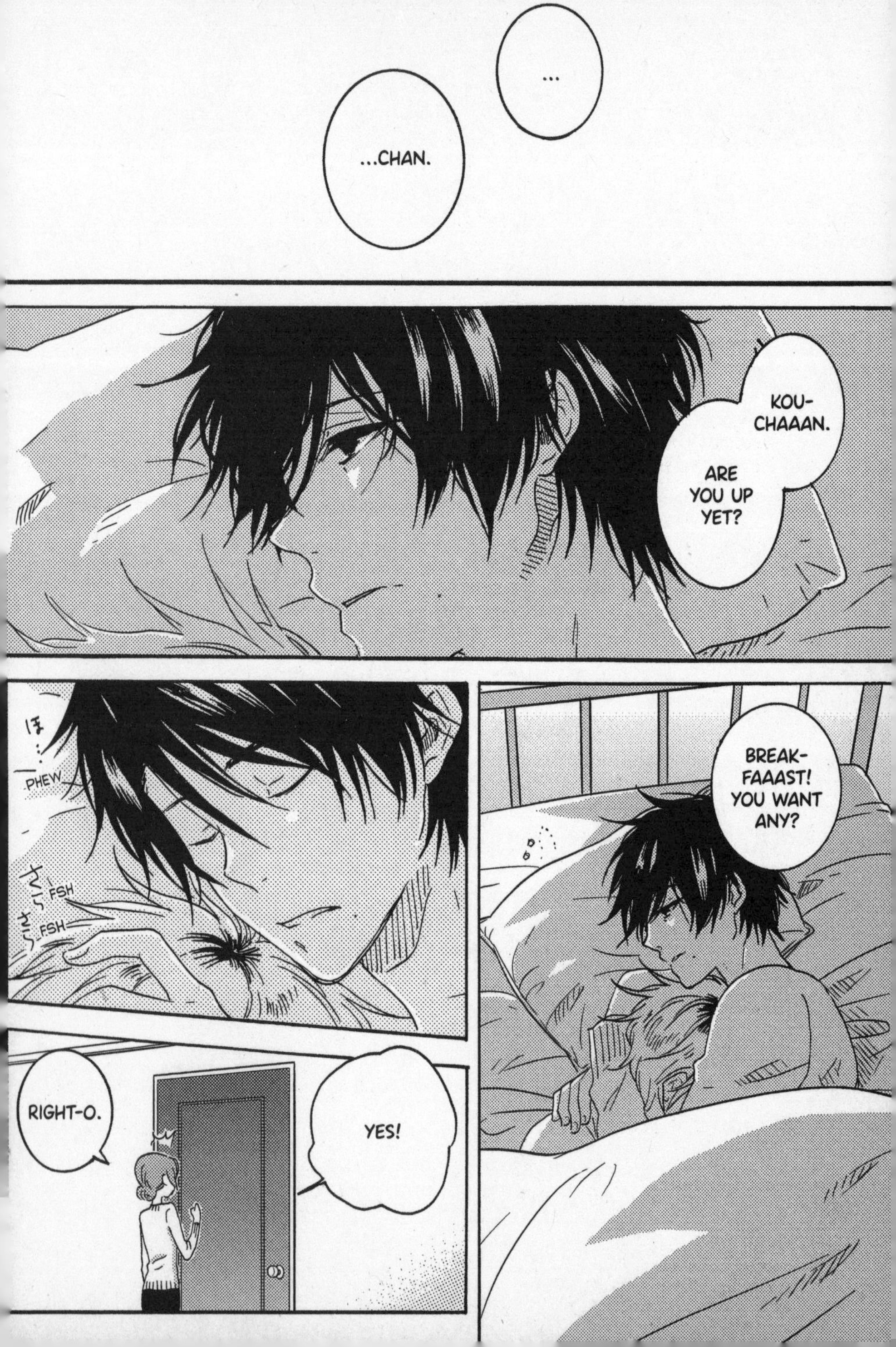
...
...CHAN.
KOU-CHAAAN.
ARE YOU UP YET?
BREAK-FAAAST! YOU WANT ANY?
PHEW
FSH
FSH
YES!
RIGHT-O.

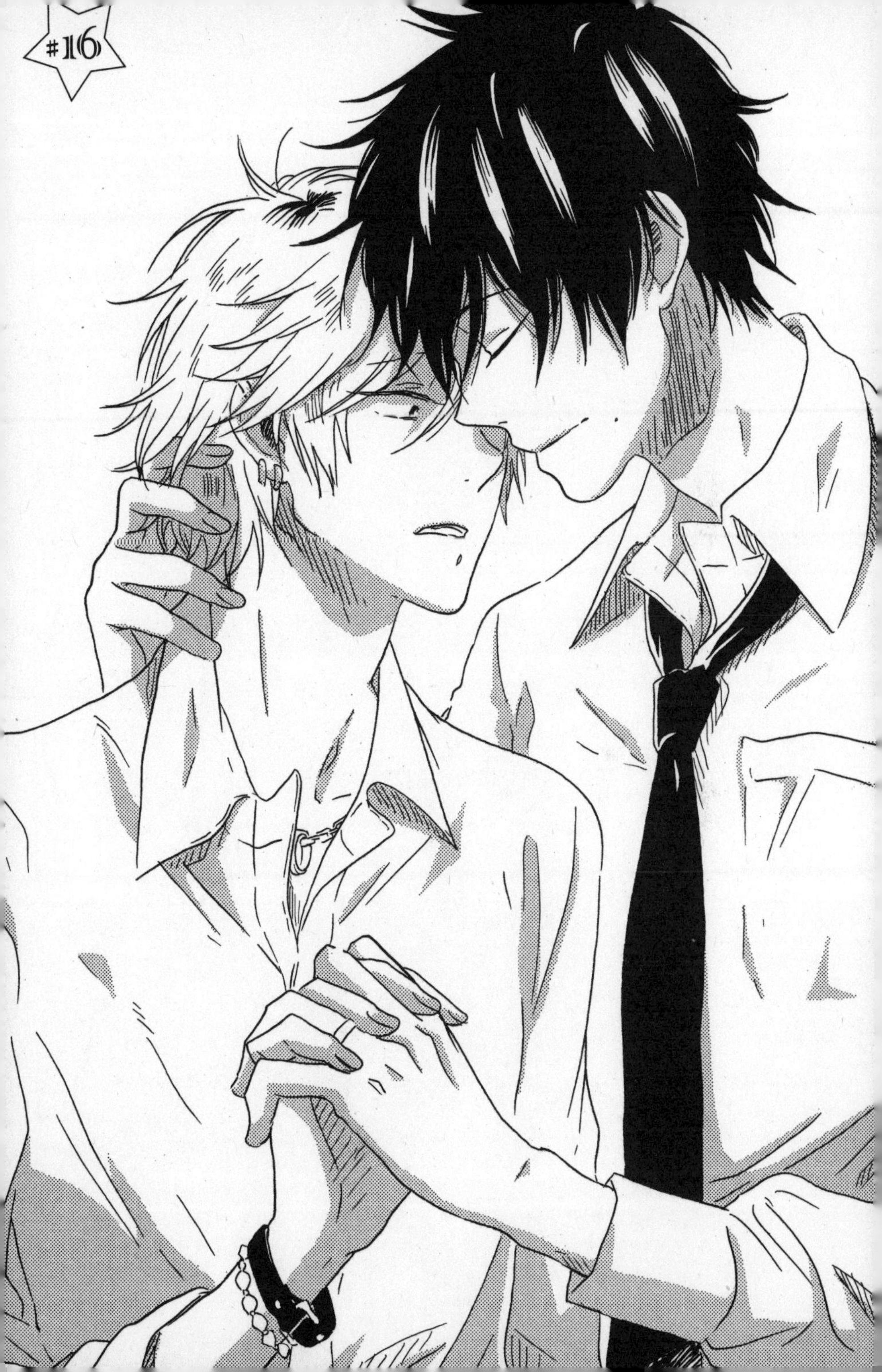
#16

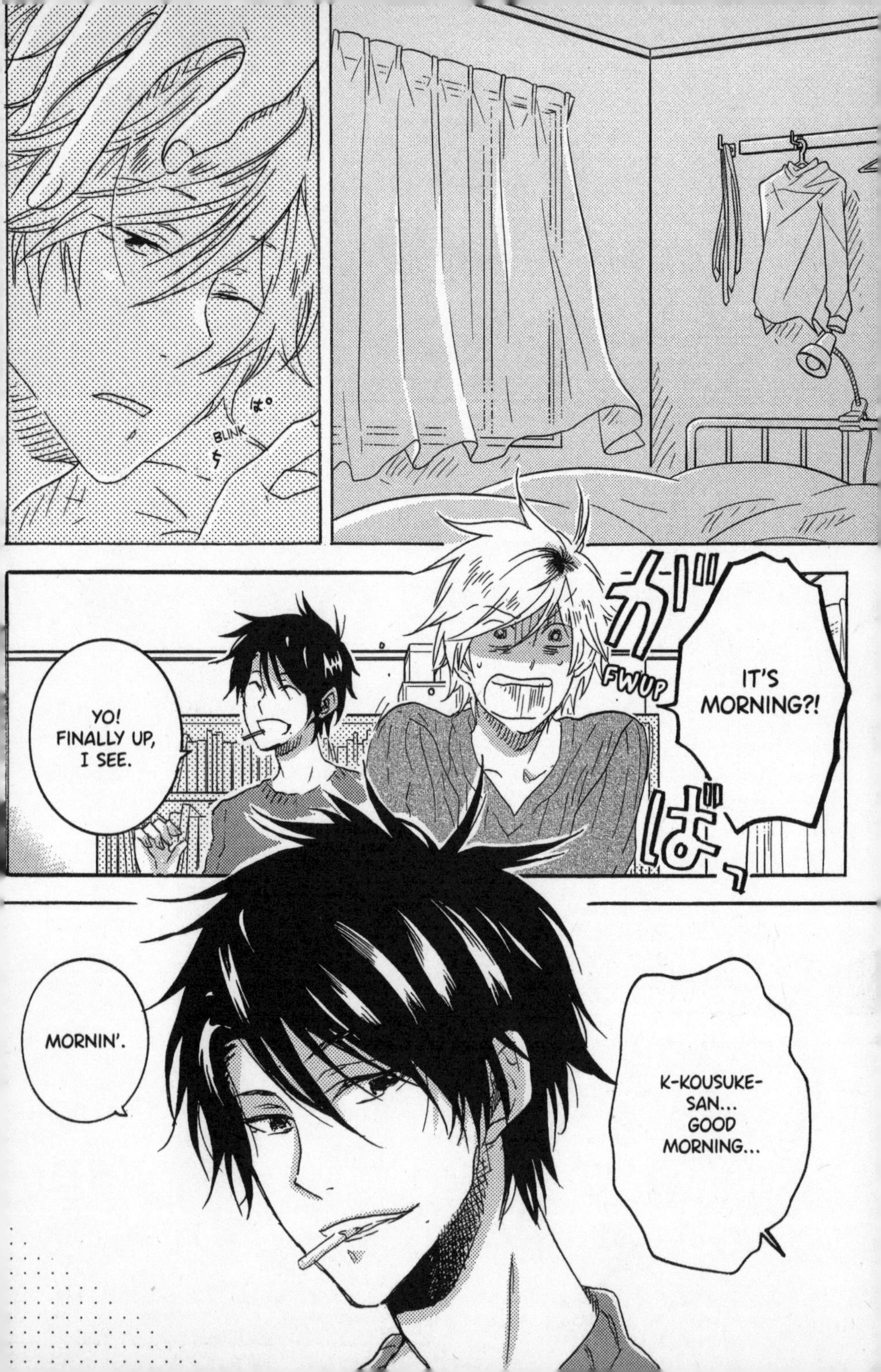
ぱ。
BLINK
がばっ
FWUP
IT'S MORNING?!
YO! FINALLY UP, I SEE.
K-KOUSUKE-SAN... GOOD MORNING...
MORNIN'.

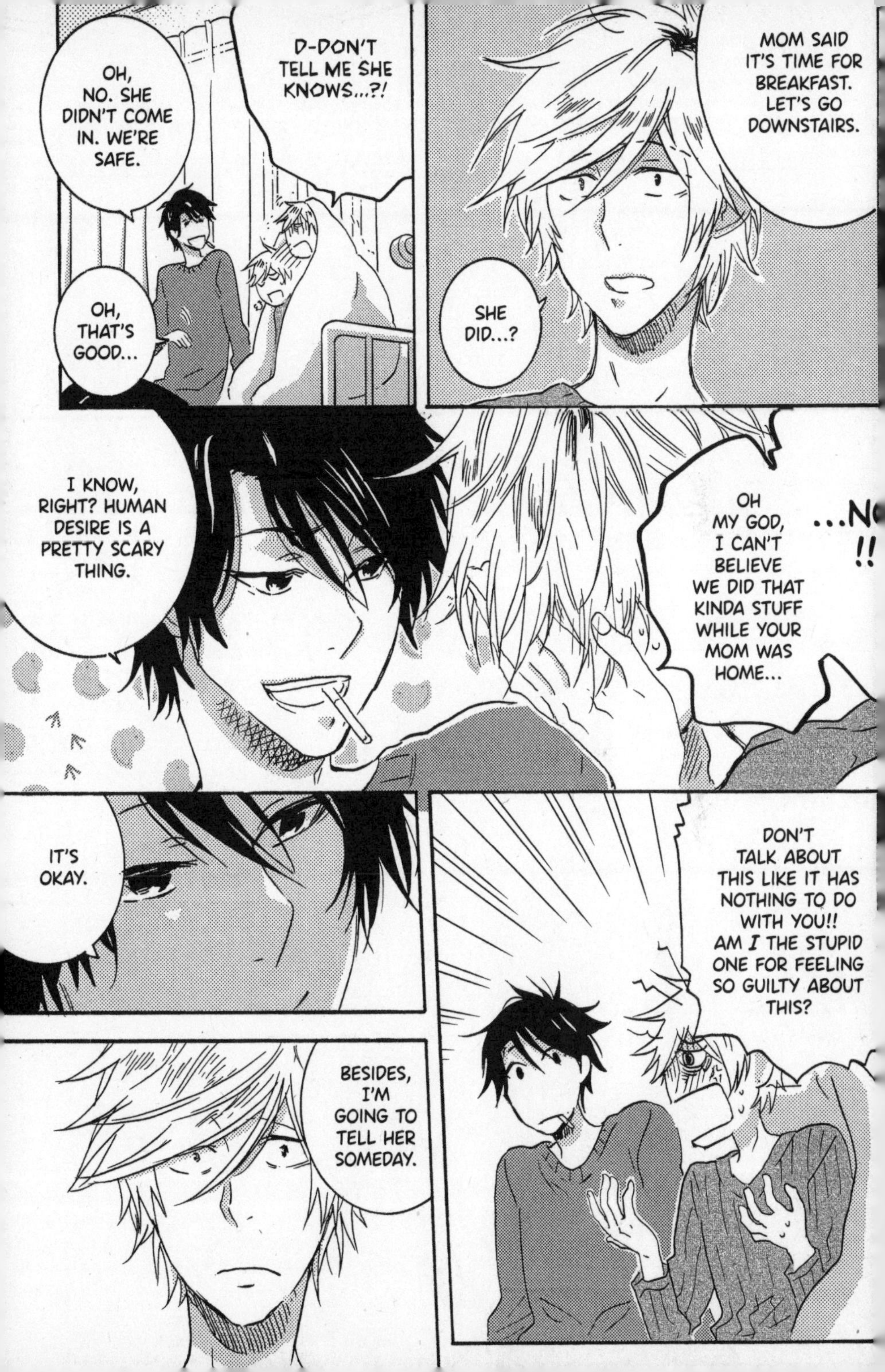
MOM SAID IT'S TIME FOR BREAKFAST. LET'S GO DOWNSTAIRS.
SHE DID...?
D-DON'T TELL ME SHE KNOWS...?!
OH, NO. SHE DIDN'T COME IN. WE'RE SAFE.
OH, THAT'S GOOD...
...N !!
OH MY GOD, I CAN'T BELIEVE WE DID THAT KINDA STUFF WHILE YOUR MOM WAS HOME...
I KNOW, RIGHT? HUMAN DESIRE IS A PRETTY SCARY THING.
DON'T TALK ABOUT THIS LIKE IT HAS NOTHING TO DO WITH YOU!! AM *I* THE STUPID ONE FOR FEELING SO GUILTY ABOUT THIS?
IT'S OKAY.
BESIDES, I'M GOING TO TELL HER SOMEDAY.

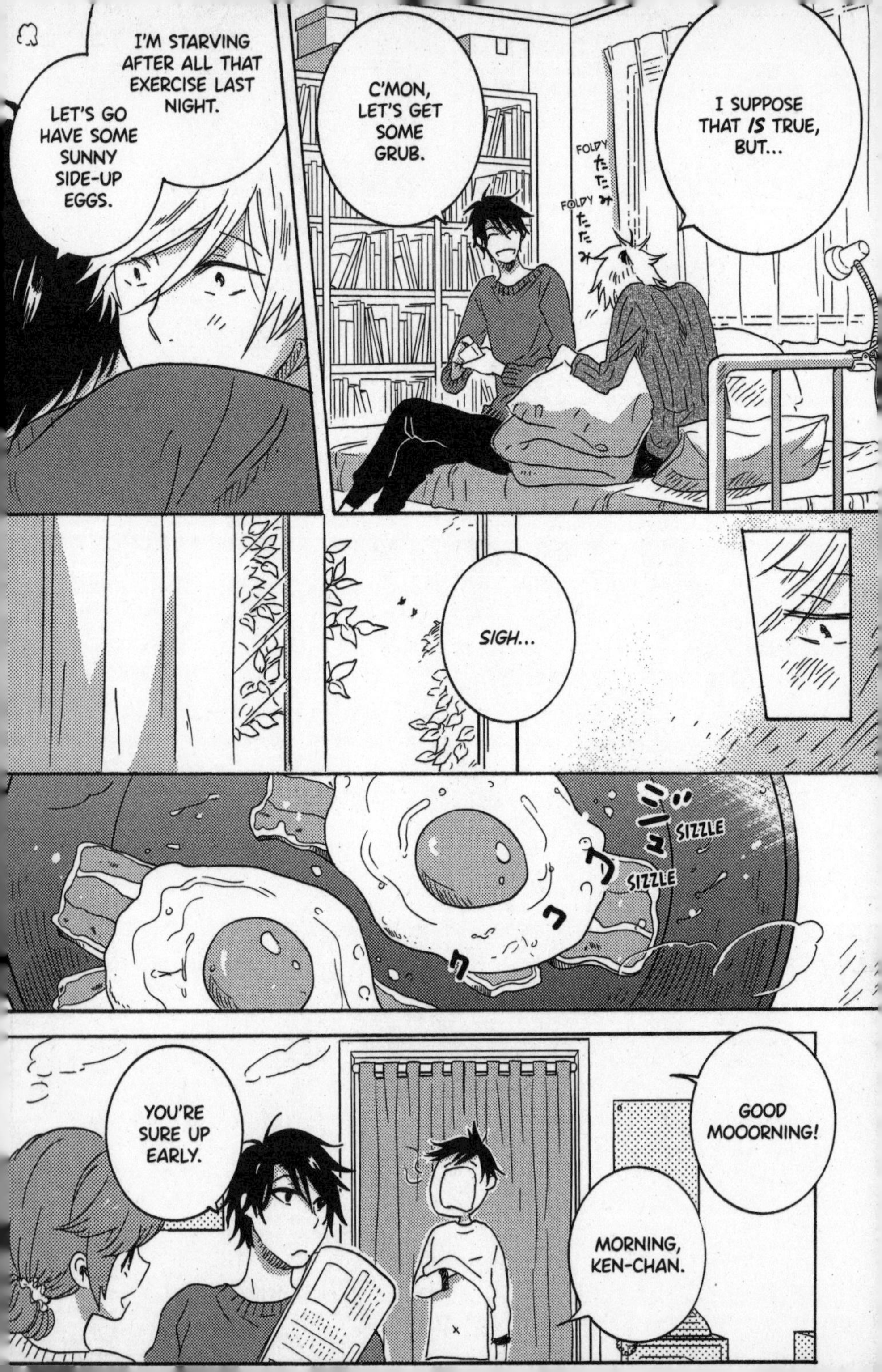
I SUPPOSE THAT *IS* TRUE, BUT...
FOLDY たたみ
FOLDY たたみ
C'MON, LET'S GET SOME GRUB.
I'M STARVING AFTER ALL THAT EXERCISE LAST NIGHT.
LET'S GO HAVE SOME SUNNY SIDE-UP EGGS.
SIGH...
SIZZLE
SIZZLE
GOOD MOOORNING!
MORNING, KEN-CHAN.
YOU'RE SURE UP EARLY.

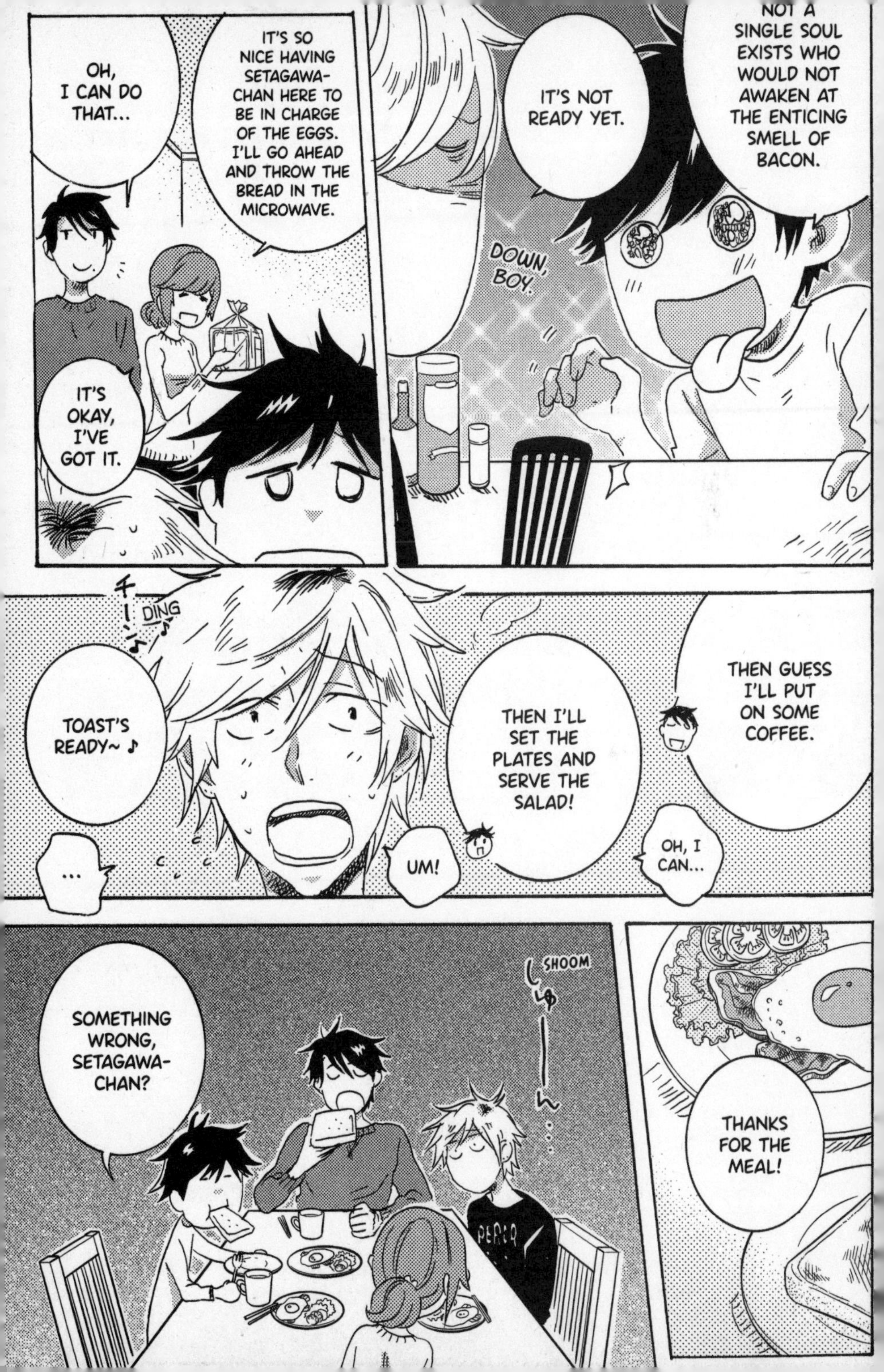
NOT A SINGLE SOUL EXISTS WHO WOULD NOT AWAKEN AT THE ENTICING SMELL OF BACON.
IT'S NOT READY YET.
DOWN, BOY.
IT'S SO NICE HAVING SETAGAWA-CHAN HERE TO BE IN CHARGE OF THE EGGS. I'LL GO AHEAD AND THROW THE BREAD IN THE MICROWAVE.
OH, I CAN DO THAT...
IT'S OKAY, I'VE GOT IT.
THEN GUESS I'LL PUT ON SOME COFFEE.
THEN I'LL SET THE PLATES AND SERVE THE SALAD!
OH, I CAN...
UM!
チーン♪ DING
TOAST'S READY~ ♪
...
THANKS FOR THE MEAL!
しゅーーん… SHOOM
SOMETHING WRONG, SETAGAWA-CHAN?

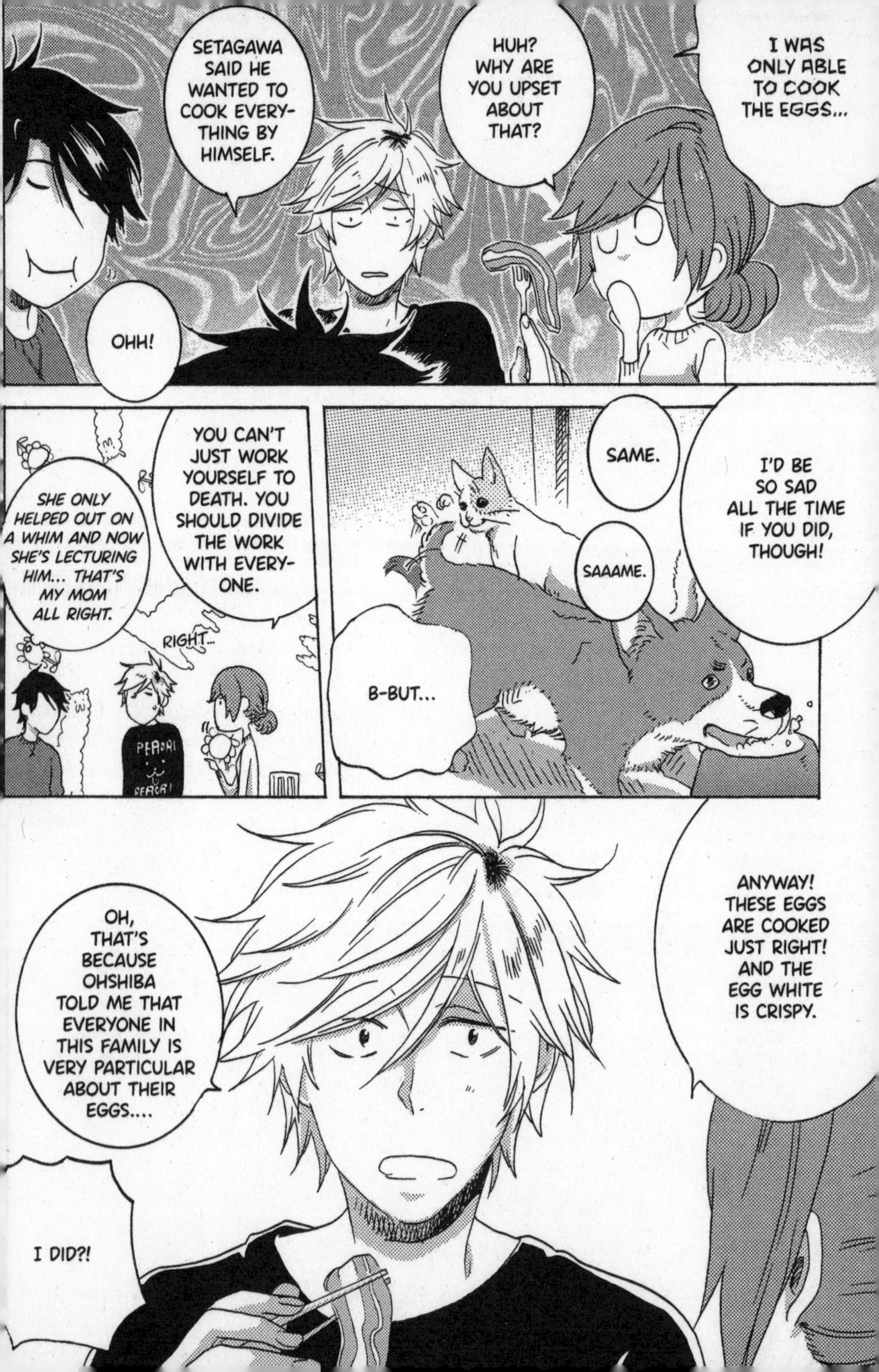
I WAS ONLY ABLE TO COOK THE EGGS...
HUH? WHY ARE YOU UPSET ABOUT THAT?
SETAGAWA SAID HE WANTED TO COOK EVERY-THING BY HIMSELF.
OHH!
I'D BE SO SAD ALL THE TIME IF YOU DID, THOUGH!
SAME.
SAAAME.
B-BUT...
YOU CAN'T JUST WORK YOURSELF TO DEATH. YOU SHOULD DIVIDE THE WORK WITH EVERY-ONE.
SHE ONLY HELPED OUT ON A WHIM AND NOW SHE'S LECTURING HIM... THAT'S MY MOM ALL RIGHT.
RIGHT...
ANYWAY! THESE EGGS ARE COOKED JUST RIGHT! AND THE EGG WHITE IS CRISPY.
OH, THAT'S BECAUSE OHSHIBA TOLD ME THAT EVERYONE IN THIS FAMILY IS VERY PARTICULAR ABOUT THEIR EGGS....
I DID?!

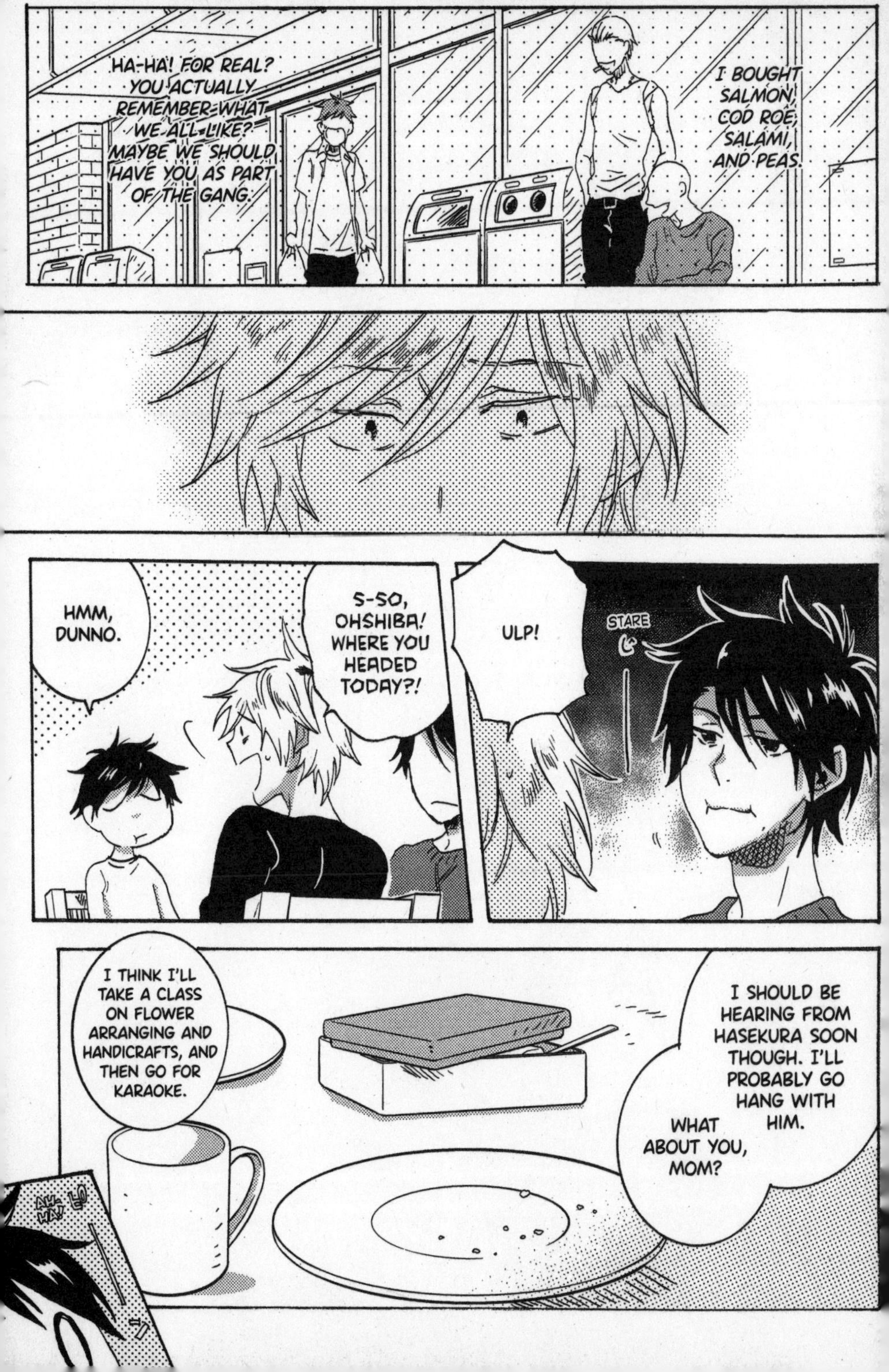
I BOUGHT SALMON, COD ROE, SALAMI, AND PEAS.
HA-HA! FOR REAL? YOU ACTUALLY REMEMBER WHAT WE ALL LIKE? MAYBE WE SHOULD HAVE YOU AS PART OF THE GANG.
STARE
ULP!
S-SO, OHSHIBA! WHERE YOU HEADED TODAY?!
HMM, DUNNO.
I SHOULD BE HEARING FROM HASEKURA SOON THOUGH. I'LL PROBABLY GO HANG WITH HIM.
WHAT ABOUT YOU, MOM?
I THINK I'LL TAKE A CLASS ON FLOWER ARRANGING AND HANDICRAFTS, AND THEN GO FOR KARAOKE.
AH-HA!

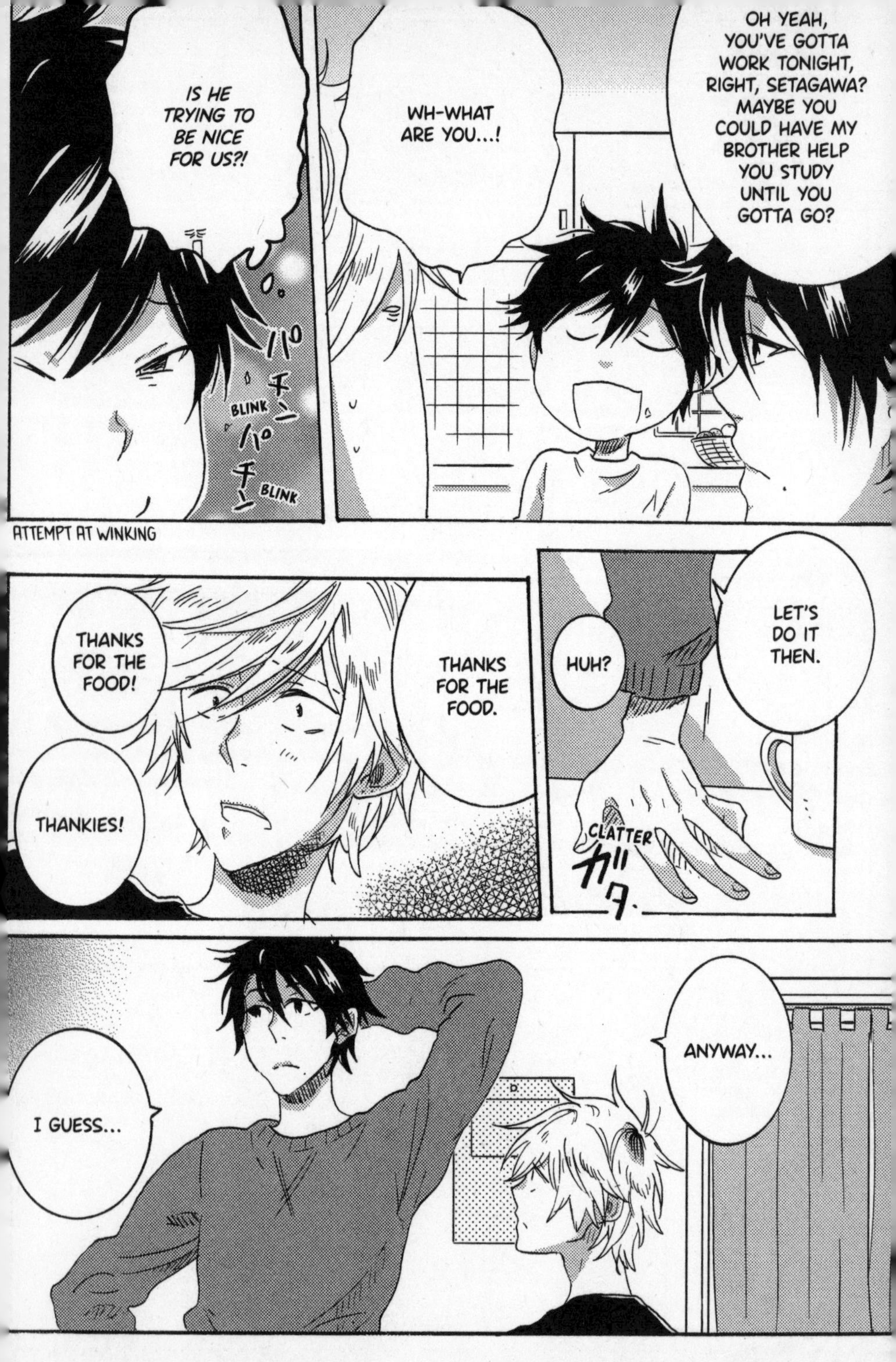
OH YEAH, YOU'VE GOTTA WORK TONIGHT, RIGHT, SETAGAWA? MAYBE YOU COULD HAVE MY BROTHER HELP YOU STUDY UNTIL YOU GOTTA GO?
WH-WHAT ARE YOU...!
IS HE TRYING TO BE NICE FOR US?!
BLINK
BLINK
ATTEMPT AT WINKING
LET'S DO IT THEN.
HUH?
CLATTER
THANKS FOR THE FOOD.
THANKS FOR THE FOOD!
THANKIES!
ANYWAY...
I GUESS...

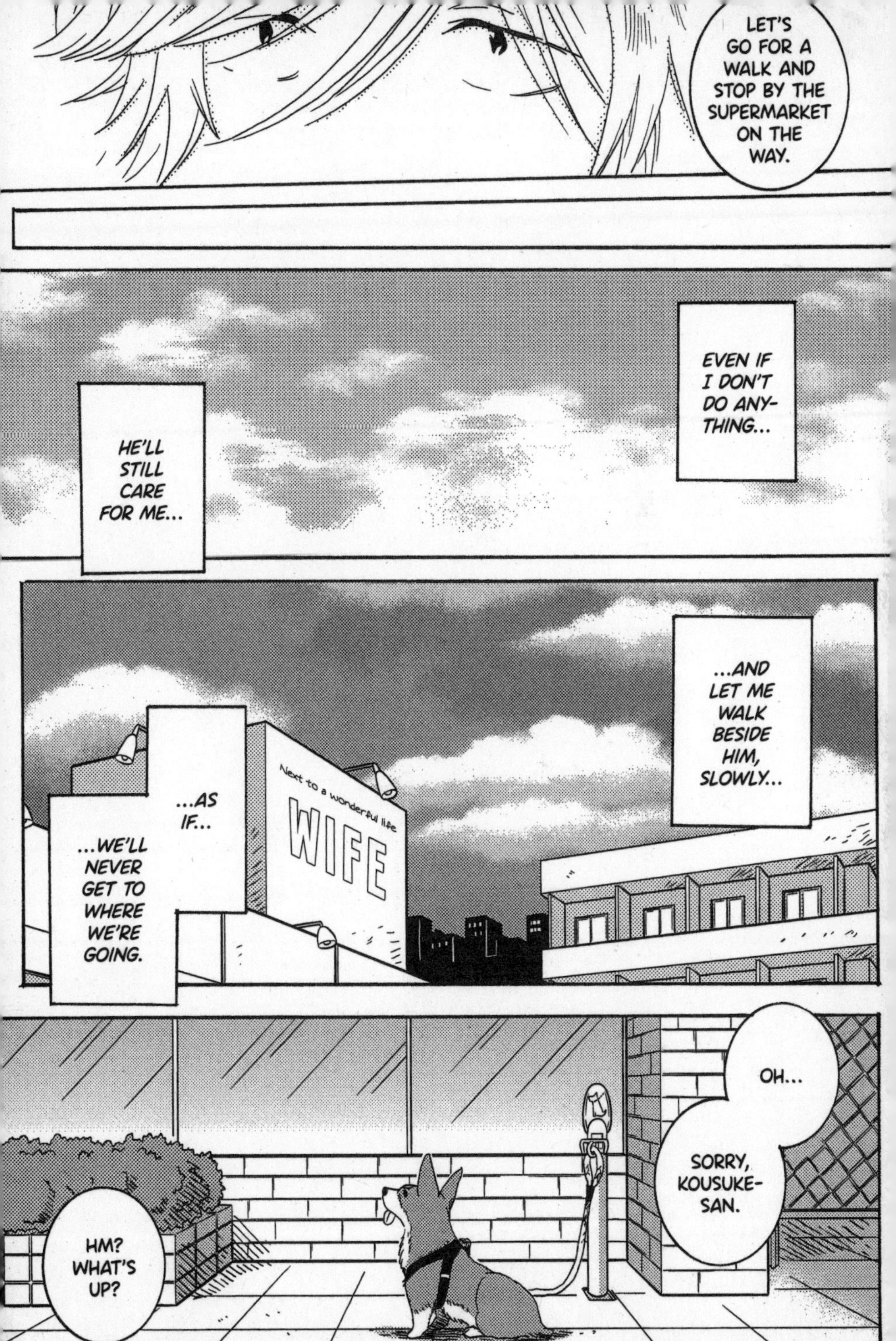
LET'S GO FOR A WALK AND STOP BY THE SUPERMARKET ON THE WAY.
EVEN IF I DON'T DO ANY-THING...
HE'LL STILL CARE FOR ME...
...AND LET ME WALK BESIDE HIM, SLOWLY...
Next to a wonderful life
WIFE
...AS IF...
...WE'LL NEVER GET TO WHERE WE'RE GOING.
OH...
SORRY, KOUSUKE-SAN.
HM? WHAT'S UP?

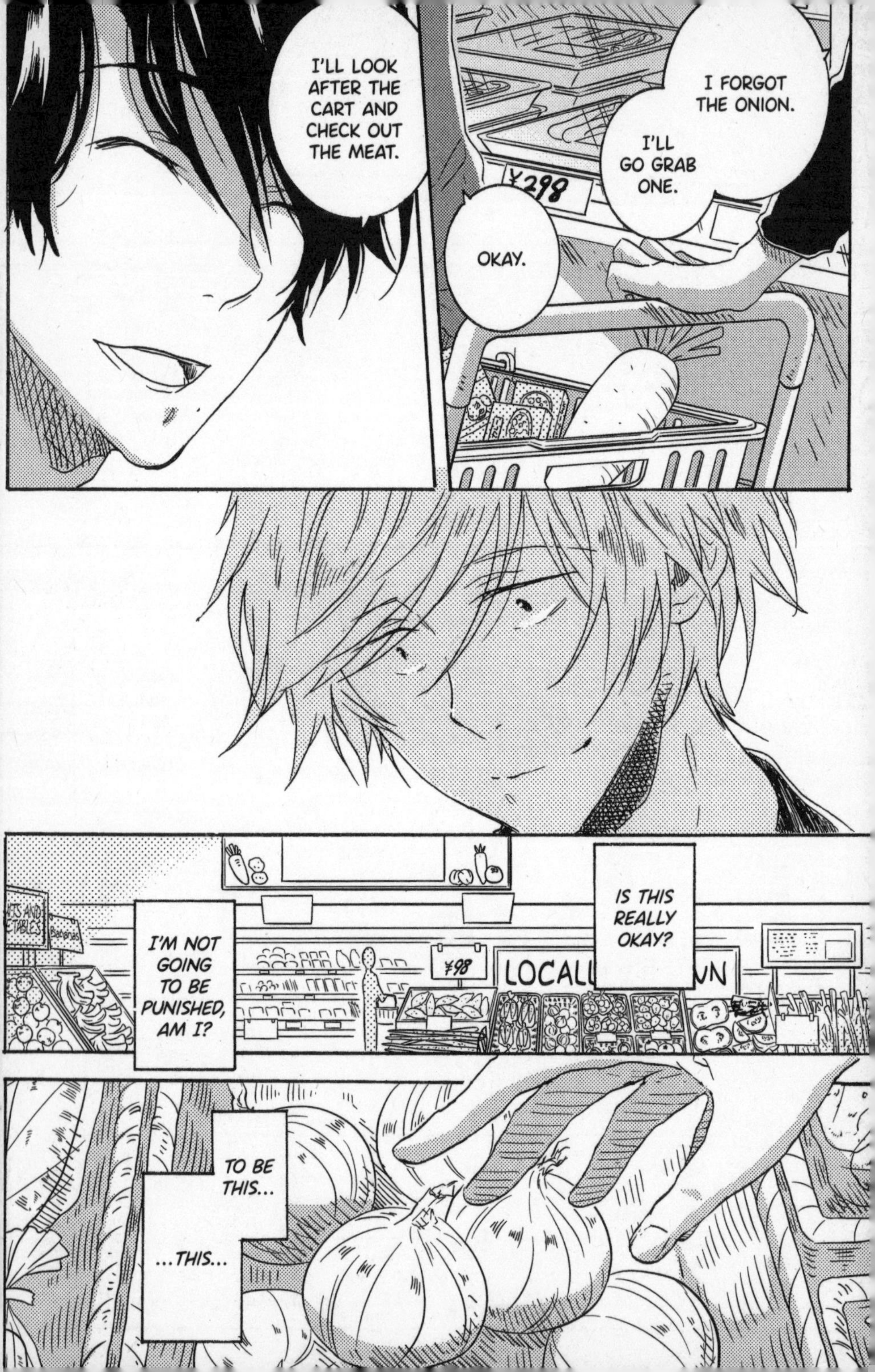

I FORGOT THE ONION.
I'LL GO GRAB ONE.
¥298
OKAY.
I'LL LOOK AFTER THE CART AND CHECK OUT THE MEAT.
IS THIS REALLY OKAY?
¥98
I'M NOT GOING TO BE PUNISHED, AM I?
TO BE THIS...
...THIS...

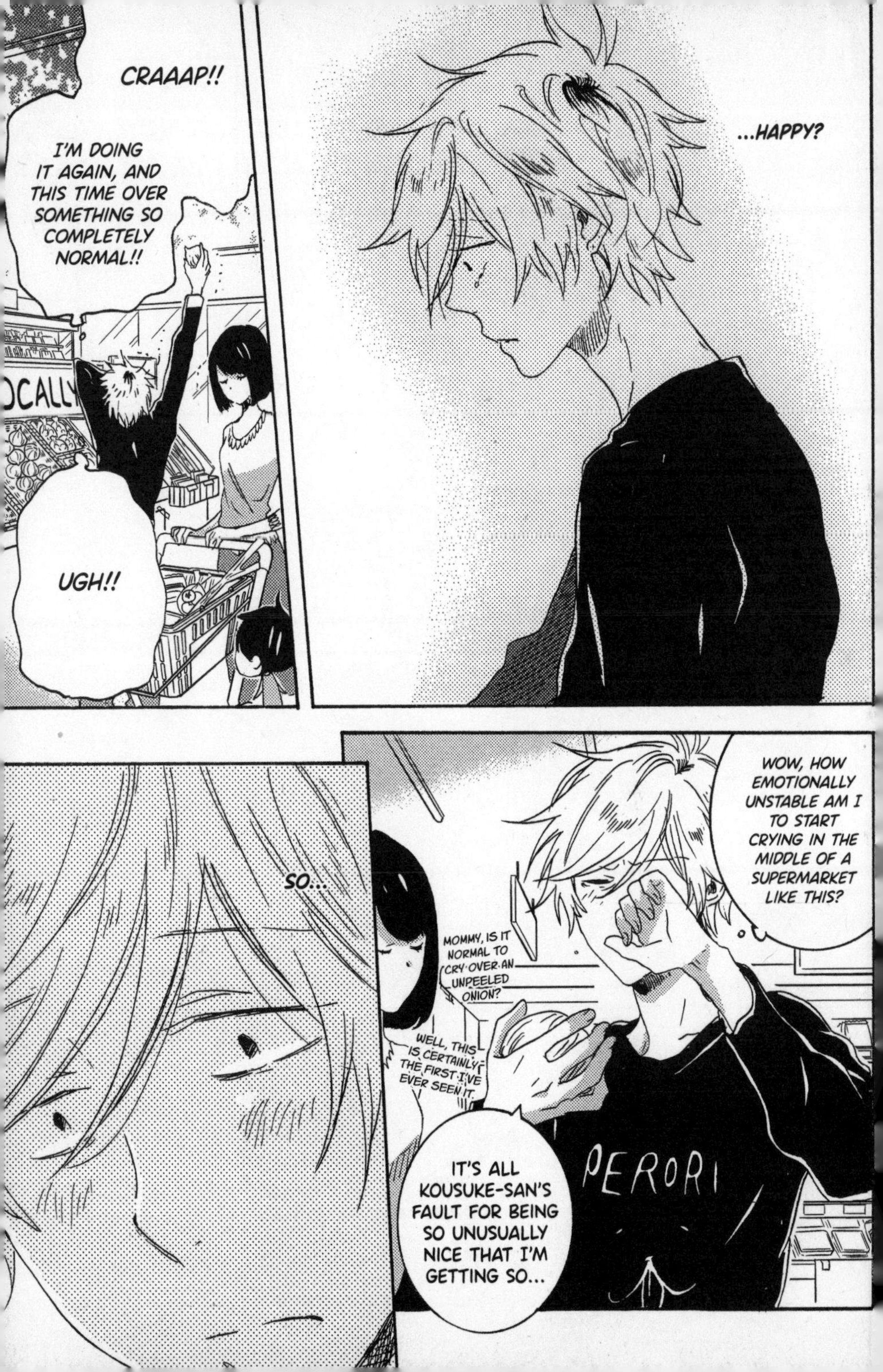
...HAPPY?
CRAAAP!!
I'M DOING IT AGAIN, AND THIS TIME OVER SOMETHING SO COMPLETELY NORMAL!!
UGH!!
WOW, HOW EMOTIONALLY UNSTABLE AM I TO START CRYING IN THE MIDDLE OF A SUPERMARKET LIKE THIS?
MOMMY, IS IT NORMAL TO CRY OVER AN UNPEELED ONION?
WELL, THIS IS CERTAINLY THE FIRST I'VE EVER SEEN IT.
IT'S ALL KOUSUKE-SAN'S FAULT FOR BEING SO UNUSUALLY NICE THAT I'M GETTING SO...
PERORI
SO...

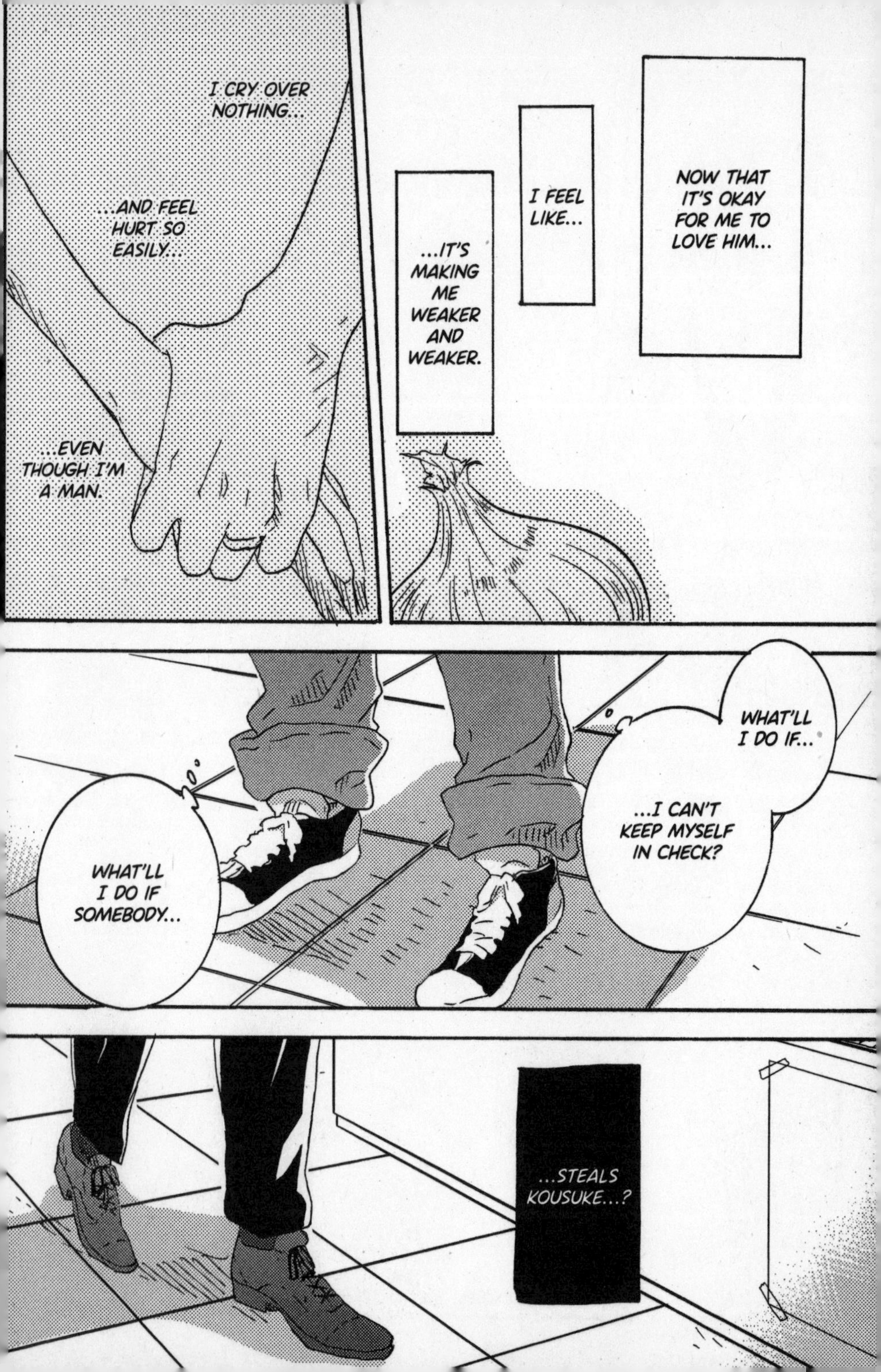
NOW THAT IT'S OKAY FOR ME TO LOVE HIM...
I FEEL LIKE...
...IT'S MAKING ME WEAKER AND WEAKER.
I CRY OVER NOTHING...
...AND FEEL HURT SO EASILY...
...EVEN THOUGH I'M A MAN.
WHAT'LL I DO IF...
...I CAN'T KEEP MYSELF IN CHECK?
WHAT'LL I DO IF SOMEBODY...
...STEALS KOUSUKE...?

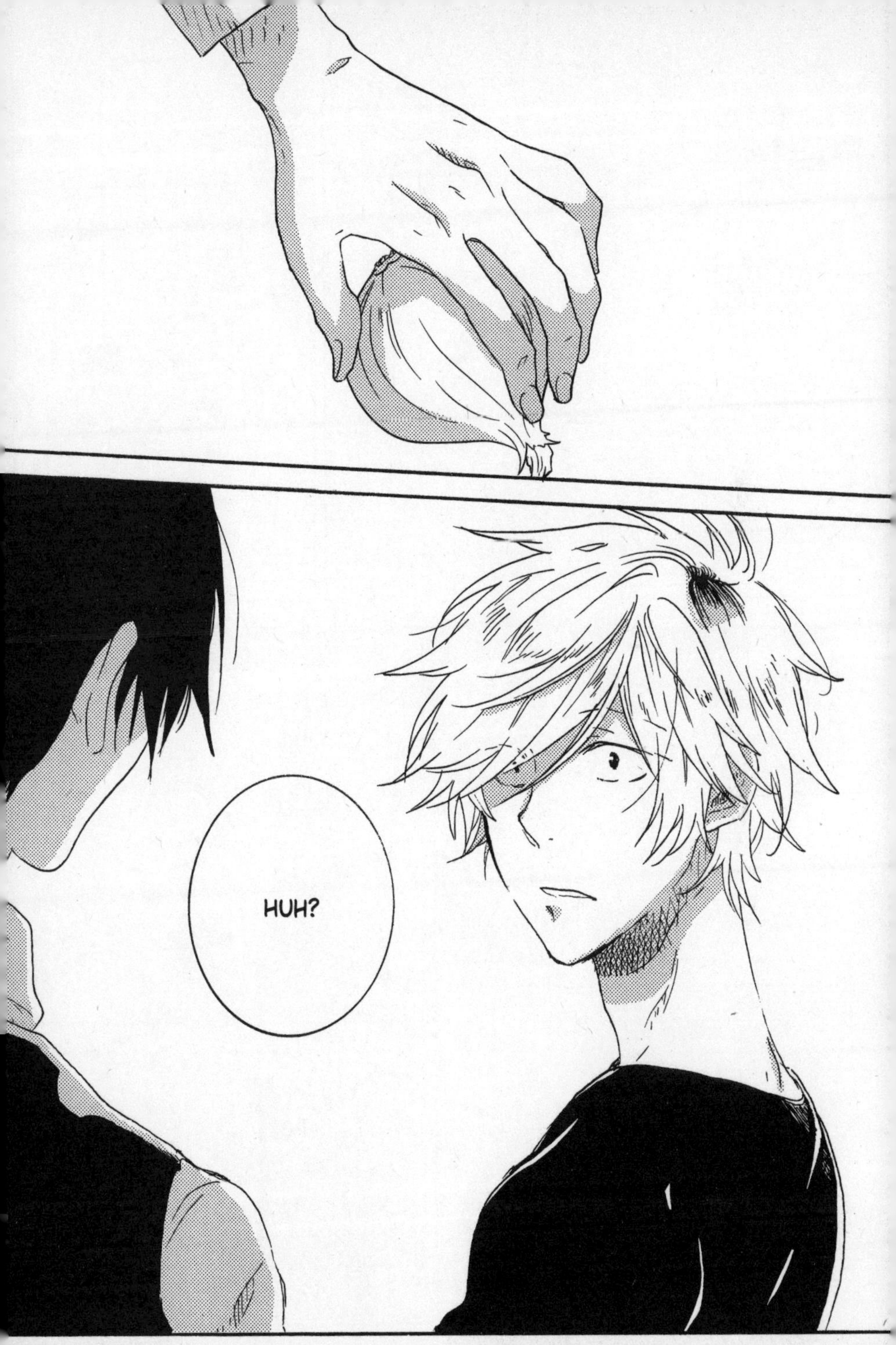
HUH?

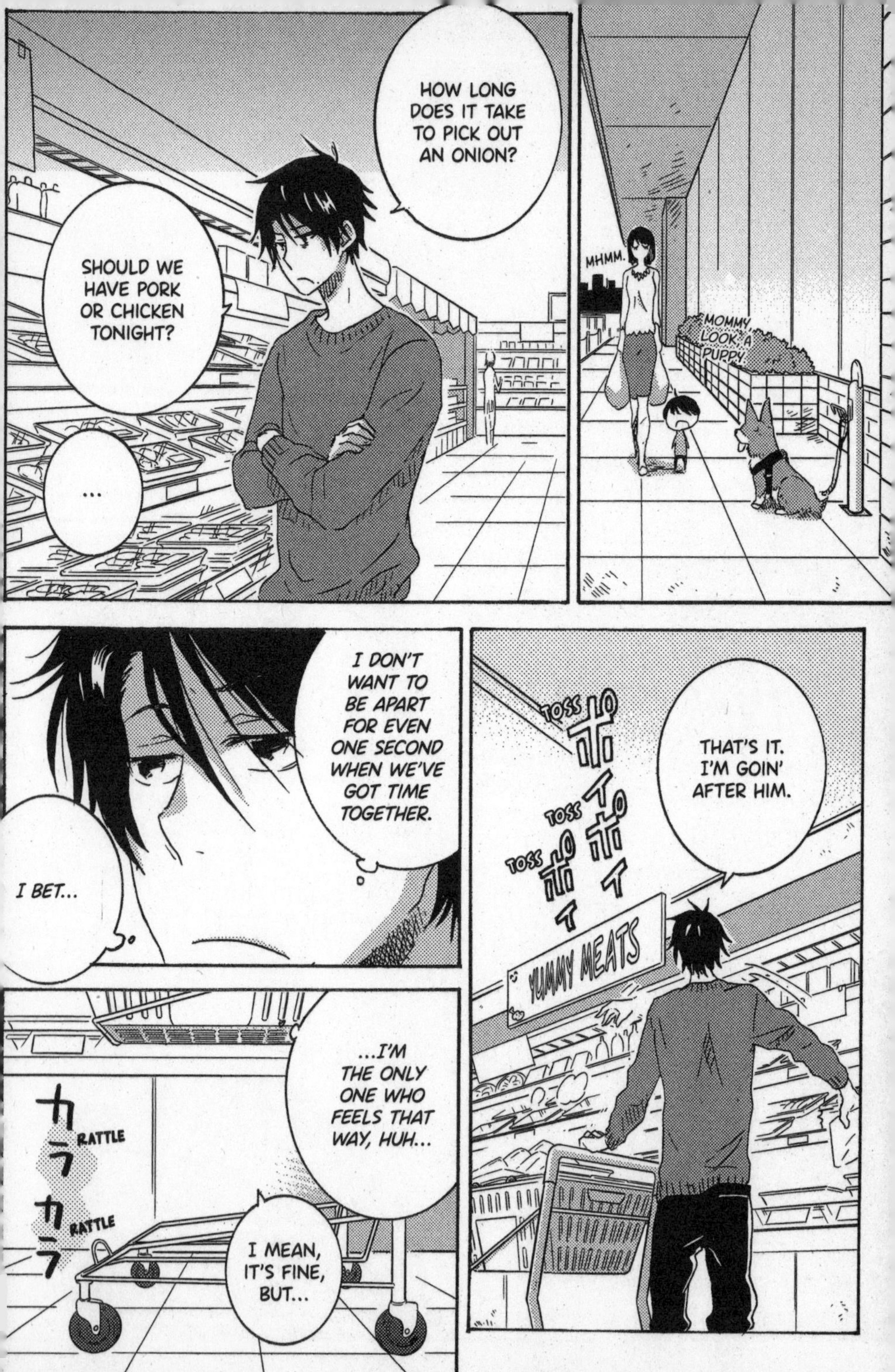
MOMMY, LOOK, A PUPPY.
MHMM.
HOW LONG DOES IT TAKE TO PICK OUT AN ONION?
SHOULD WE HAVE PORK OR CHICKEN TONIGHT?
...
ポイポイポイ
TOSS TOSS TOSS
THAT'S IT. I'M GOIN' AFTER HIM.
YUMMY MEATS
I DON'T WANT TO BE APART FOR EVEN ONE SECOND WHEN WE'VE GOT TIME TOGETHER.
I BET...
...I'M THE ONLY ONE WHO FEELS THAT WAY, HUH...
I MEAN, IT'S FINE, BUT...
カラカラ
RATTLE RATTLE

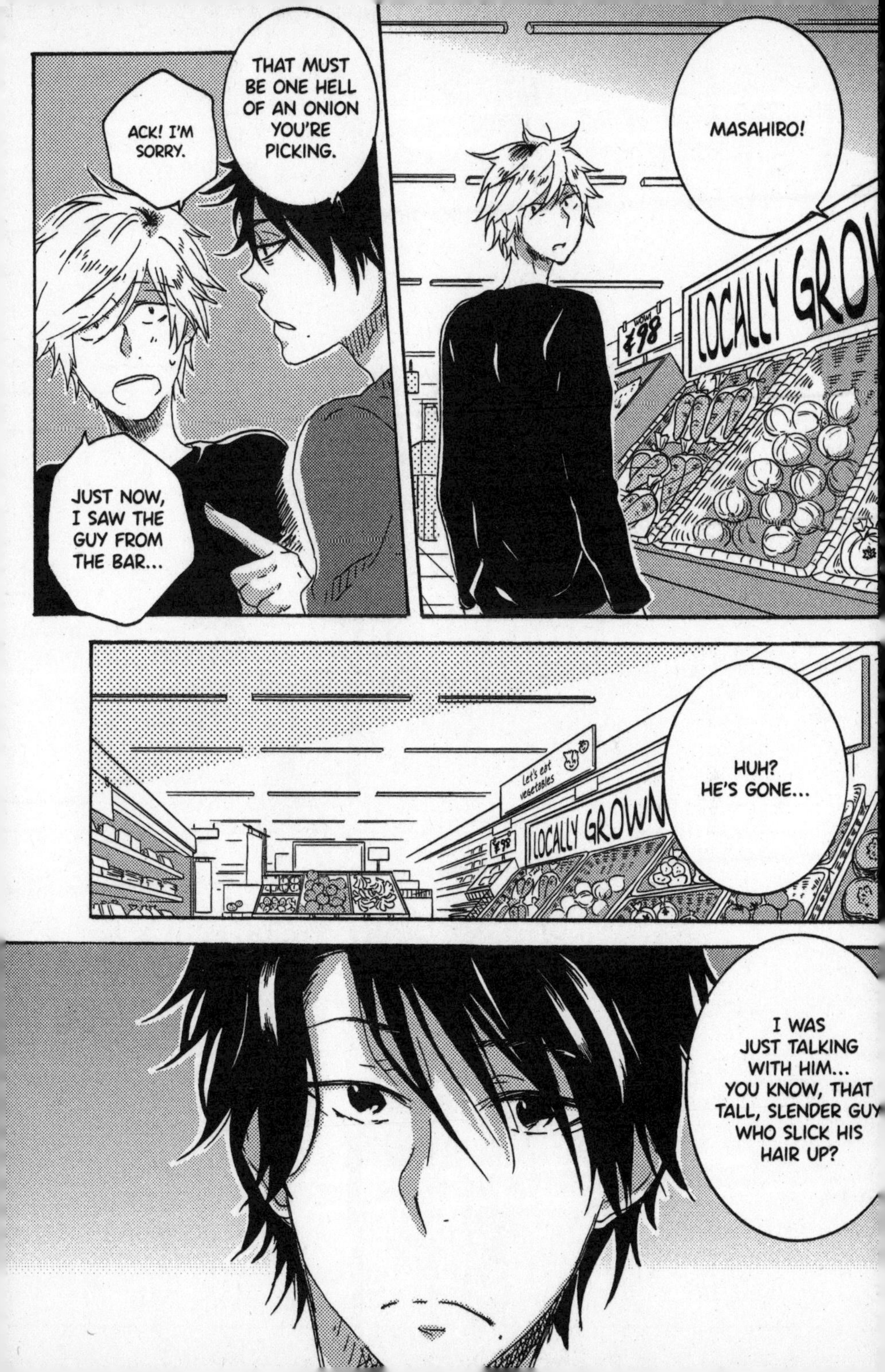
MASAHIRO!
LOCALLY GROW
WOW
¥98
THAT MUST BE ONE HELL OF AN ONION YOU'RE PICKING.
ACK! I'M SORRY.
JUST NOW, I SAW THE GUY FROM THE BAR...
HUH? HE'S GONE...
Let's eat vegetables
LOCALLY GROWN
¥98
I WAS JUST TALKING WITH HIM... YOU KNOW, THAT TALL, SLENDER GUY WHO SLICK HIS HAIR UP?

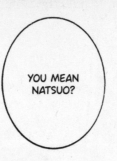

YOU MEAN NATSUO?

DOGS ARE SUCH PITIFUL CREATURES.

...

IS SUCKING UP TO YOUR MASTER ALL YOU CAN DO?

Hitorijime
My Hero

A bonus Christmas story starts on the next page. I even got to draw a Christmas-themed cover for *gateau*.

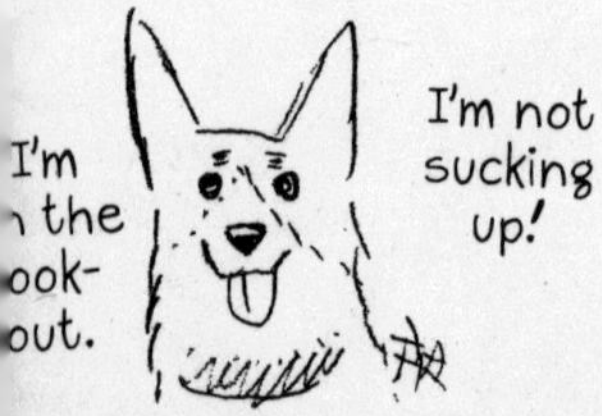
I'm not sucking up!
I'm the ook- out.

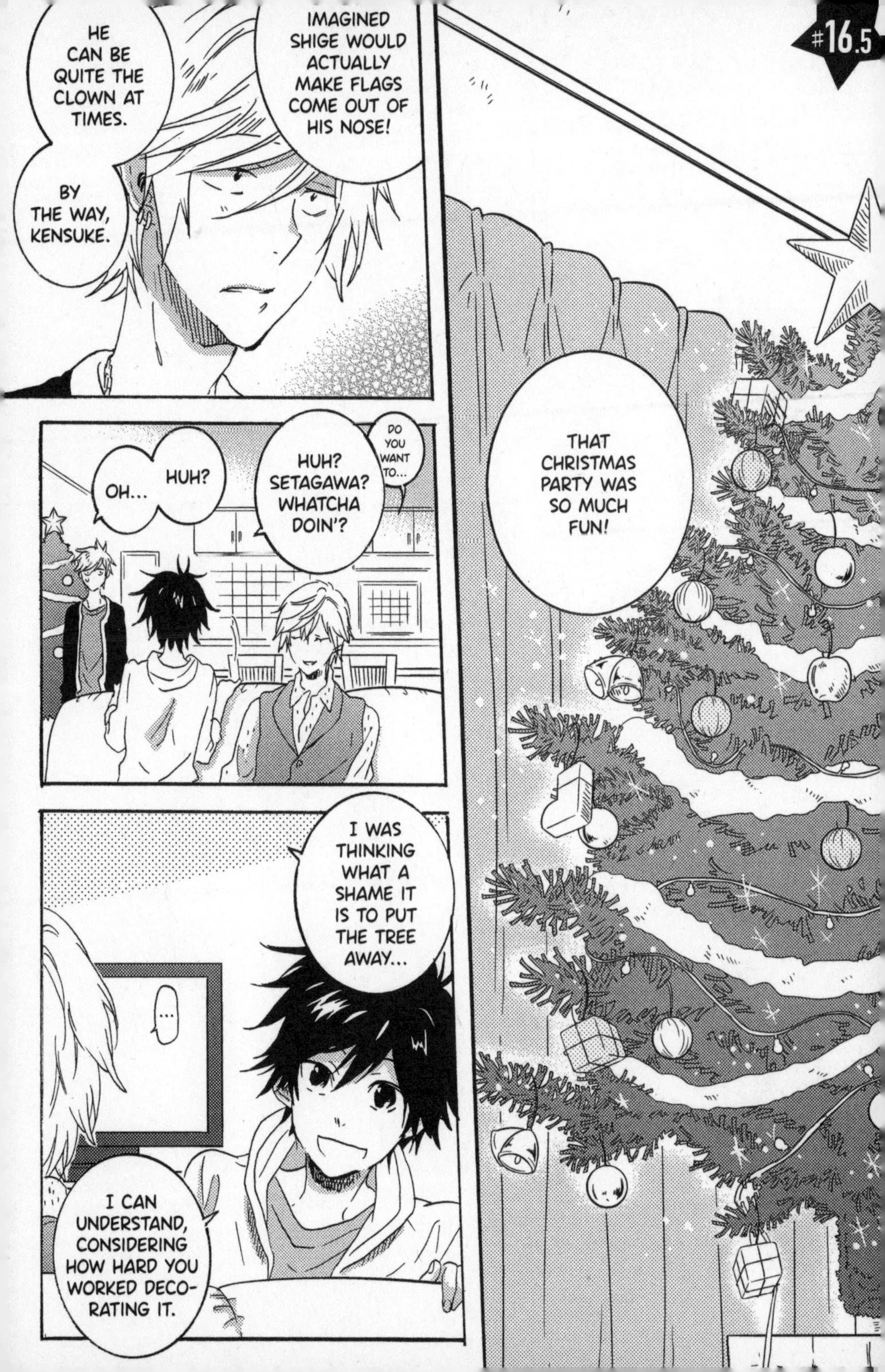
#16.5
THAT CHRISTMAS PARTY WAS SO MUCH FUN!
IMAGINED SHIGE WOULD ACTUALLY MAKE FLAGS COME OUT OF HIS NOSE!
HE CAN BE QUITE THE CLOWN AT TIMES.
BY THE WAY, KENSUKE.
DO YOU WANT TO...
HUH? SETAGAWA? WHATCHA DOIN'?
HUH?
OH...
I WAS THINKING WHAT A SHAME IT IS TO PUT THE TREE AWAY...
...
I CAN UNDERSTAND, CONSIDERING HOW HARD YOU WORKED DECO-RATING IT.

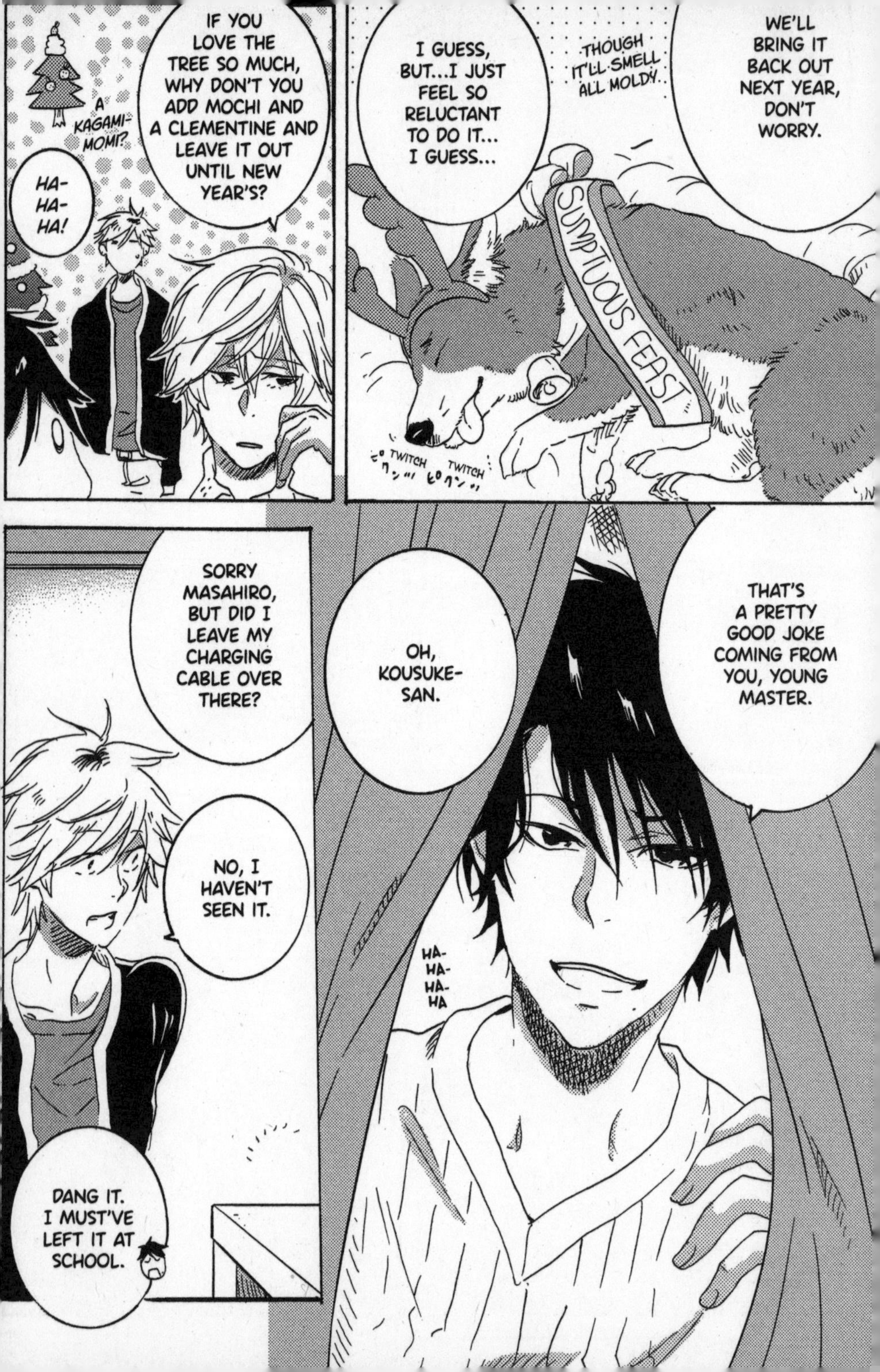
WE'LL BRING IT BACK OUT NEXT YEAR, DON'T WORRY.
THOUGH IT'LL SMELL ALL MOLDY.
I GUESS, BUT...I JUST FEEL SO RELUCTANT TO DO IT... I GUESS...
SUMPTUOUS FEAST
TWITCH TWITCH
IF YOU LOVE THE TREE SO MUCH, WHY DON'T YOU ADD MOCHI AND A CLEMENTINE AND LEAVE IT OUT UNTIL NEW YEAR'S?
A KAGAMI-MOMI?
HA-HA-HA!
THAT'S A PRETTY GOOD JOKE COMING FROM YOU, YOUNG MASTER.
OH, KOUSUKE-SAN.
HA-HA-HA-HA
SORRY MASAHIRO, BUT DID I LEAVE MY CHARGING CABLE OVER THERE?
NO, I HAVEN'T SEEN IT.
DANG IT. I MUST'VE LEFT IT AT SCHOOL.

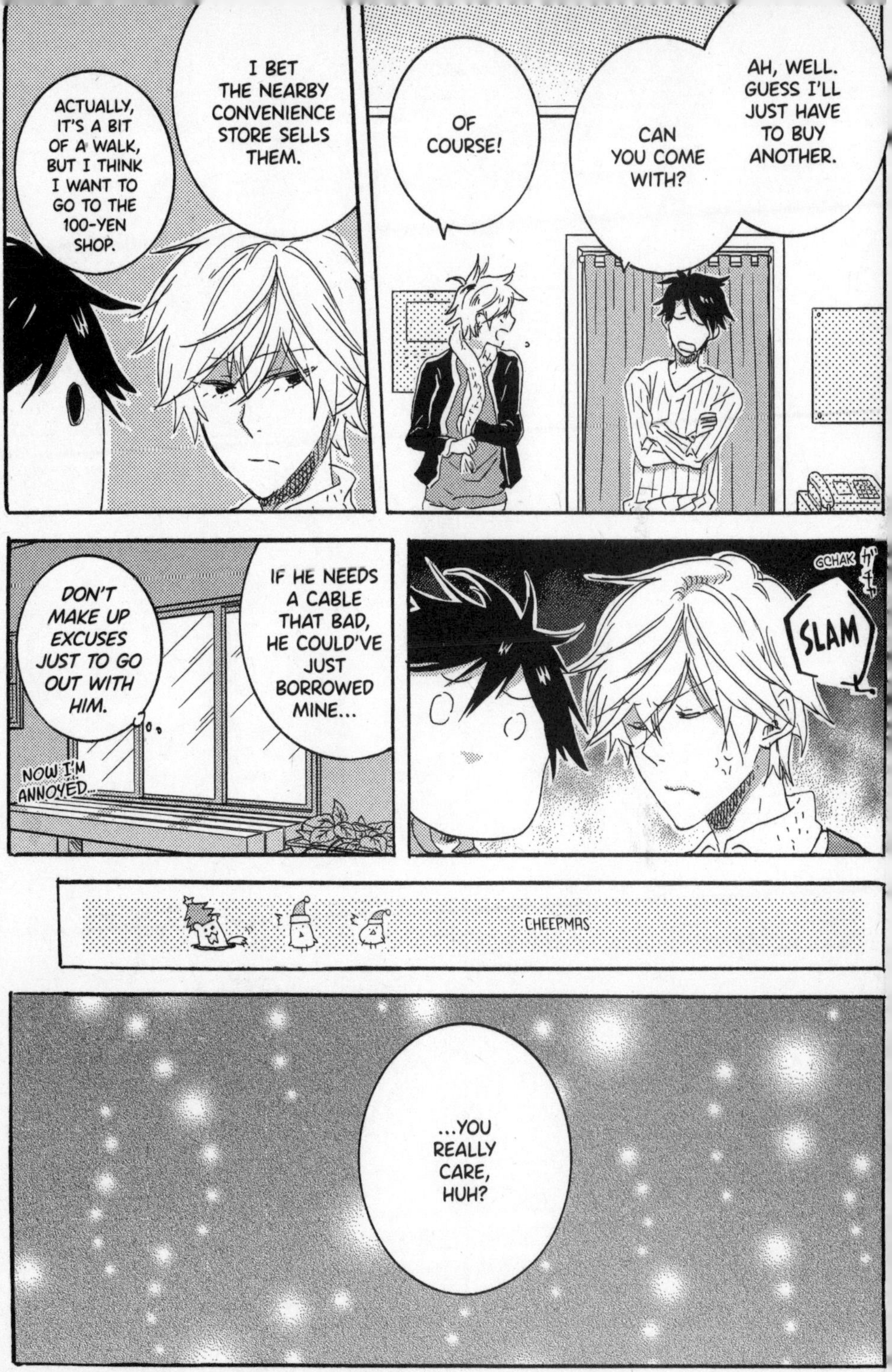
AH, WELL. GUESS I'LL JUST HAVE TO BUY ANOTHER.
CAN YOU COME WITH?
OF COURSE!
I BET THE NEARBY CONVENIENCE STORE SELLS THEM.
ACTUALLY, IT'S A BIT OF A WALK, BUT I THINK I WANT TO GO TO THE 100-YEN SHOP.
GCHAK
SLAM
IF HE NEEDS A CABLE THAT BAD, HE COULD'VE JUST BORROWED MINE...
DON'T MAKE UP EXCUSES JUST TO GO OUT WITH HIM.
NOW I'M ANNOYED...
CHEEPMAS
...YOU REALLY CARE, HUH?

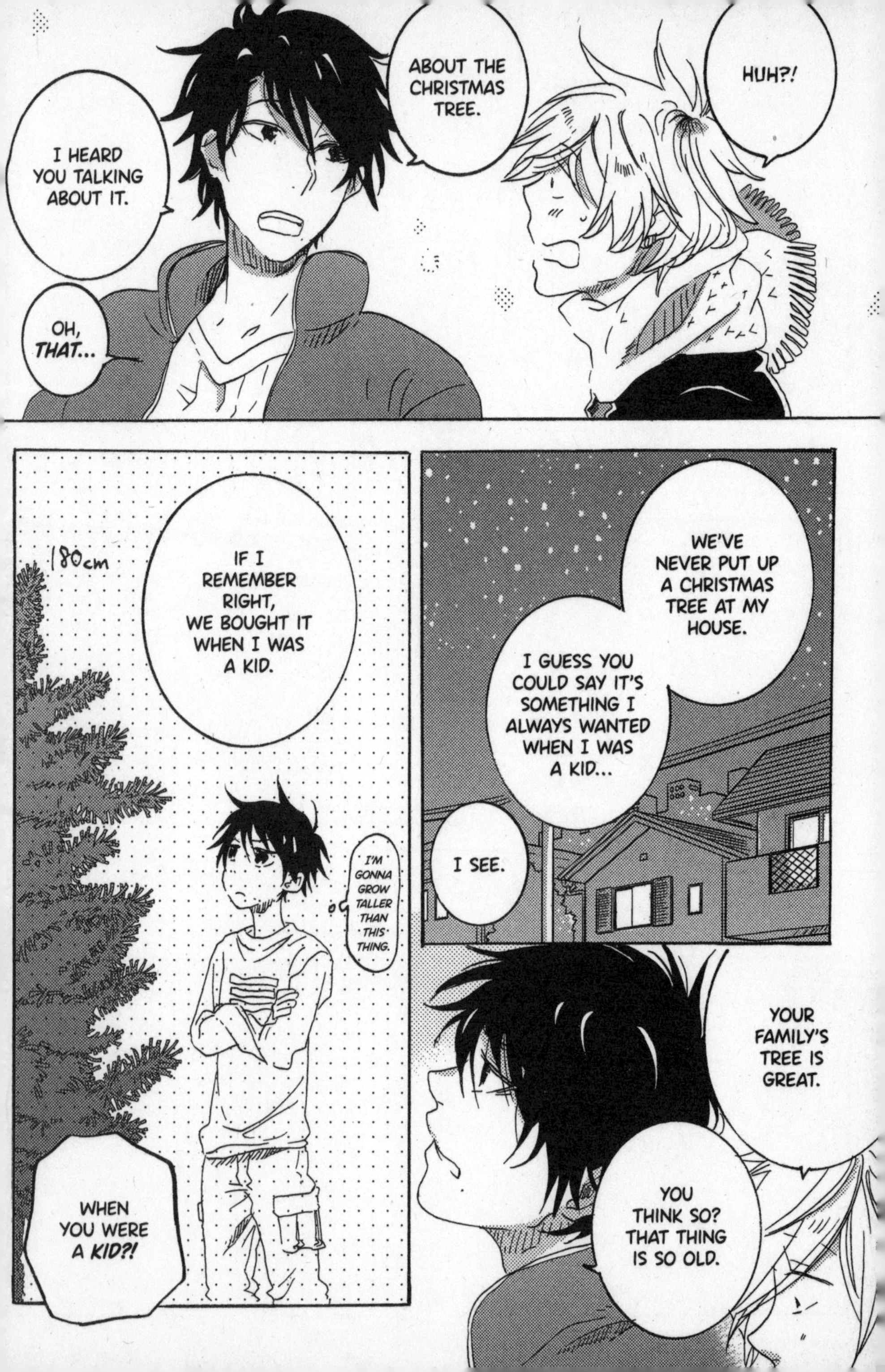
HUH?!
ABOUT THE CHRISTMAS TREE.
I HEARD YOU TALKING ABOUT IT.
OH, *THAT*...
WE'VE NEVER PUT UP A CHRISTMAS TREE AT MY HOUSE.
I GUESS YOU COULD SAY IT'S SOMETHING I ALWAYS WANTED WHEN I WAS A KID...
I SEE.
YOUR FAMILY'S TREE IS GREAT.
YOU THINK SO? THAT THING IS SO OLD.
IF I REMEMBER RIGHT, WE BOUGHT IT WHEN I WAS A KID.
180cm
I'M GONNA GROW TALLER THAN THIS THING.
WHEN YOU WERE A *KID?!*

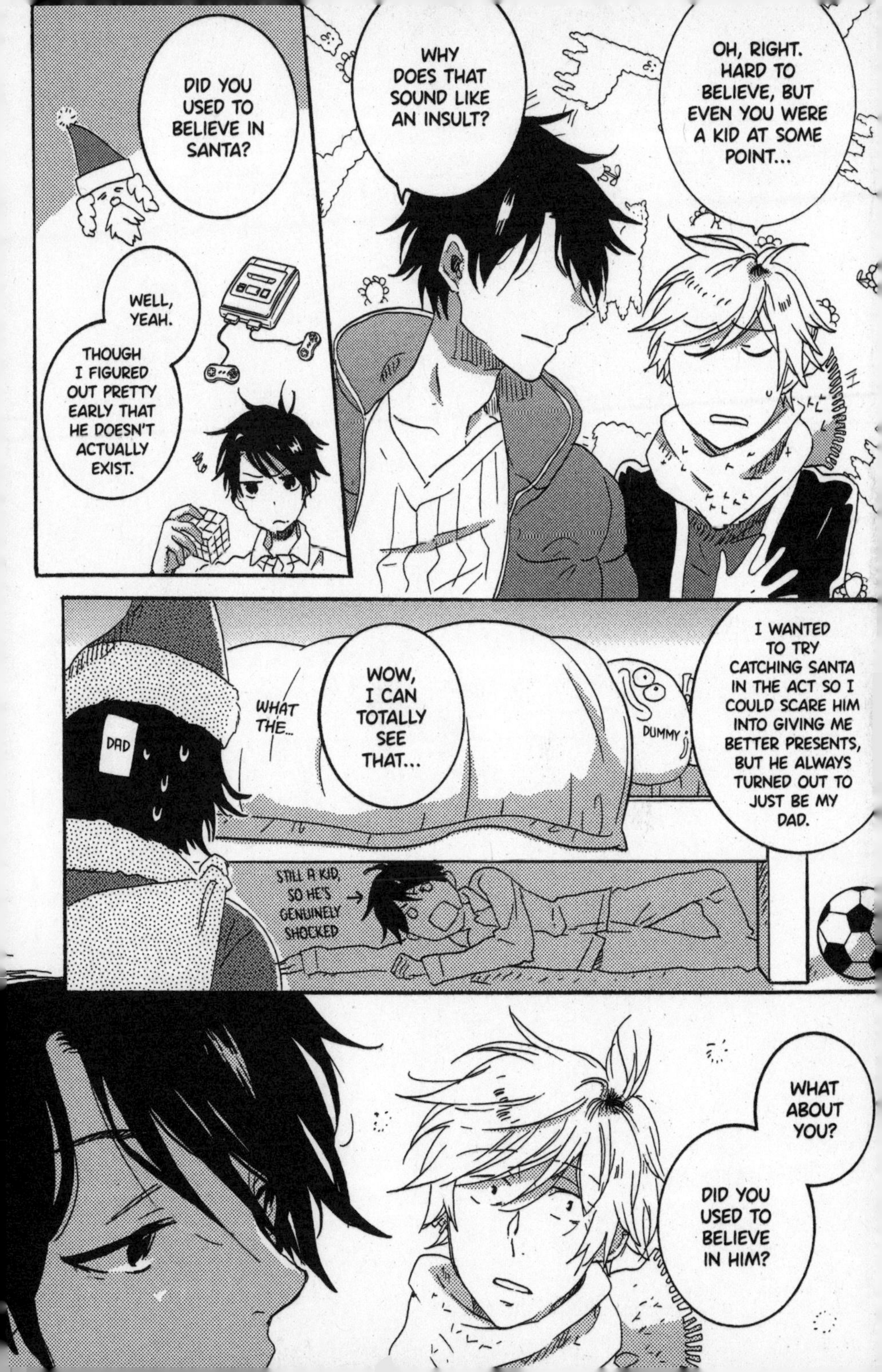
OH, RIGHT. HARD TO BELIEVE, BUT EVEN YOU WERE A KID AT SOME POINT...
WHY DOES THAT SOUND LIKE AN INSULT?
DID YOU USED TO BELIEVE IN SANTA?
WELL, YEAH.
THOUGH I FIGURED OUT PRETTY EARLY THAT HE DOESN'T ACTUALLY EXIST.
I WANTED TO TRY CATCHING SANTA IN THE ACT SO I COULD SCARE HIM INTO GIVING ME BETTER PRESENTS, BUT HE ALWAYS TURNED OUT TO JUST BE MY DAD.
DUMMY
WOW, I CAN TOTALLY SEE THAT...
WHAT THE...
DAD
STILL A KID, SO HE'S GENUINELY SHOCKED
WHAT ABOUT YOU?
DID YOU USED TO BELIEVE IN HIM?

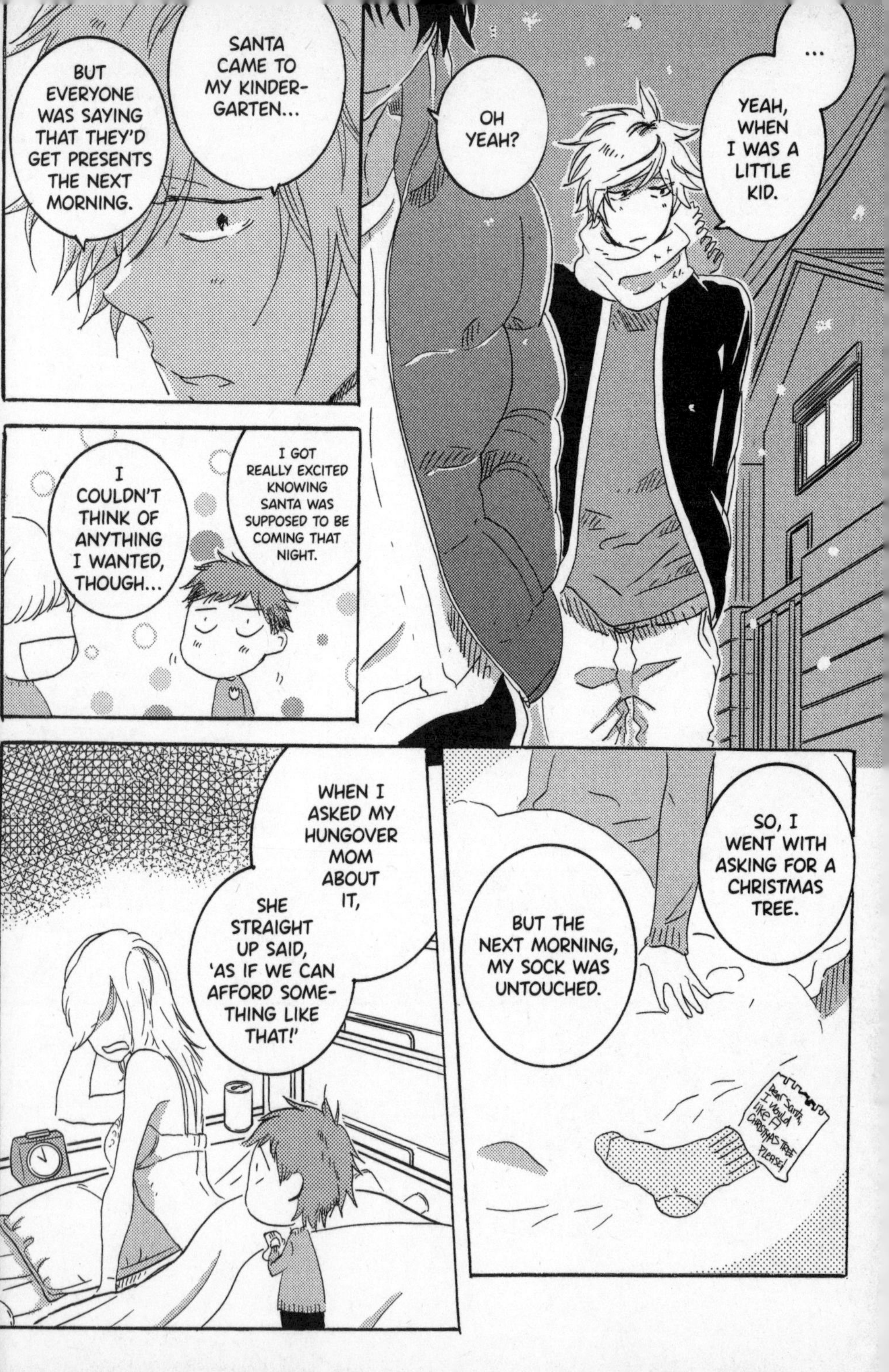
...
YEAH, WHEN I WAS A LITTLE KID.
OH YEAH?
SANTA CAME TO MY KINDER-GARTEN...
BUT EVERYONE WAS SAYING THAT THEY'D GET PRESENTS THE NEXT MORNING.
I GOT REALLY EXCITED KNOWING SANTA WAS SUPPOSED TO BE COMING THAT NIGHT.
I COULDN'T THINK OF ANYTHING I WANTED, THOUGH...
SO, I WENT WITH ASKING FOR A CHRISTMAS TREE.
BUT THE NEXT MORNING, MY SOCK WAS UNTOUCHED.
Dear Santa, I would like A CHRISTMAS TREE please!
WHEN I ASKED MY HUNGOVER MOM ABOUT IT,
SHE STRAIGHT UP SAID, 'AS IF WE CAN AFFORD SOME-THING LIKE THAT!'

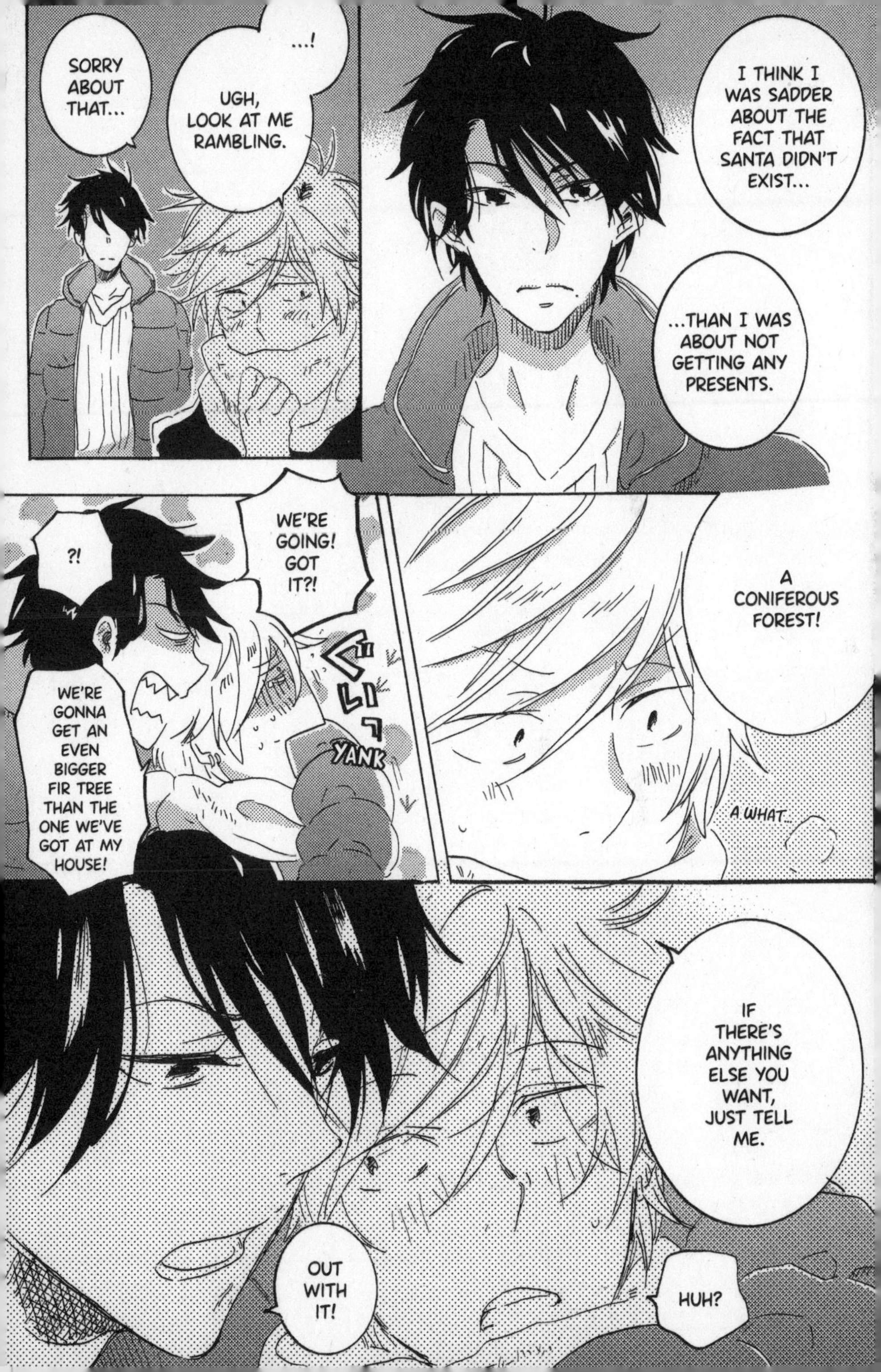
I THINK I WAS SADDER ABOUT THE FACT THAT SANTA DIDN'T EXIST...
...THAN I WAS ABOUT NOT GETTING ANY PRESENTS.
...!
UGH, LOOK AT ME RAMBLING.
SORRY ABOUT THAT...
A CONIFEROUS FOREST!
A WHAT...
WE'RE GOING! GOT IT?!
?!
YANK
WE'RE GONNA GET AN EVEN BIGGER FIR TREE THAN THE ONE WE'VE GOT AT MY HOUSE!
IF THERE'S ANYTHING ELSE YOU WANT, JUST TELL ME.
HUH?
OUT WITH IT!

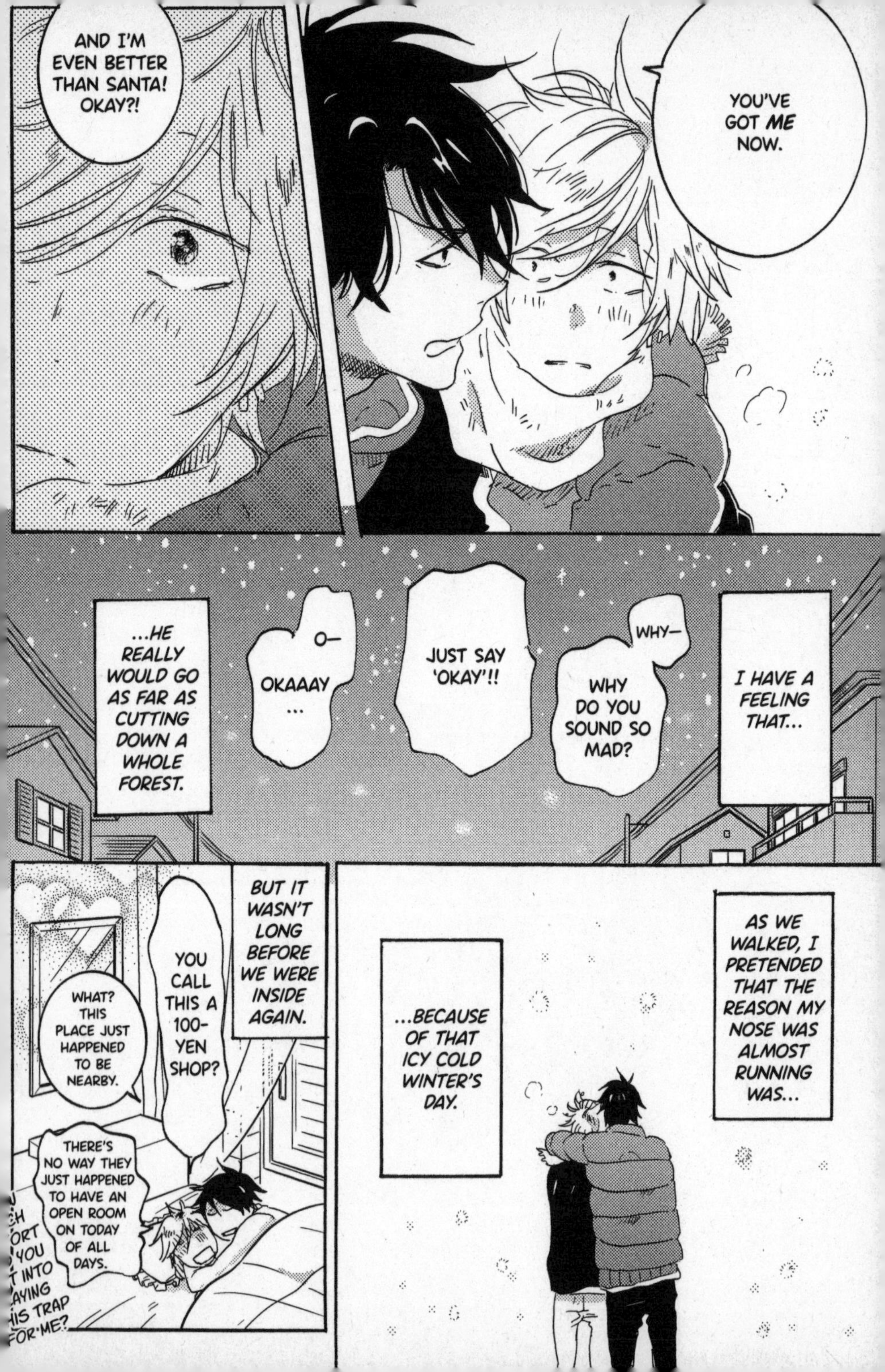
YOU'VE GOT ME NOW.
AND I'M EVEN BETTER THAN SANTA! OKAY?!
I HAVE A FEELING THAT...
WHY—
WHY DO YOU SOUND SO MAD?
JUST SAY 'OKAY'!!
O—
OKAAAY ...
...HE REALLY WOULD GO AS FAR AS CUTTING DOWN A WHOLE FOREST.
AS WE WALKED, I PRETENDED THAT THE REASON MY NOSE WAS ALMOST RUNNING WAS...
...BECAUSE OF THAT ICY COLD WINTER'S DAY.
BUT IT WASN'T LONG BEFORE WE WERE INSIDE AGAIN.
YOU CALL THIS A 100-YEN SHOP?
WHAT? THIS PLACE JUST HAPPENED TO BE NEARBY.
THERE'S NO WAY THEY JUST HAPPENED TO HAVE AN OPEN ROOM ON TODAY OF ALL DAYS.

Hitorijime
My Hero

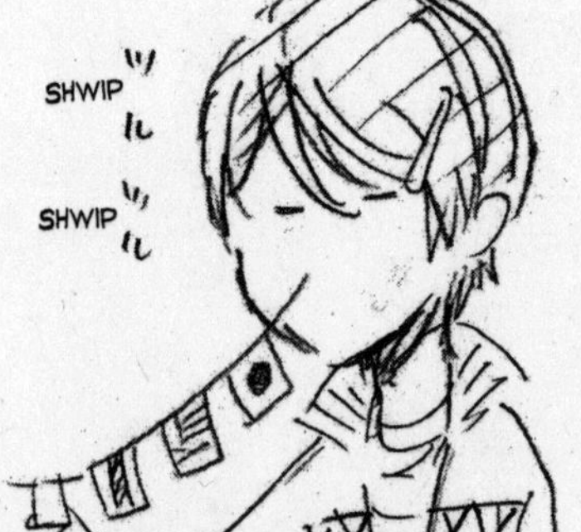
SHWIP
SHWIP

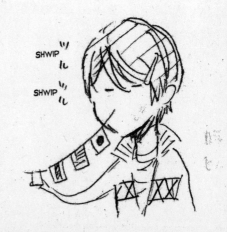

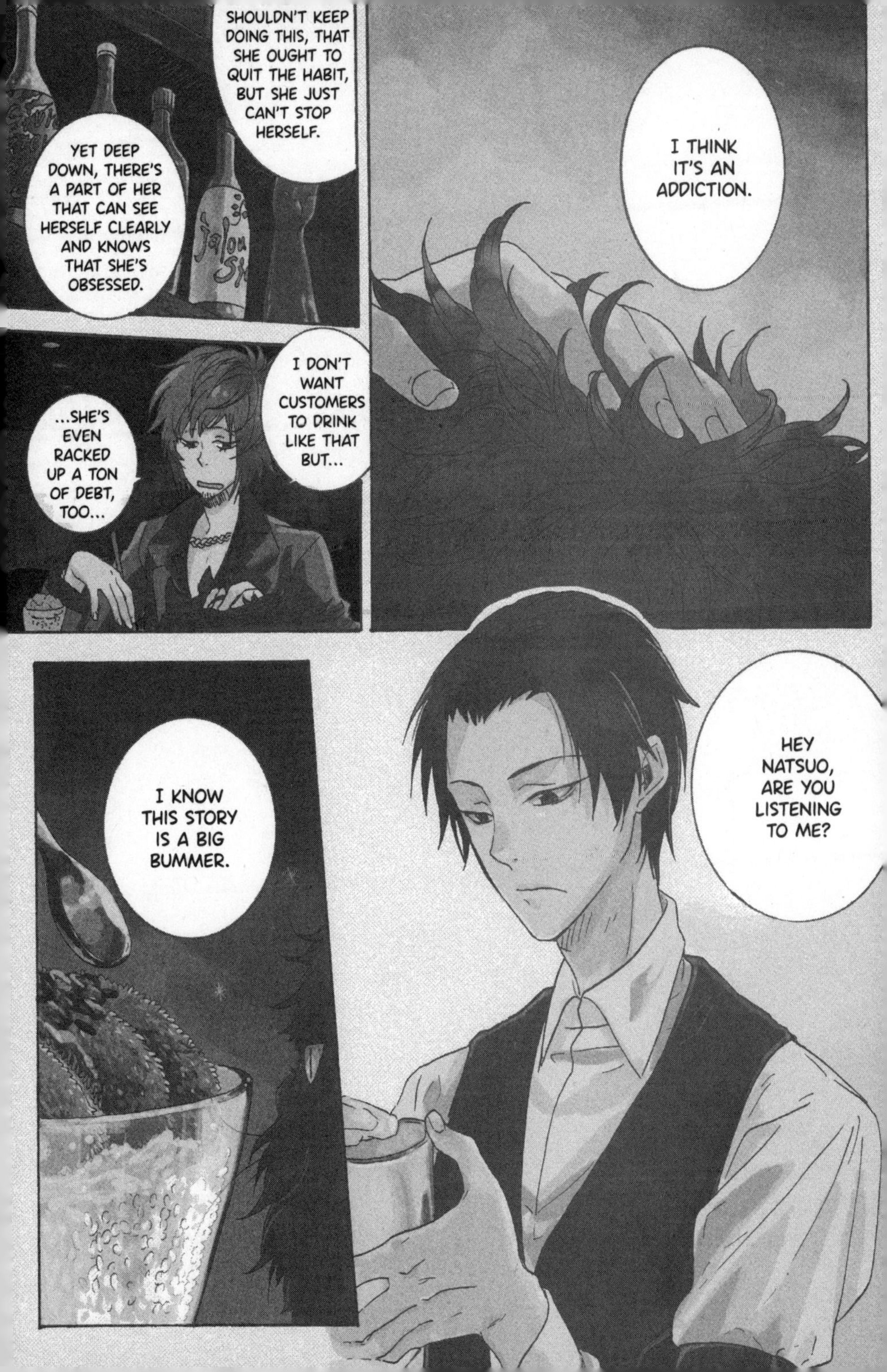
I THINK IT'S AN ADDICTION.
SHOULDN'T KEEP DOING THIS, THAT SHE OUGHT TO QUIT THE HABIT, BUT SHE JUST CAN'T STOP HERSELF.
YET DEEP DOWN, THERE'S A PART OF HER THAT CAN SEE HERSELF CLEARLY AND KNOWS THAT SHE'S OBSESSED.
I DON'T WANT CUSTOMERS TO DRINK LIKE THAT BUT...
...SHE'S EVEN RACKED UP A TON OF DEBT, TOO...
HEY NATSUO, ARE YOU LISTENING TO ME?
I KNOW THIS STORY IS A BIG BUMMER.

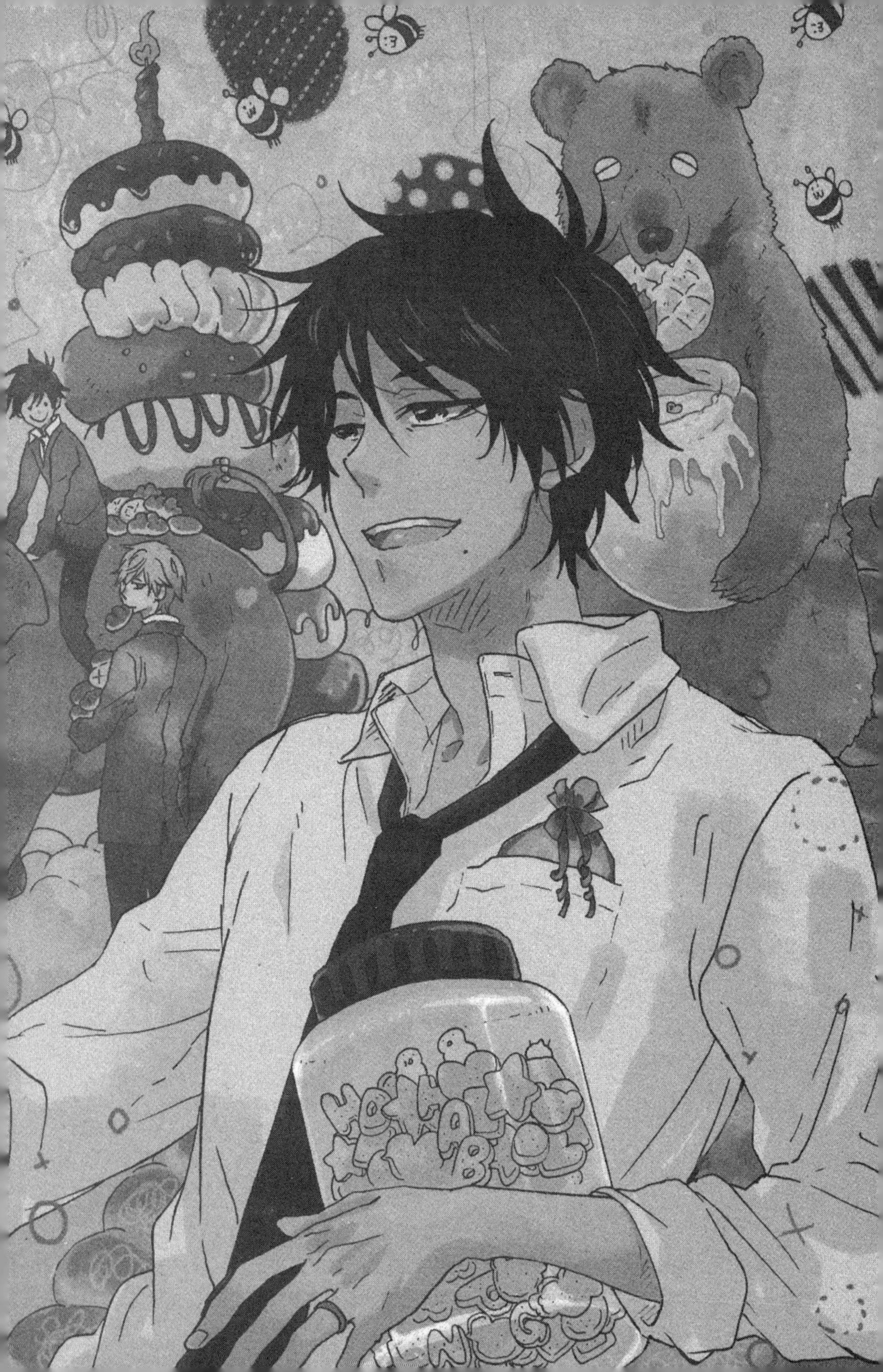

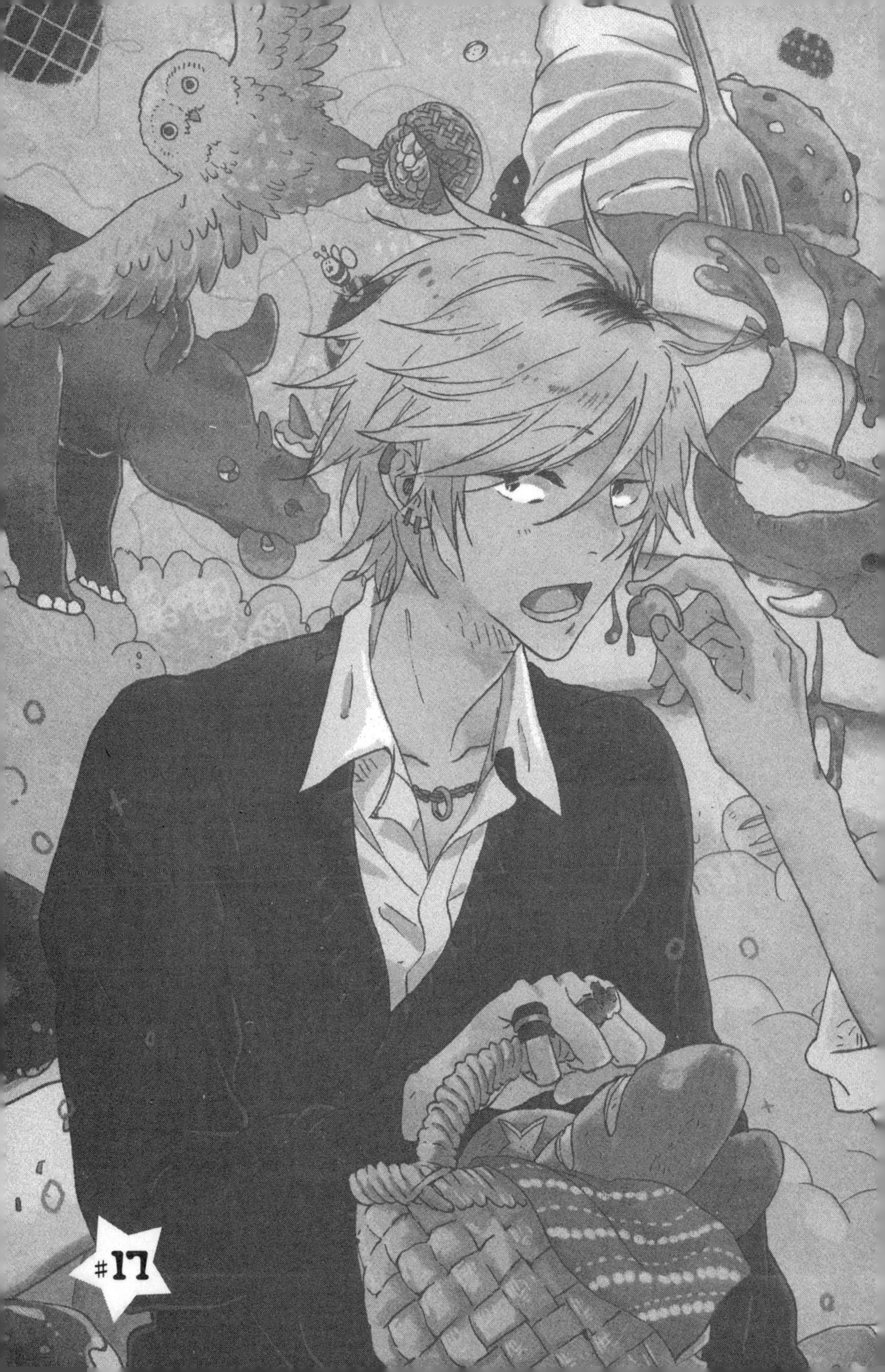
#17

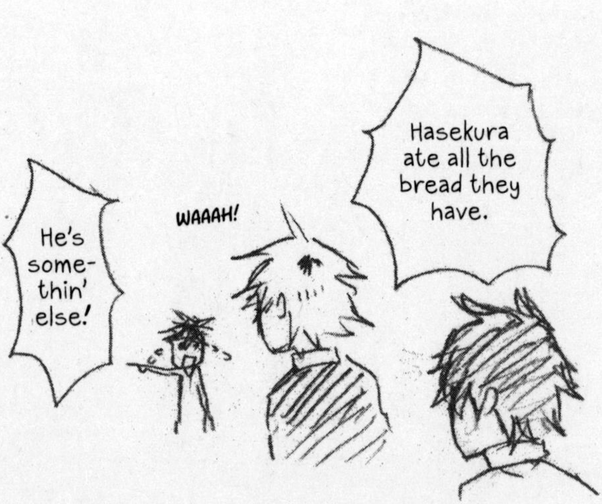
Hasekura ate all the bread they have.
WAAAH!
He's some-thin' else!

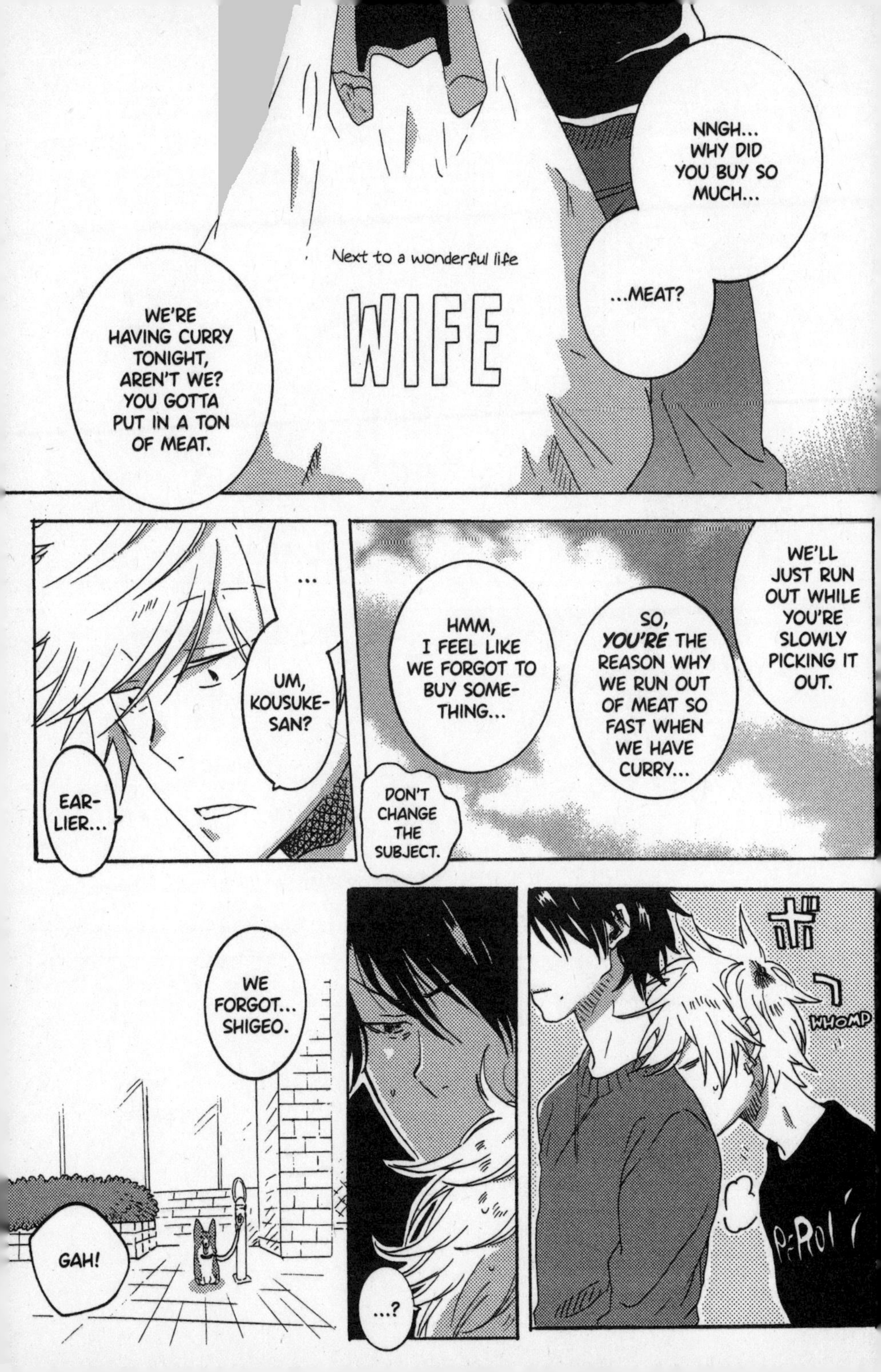
NNGH... WHY DID YOU BUY SO MUCH...
...MEAT?
Next to a wonderful life
WIFE
WE'RE HAVING CURRY TONIGHT, AREN'T WE? YOU GOTTA PUT IN A TON OF MEAT.
WE'LL JUST RUN OUT WHILE YOU'RE SLOWLY PICKING IT OUT.
SO, *YOU'RE* THE REASON WHY WE RUN OUT OF MEAT SO FAST WHEN WE HAVE CURRY...
HMM, I FEEL LIKE WE FORGOT TO BUY SOME-THING...
DON'T CHANGE THE SUBJECT.
...
UM, KOUSUKE-SAN?
EAR-LIER...
ボフ
WHOMP
...?
WE FORGOT... SHIGEO.
GAH!

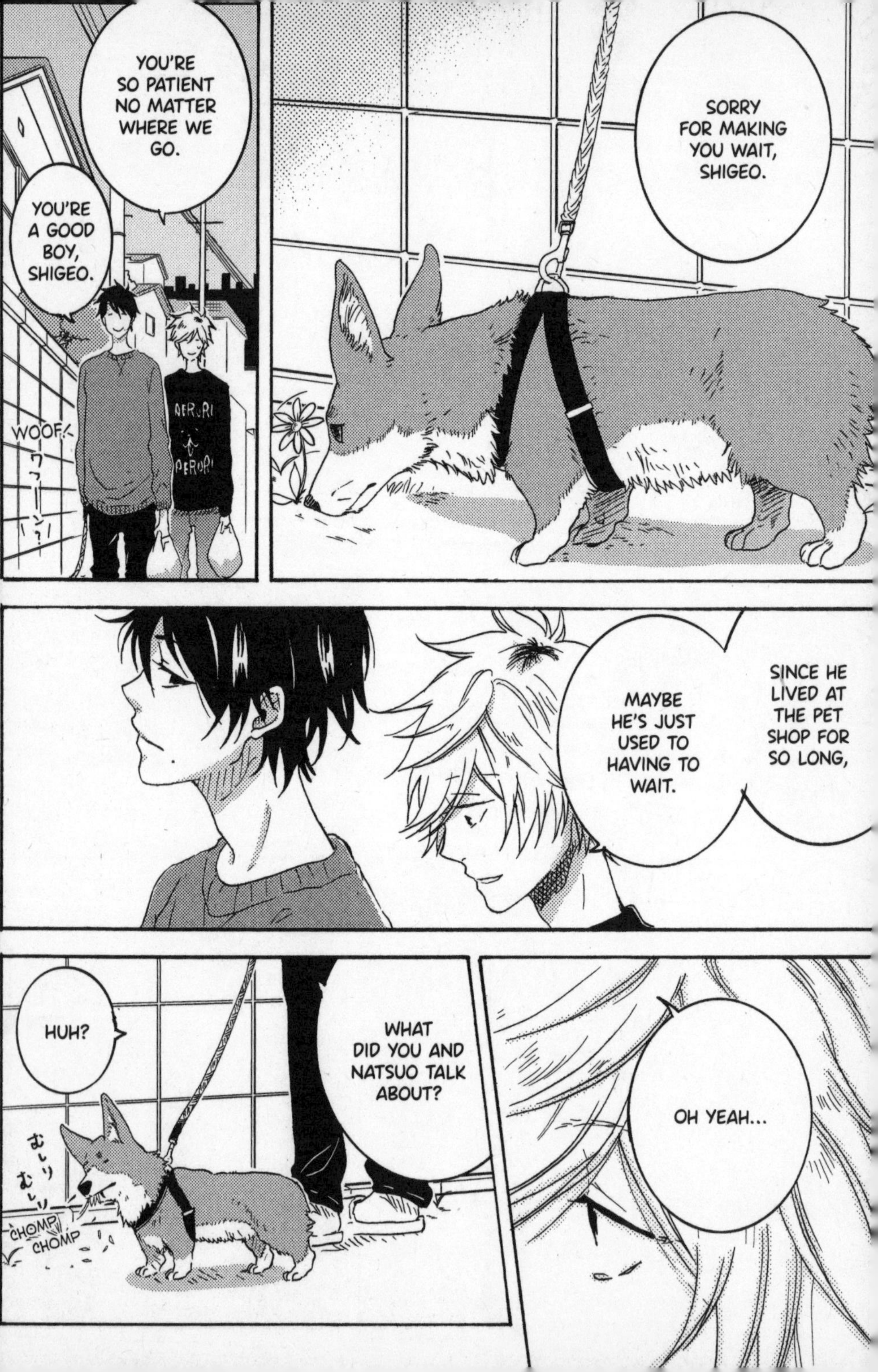
SORRY FOR MAKING YOU WAIT, SHIGEO.
YOU'RE SO PATIENT NO MATTER WHERE WE GO.
YOU'RE A GOOD BOY, SHIGEO.
WOOF!
SINCE HE LIVED AT THE PET SHOP FOR SO LONG,
MAYBE HE'S JUST USED TO HAVING TO WAIT.
OH YEAH...
WHAT DID YOU AND NATSUO TALK ABOUT?
HUH?
むしり むしり
CHOMP CHOMP

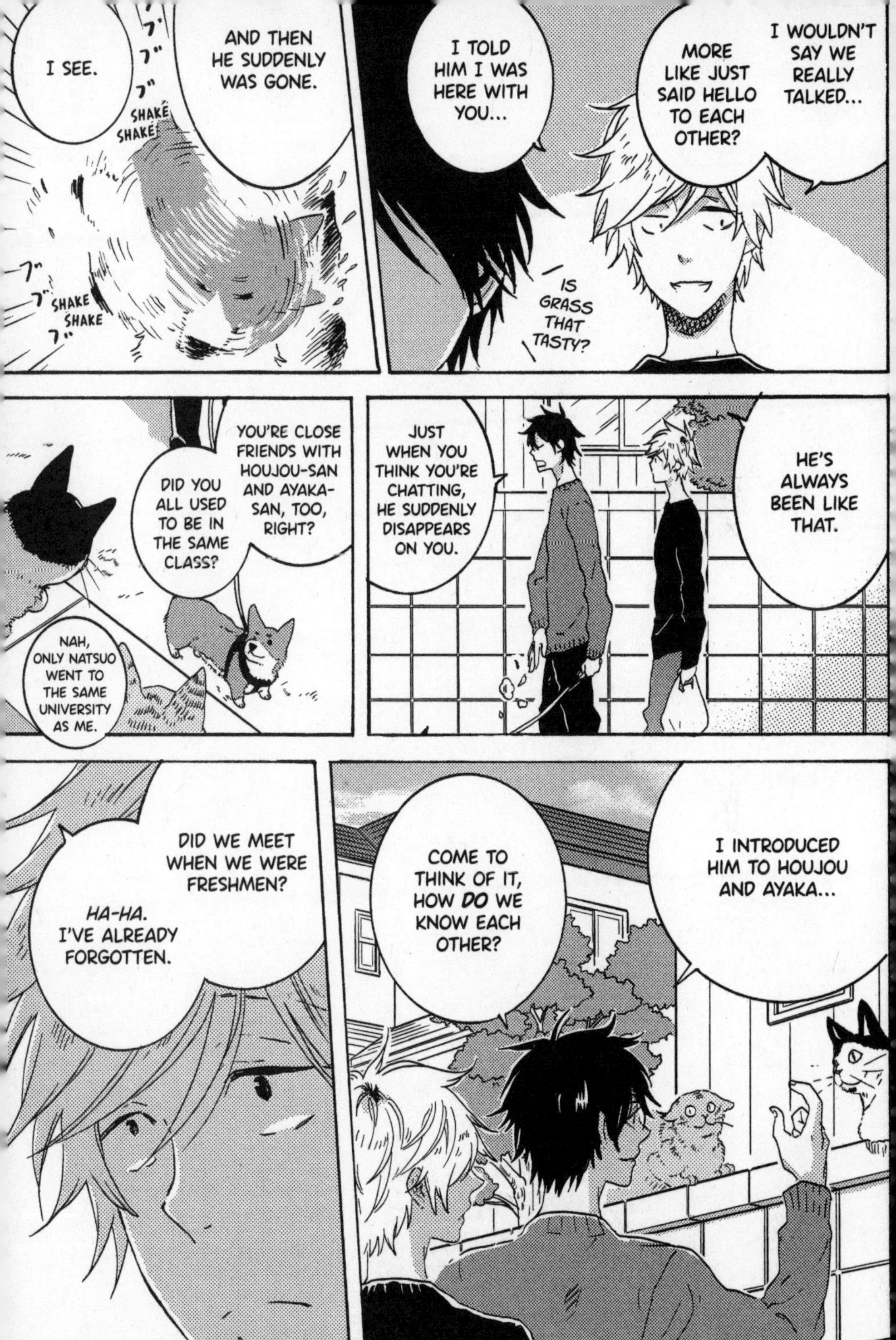
I WOULDN'T SAY WE REALLY TALKED...
MORE LIKE JUST SAID HELLO TO EACH OTHER?
I TOLD HIM I WAS HERE WITH YOU...
IS GRASS THAT TASTY?
AND THEN HE SUDDENLY WAS GONE.
I SEE.
SHAKE SHAKE
SHAKE SHAKE
HE'S ALWAYS BEEN LIKE THAT.
JUST WHEN YOU THINK YOU'RE CHATTING, HE SUDDENLY DISAPPEARS ON YOU.
YOU'RE CLOSE FRIENDS WITH HOUJOU-SAN AND AYAKA-SAN, TOO, RIGHT?
DID YOU ALL USED TO BE IN THE SAME CLASS?
NAH, ONLY NATSUO WENT TO THE SAME UNIVERSITY AS ME.
I INTRODUCED HIM TO HOUJOU AND AYAKA...
COME TO THINK OF IT, HOW *DO* WE KNOW EACH OTHER?
DID WE MEET WHEN WE WERE FRESHMEN?
HA-HA. I'VE ALREADY FORGOTTEN.

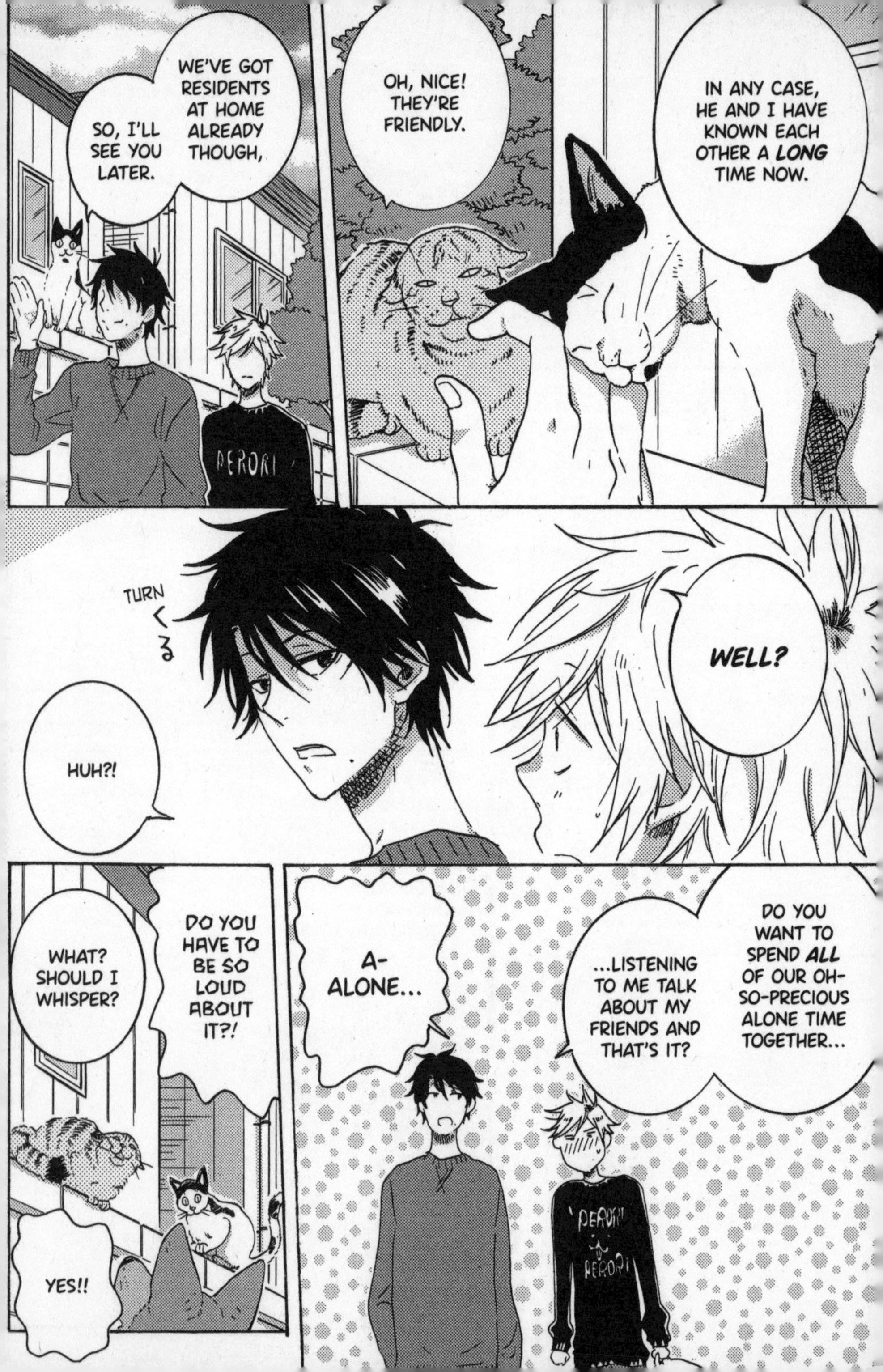
IN ANY CASE, HE AND I HAVE KNOWN EACH OTHER A *LONG* TIME NOW.
OH, NICE! THEY'RE FRIENDLY.
WE'VE GOT RESIDENTS AT HOME ALREADY THOUGH,
SO, I'LL SEE YOU LATER.
PERORI
WELL?
TURN くる
HUH?!
DO YOU WANT TO SPEND *ALL* OF OUR OH-SO-PRECIOUS ALONE TIME TOGETHER...
...LISTENING TO ME TALK ABOUT MY FRIENDS AND THAT'S IT?
A-ALONE...
PERORI PERORI
DO YOU HAVE TO BE SO LOUD ABOUT IT?!
WHAT? SHOULD I WHISPER?
YES!!

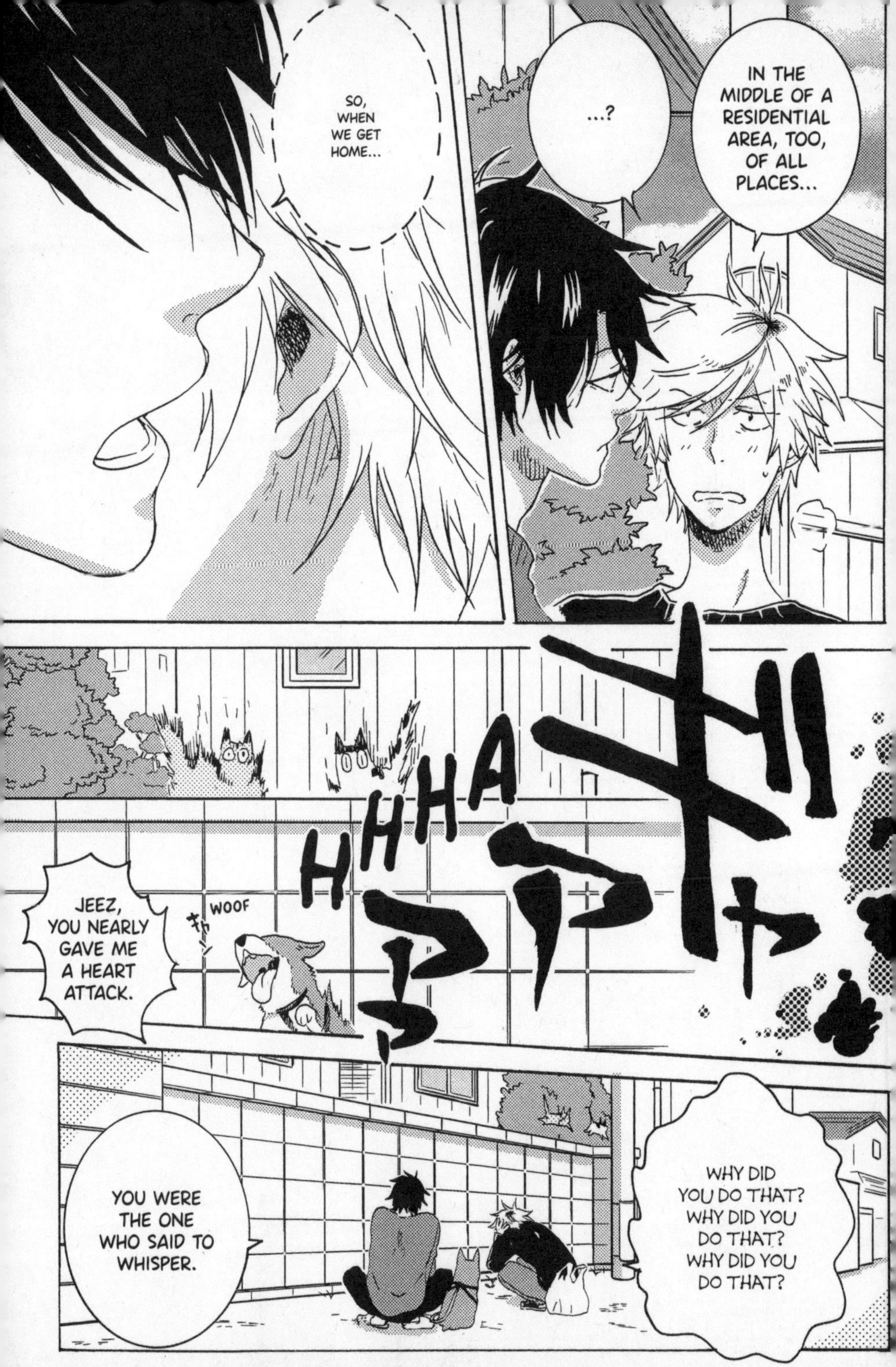
IN THE MIDDLE OF A RESIDENTIAL AREA, TOO, OF ALL PLACES...
...?
SO, WHEN WE GET HOME...
HHHA
WOOF
JEEZ, YOU NEARLY GAVE ME A HEART ATTACK.
WHY DID YOU DO THAT? WHY DID YOU DO THAT? WHY DID YOU DO THAT?
YOU WERE THE ONE WHO SAID TO WHISPER.

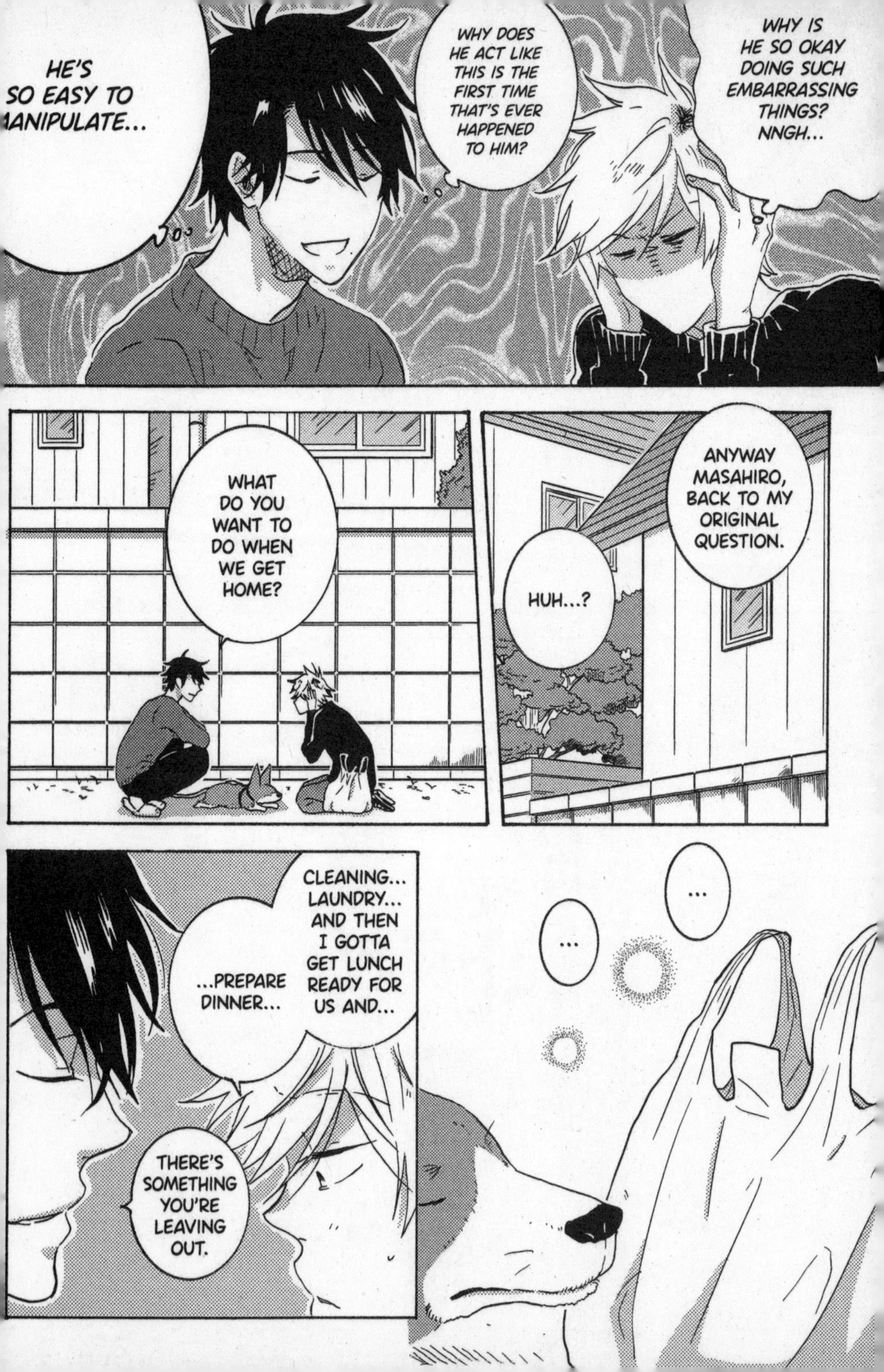
WHY IS HE SO OKAY DOING SUCH EMBARRASSING THINGS? NNGH...
WHY DOES HE ACT LIKE THIS IS THE FIRST TIME THAT'S EVER HAPPENED TO HIM?
HE'S SO EASY TO MANIPULATE...
ANYWAY MASAHIRO, BACK TO MY ORIGINAL QUESTION.
HUH...?
WHAT DO YOU WANT TO DO WHEN WE GET HOME?
...
...
CLEANING... LAUNDRY... AND THEN I GOTTA GET LUNCH READY FOR US AND...
...PREPARE DINNER...
THERE'S SOMETHING YOU'RE LEAVING OUT.

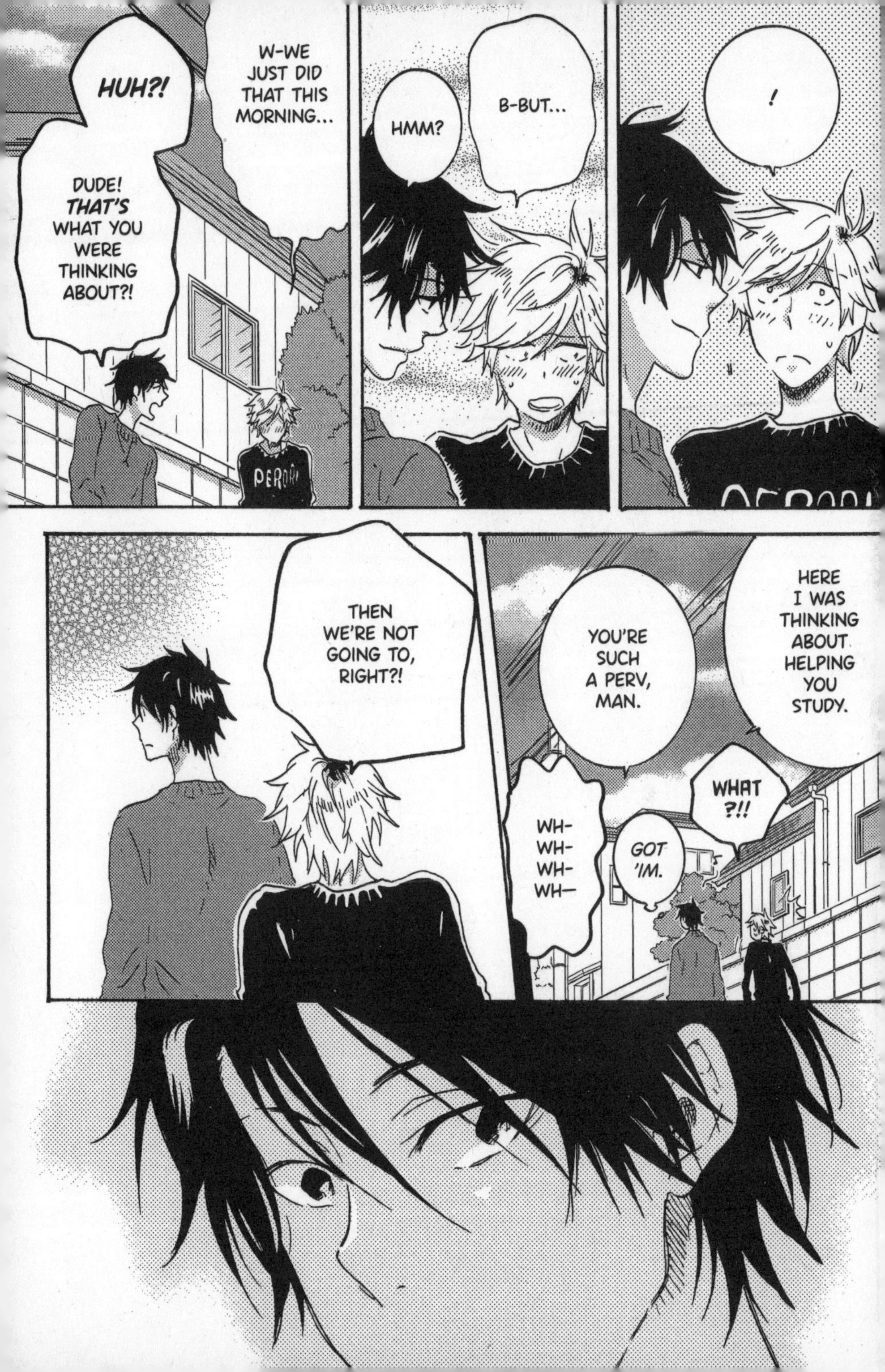
!
B-BUT...
HMM?
W-WE JUST DID THAT THIS MORNING...
HUH?!
DUDE! THAT'S WHAT YOU WERE THINKING ABOUT?!
HERE I WAS THINKING ABOUT HELPING YOU STUDY.
YOU'RE SUCH A PERV, MAN.
WHAT ?!!
GOT 'IM.
WH- WH- WH- WH—
THEN WE'RE NOT GOING TO, RIGHT?!

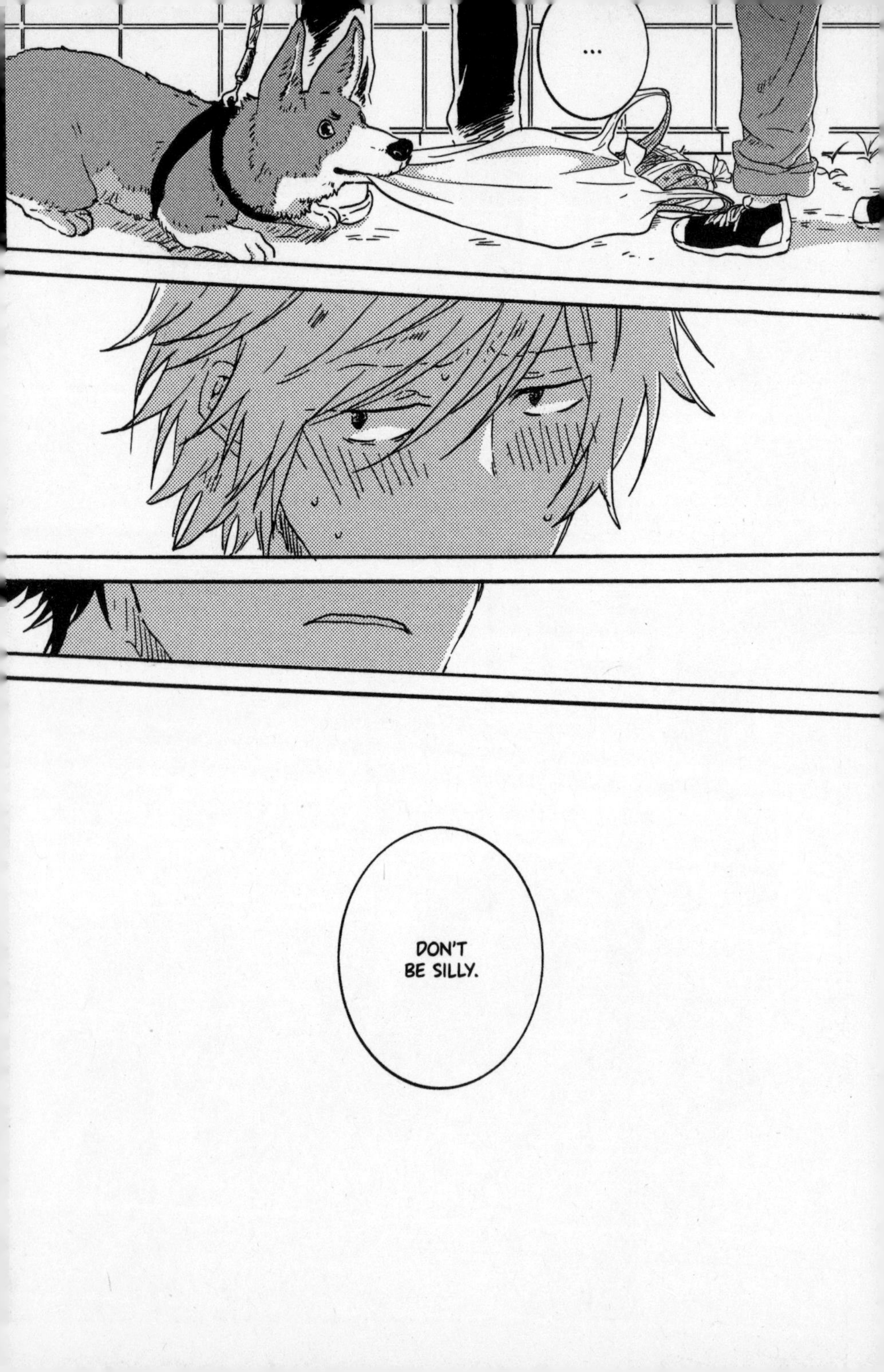
...
DON'T
BE SILLY.

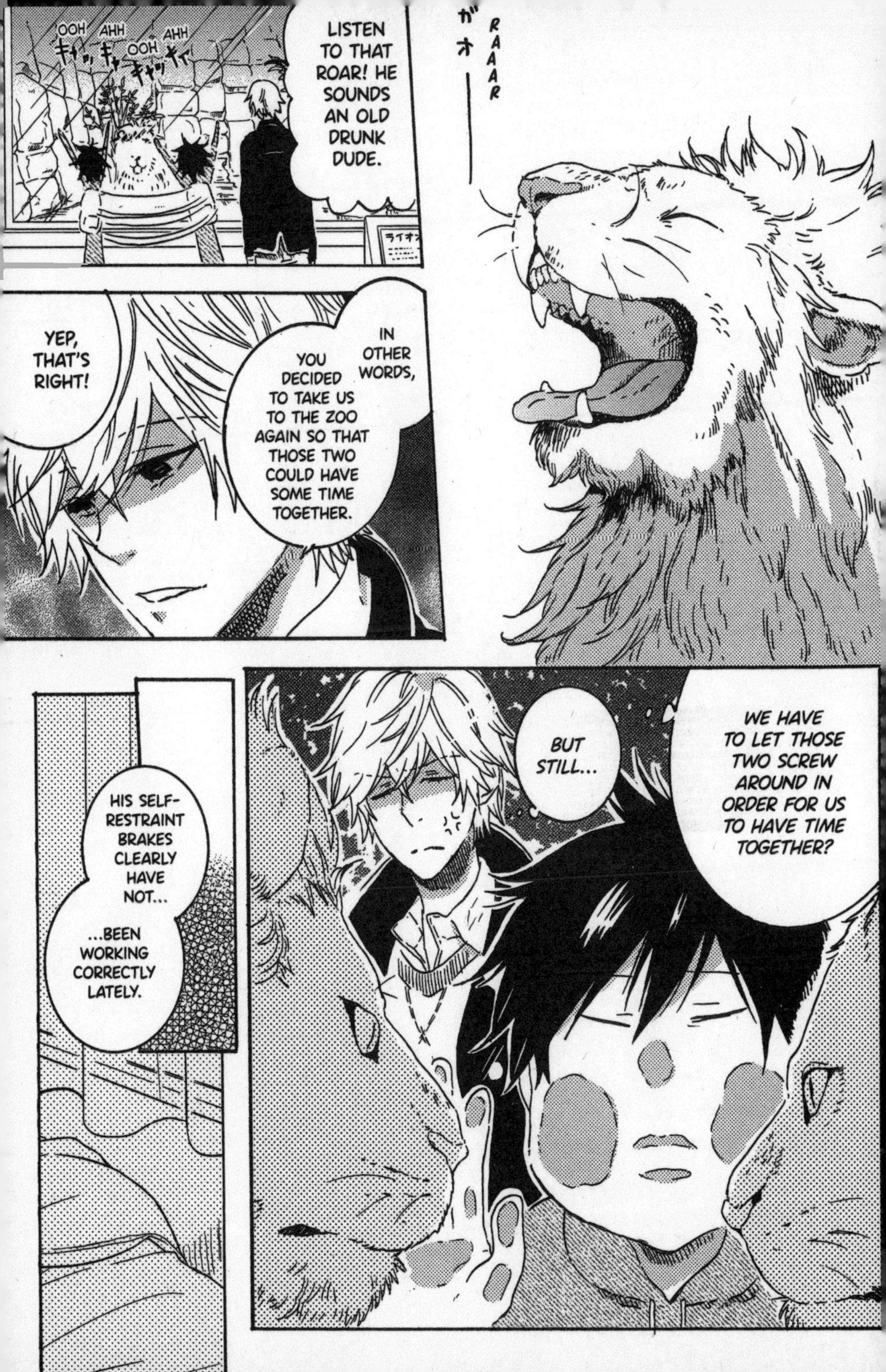
ガオ
RAAAR
OOH AHH OOH AHH
キャッキャ キャッキャ
LISTEN TO THAT ROAR! HE SOUNDS AN OLD DRUNK DUDE.
IN OTHER WORDS, YOU DECIDED TO TAKE US TO THE ZOO AGAIN SO THAT THOSE TWO COULD HAVE SOME TIME TOGETHER.
YEP, THAT'S RIGHT!
WE HAVE TO LET THOSE TWO SCREW AROUND IN ORDER FOR US TO HAVE TIME TOGETHER?
BUT STILL...
HIS SELF-RESTRAINT BRAKES CLEARLY HAVE NOT...
...BEEN WORKING CORRECTLY LATELY.

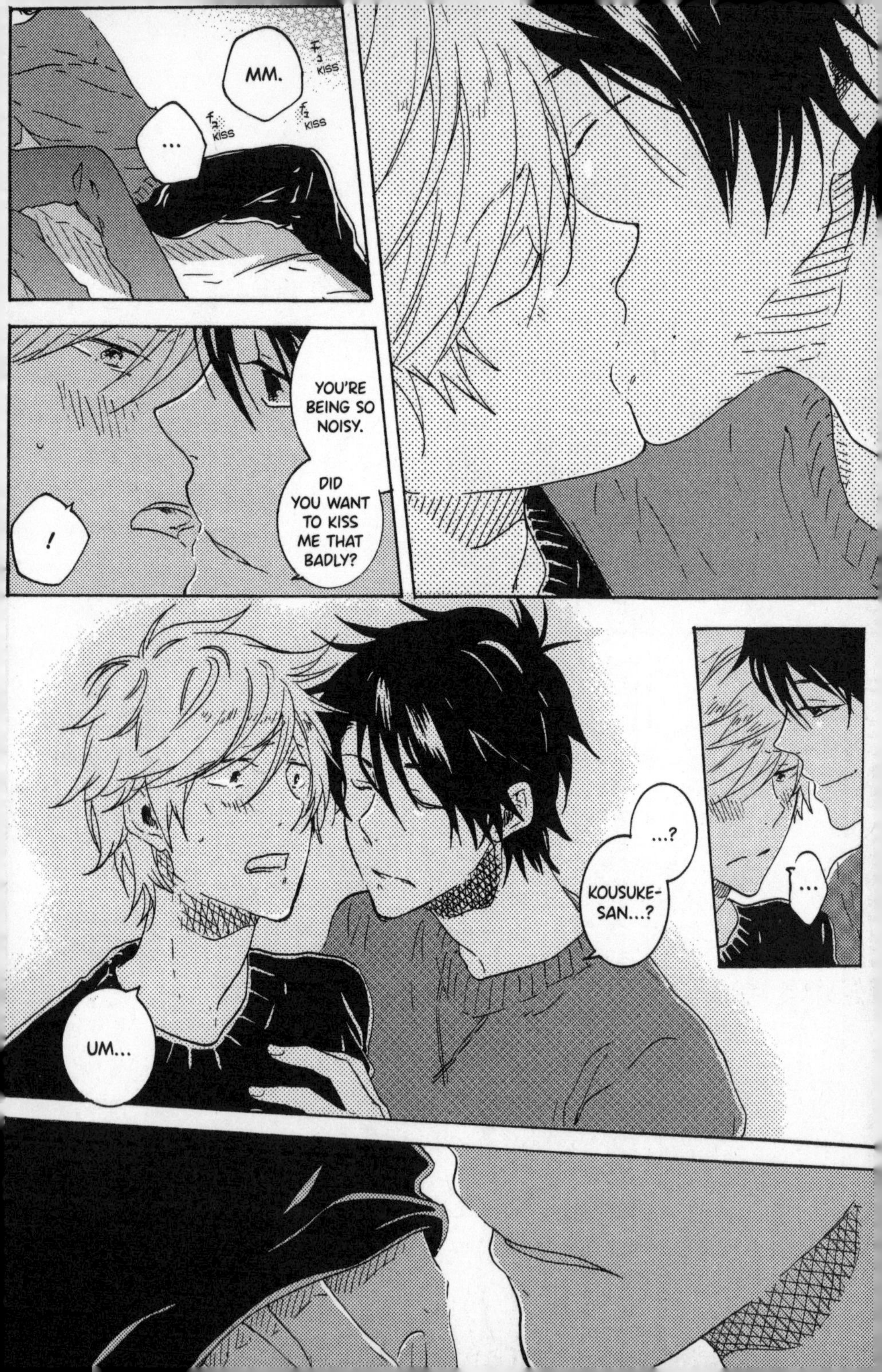
KISS
MM.
KISS
KISS
...
YOU'RE BEING SO NOISY.
DID YOU WANT TO KISS ME THAT BADLY?
!
...
...?
KOUSUKE-SAN...?
UM...

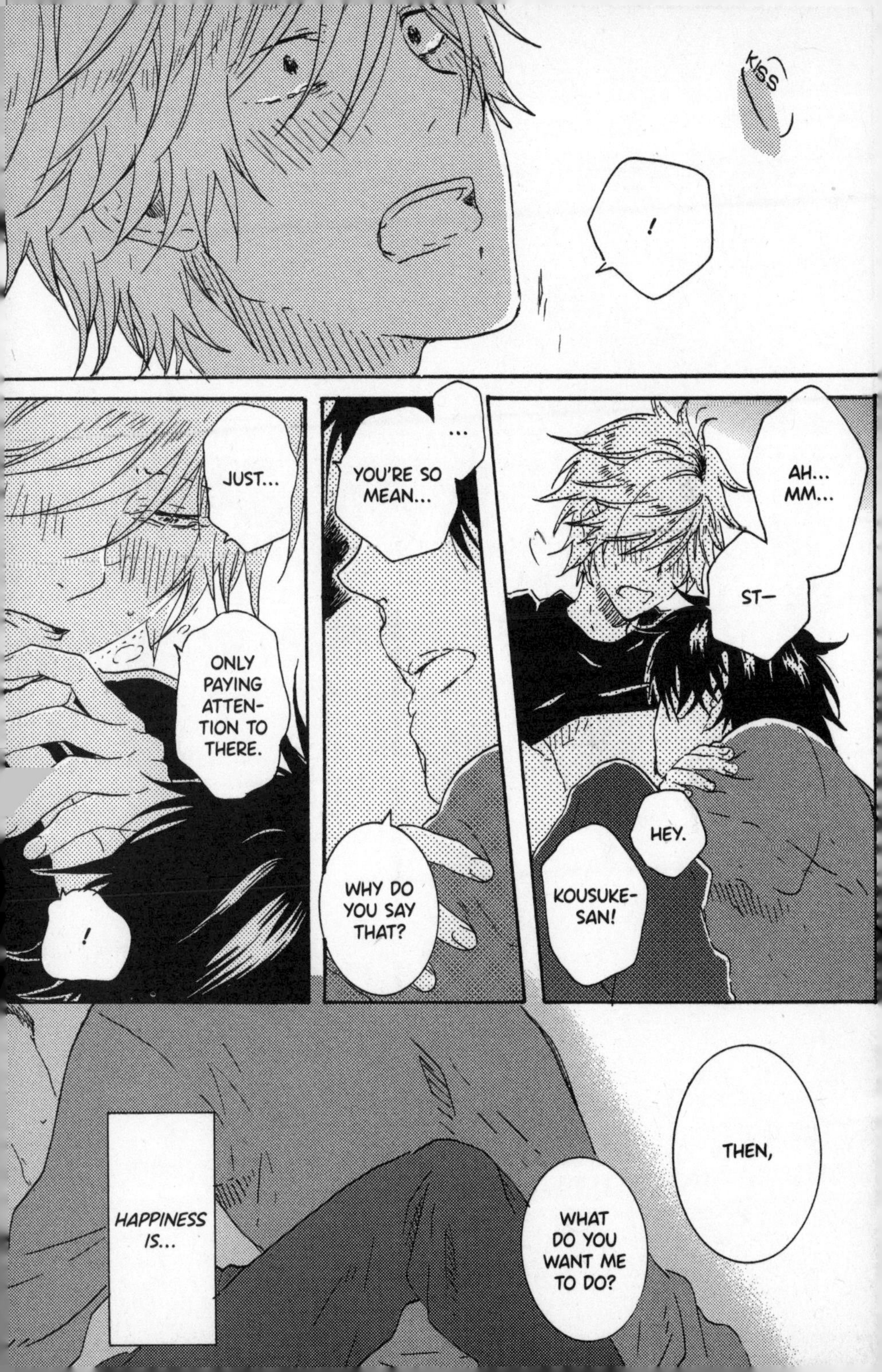
KISS
!
AH... MM...
ST—
HEY.
KOUSUKE-SAN!
...
YOU'RE SO MEAN...
WHY DO YOU SAY THAT?
JUST...
ONLY PAYING ATTEN-TION TO THERE.
!
THEN,
WHAT DO YOU WANT ME TO DO?
HAPPINESS IS...

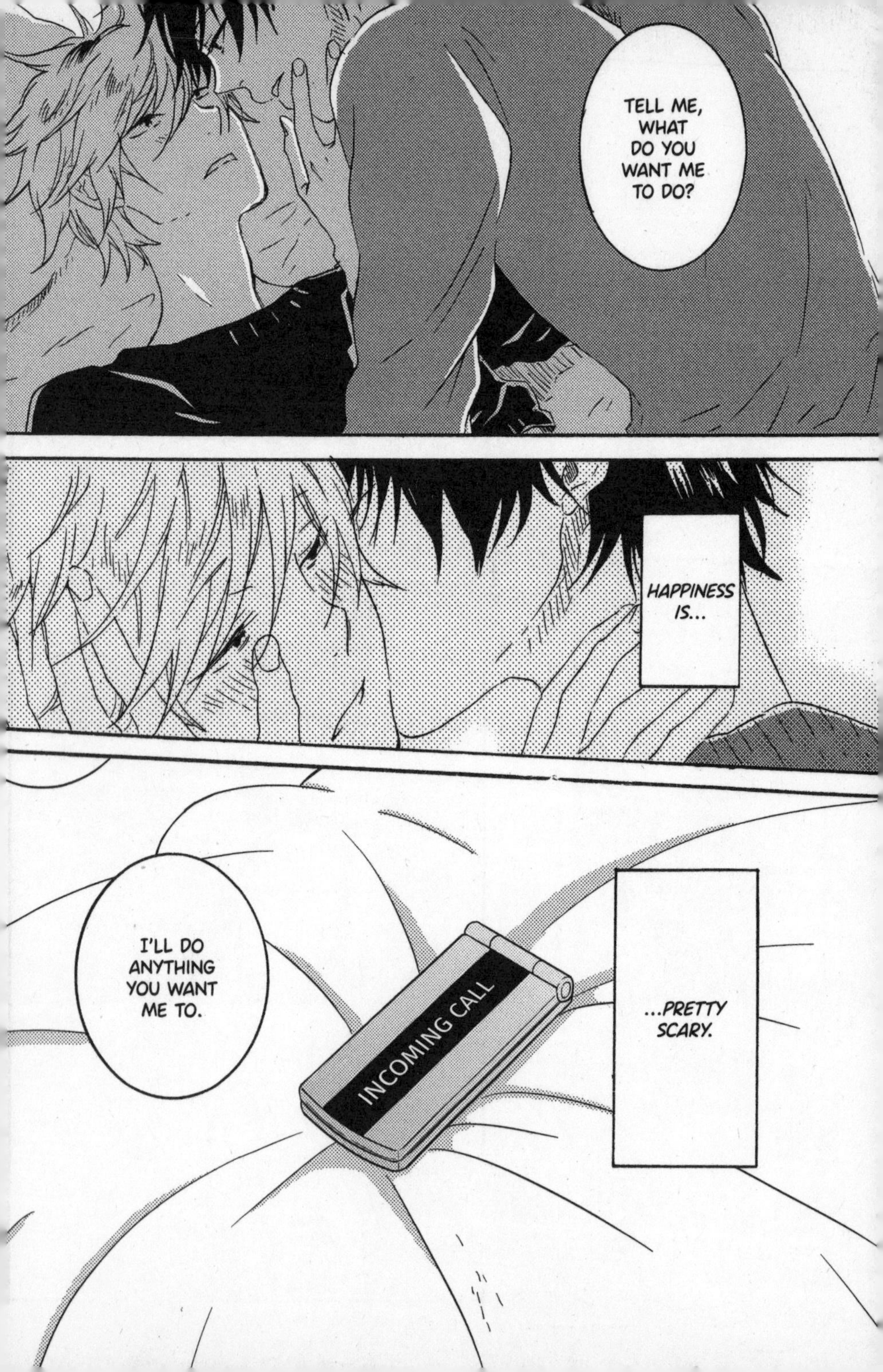
TELL ME, WHAT DO YOU WANT ME TO DO?
HAPPINESS IS...
...PRETTY SCARY.
I'LL DO ANYTHING YOU WANT ME TO.
INCOMING CALL

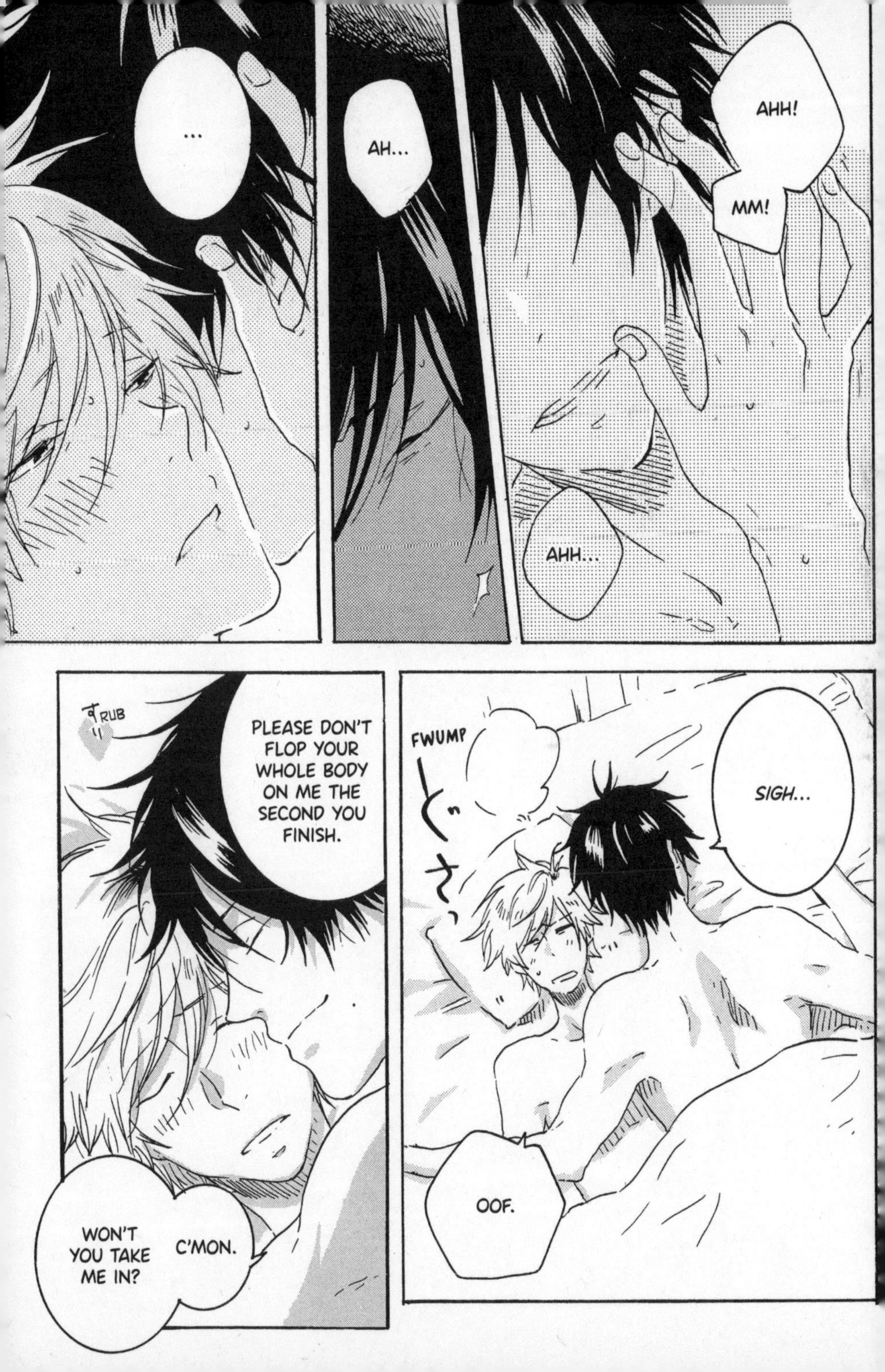
AHH!
MM!
AHH...
AH...
...
SIGH...
FWUMP
OOF.
PLEASE DON'T FLOP YOUR WHOLE BODY ON ME THE SECOND YOU FINISH.
RUB
C'MON.
WON'T YOU TAKE ME IN?

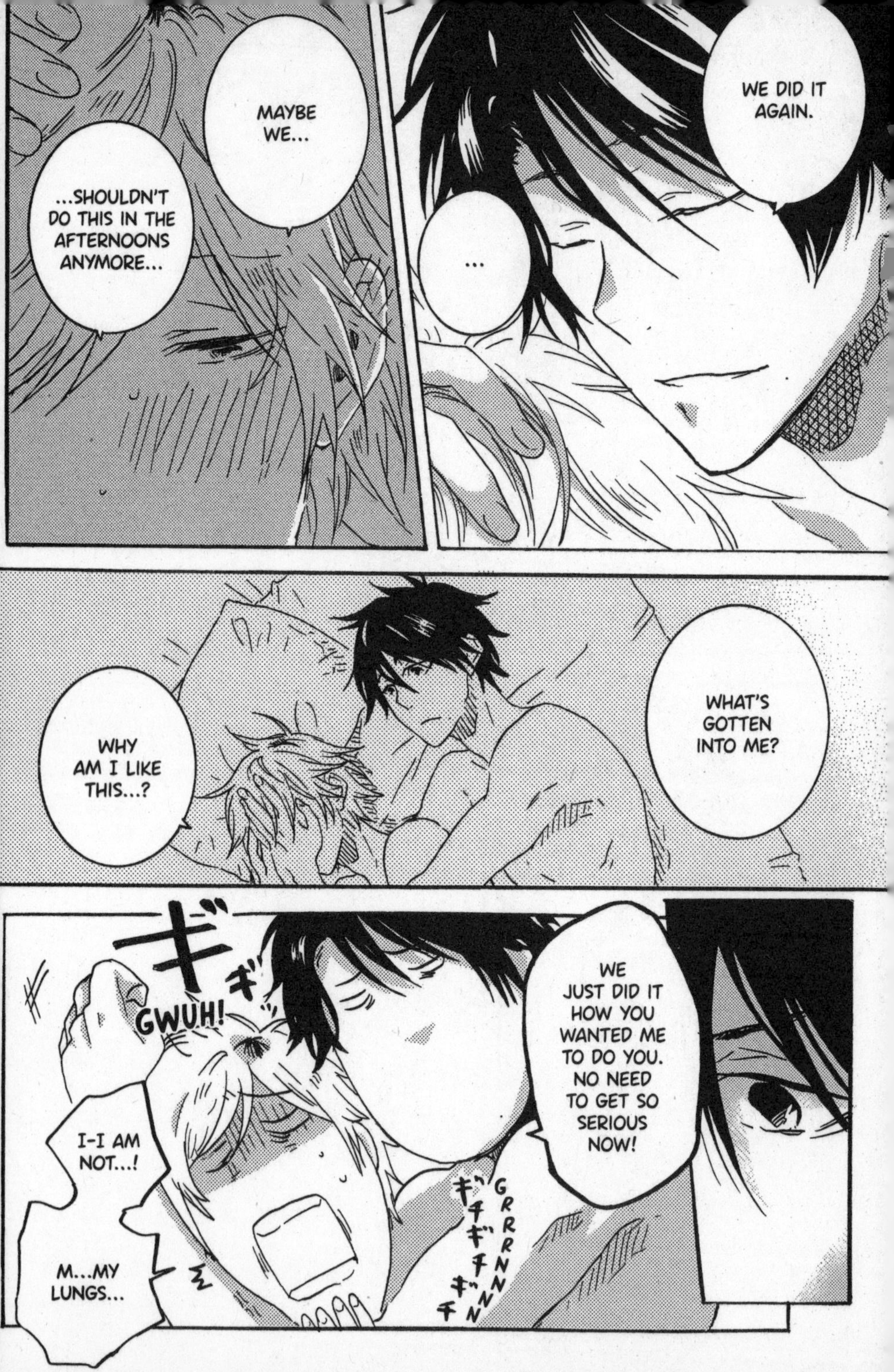
WE DID IT AGAIN.
...
MAYBE WE...
...SHOULDN'T DO THIS IN THE AFTERNOONS ANYMORE...
WHAT'S GOTTEN INTO ME?
WHY AM I LIKE THIS...?
WE JUST DID IT HOW YOU WANTED ME TO DO YOU. NO NEED TO GET SO SERIOUS NOW!
ギギ
GWUH!
I-I AM NOT...!
GRRRNNN
M...MY LUNGS...

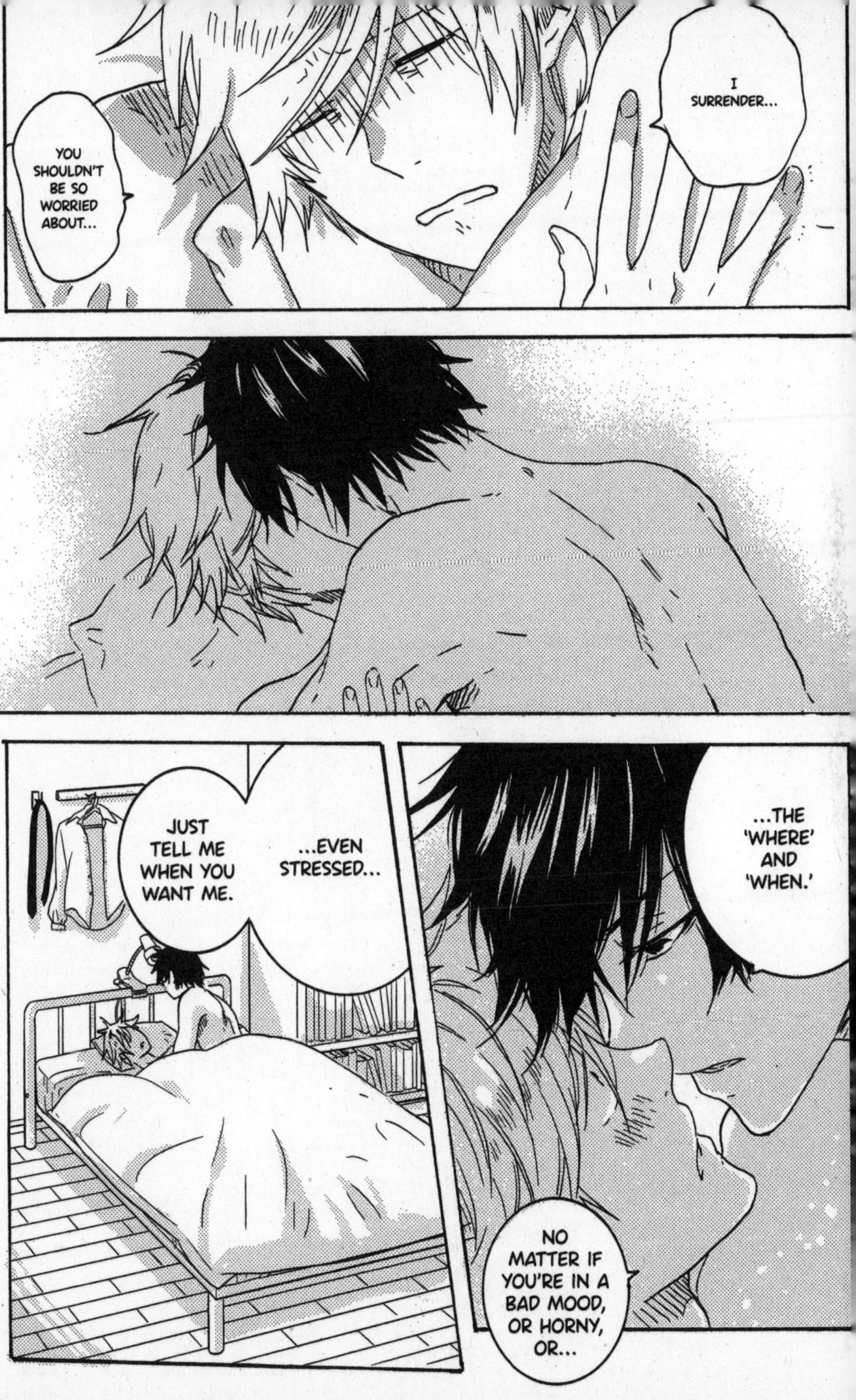
I SURRENDER...
YOU SHOULDN'T BE SO WORRIED ABOUT...
...THE 'WHERE' AND 'WHEN.'
NO MATTER IF YOU'RE IN A BAD MOOD, OR HORNY, OR...
...EVEN STRESSED...
JUST TELL ME WHEN YOU WANT ME.

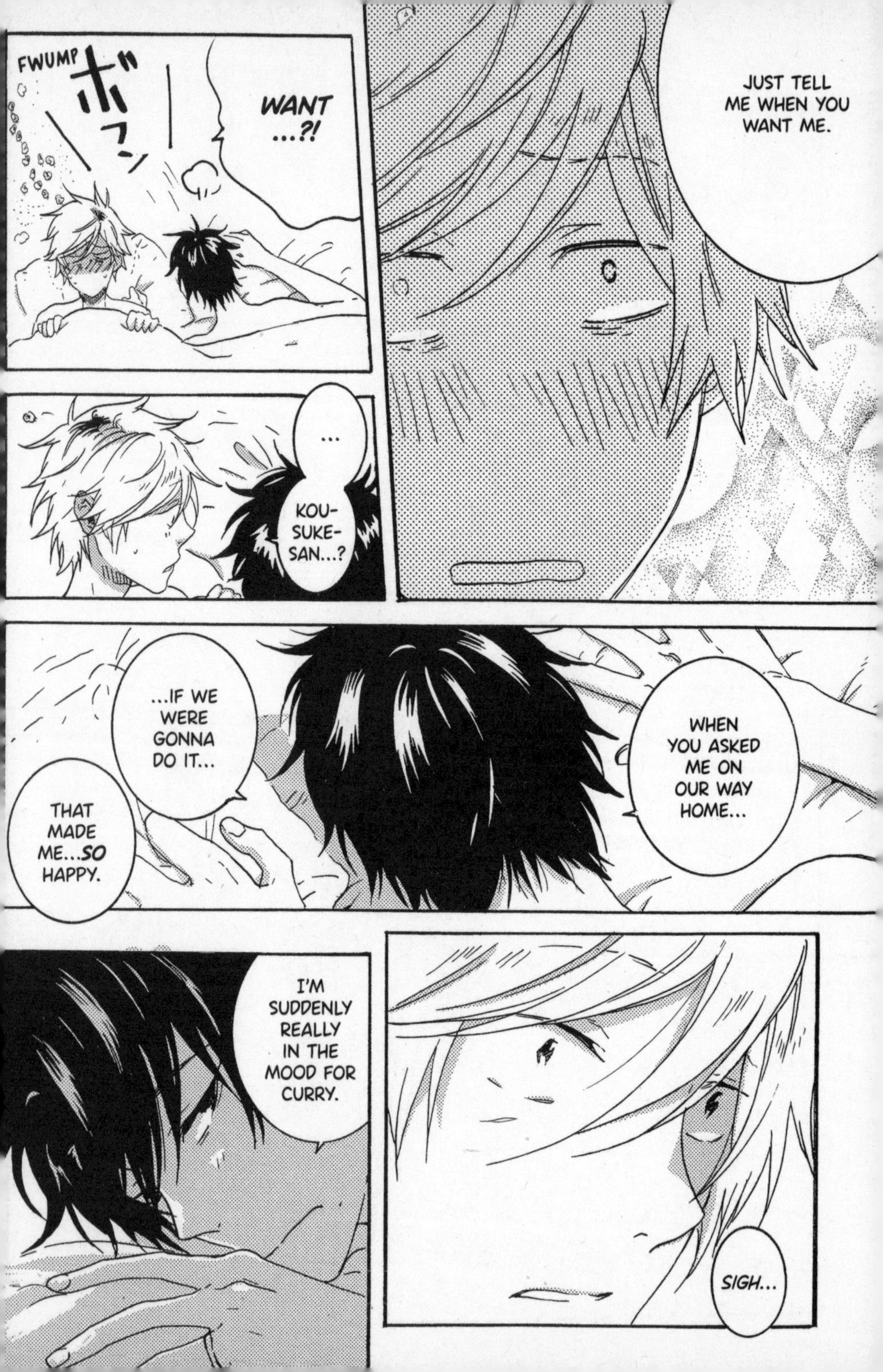

JUST TELL ME WHEN YOU WANT ME.
FWUMP
ボフン
WANT ...?!
...
KOU-SUKE-SAN...?
WHEN YOU ASKED ME ON OUR WAY HOME...
...IF WE WERE GONNA DO IT...
THAT MADE ME...SO HAPPY.
SIGH...
I'M SUDDENLY REALLY IN THE MOOD FOR CURRY.

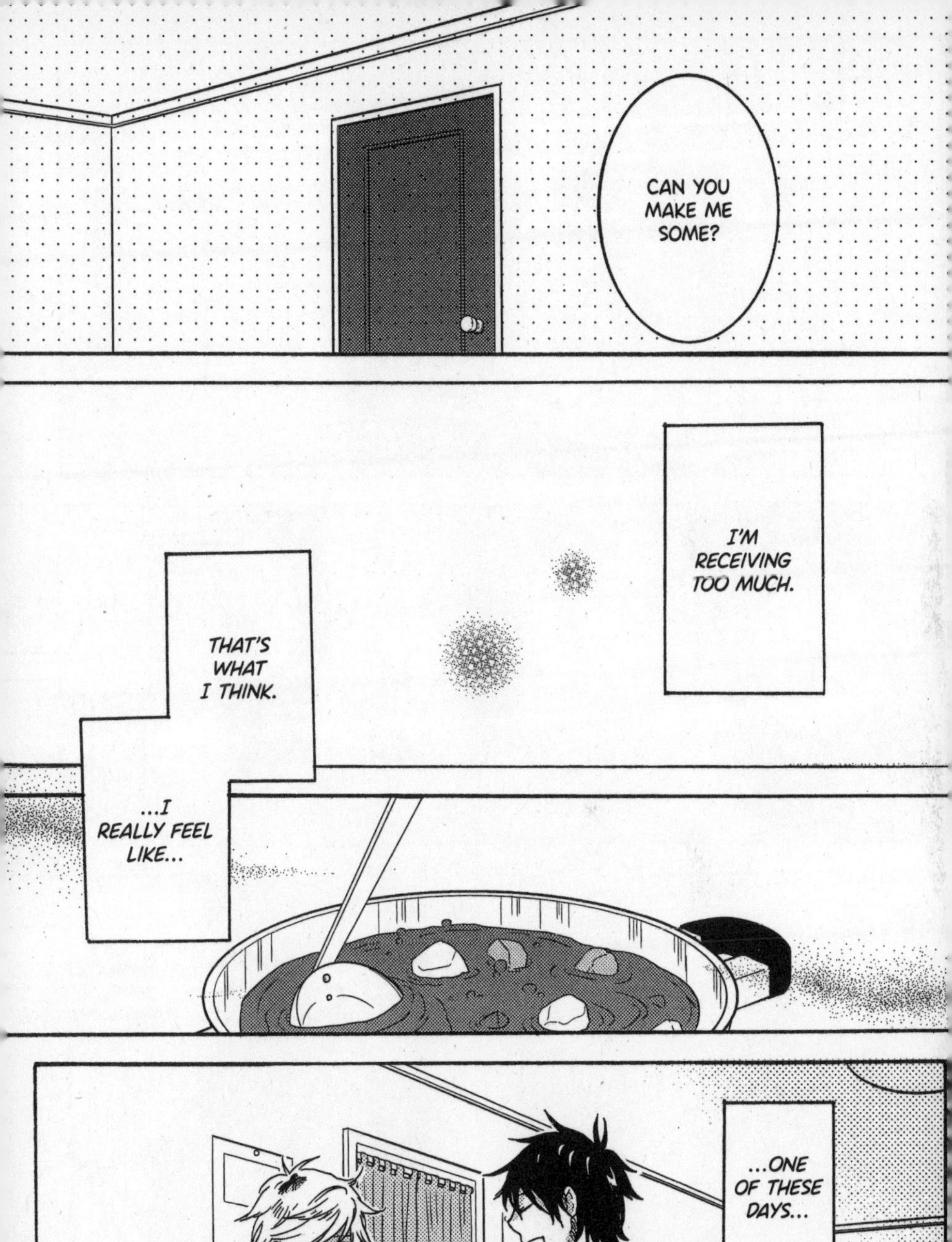
CAN YOU MAKE ME SOME?
I'M RECEIVING TOO MUCH.
THAT'S WHAT I THINK.
...I REALLY FEEL LIKE...
...ONE OF THESE DAYS...

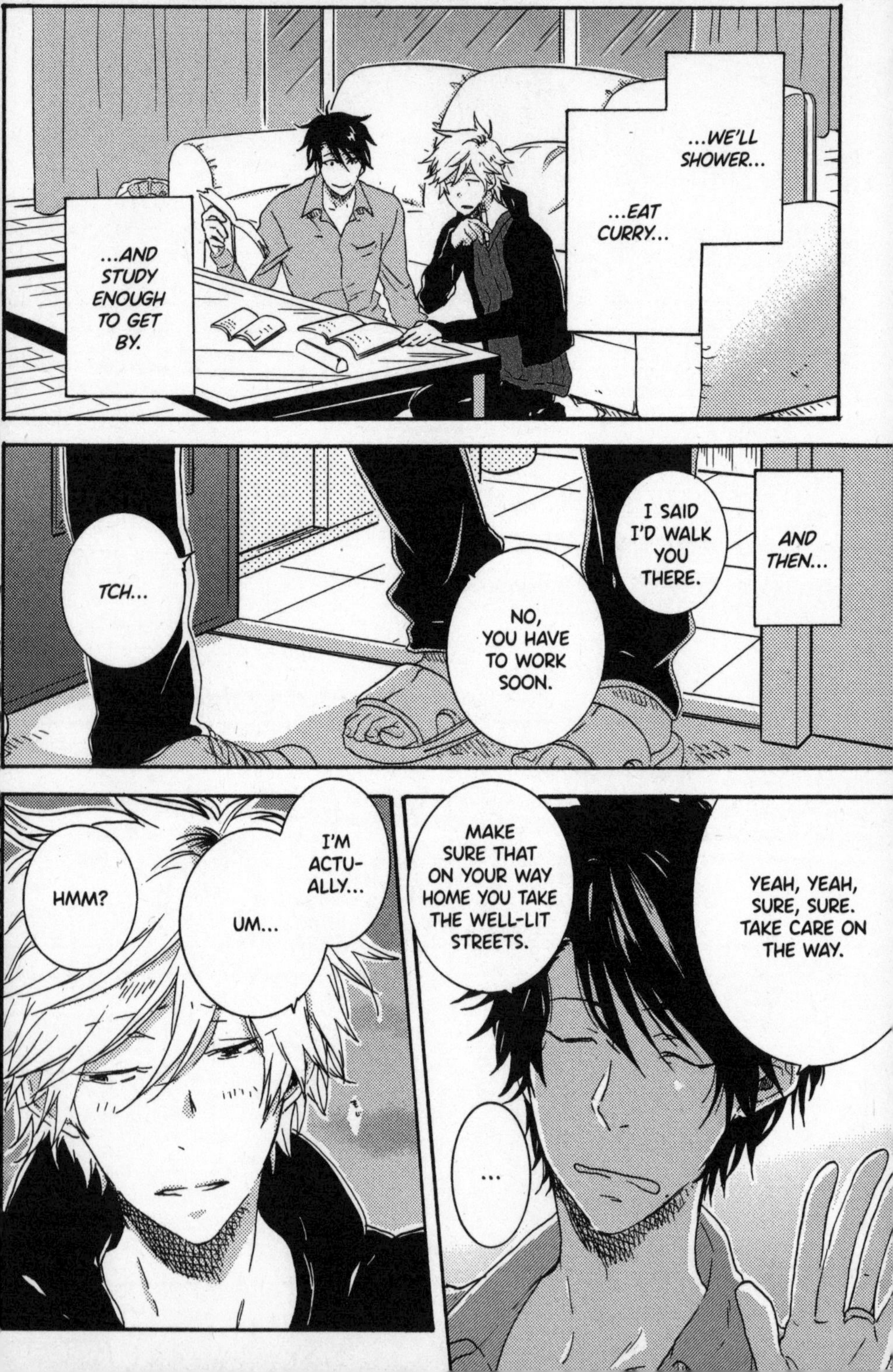
...WE'LL SHOWER...
...EAT CURRY...
...AND STUDY ENOUGH TO GET BY.
AND THEN...
I SAID I'D WALK YOU THERE.
NO, YOU HAVE TO WORK SOON.
TCH...
YEAH, YEAH, SURE, SURE. TAKE CARE ON THE WAY.
MAKE SURE THAT ON YOUR WAY HOME YOU TAKE THE WELL-LIT STREETS.
...
I'M ACTU-ALLY...
UM...
HMM?

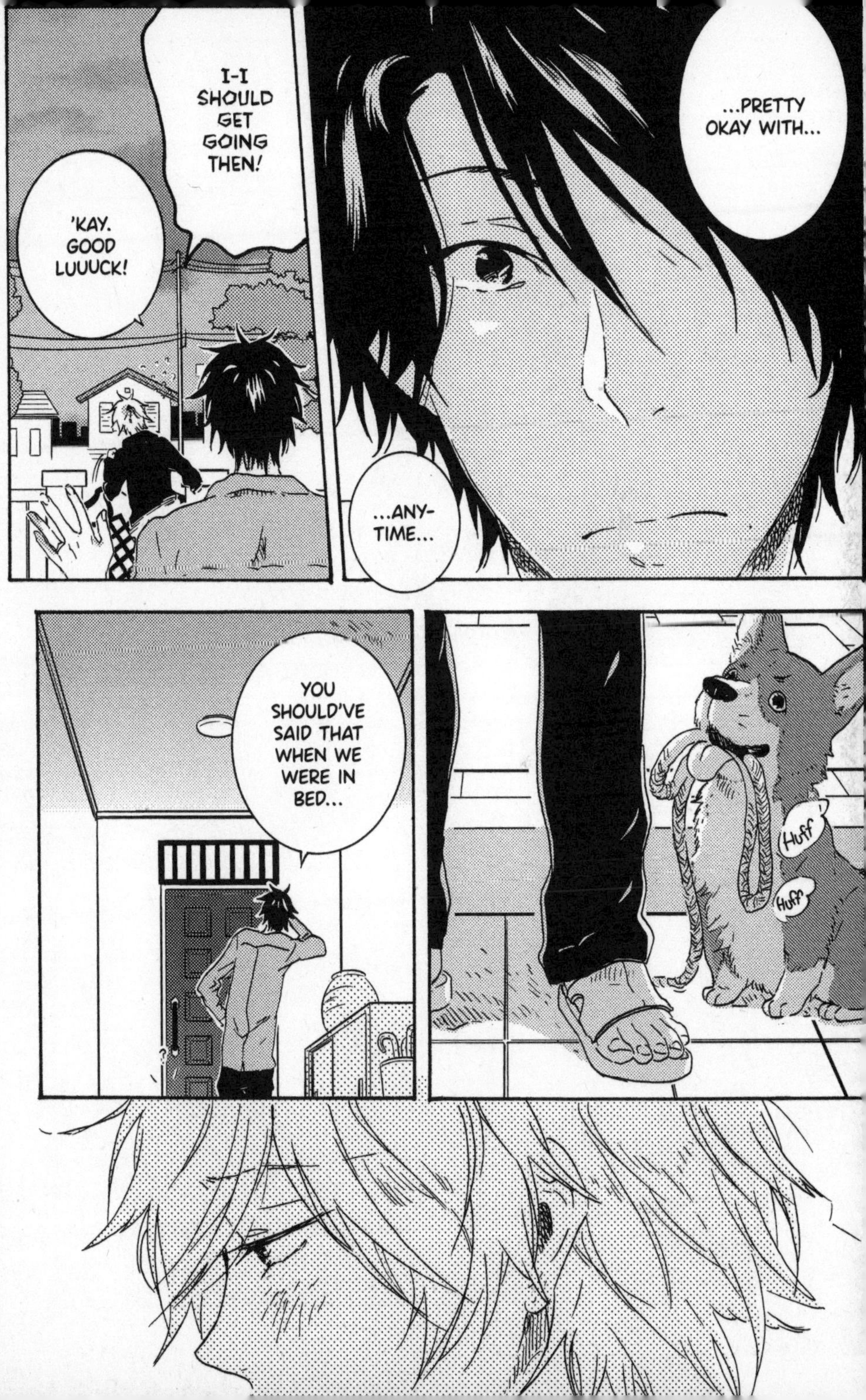
...PRETTY OKAY WITH...
...ANY-TIME...
I-I SHOULD GET GOING THEN!
'KAY. GOOD LUUUCK!
Huff
Huff
YOU SHOULD'VE SAID THAT WHEN WE WERE IN BED...

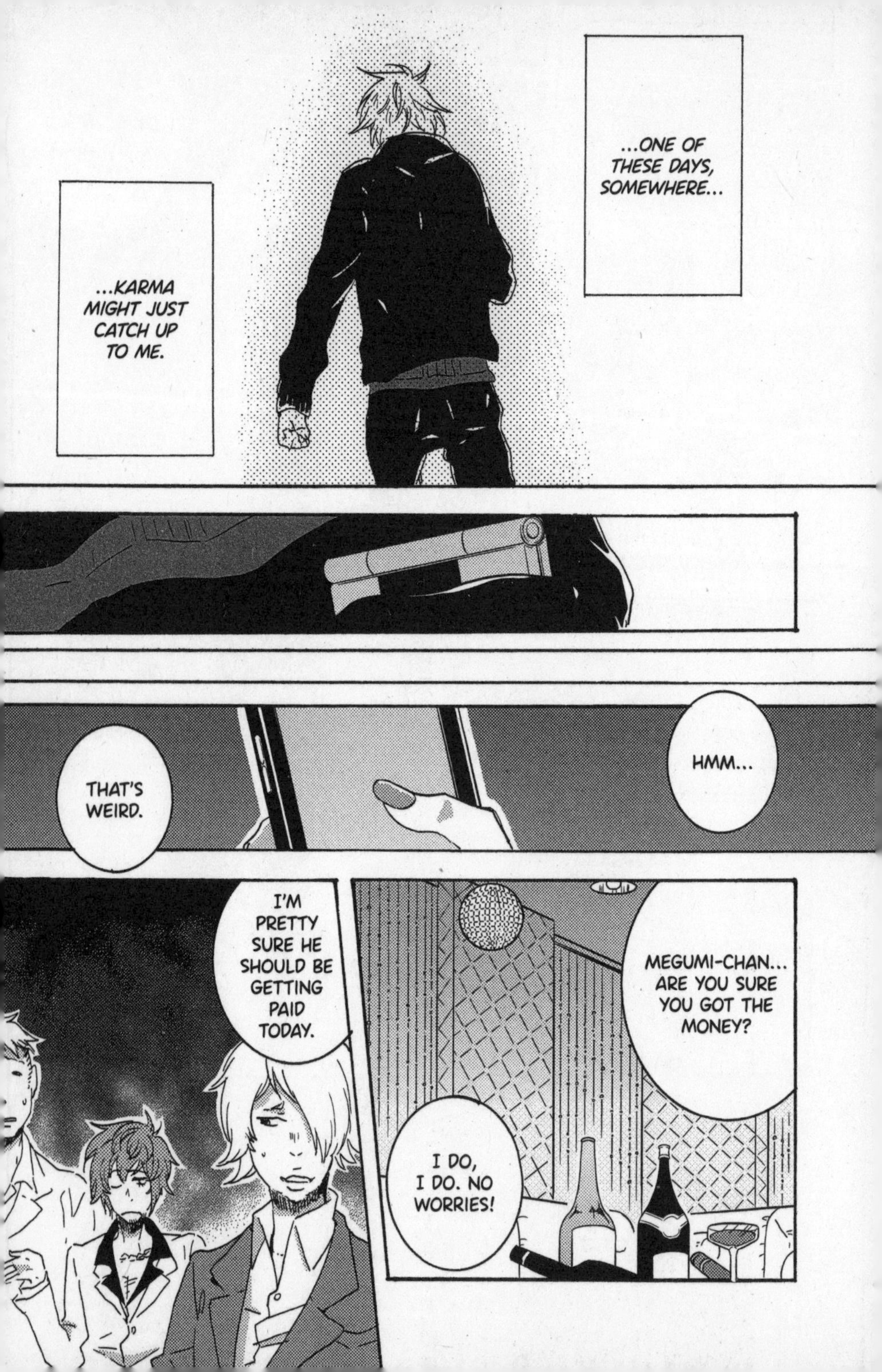
...ONE OF THESE DAYS, SOMEWHERE...
...KARMA MIGHT JUST CATCH UP TO ME.
HMM...
THAT'S WEIRD.
MEGUMI-CHAN... ARE YOU SURE YOU GOT THE MONEY?
I DO, I DO. NO WORRIES!
I'M PRETTY SURE HE SHOULD BE GETTING PAID TODAY.

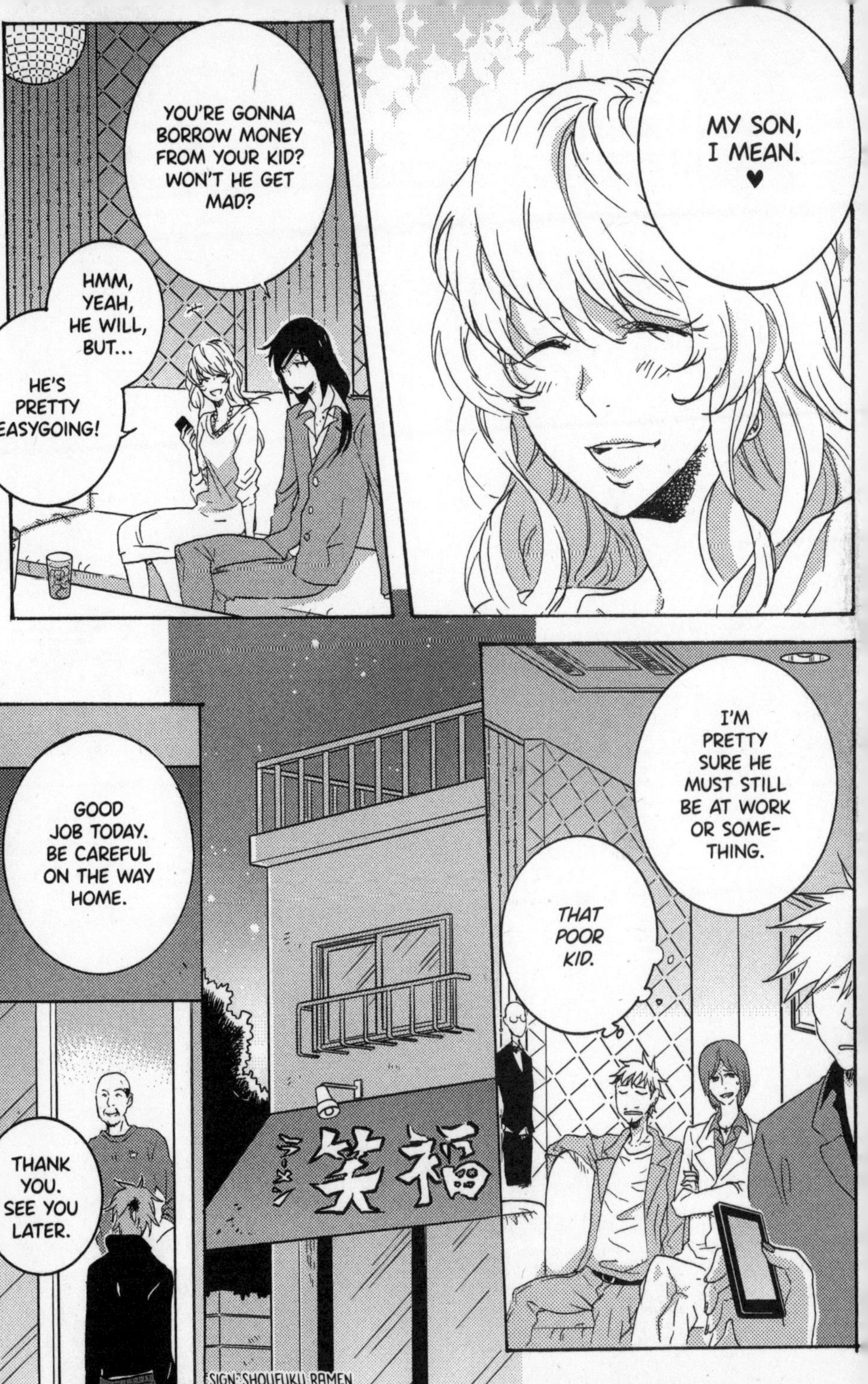
MY SON, I MEAN. ♥
YOU'RE GONNA BORROW MONEY FROM YOUR KID? WON'T HE GET MAD?
HMM, YEAH, HE WILL, BUT...
HE'S PRETTY EASYGOING!
I'M PRETTY SURE HE MUST STILL BE AT WORK OR SOME-THING.
THAT POOR KID.
ラーメン 笑福
GOOD JOB TODAY. BE CAREFUL ON THE WAY HOME.
THANK YOU. SEE YOU LATER.
SIGN: SHOUFUKU RAMEN

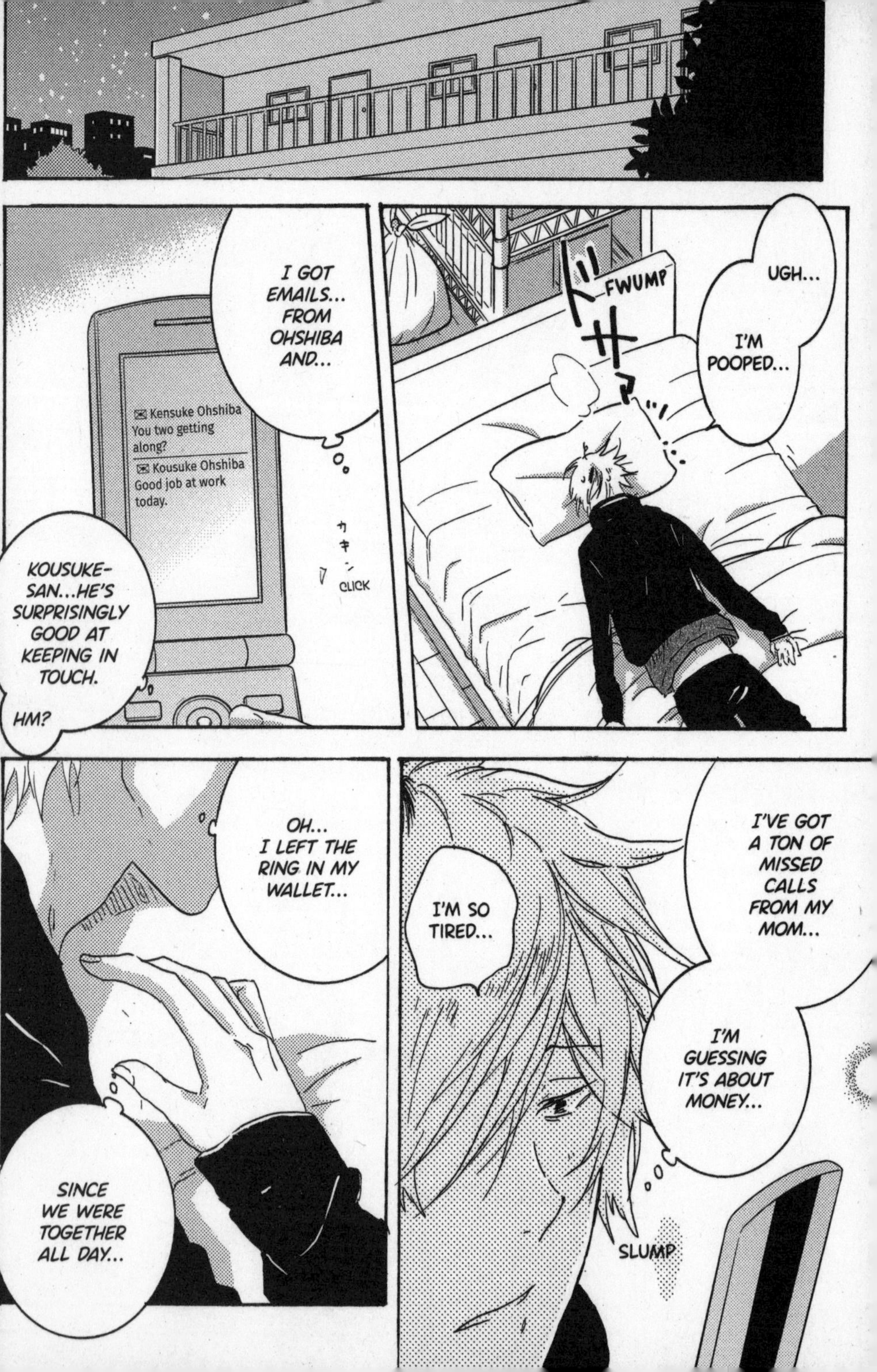
FWUMP
UGH... I'M POOPED...
I GOT EMAILS... FROM OHSHIBA AND...
Kensuke Ohshiba You two getting along?
Kousuke Ohshiba Good job at work today.
CLICK
KOUSUKE-SAN...HE'S SURPRISINGLY GOOD AT KEEPING IN TOUCH.
HM?
I'VE GOT A TON OF MISSED CALLS FROM MY MOM...
I'M SO TIRED...
I'M GUESSING IT'S ABOUT MONEY...
SLUMP
OH... I LEFT THE RING IN MY WALLET...
SINCE WE WERE TOGETHER ALL DAY...

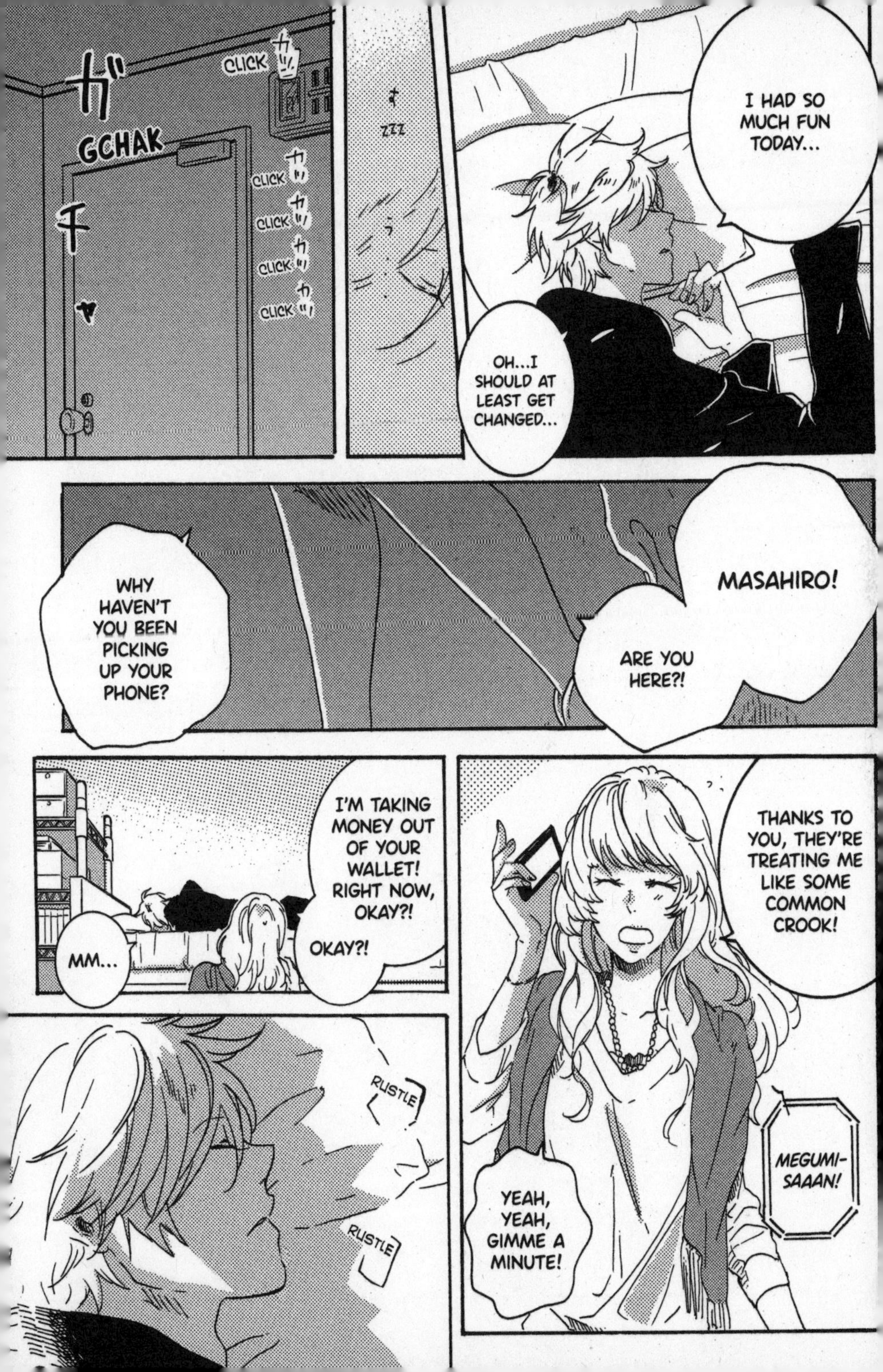
I HAD SO MUCH FUN TODAY...
OH...I SHOULD AT LEAST GET CHANGED...
ZZZ
CLICK
GCHAK
CLICK
CLICK
CLICK
CLICK
MASAHIRO!
ARE YOU HERE?!
WHY HAVEN'T YOU BEEN PICKING UP YOUR PHONE?
THANKS TO YOU, THEY'RE TREATING ME LIKE SOME COMMON CROOK!
MEGUMI-SAAAN!
YEAH, YEAH, GIMME A MINUTE!
I'M TAKING MONEY OUT OF YOUR WALLET! RIGHT NOW, OKAY?!
OKAY?!
MM...
RUSTLE
RUSTLE

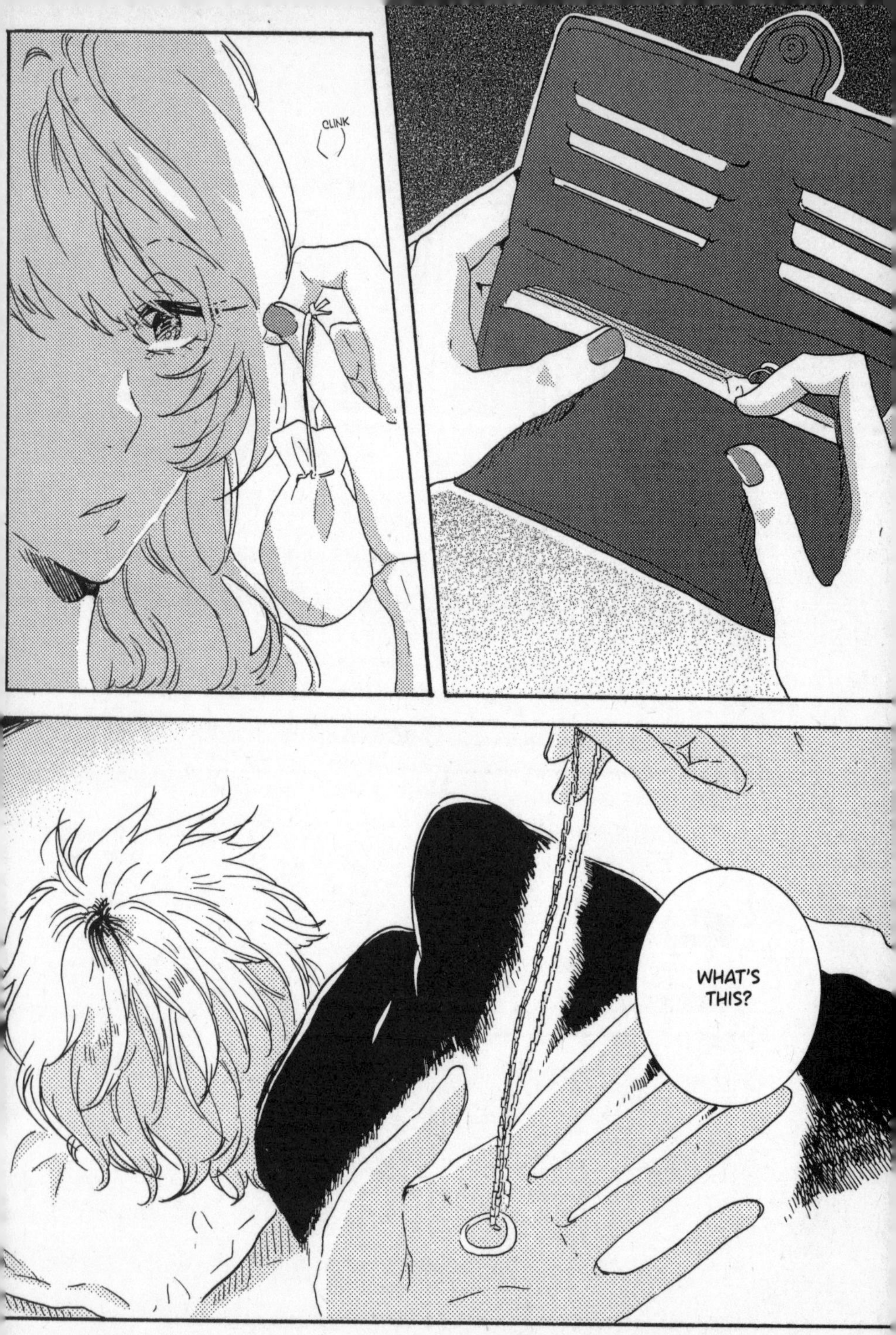
CLINK
WHAT'S THIS?

Hitorijime
My Hero

Q.
Huh?
You weren't
at Tohru-kun's
place?

A. I was looking for work.

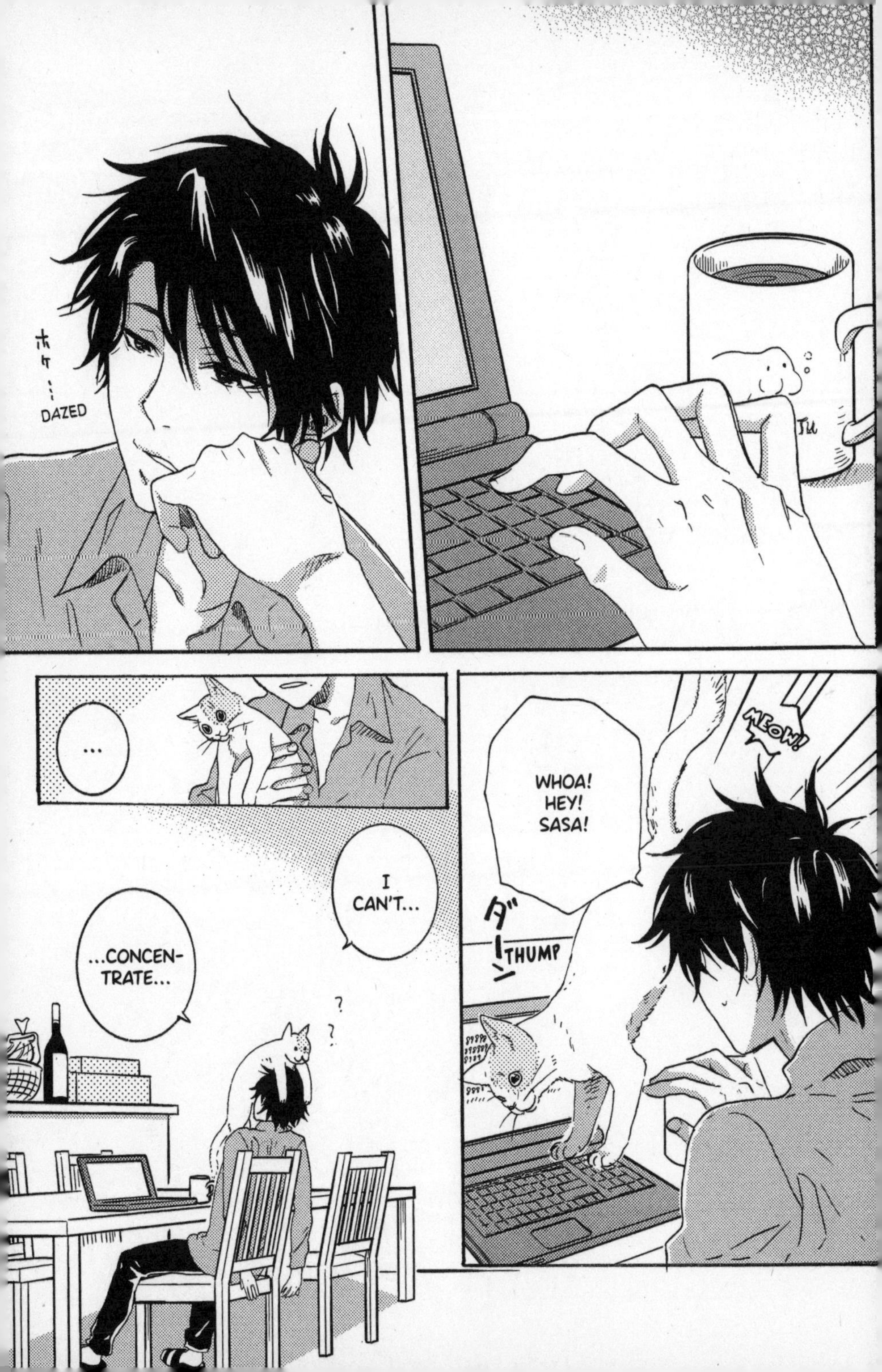
ホケ…
DAZED
MEOW!
WHOA! HEY! SASA!
ダーン
THUMP
...
I CAN'T...
...CONCENTRATE...
?
?

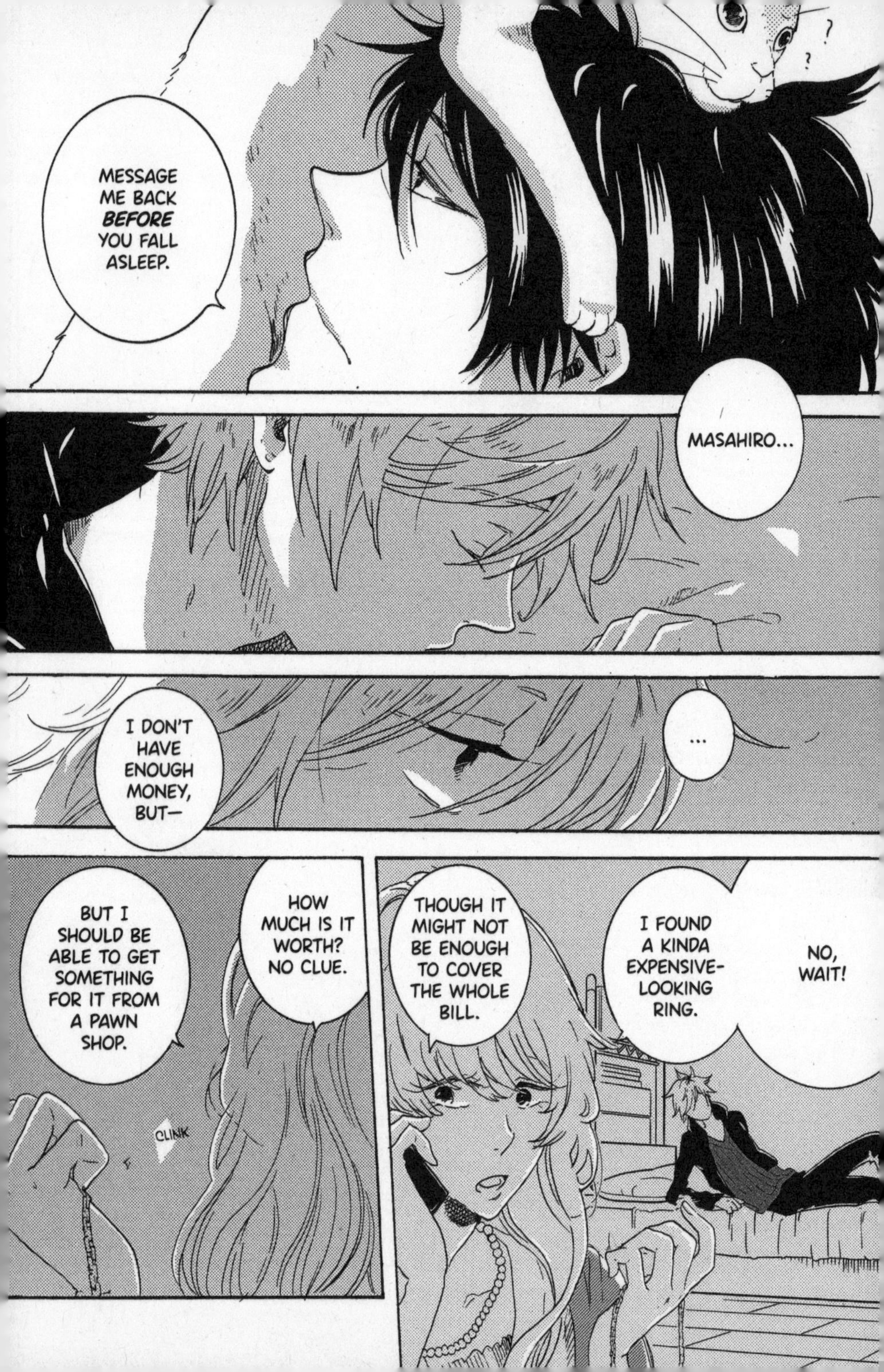
MESSAGE ME BACK ***BEFORE*** YOU FALL ASLEEP.
MASAHIRO...
...
I DON'T HAVE ENOUGH MONEY, BUT—
NO, WAIT!
I FOUND A KINDA EXPENSIVE-LOOKING RING.
THOUGH IT MIGHT NOT BE ENOUGH TO COVER THE WHOLE BILL.
HOW MUCH IS IT WORTH? NO CLUE.
BUT I SHOULD BE ABLE TO GET SOMETHING FOR IT FROM A PAWN SHOP.
CLINK

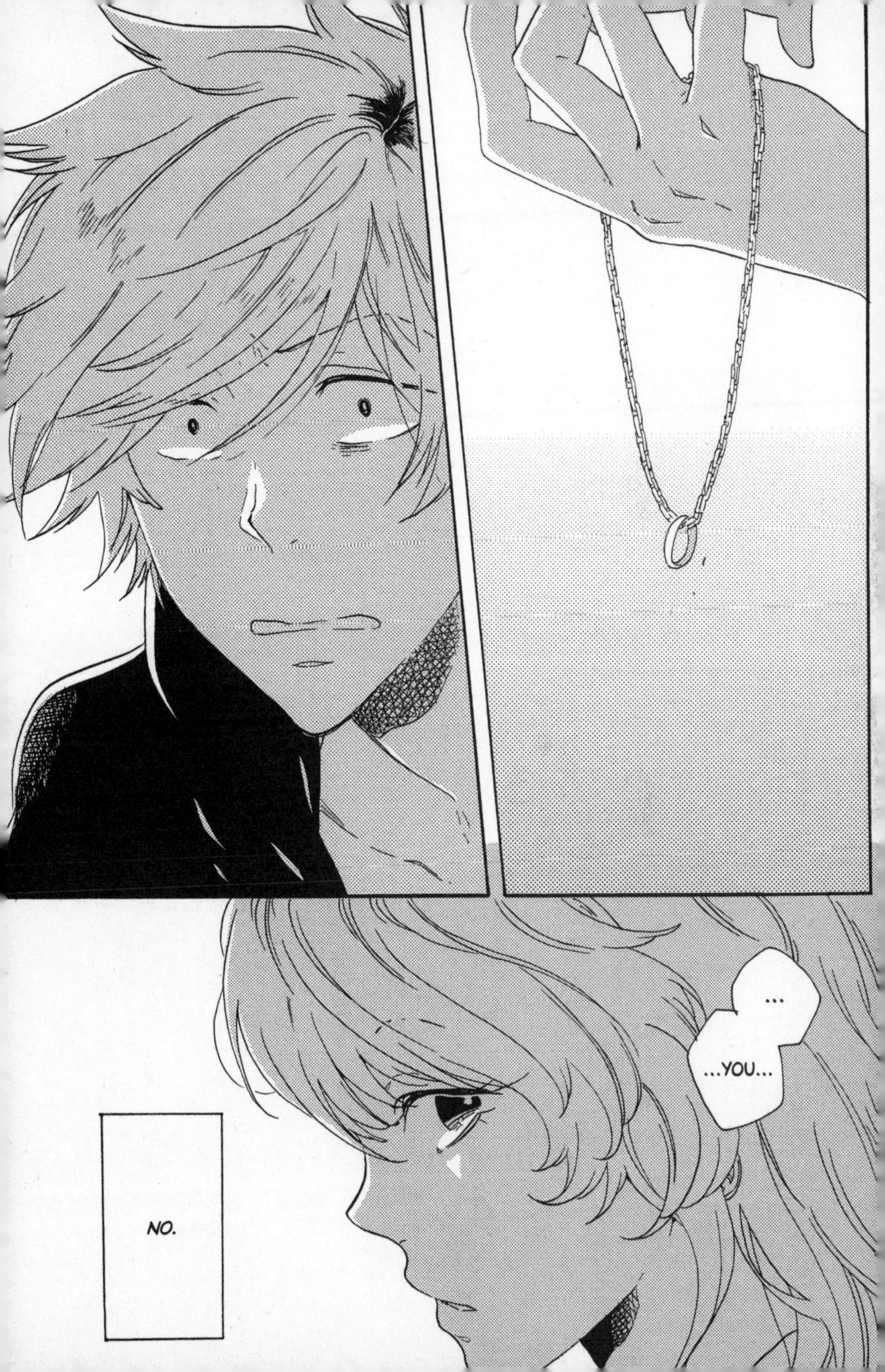
...
...YOU...
NO.

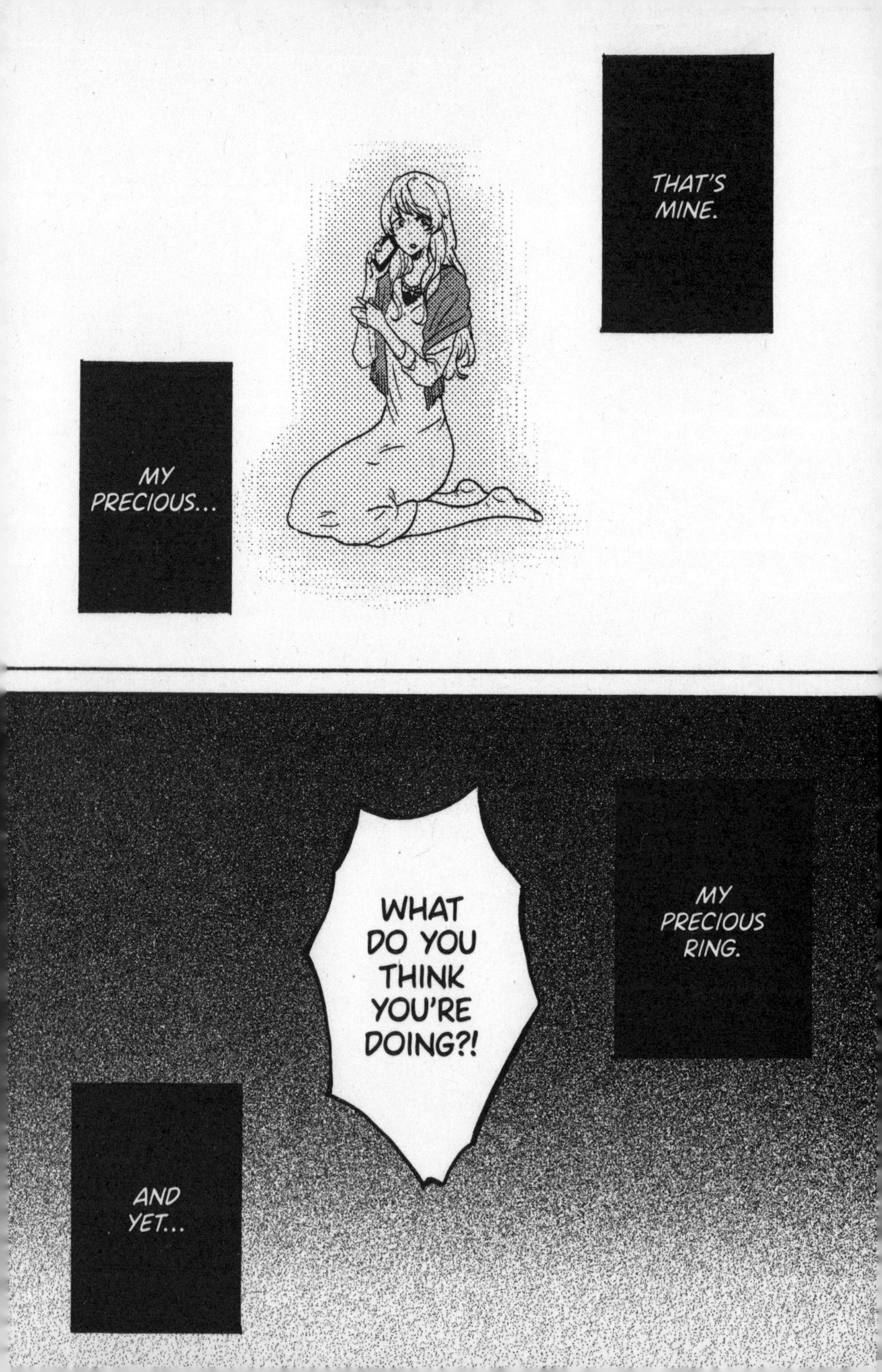
THAT'S MINE.
MY PRECIOUS...
MY PRECIOUS RING.
WHAT DO YOU THINK YOU'RE DOING?!
AND YET...

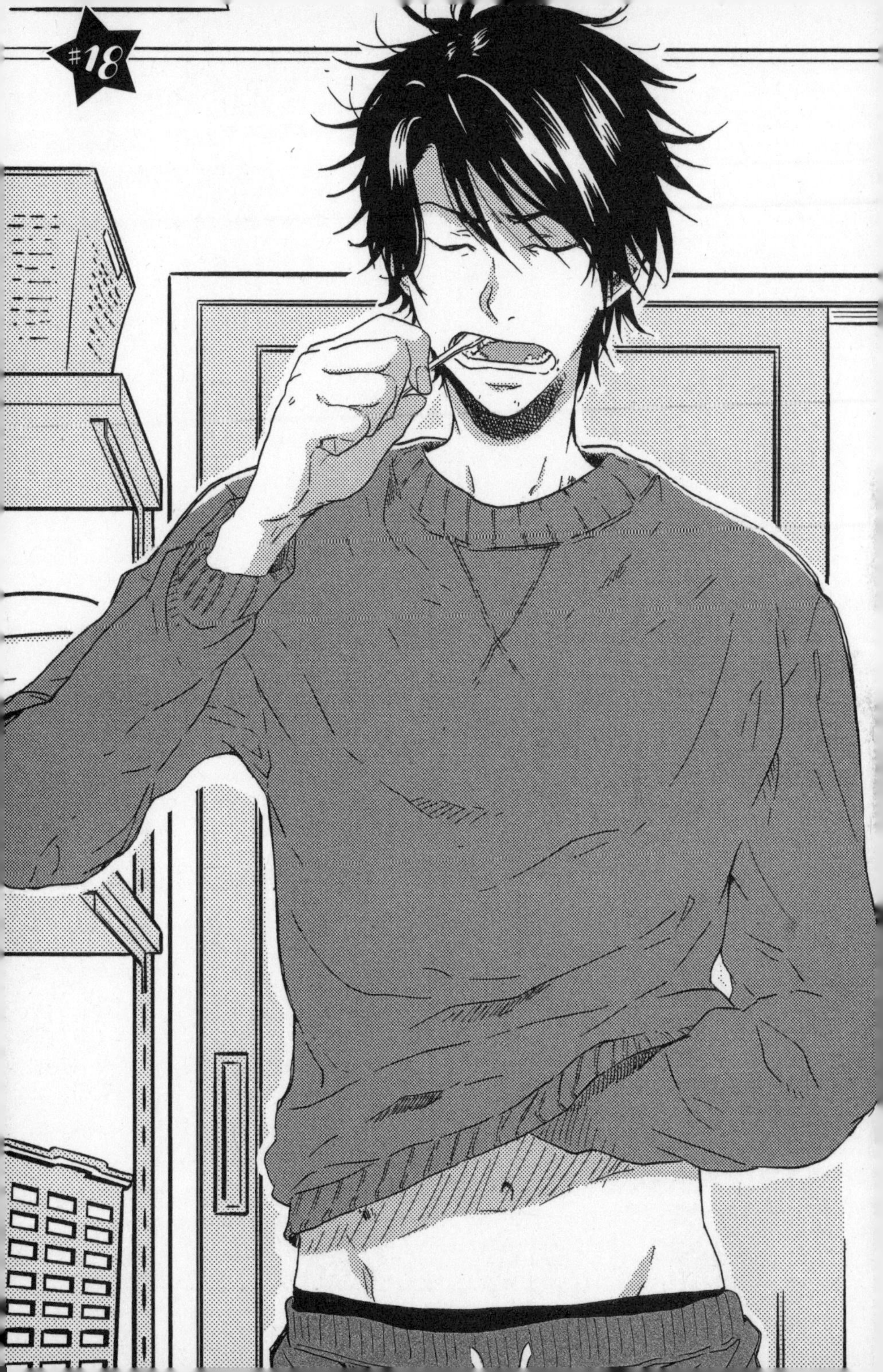
#18

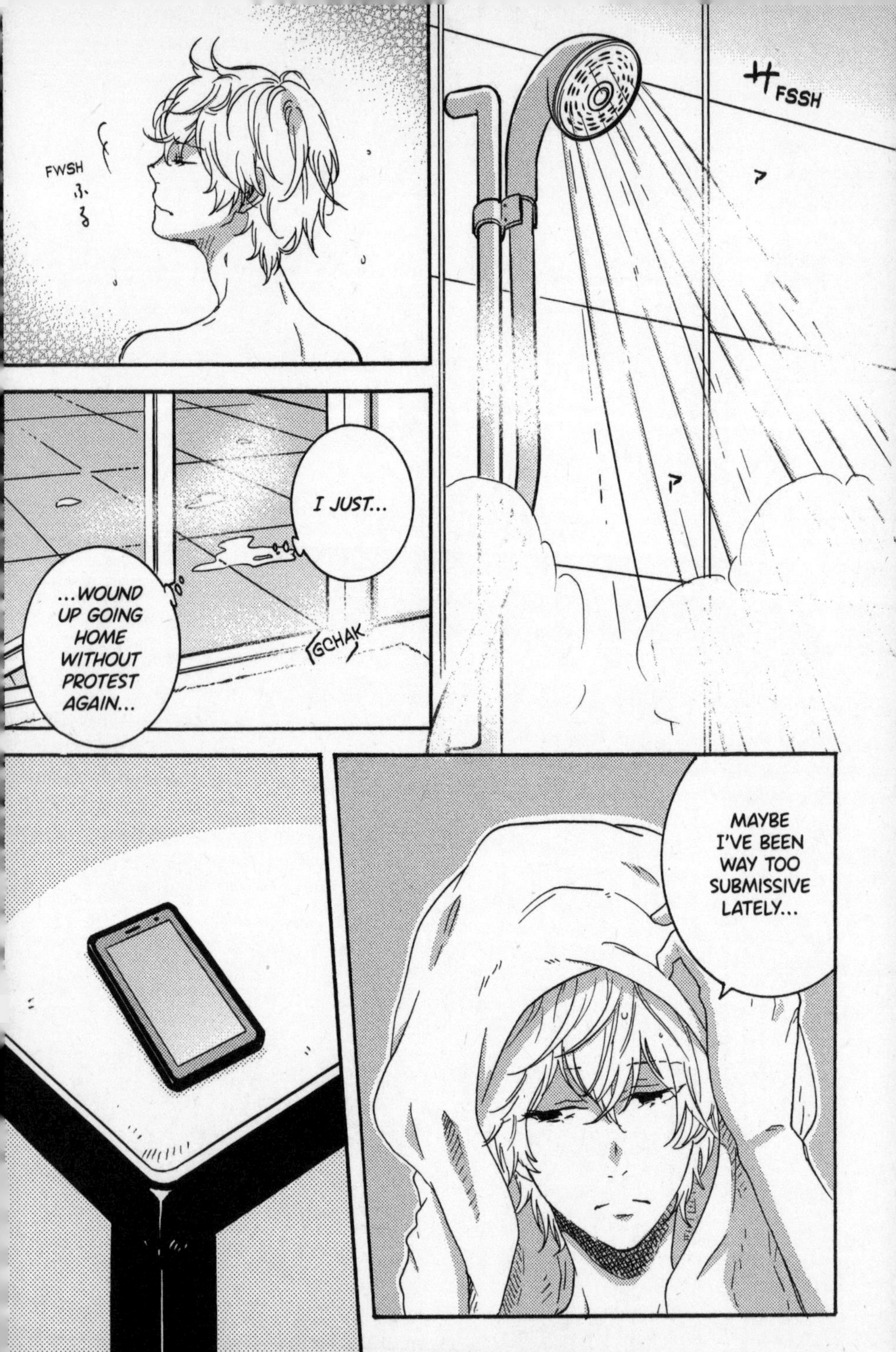
FSSH
FWSH
ふる
I JUST...
...WOUND UP GOING HOME WITHOUT PROTEST AGAIN...
GCHAK
MAYBE I'VE BEEN WAY TOO SUBMISSIVE LATELY...

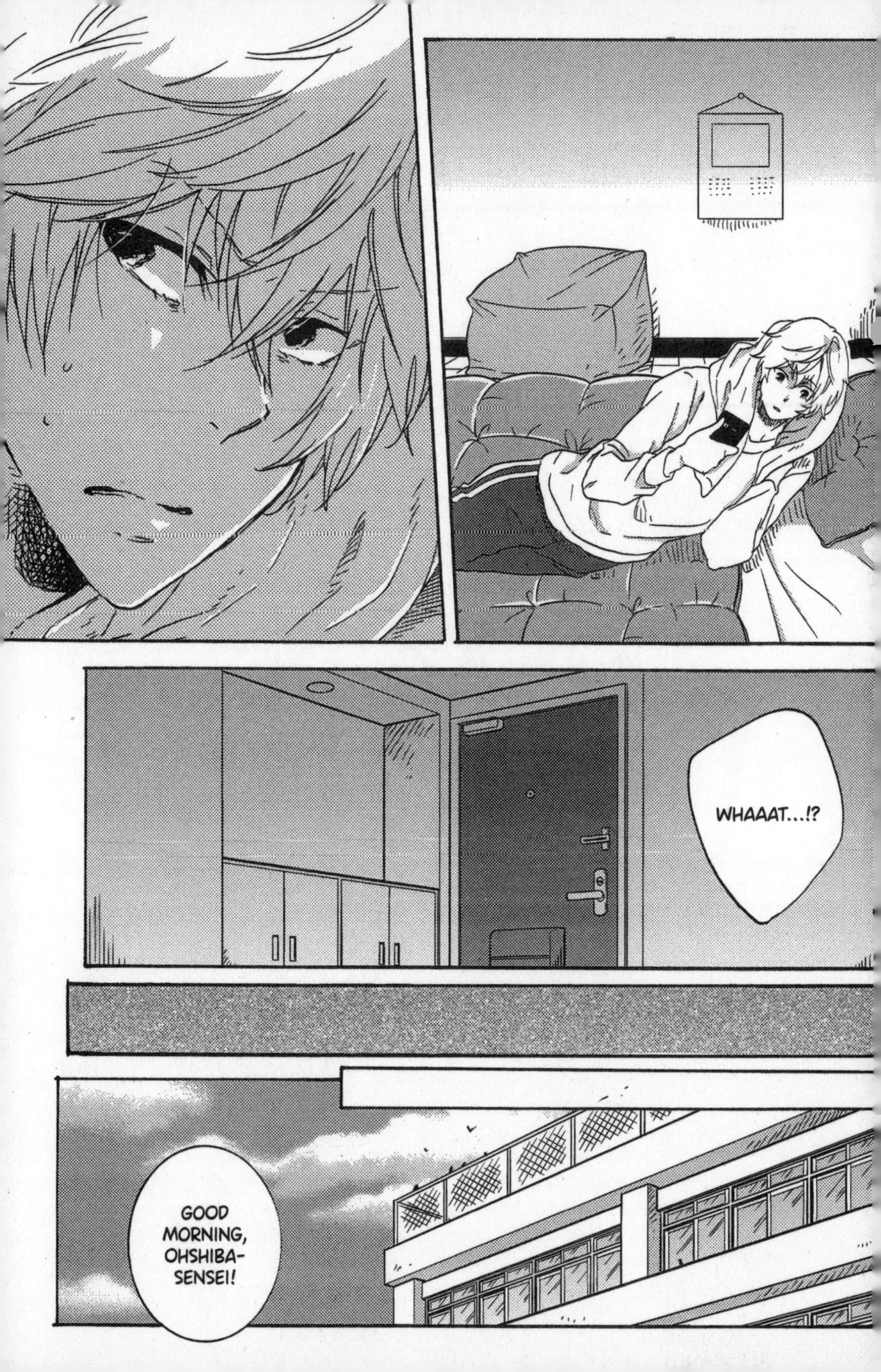
WHAAAT...!?
GOOD MORNING, OHSHIBA-SENSEI!

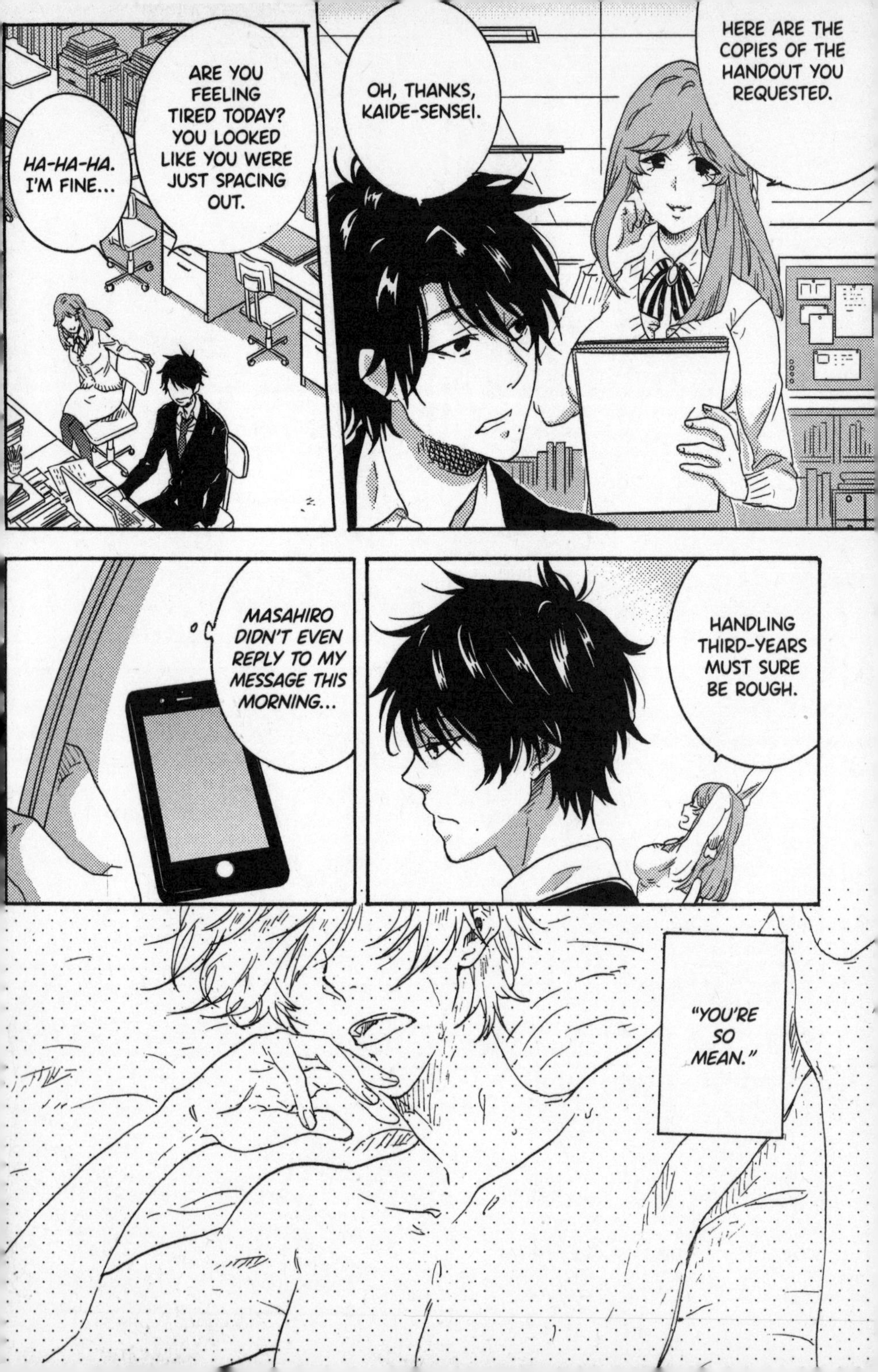
HERE ARE THE COPIES OF THE HANDOUT YOU REQUESTED.
OH, THANKS, KAIDE-SENSEI.
ARE YOU FEELING TIRED TODAY? YOU LOOKED LIKE YOU WERE JUST SPACING OUT.
HA-HA-HA. I'M FINE...
HANDLING THIRD-YEARS MUST SURE BE ROUGH.
MASAHIRO DIDN'T EVEN REPLY TO MY MESSAGE THIS MORNING...
"YOU'RE SO MEAN."

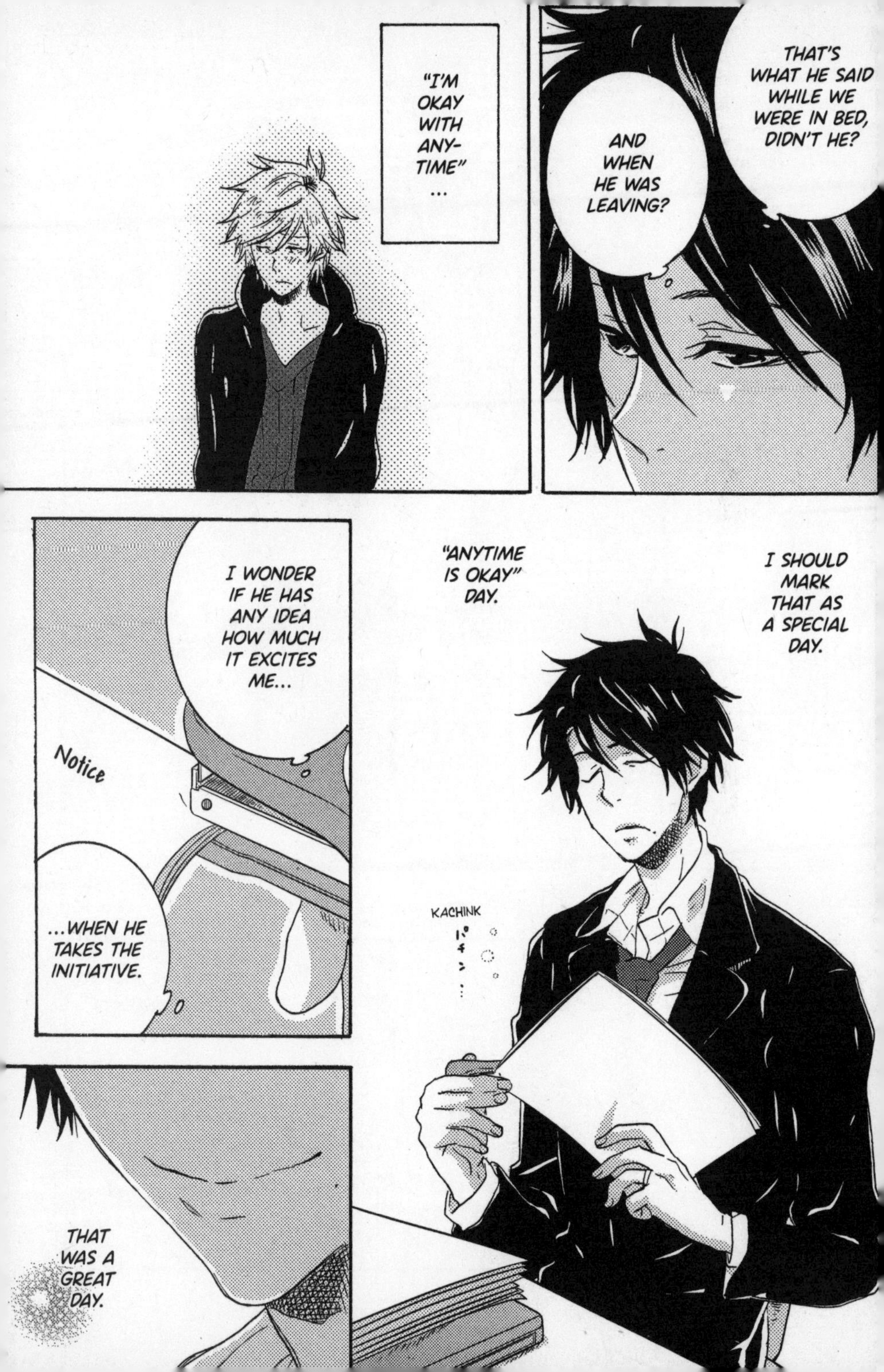
THAT'S WHAT HE SAID WHILE WE WERE IN BED, DIDN'T HE?
AND WHEN HE WAS LEAVING?
"I'M OKAY WITH ANY-TIME" ...
I SHOULD MARK THAT AS A SPECIAL DAY.
"ANYTIME IS OKAY" DAY.
KACHINK
パチン
I WONDER IF HE HAS ANY IDEA HOW MUCH IT EXCITES ME...
Notice
...WHEN HE TAKES THE INITIATIVE.
THAT WAS A GREAT DAY.

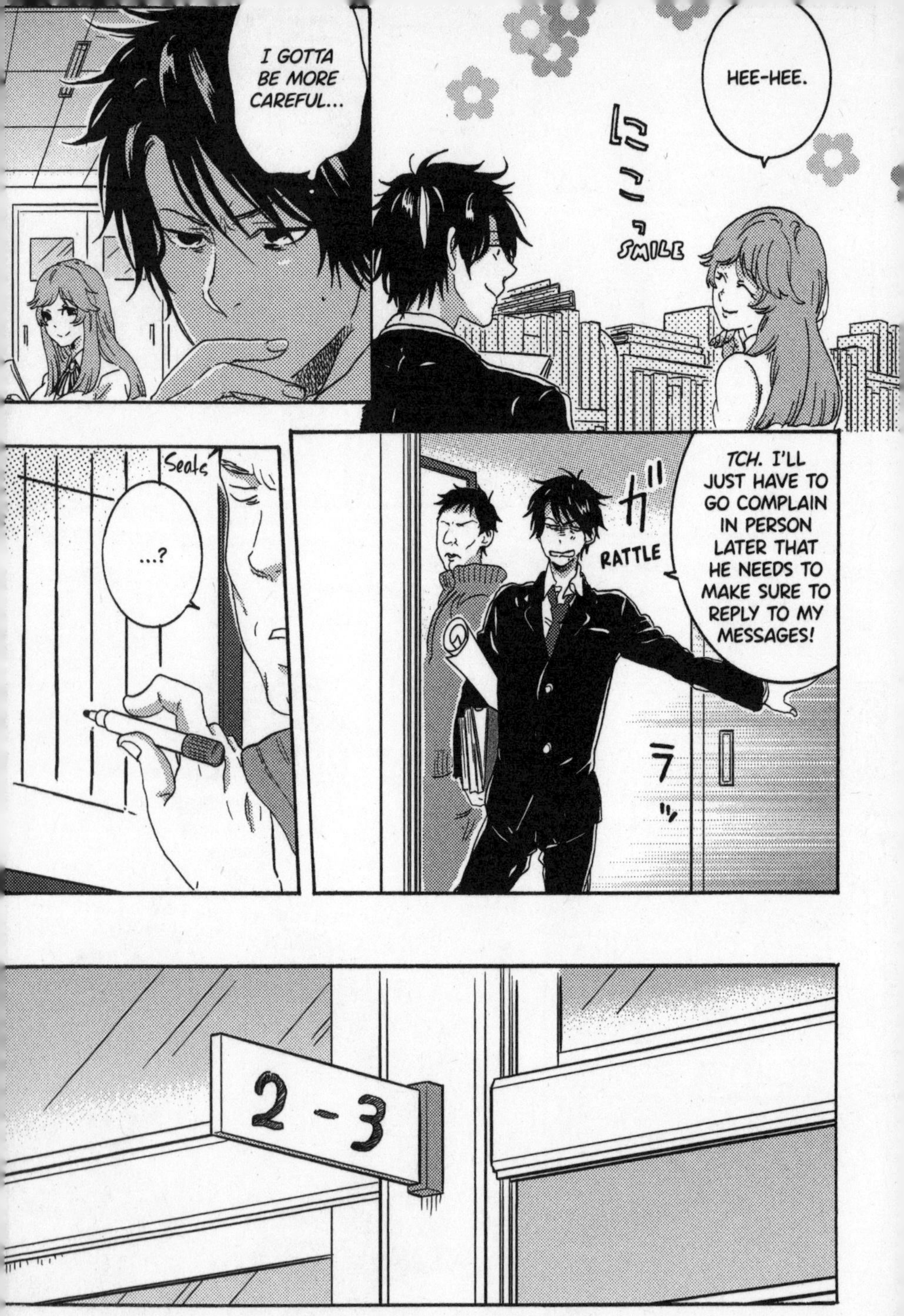
HEE-HEE.
にこっ
SMILE
I GOTTA BE MORE CAREFUL...
ガラッ
RATTLE
TCH. I'LL JUST HAVE TO GO COMPLAIN IN PERSON LATER THAT HE NEEDS TO MAKE SURE TO REPLY TO MY MESSAGES!
Seats
...?
2-3

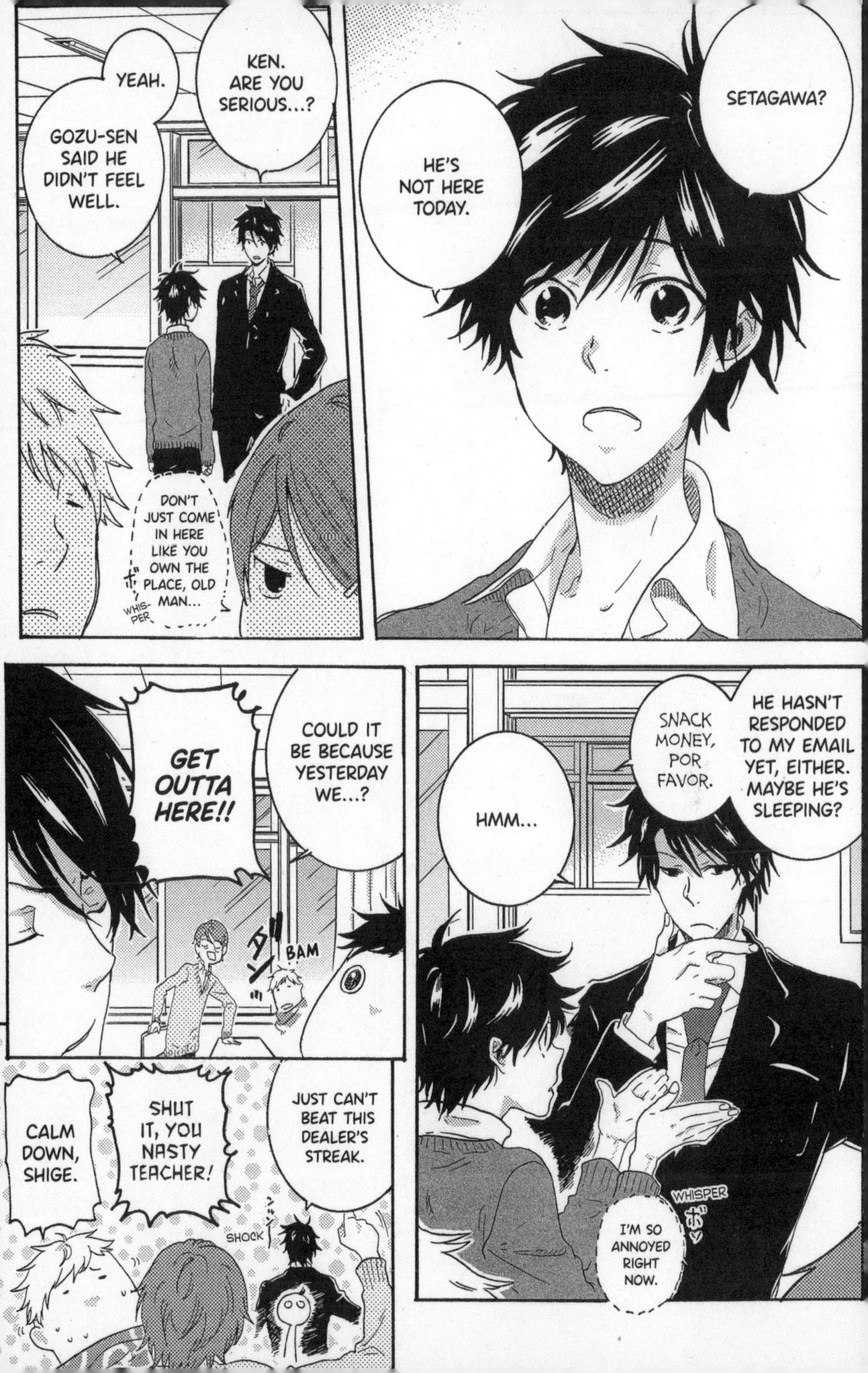
SETAGAWA?
HE'S NOT HERE TODAY.
KEN. ARE YOU SERIOUS...?
YEAH.
GOZU-SEN SAID HE DIDN'T FEEL WELL.
DON'T JUST COME IN HERE LIKE YOU OWN THE PLACE, OLD MAN...
WHISPER
HE HASN'T RESPONDED TO MY EMAIL YET, EITHER. MAYBE HE'S SLEEPING?
SNACK MONEY, POR FAVOR.
HMM...
WHISPER
I'M SO ANNOYED RIGHT NOW.
COULD IT BE BECAUSE YESTERDAY WE...?
GET OUTTA HERE!!
BAM
JUST CAN'T BEAT THIS DEALER'S STREAK.
SHUT IT, YOU NASTY TEACHER!
CALM DOWN, SHIGE.
SHOCK

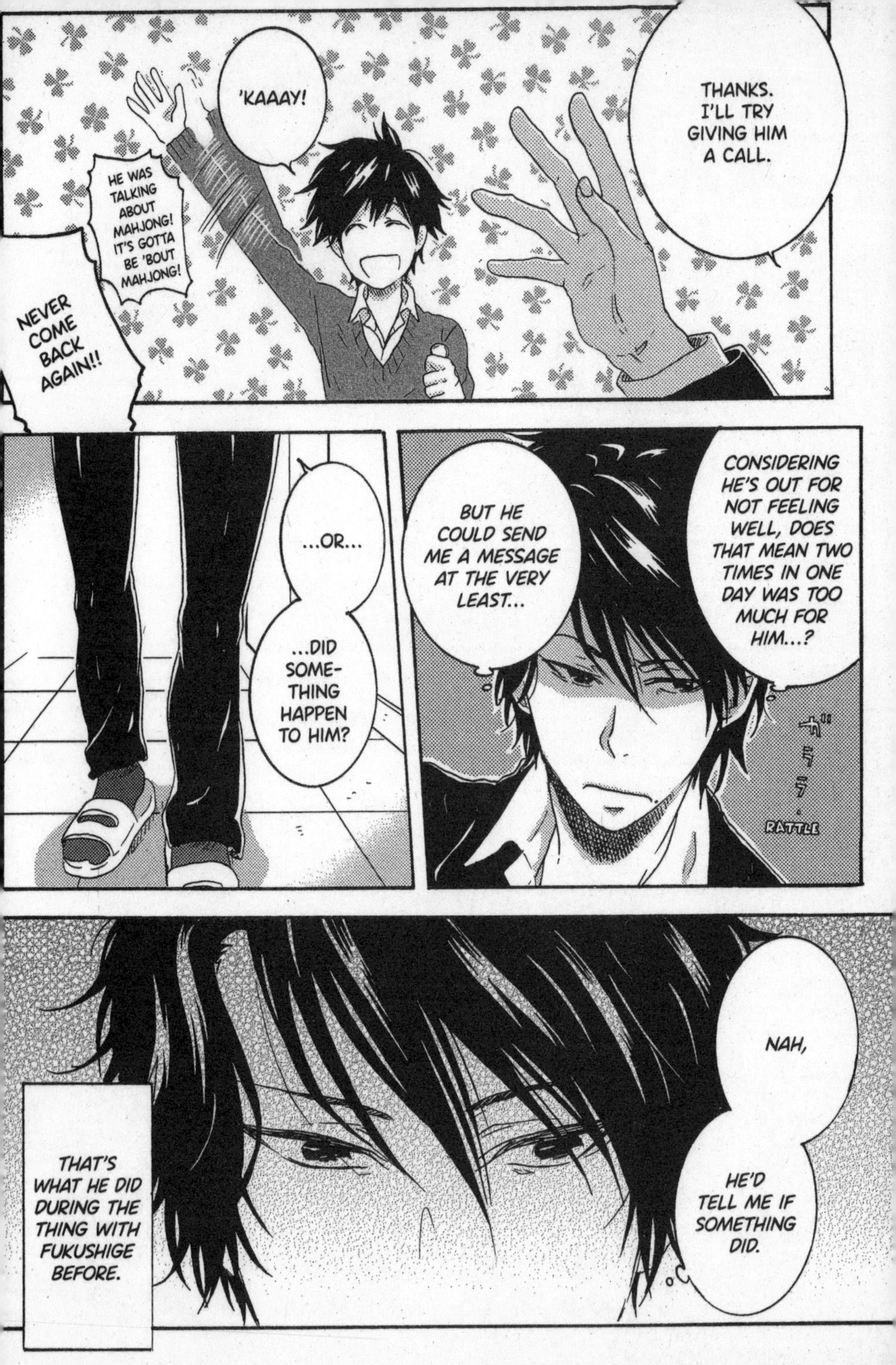
THANKS. I'LL TRY GIVING HIM A CALL.
'KAAAY!
HE WAS TALKING ABOUT MAHJONG! IT'S GOTTA BE 'BOUT MAHJONG!
NEVER COME BACK AGAIN!!
CONSIDERING HE'S OUT FOR NOT FEELING WELL, DOES THAT MEAN TWO TIMES IN ONE DAY WAS TOO MUCH FOR HIM...?
BUT HE COULD SEND ME A MESSAGE AT THE VERY LEAST...
RATTLE
...OR...
...DID SOMETHING HAPPEN TO HIM?
NAH,
HE'D TELL ME IF SOMETHING DID.
THAT'S WHAT HE DID DURING THE THING WITH FUKUSHIGE BEFORE.

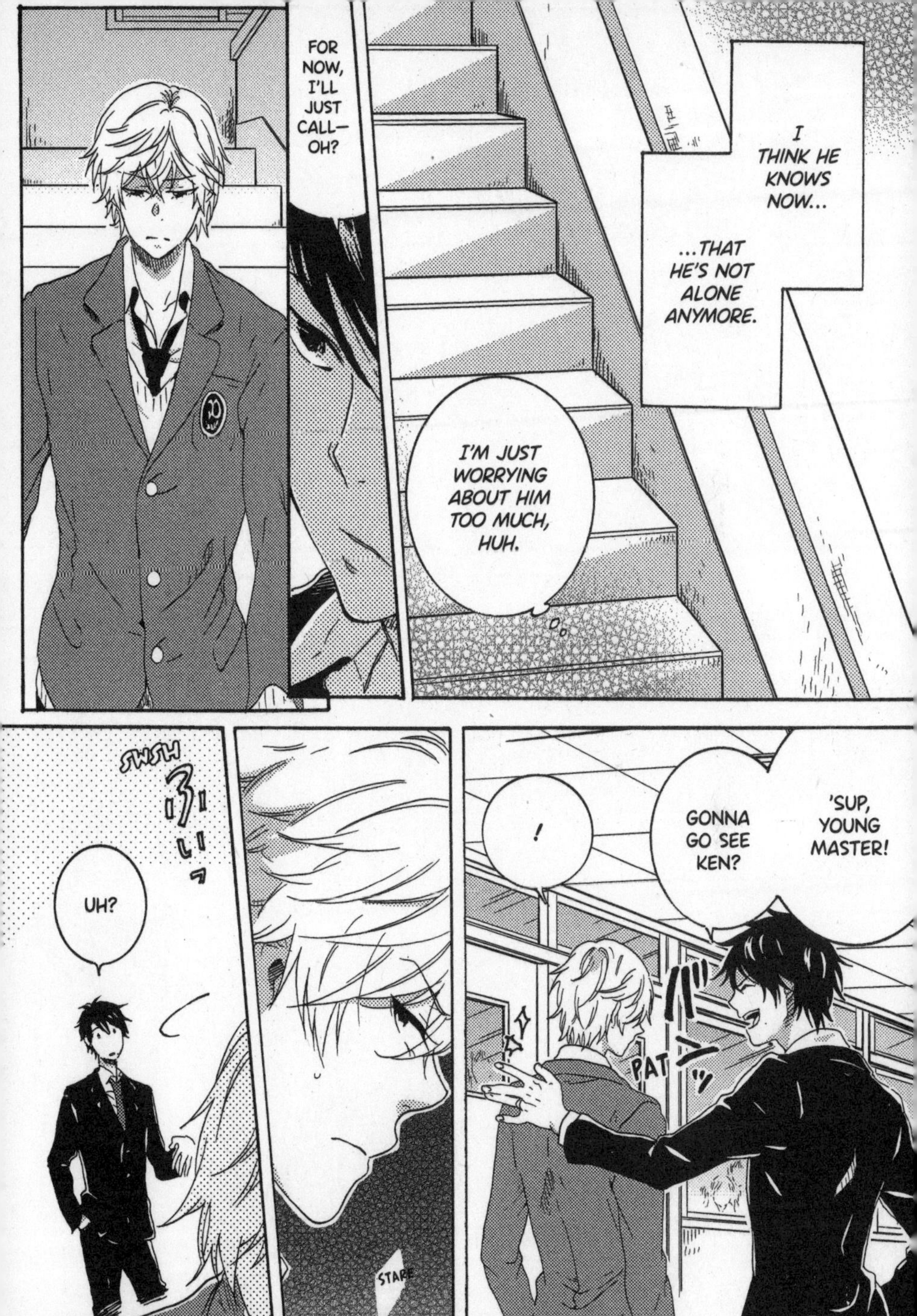
I THINK HE KNOWS NOW...
...THAT HE'S NOT ALONE ANYMORE.
I'M JUST WORRYING ABOUT HIM TOO MUCH, HUH.
FOR NOW, I'LL JUST CALL—OH?
'SUP, YOUNG MASTER!
GONNA GO SEE KEN?
!
PAT
STARE
SWSH
UH?

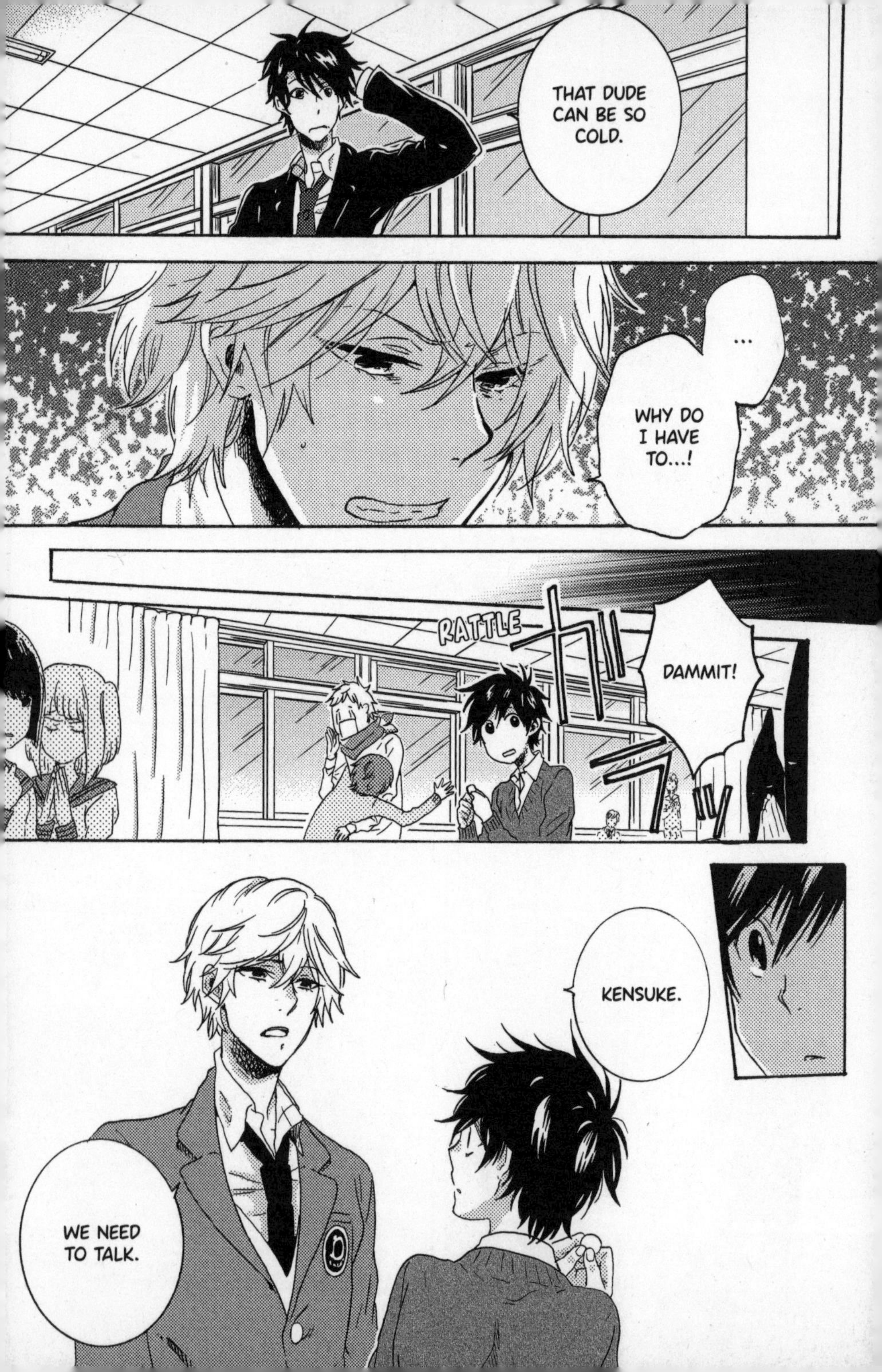
THAT DUDE CAN BE SO COLD.
...
WHY DO I HAVE TO...!
DAMMIT!
RATTLE
KENSUKE.
WE NEED TO TALK.

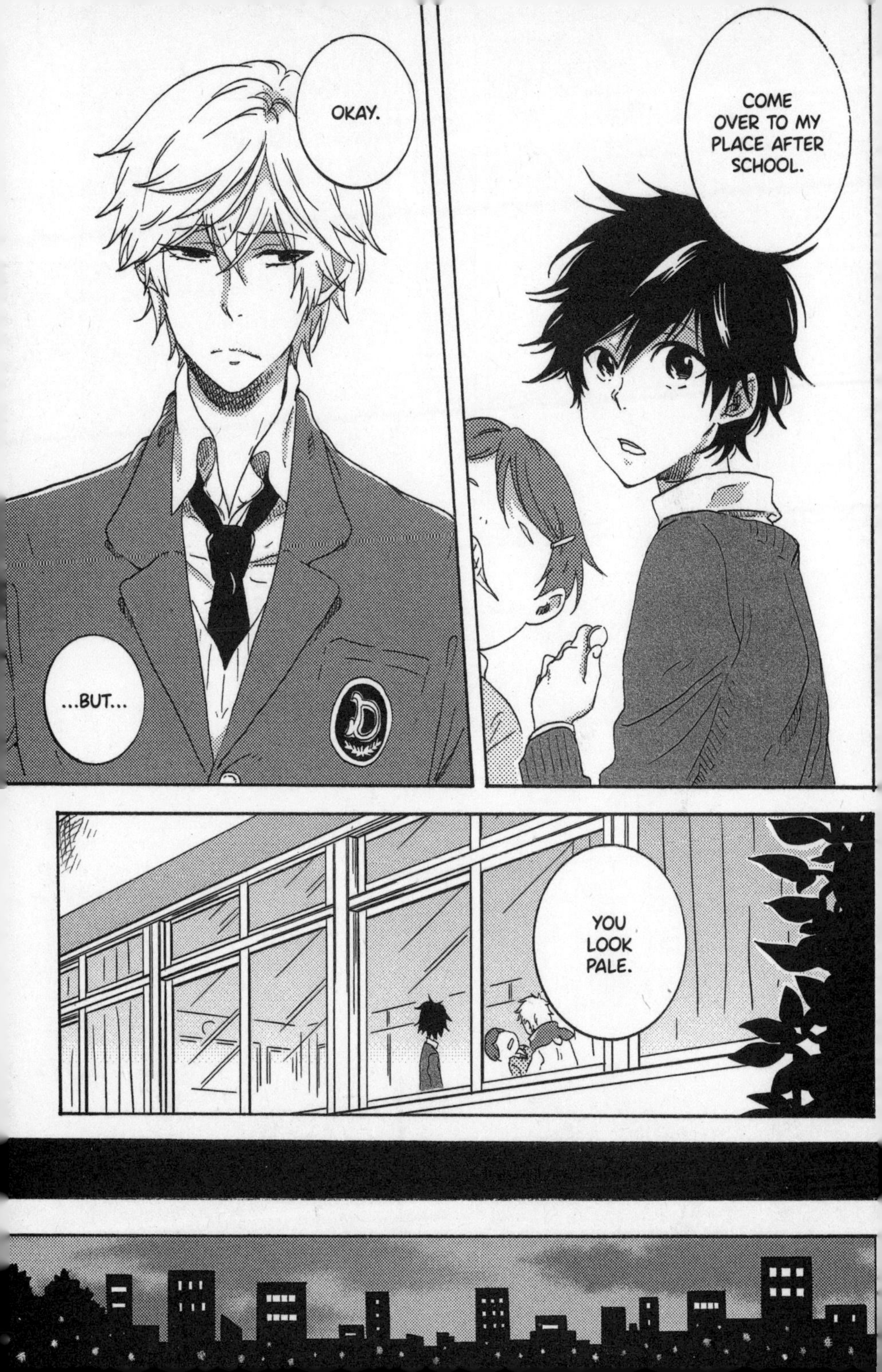
COME OVER TO MY PLACE AFTER SCHOOL.
OKAY.
...BUT...
YOU LOOK PALE.

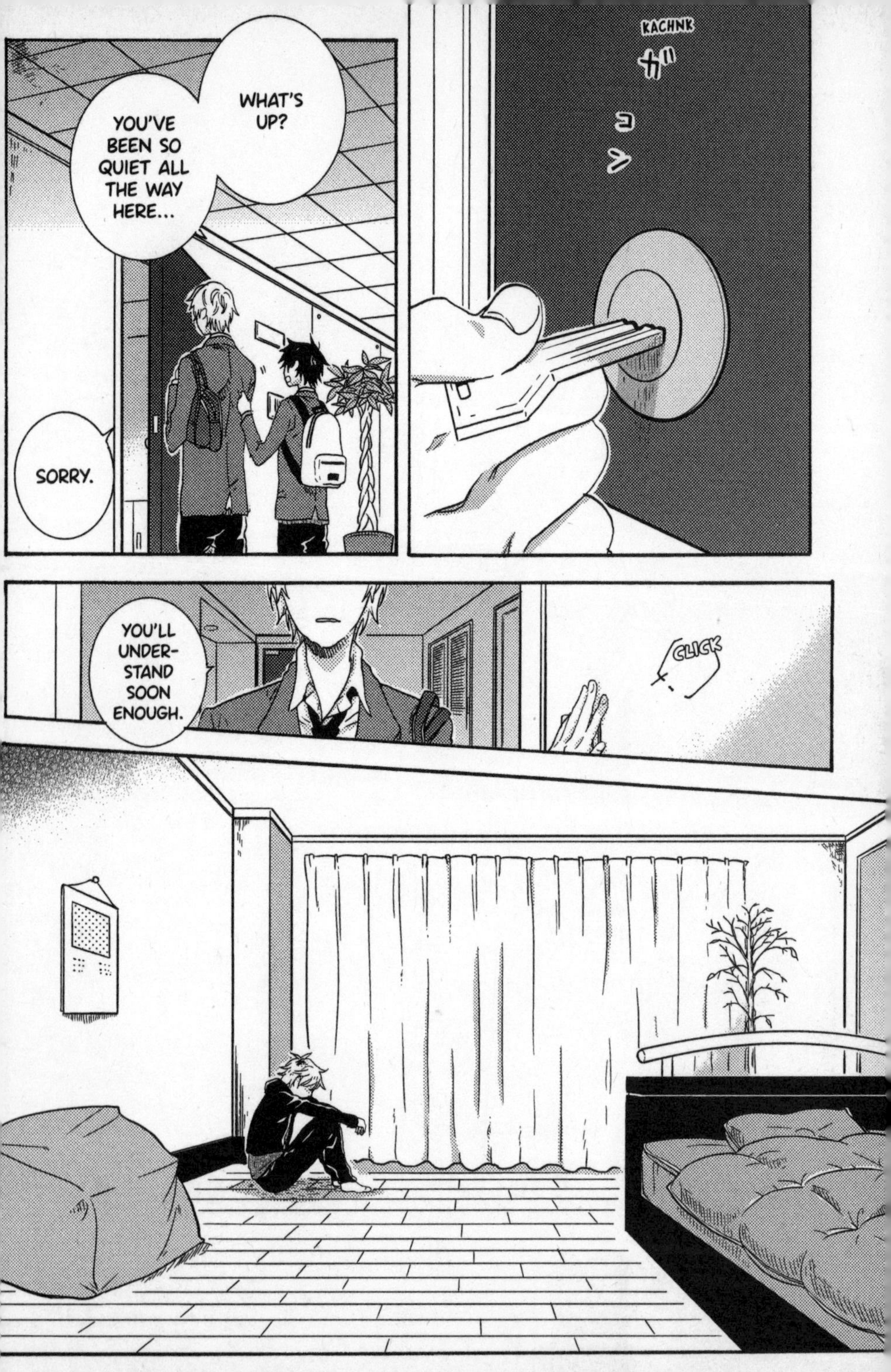
KACHNK
ガコン
WHAT'S UP?
YOU'VE BEEN SO QUIET ALL THE WAY HERE...
SORRY.
CLICK
YOU'LL UNDER-STAND SOON ENOUGH.

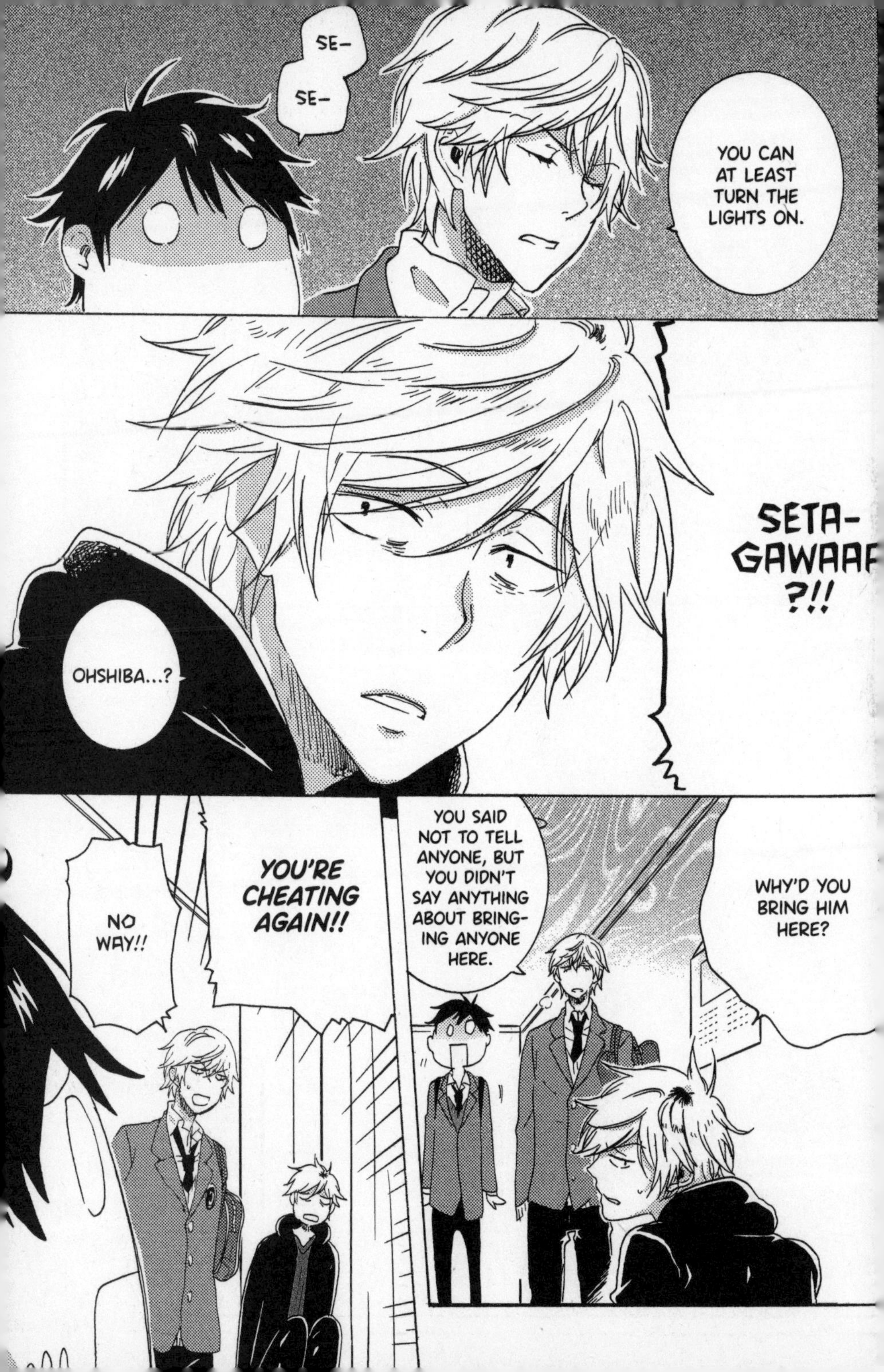
YOU CAN AT LEAST TURN THE LIGHTS ON.
SE-
SE-
SETA-GAWAAA?!!
OHSHIBA...?
WHY'D YOU BRING HIM HERE?
YOU SAID NOT TO TELL ANYONE, BUT YOU DIDN'T SAY ANYTHING ABOUT BRING-ING ANYONE HERE.
YOU'RE CHEATING AGAIN!!
NO WAY!!

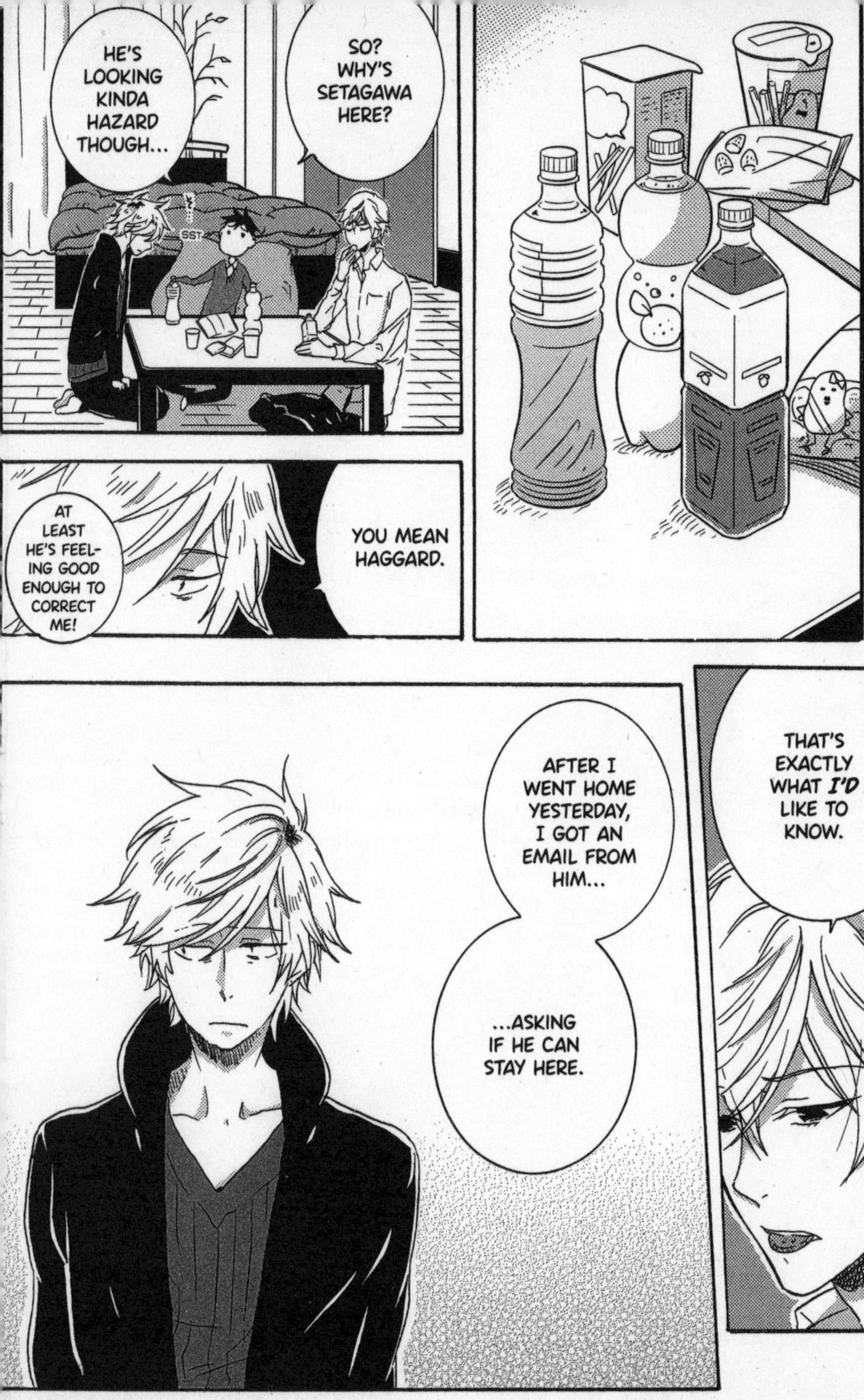
SO? WHY'S SETAGAWA HERE?
HE'S LOOKING KINDA HAZARD THOUGH...
SST
YOU MEAN HAGGARD.
AT LEAST HE'S FEEL-ING GOOD ENOUGH TO CORRECT ME!
THAT'S EXACTLY WHAT *I'D* LIKE TO KNOW.
AFTER I WENT HOME YESTERDAY, I GOT AN EMAIL FROM HIM...
...ASKING IF HE CAN STAY HERE.

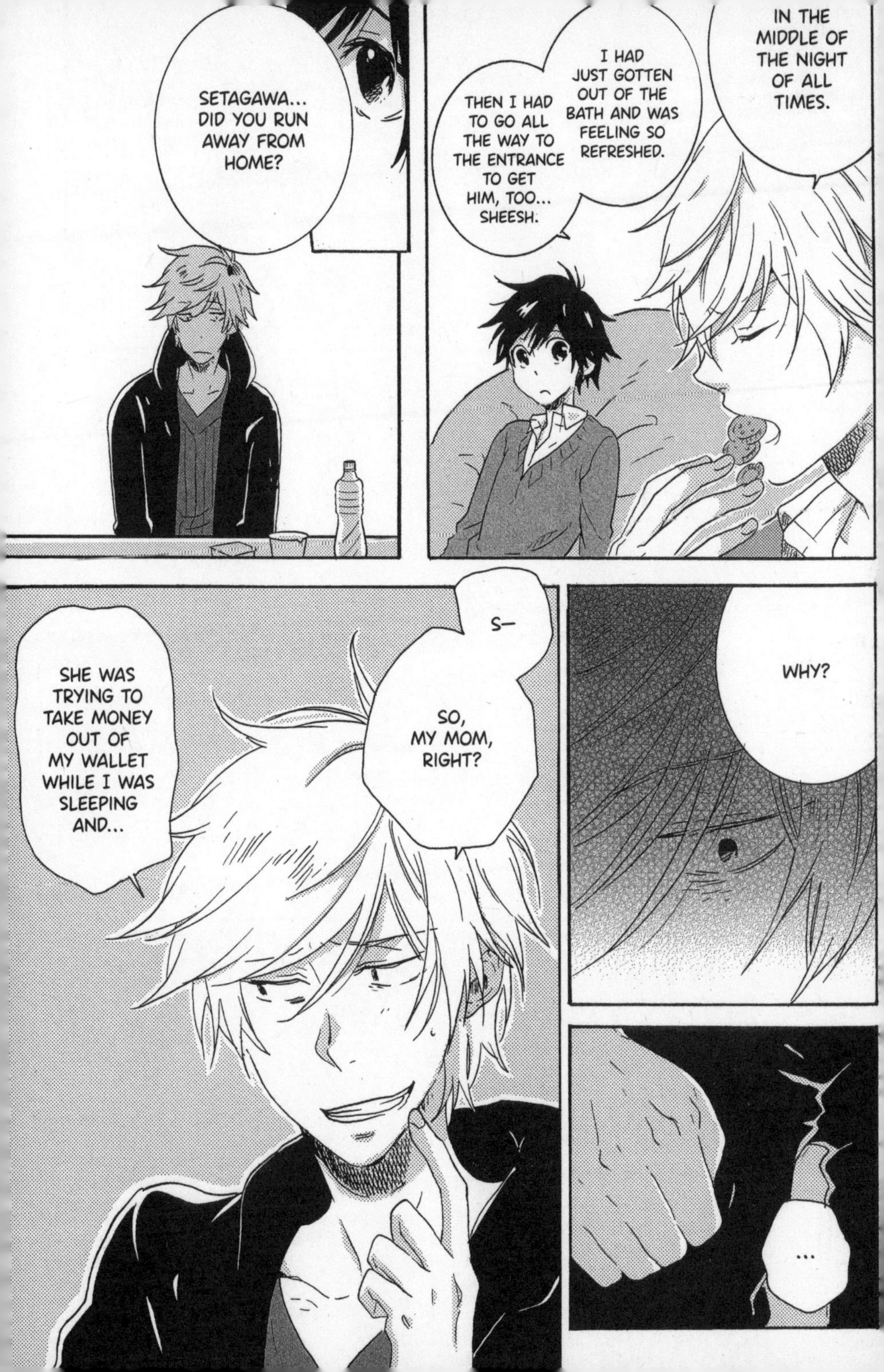
IN THE MIDDLE OF THE NIGHT OF ALL TIMES.
I HAD JUST GOTTEN OUT OF THE BATH AND WAS FEELING SO REFRESHED.
THEN I HAD TO GO ALL THE WAY TO THE ENTRANCE TO GET HIM, TOO... SHEESH.
SETAGAWA... DID YOU RUN AWAY FROM HOME?
WHY?
...
S—
SO, MY MOM, RIGHT?
SHE WAS TRYING TO TAKE MONEY OUT OF MY WALLET WHILE I WAS SLEEPING AND...

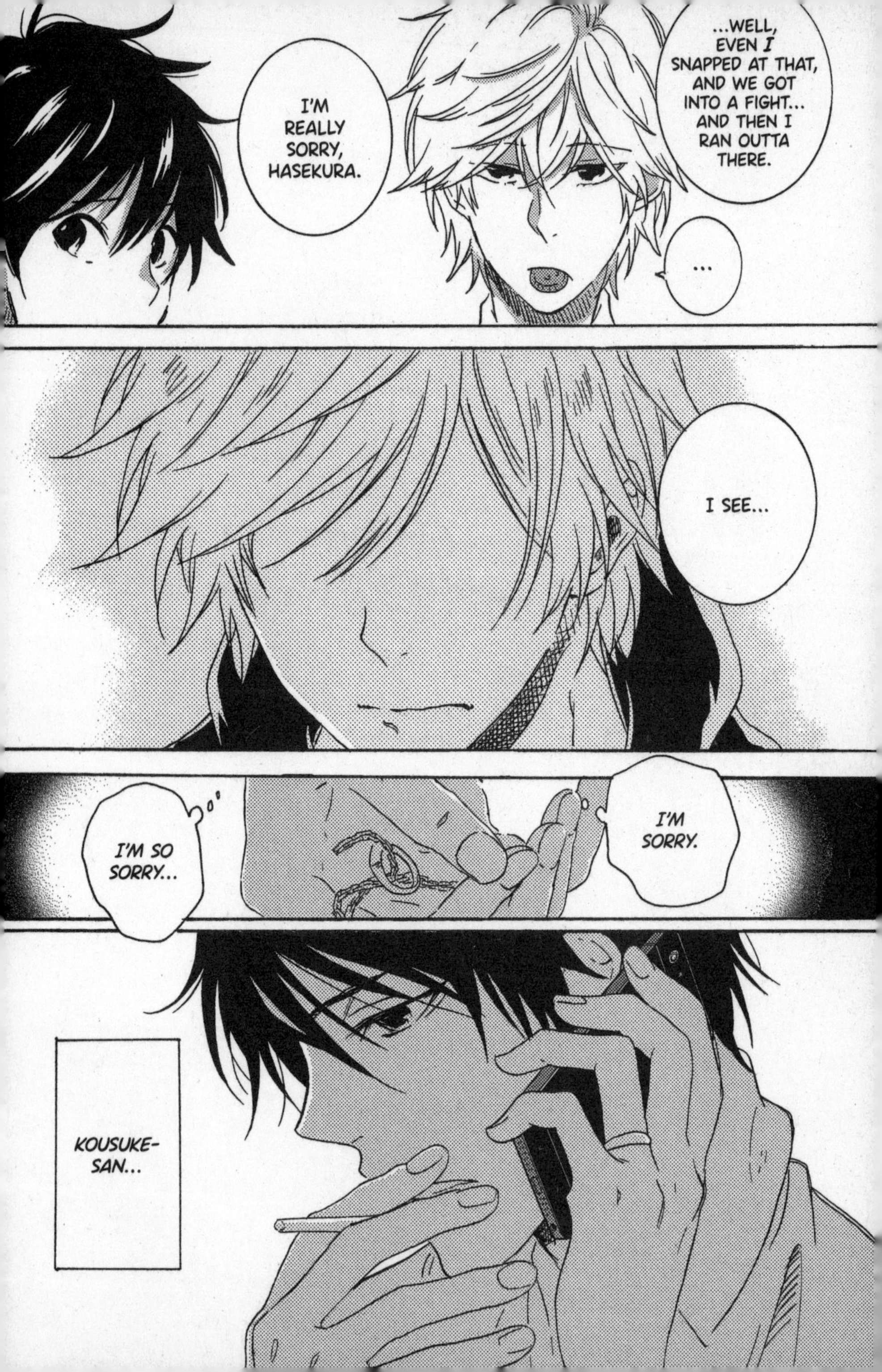
...WELL, EVEN *I* SNAPPED AT THAT, AND WE GOT INTO A FIGHT... AND THEN I RAN OUTTA THERE.
...
I'M REALLY SORRY, HASEKURA.
I SEE...
I'M SORRY.
I'M SO SORRY...
KOUSUKE-SAN...

Hitorijime My Hero

~Hasekuraism~

A religion that worships Hasekura.

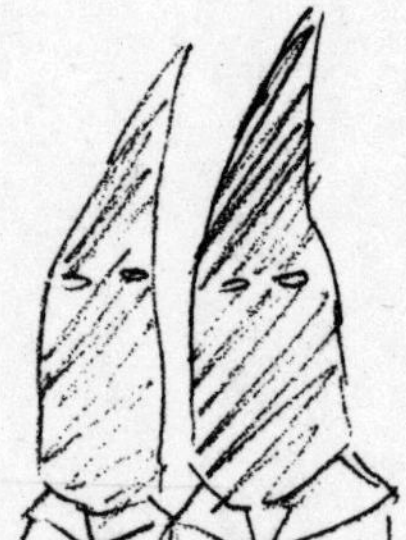

Hasekura-san pretends not to notice the women who worship him (because he's scared of them).

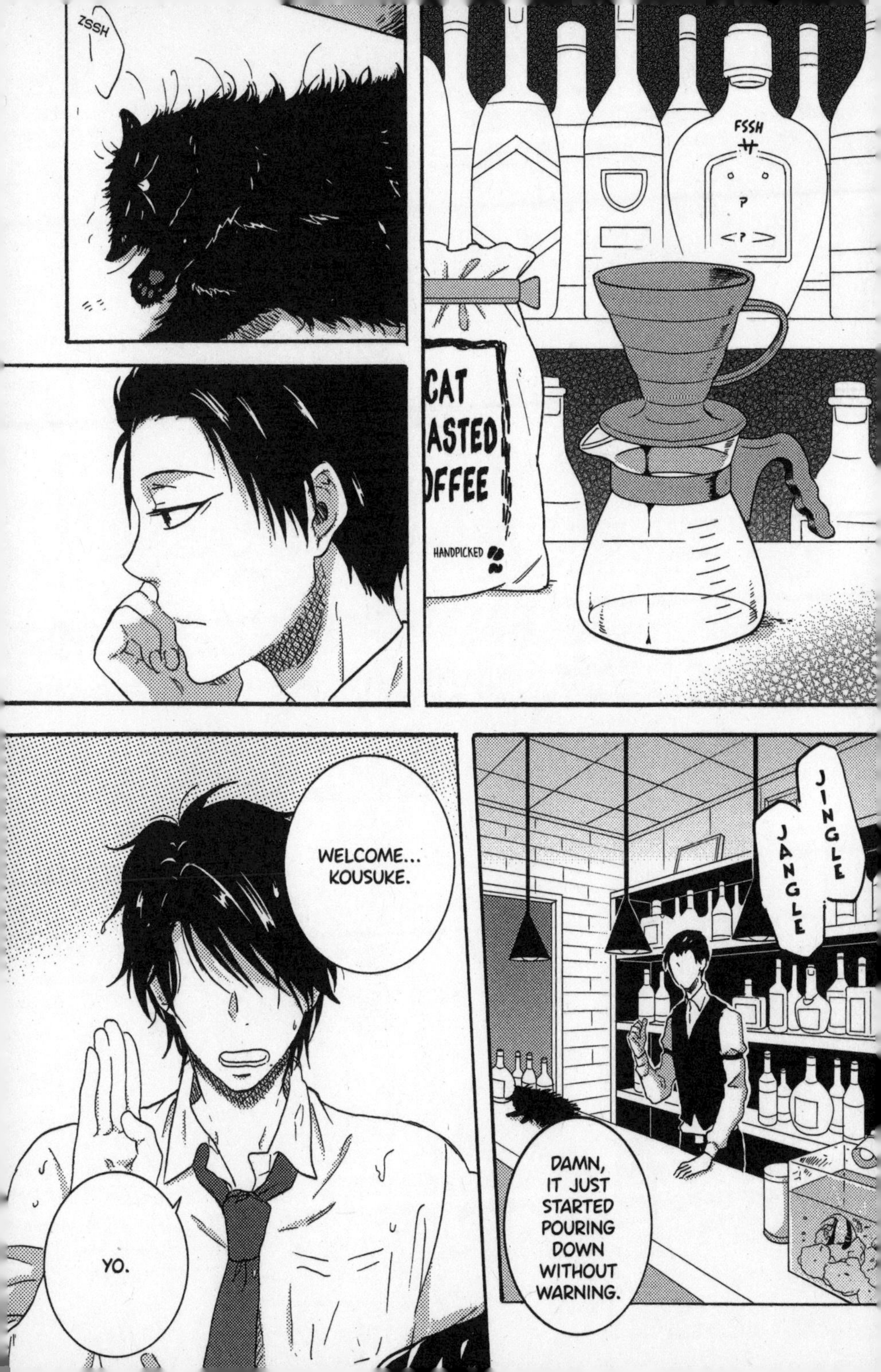
FSSH
CAT
ASTED
OFFEE
HANDPICKED
ZSSH
JINGLE
JANGLE
DAMN, IT JUST STARTED POURING DOWN WITHOUT WARNING.
WELCOME... KOUSUKE.
YO.

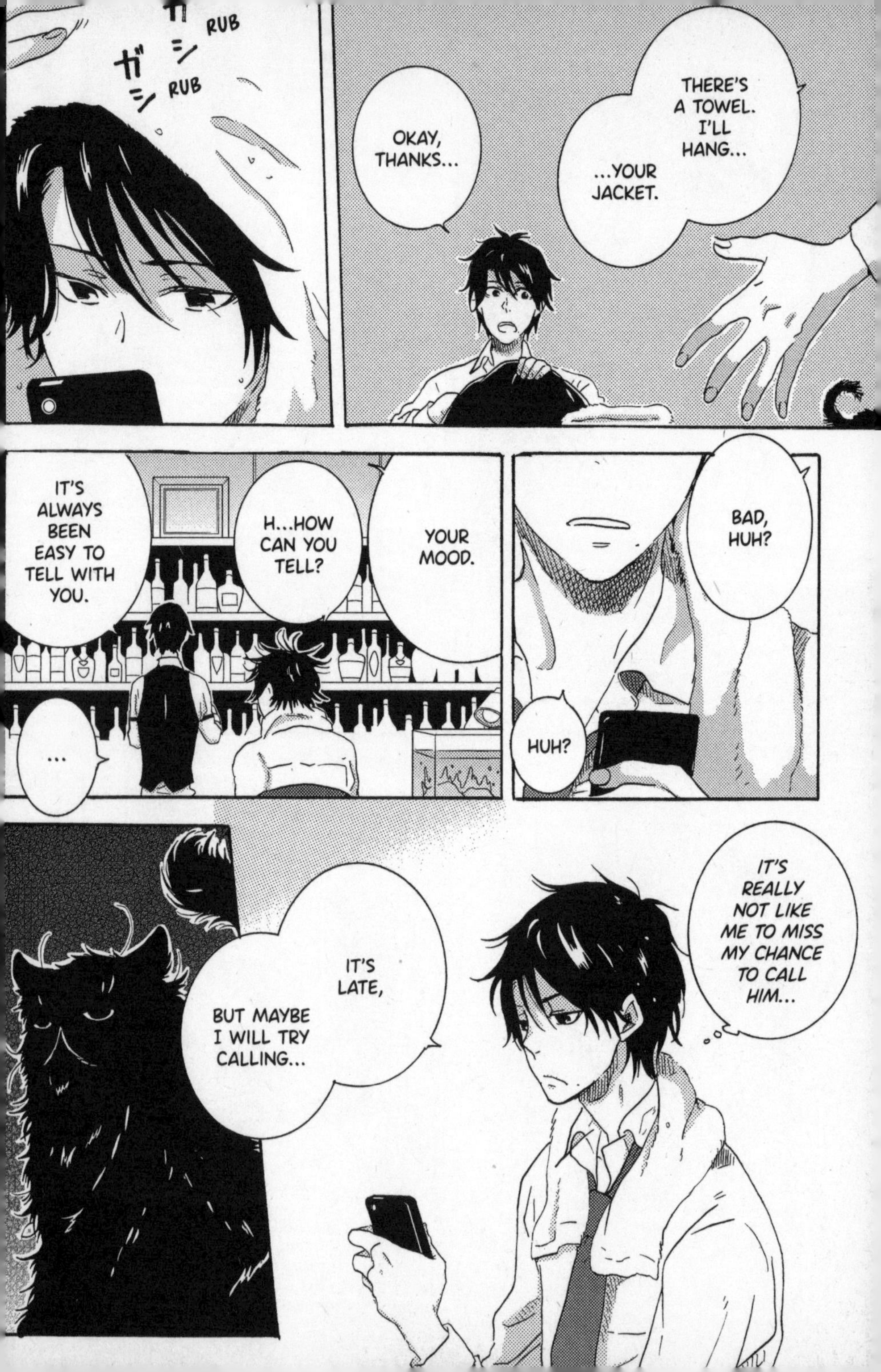
THERE'S A TOWEL. I'LL HANG...
...YOUR JACKET.
OKAY, THANKS...
ガシガシ
RUB RUB
BAD, HUH?
HUH?
YOUR MOOD.
H...HOW CAN YOU TELL?
IT'S ALWAYS BEEN EASY TO TELL WITH YOU.
...
IT'S REALLY NOT LIKE ME TO MISS MY CHANCE TO CALL HIM...
IT'S LATE,
BUT MAYBE I WILL TRY CALLING...

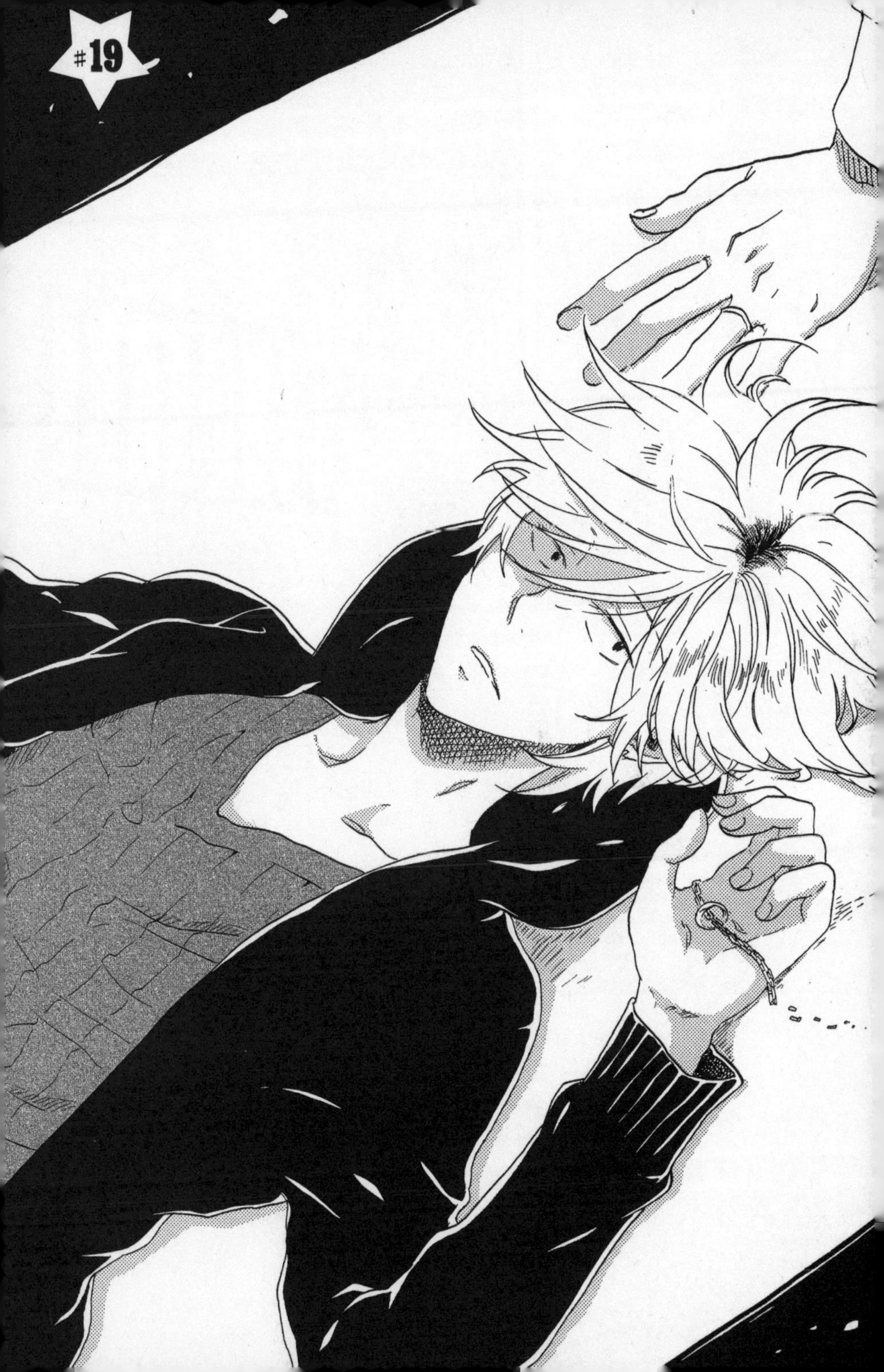
#19

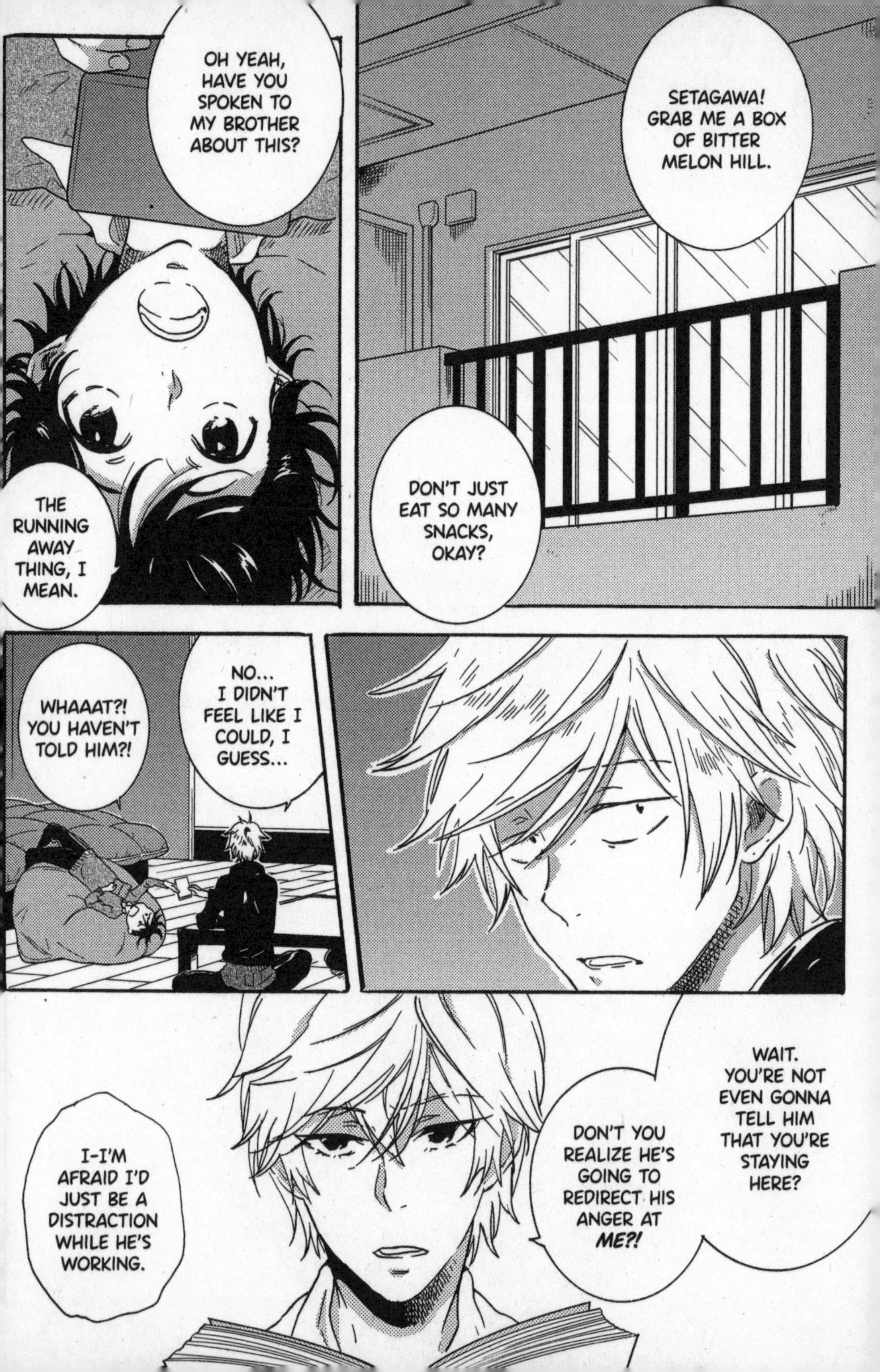
SETAGAWA! GRAB ME A BOX OF BITTER MELON HILL.
DON'T JUST EAT SO MANY SNACKS, OKAY?
OH YEAH, HAVE YOU SPOKEN TO MY BROTHER ABOUT THIS?
THE RUNNING AWAY THING, I MEAN.
NO... I DIDN'T FEEL LIKE I COULD, I GUESS...
WHAAAT?! YOU HAVEN'T TOLD HIM?!
WAIT. YOU'RE NOT EVEN GONNA TELL HIM THAT YOU'RE STAYING HERE?
DON'T YOU REALIZE HE'S GOING TO REDIRECT HIS ANGER AT *ME?!*
I-I'M AFRAID I'D JUST BE A DISTRACTION WHILE HE'S WORKING.

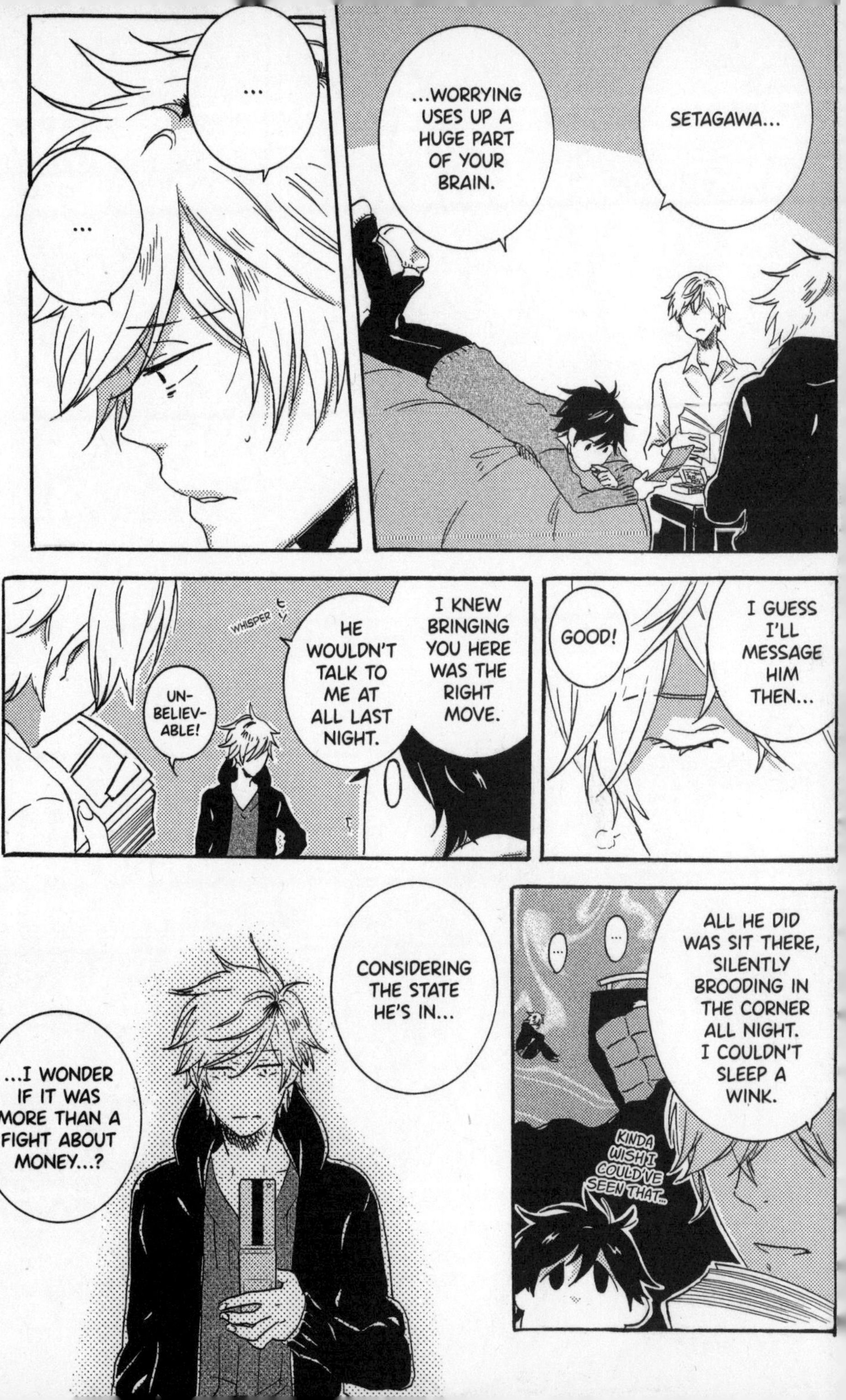
SETAGAWA...
...WORRYING USES UP A HUGE PART OF YOUR BRAIN.
...
...
I GUESS I'LL MESSAGE HIM THEN...
GOOD!
I KNEW BRINGING YOU HERE WAS THE RIGHT MOVE.
HE WOULDN'T TALK TO ME AT ALL LAST NIGHT.
WHISPER
UN-BELIEV-ABLE!
ALL HE DID WAS SIT THERE, SILENTLY BROODING IN THE CORNER ALL NIGHT. I COULDN'T SLEEP A WINK.
...
...
KINDA WISH I COULD'VE SEEN THAT...
CONSIDERING THE STATE HE'S IN...
...I WONDER IF IT WAS MORE THAN A FIGHT ABOUT MONEY...?

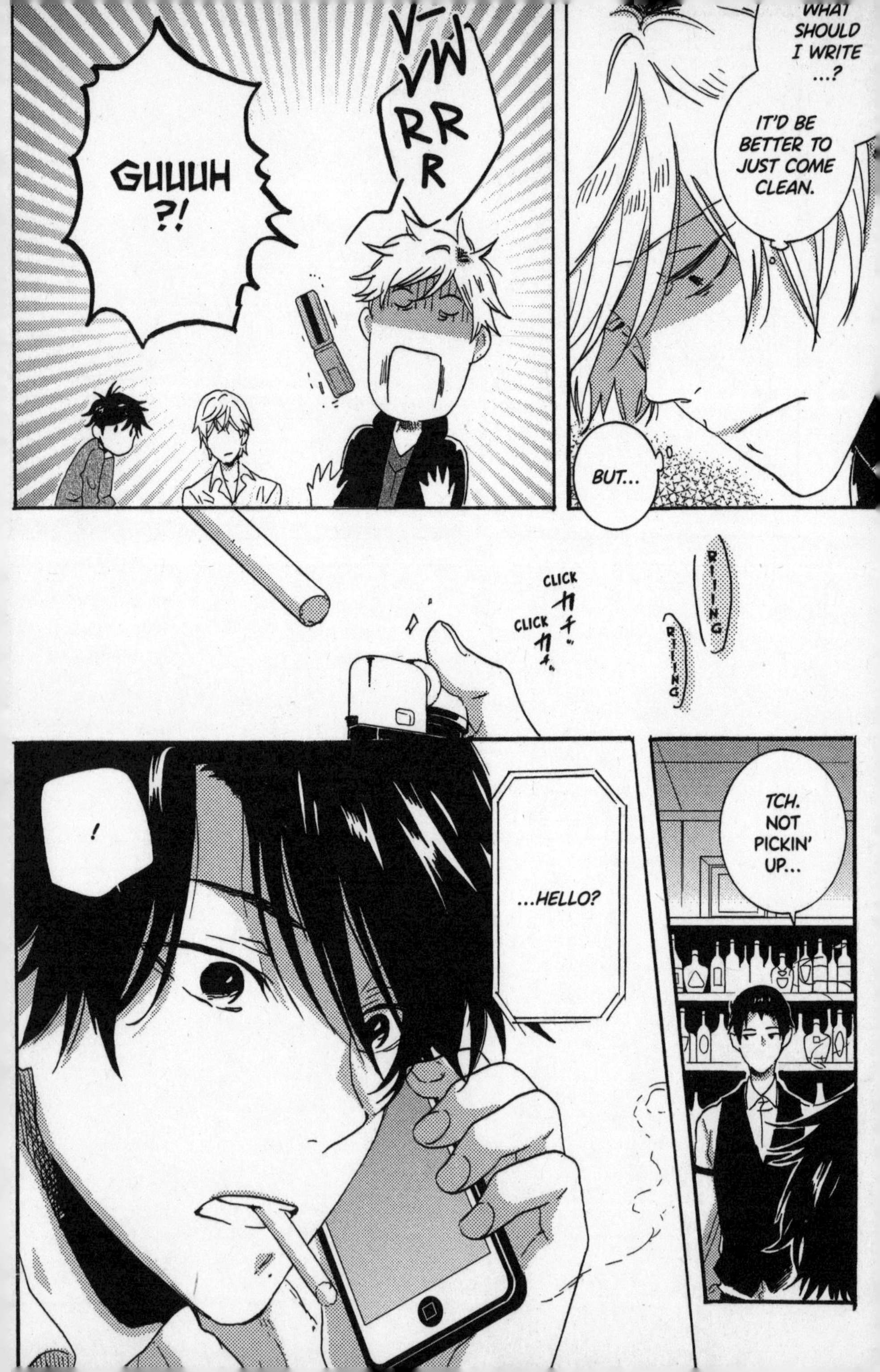
WHAT SHOULD I WRITE ...?
IT'D BE BETTER TO JUST COME CLEAN.
BUT...
V-VWRRR
GUUUH ?!
RIIING
RIIING
CLICK カチ
CLICK カチ
TCH. NOT PICKIN' UP...
...HELLO?
!

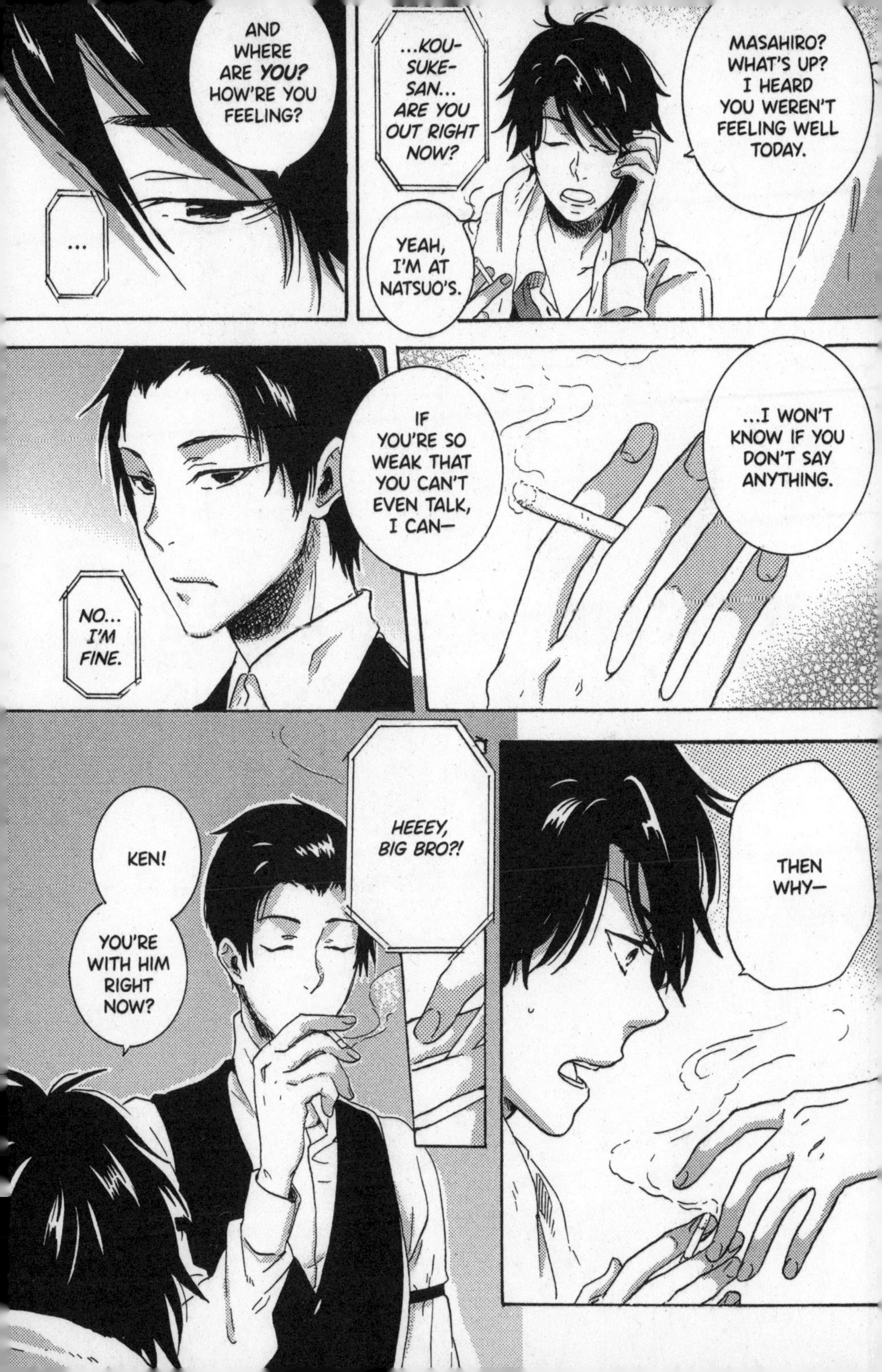
MASAHIRO? WHAT'S UP? I HEARD YOU WEREN'T FEELING WELL TODAY.
...KOU-SUKE-SAN... ARE YOU OUT RIGHT NOW?
YEAH, I'M AT NATSUO'S.
AND WHERE ARE *YOU?* HOW'RE YOU FEELING?
...
...I WON'T KNOW IF YOU DON'T SAY ANYTHING.
IF YOU'RE SO WEAK THAT YOU CAN'T EVEN TALK, I CAN—
NO... I'M FINE.
THEN WHY—
HEEEY, BIG BRO?!
KEN!
YOU'RE WITH HIM RIGHT NOW?

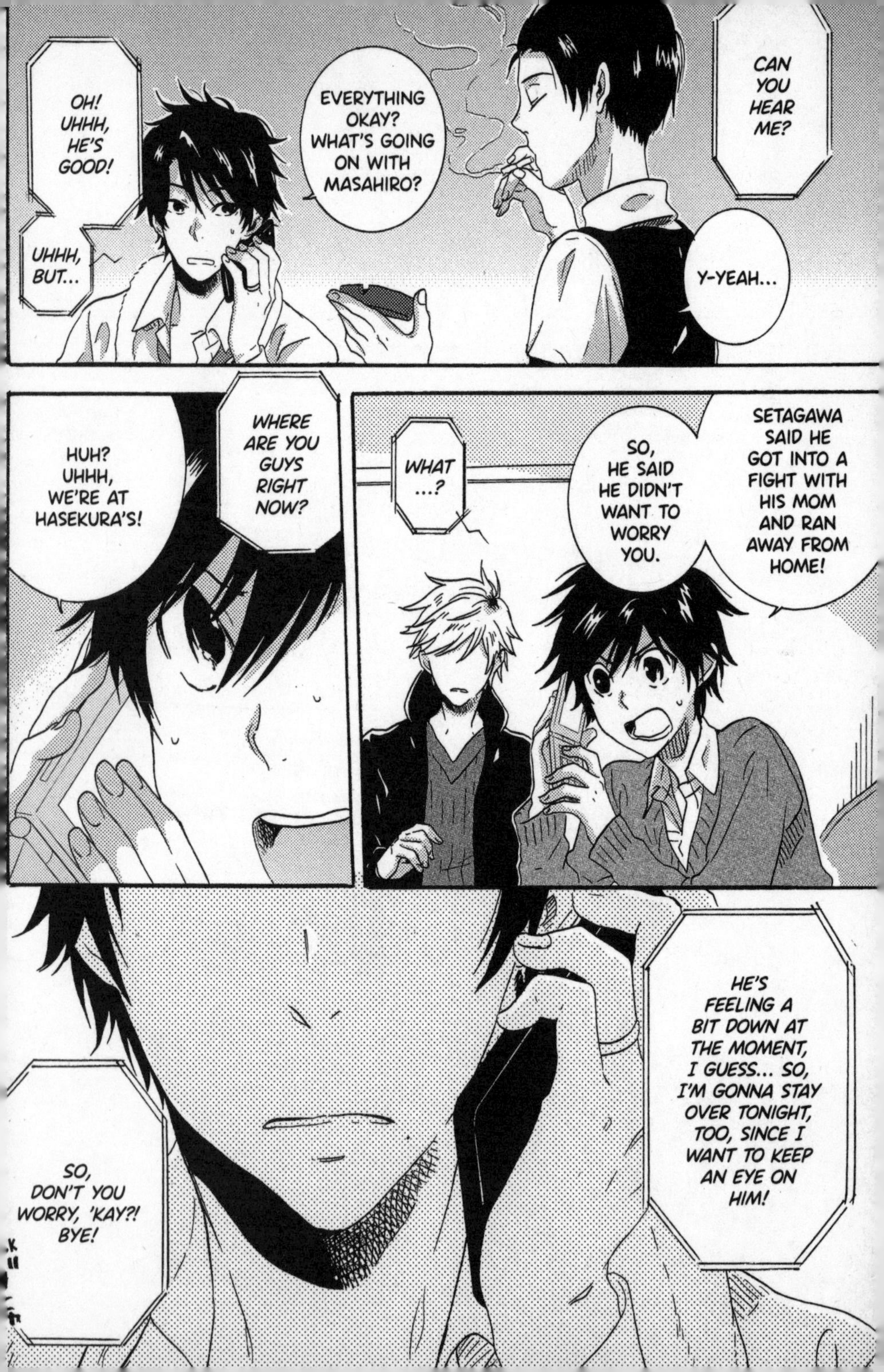
CAN YOU HEAR ME?
Y-YEAH...
EVERYTHING OKAY? WHAT'S GOING ON WITH MASAHIRO?
OH! UHHH, HE'S GOOD!
UHHH, BUT...
SETAGAWA SAID HE GOT INTO A FIGHT WITH HIS MOM AND RAN AWAY FROM HOME!
SO, HE SAID HE DIDN'T WANT TO WORRY YOU.
WHAT ...?
WHERE ARE YOU GUYS RIGHT NOW?
HUH? UHHH, WE'RE AT HASEKURA'S!
HE'S FEELING A BIT DOWN AT THE MOMENT, I GUESS... SO, I'M GONNA STAY OVER TONIGHT, TOO, SINCE I WANT TO KEEP AN EYE ON HIM!
SO, DON'T YOU WORRY, 'KAY?! BYE!

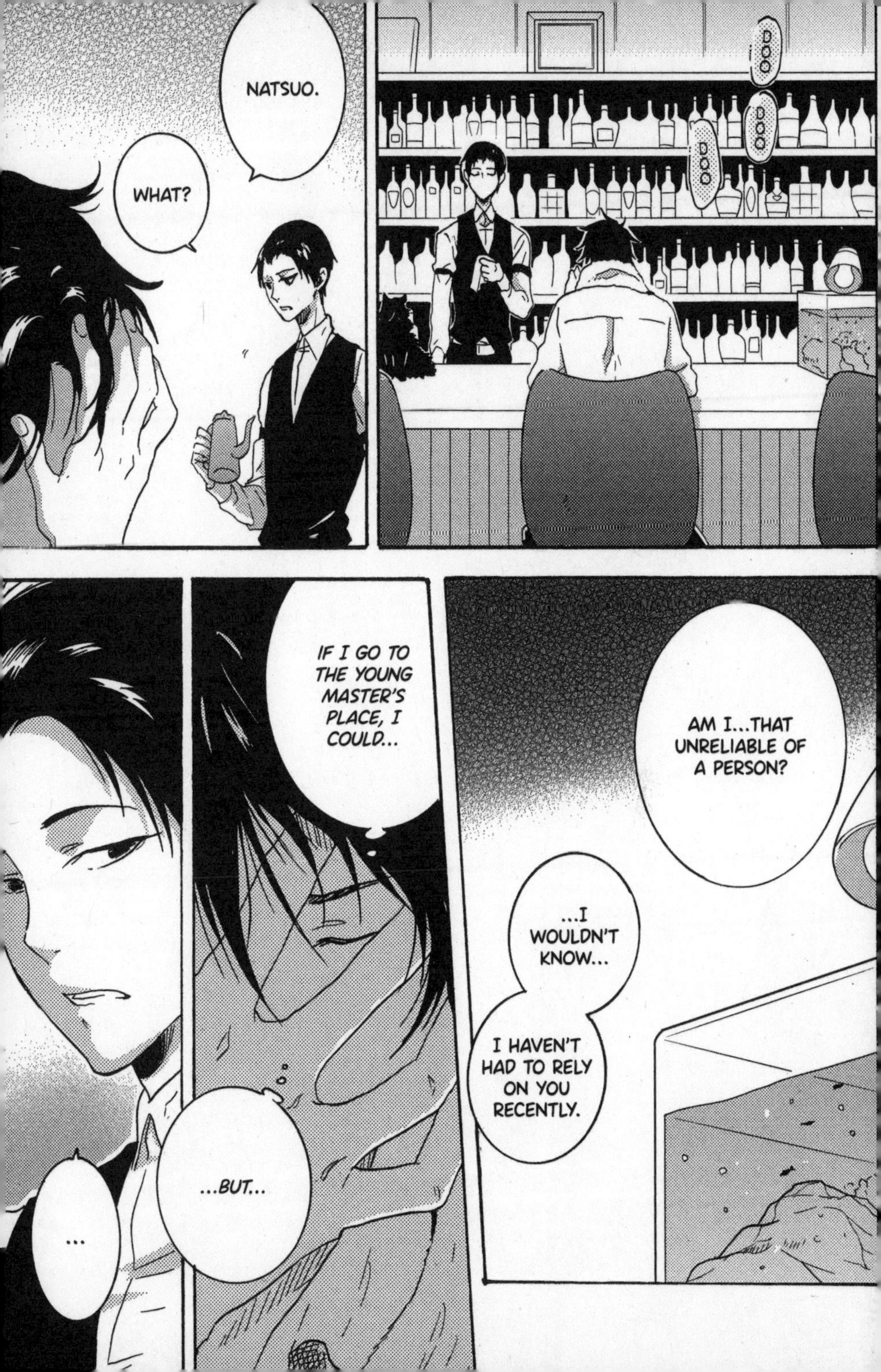
DOO
DOO
DOO
NATSUO.
WHAT?
AM I...THAT UNRELIABLE OF A PERSON?
...I WOULDN'T KNOW...
I HAVEN'T HAD TO RELY ON YOU RECENTLY.
IF I GO TO THE YOUNG MASTER'S PLACE, I COULD...
...BUT...
...

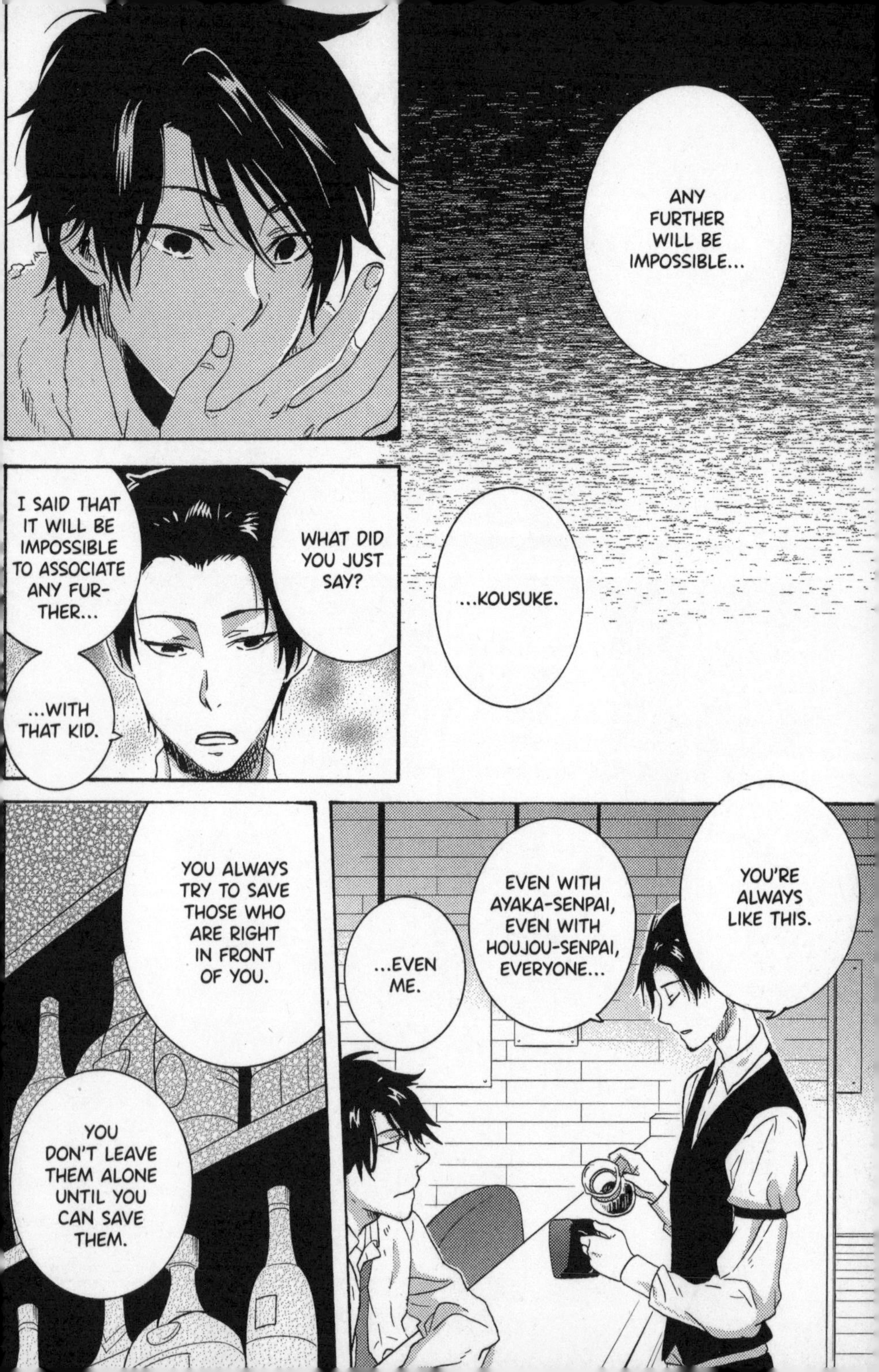
ANY FURTHER WILL BE IMPOSSIBLE...
...KOUSUKE.
WHAT DID YOU JUST SAY?
I SAID THAT IT WILL BE IMPOSSIBLE TO ASSOCIATE ANY FUR-THER...
...WITH THAT KID.
YOU'RE ALWAYS LIKE THIS.
EVEN WITH AYAKA-SENPAI, EVEN WITH HOUJOU-SENPAI, EVERYONE...
...EVEN ME.
YOU ALWAYS TRY TO SAVE THOSE WHO ARE RIGHT IN FRONT OF YOU.
YOU DON'T LEAVE THEM ALONE UNTIL YOU CAN SAVE THEM.

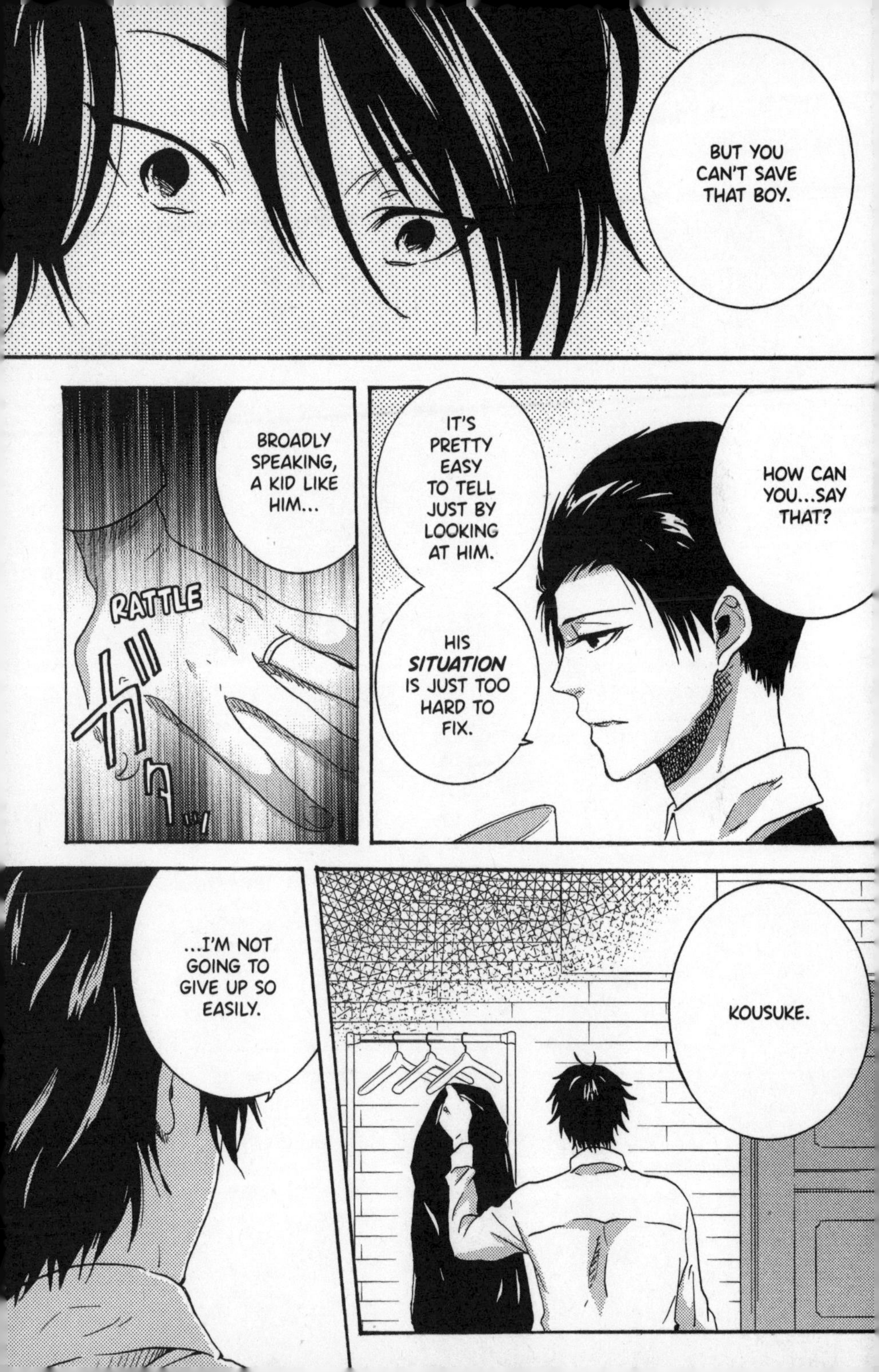
BUT YOU CAN'T SAVE THAT BOY.
HOW CAN YOU...SAY THAT?
IT'S PRETTY EASY TO TELL JUST BY LOOKING AT HIM.
HIS *SITUATION* IS JUST TOO HARD TO FIX.
BROADLY SPEAKING, A KID LIKE HIM...
RATTLE
KOUSUKE.
...I'M NOT GOING TO GIVE UP SO EASILY.

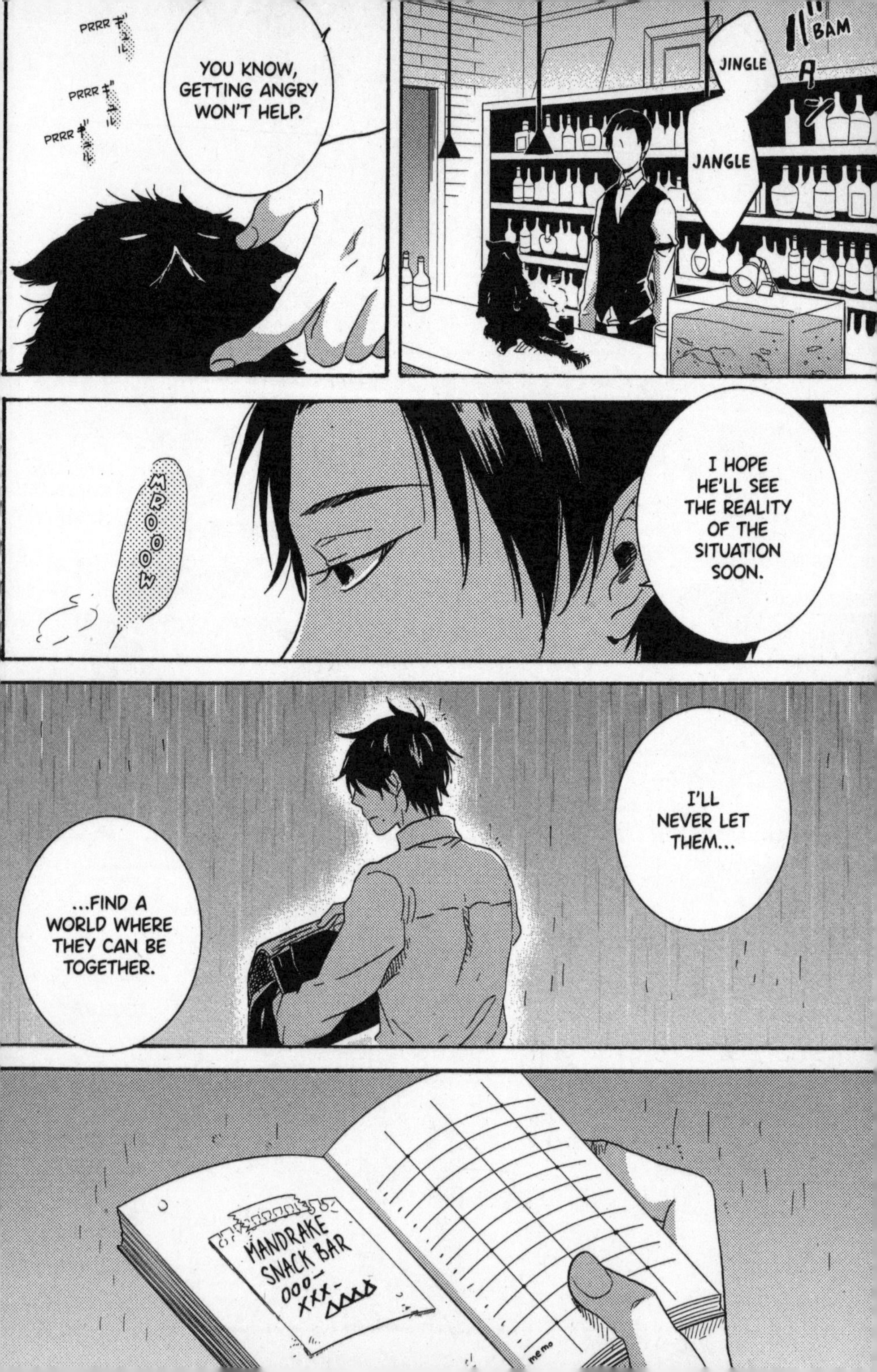
JINGLE
JANGLE
BAM
YOU KNOW, GETTING ANGRY WON'T HELP.
PRRR
PRRR
PRRR
I HOPE HE'LL SEE THE REALITY OF THE SITUATION SOON.
MROOOW
I'LL NEVER LET THEM...
...FIND A WORLD WHERE THEY CAN BE TOGETHER.
MANDRAKE SNACK BAR 000-XXX-ΔΔΔΔ
memo

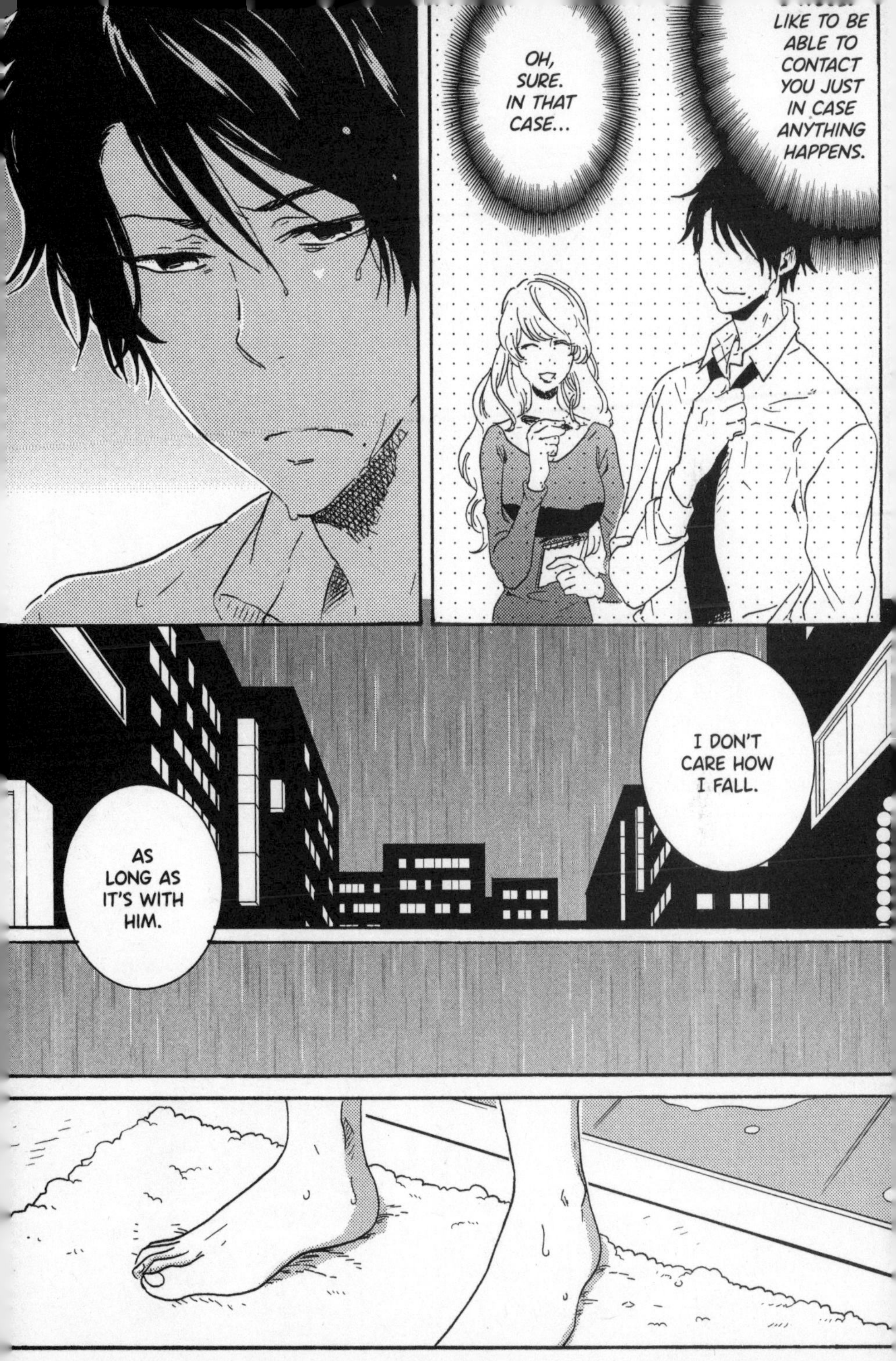
LIKE TO BE ABLE TO CONTACT YOU JUST IN CASE ANYTHING HAPPENS.
OH, SURE. IN THAT CASE...
I DON'T CARE HOW I FALL.
AS LONG AS IT'S WITH HIM.

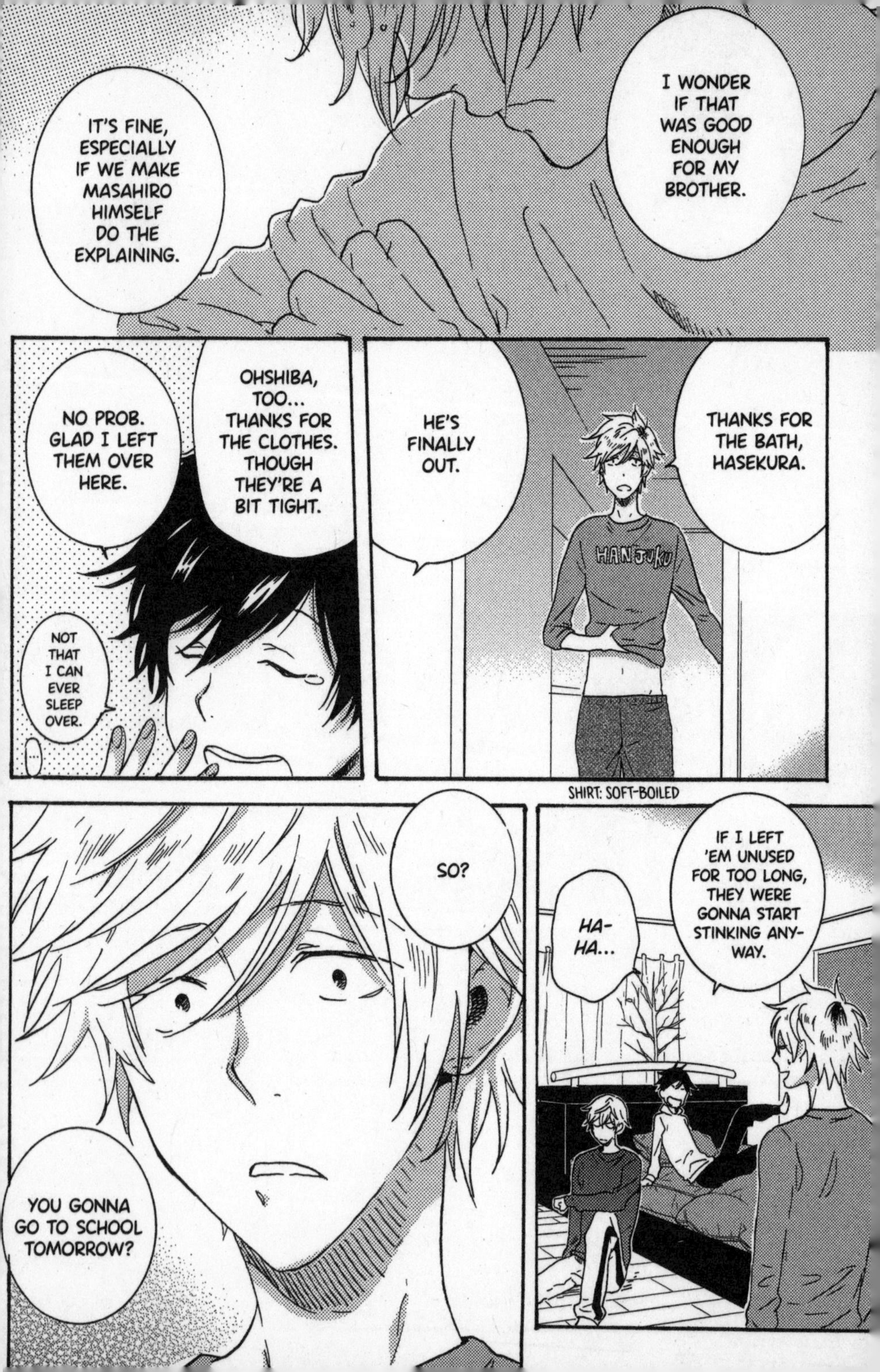
I WONDER IF THAT WAS GOOD ENOUGH FOR MY BROTHER.
IT'S FINE, ESPECIALLY IF WE MAKE MASAHIRO HIMSELF DO THE EXPLAINING.
THANKS FOR THE BATH, HASEKURA.
HANJUKU
HE'S FINALLY OUT.
SHIRT: SOFT-BOILED
OHSHIBA, TOO... THANKS FOR THE CLOTHES. THOUGH THEY'RE A BIT TIGHT.
NO PROB. GLAD I LEFT THEM OVER HERE.
NOT THAT I CAN EVER SLEEP OVER.
...
IF I LEFT 'EM UNUSED FOR TOO LONG, THEY WERE GONNA START STINKING ANY-WAY.
HA-HA...
SO?
YOU GONNA GO TO SCHOOL TOMORROW?

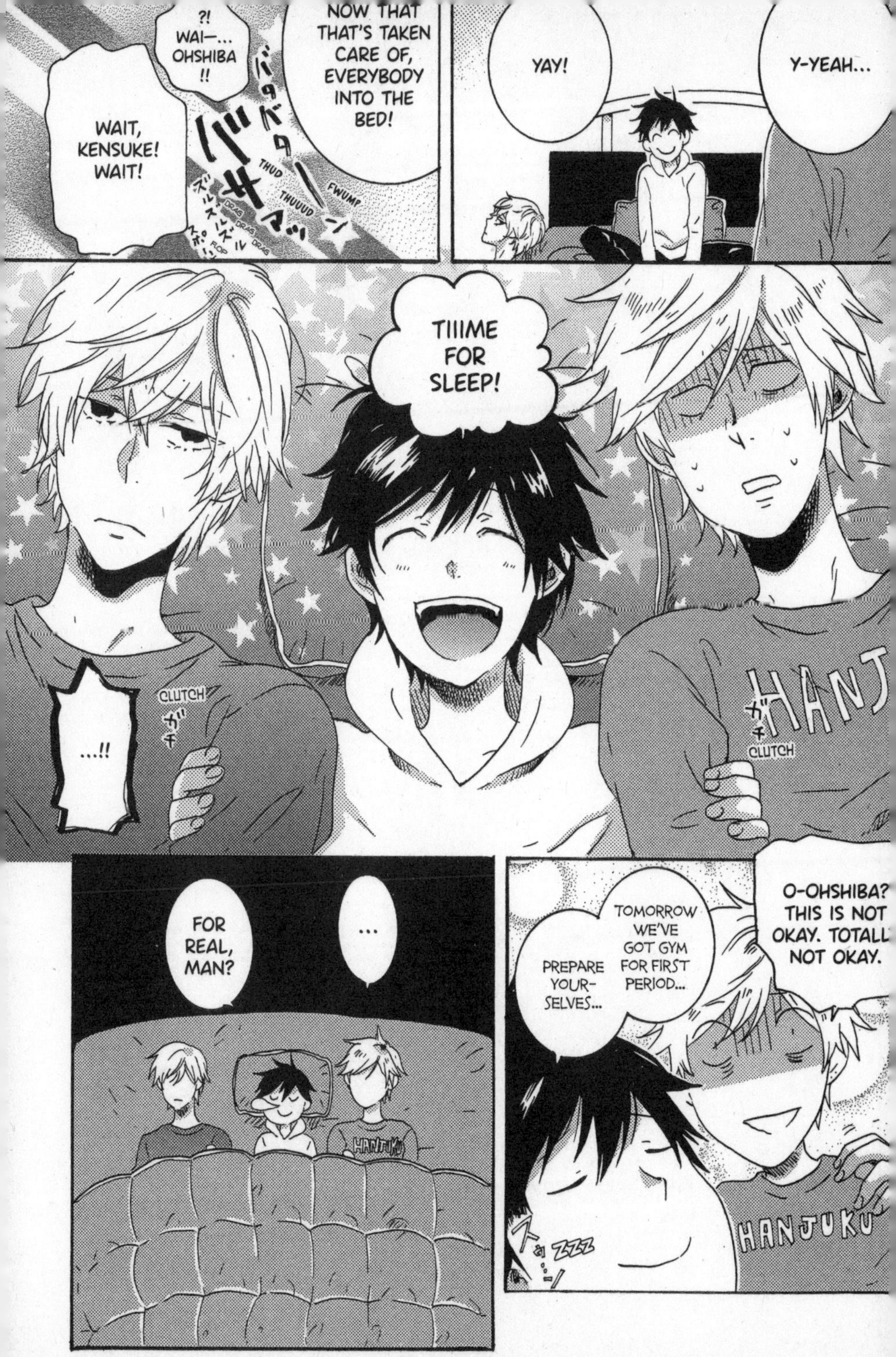
Y-YEAH...
YAY!
NOW THAT THAT'S TAKEN CARE OF, EVERYBODY INTO THE BED!
?! WAI—... OHSHIBA !!
WAIT, KENSUKE! WAIT!
FWUMP
THUD
THUUUD
DRAG
DRAG
DRAG
FLOP
TIIIME FOR SLEEP!
HANJ
CLUTCH
CLUTCH
...!!
O-OHSHIBA? THIS IS NOT OKAY. TOTALL NOT OKAY.
TOMORROW WE'VE GOT GYM FOR FIRST PERIOD...
PREPARE YOUR-SELVES...
HANJUKU
ZZZ
...
FOR REAL, MAN?
HANJUKU

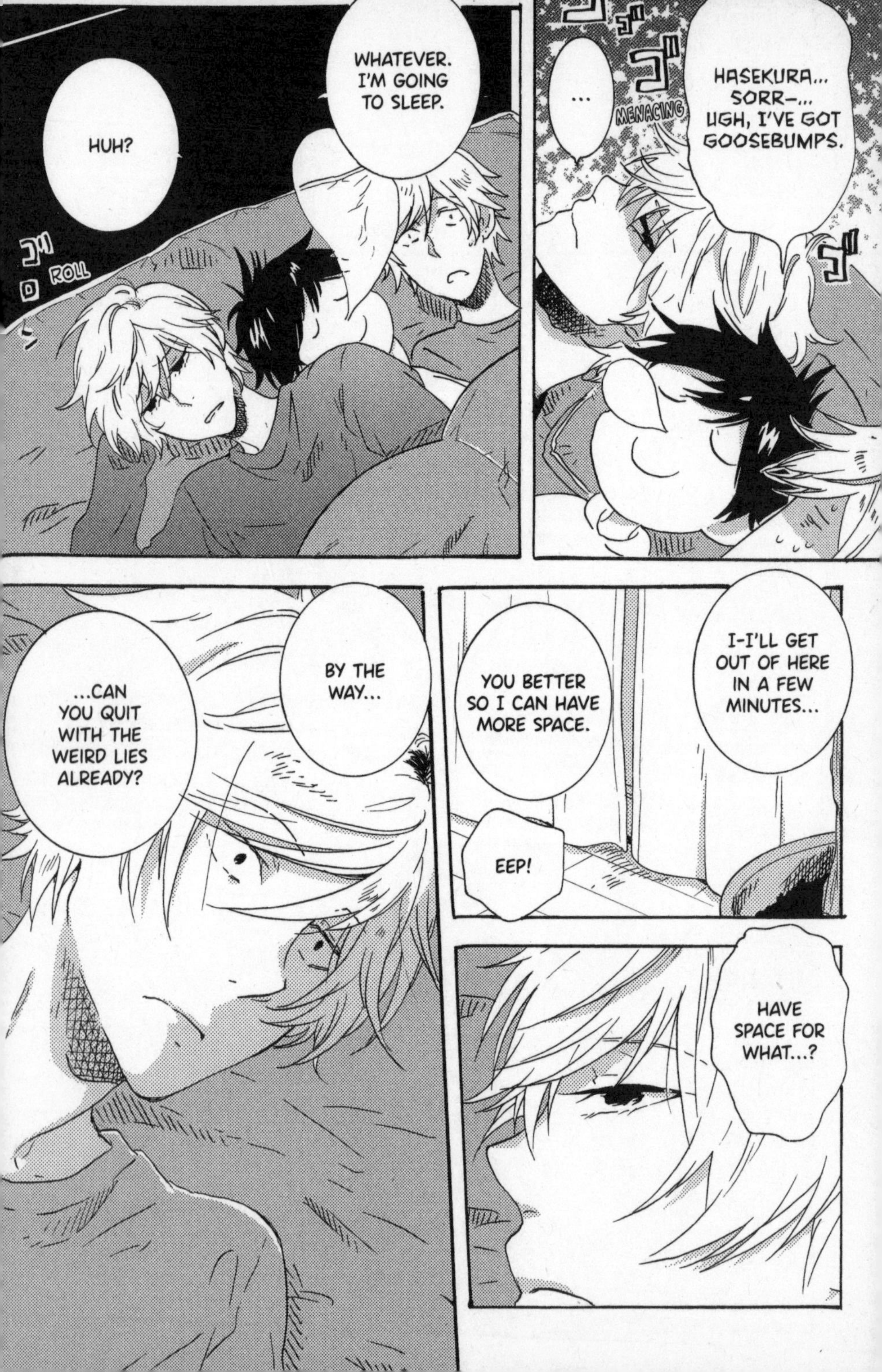
HASEKURA... SORR-... UGH, I'VE GOT GOOSEBUMPS.
...
MENACING
WHATEVER. I'M GOING TO SLEEP.
HUH?
ROLL
I-I'LL GET OUT OF HERE IN A FEW MINUTES...
YOU BETTER SO I CAN HAVE MORE SPACE.
EEP!
HAVE SPACE FOR WHAT...?
BY THE WAY...
...CAN YOU QUIT WITH THE WEIRD LIES ALREADY?

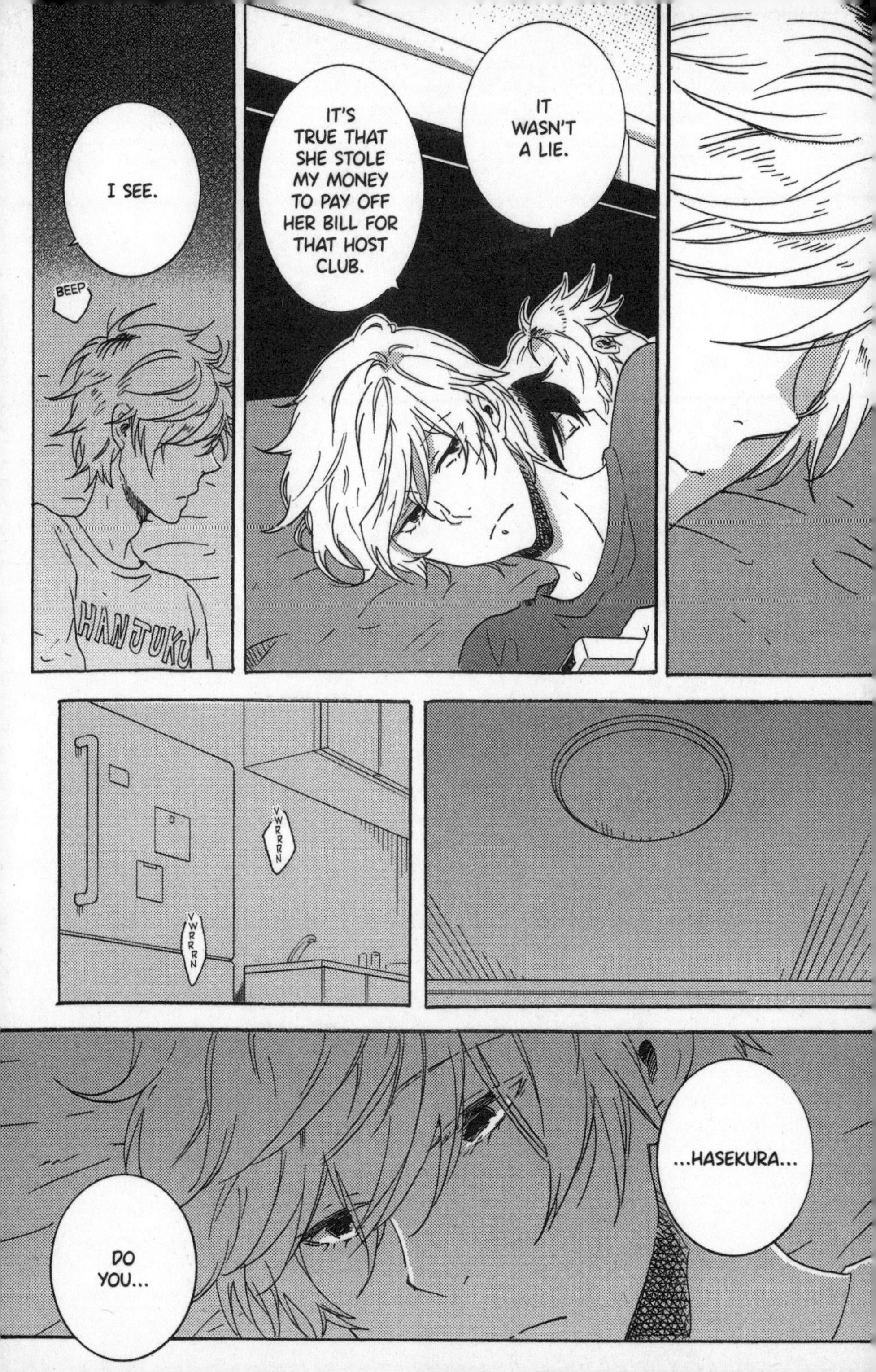
IT WASN'T A LIE.
IT'S TRUE THAT SHE STOLE MY MONEY TO PAY OFF HER BILL FOR THAT HOST CLUB.
I SEE.
BEEP
HANJUKU
VWRRN
VWRRN
...HASEKURA...
DO YOU...

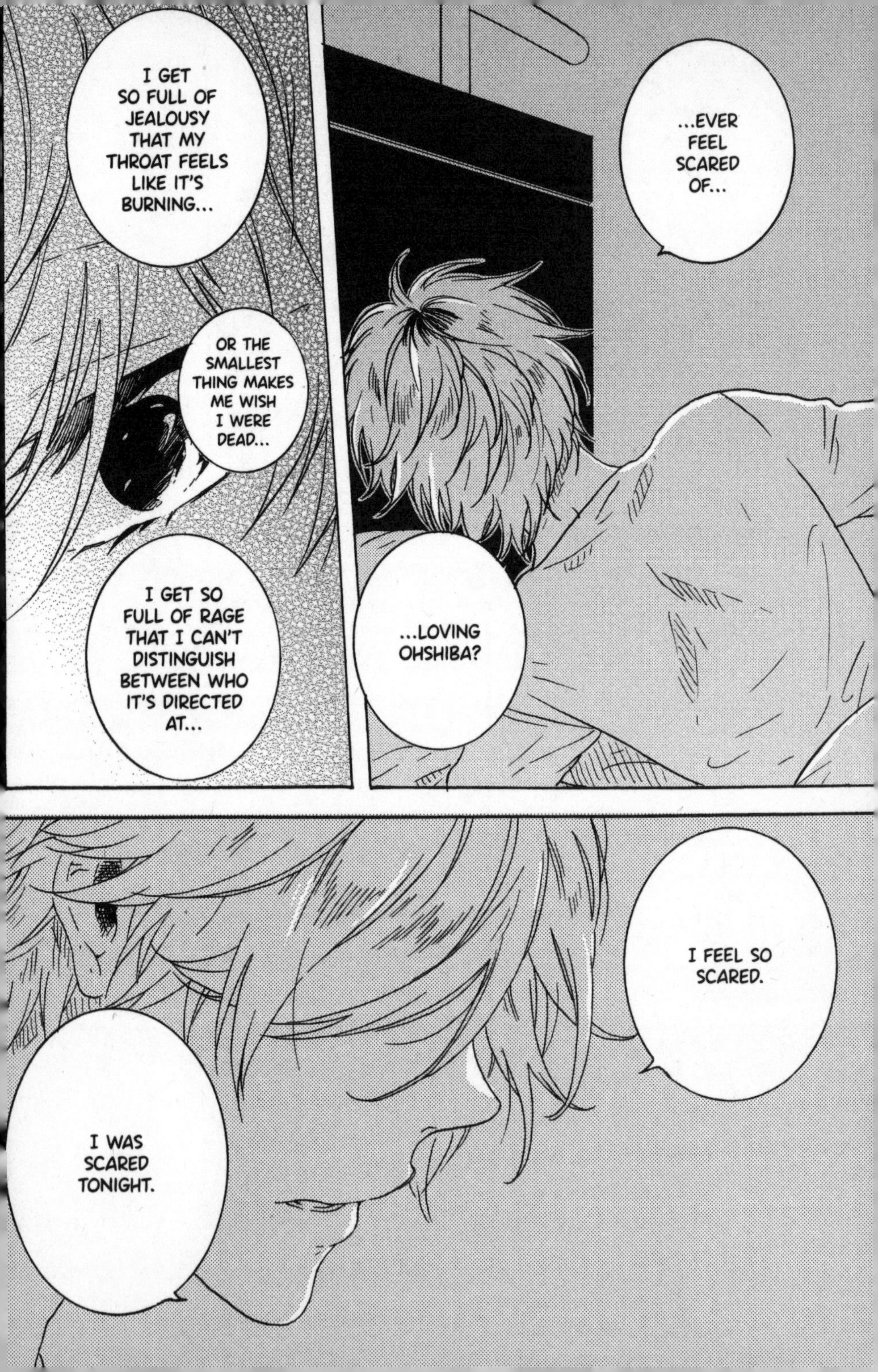

...EVER FEEL SCARED OF...
...LOVING OHSHIBA?
I GET SO FULL OF JEALOUSY THAT MY THROAT FEELS LIKE IT'S BURNING...
OR THE SMALLEST THING MAKES ME WISH I WERE DEAD...
I GET SO FULL OF RAGE THAT I CAN'T DISTINGUISH BETWEEN WHO IT'S DIRECTED AT...
I FEEL SO SCARED.
I WAS SCARED TONIGHT.

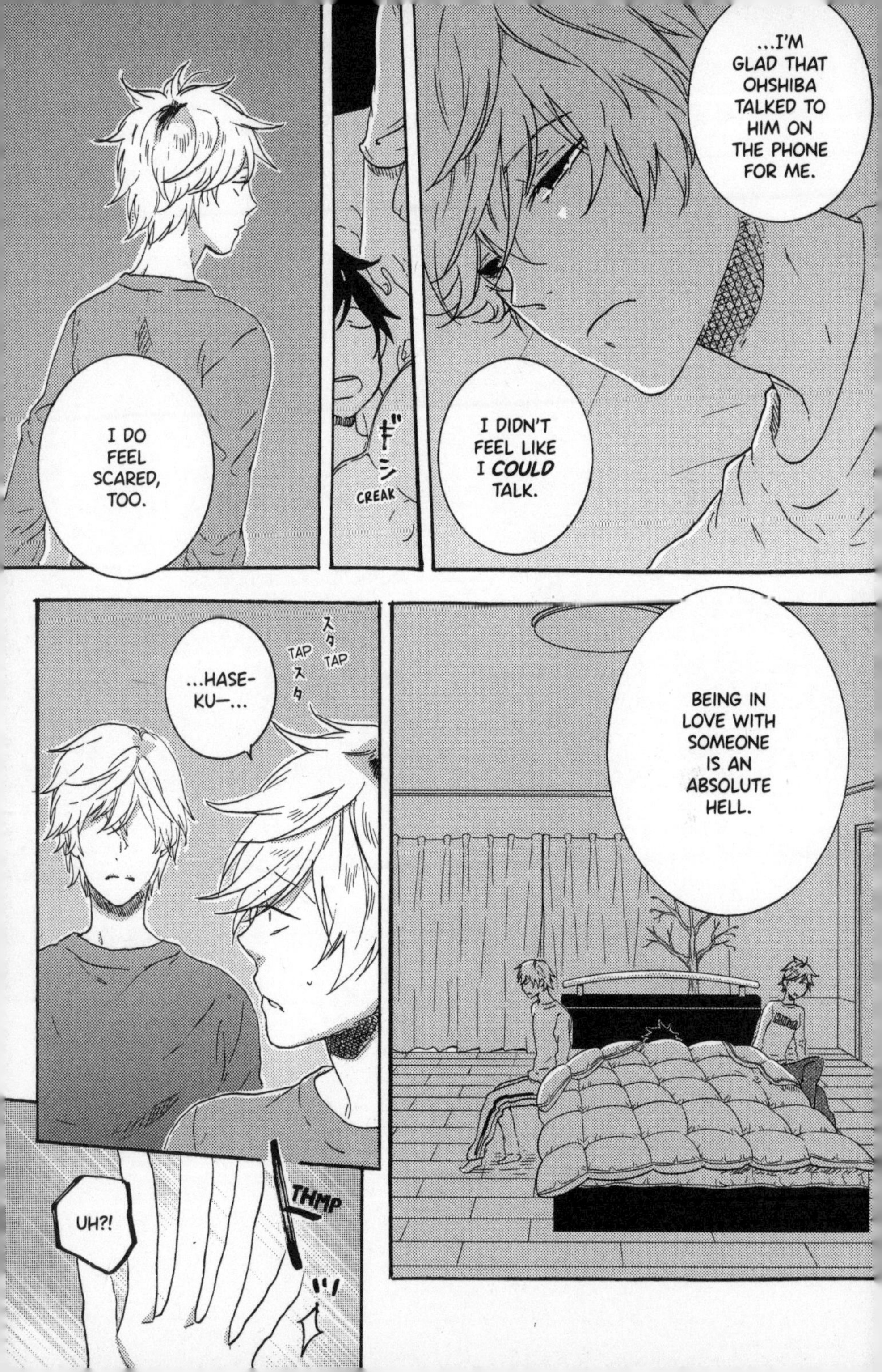
...I'M GLAD THAT OHSHIBA TALKED TO HIM ON THE PHONE FOR ME.
I DIDN'T FEEL LIKE I COULD TALK.
ギシ
CREAK
I DO FEEL SCARED, TOO.
BEING IN LOVE WITH SOMEONE IS AN ABSOLUTE HELL.
スタスタ
TAP TAP
...HASE-KU—...
THMP
UH?!

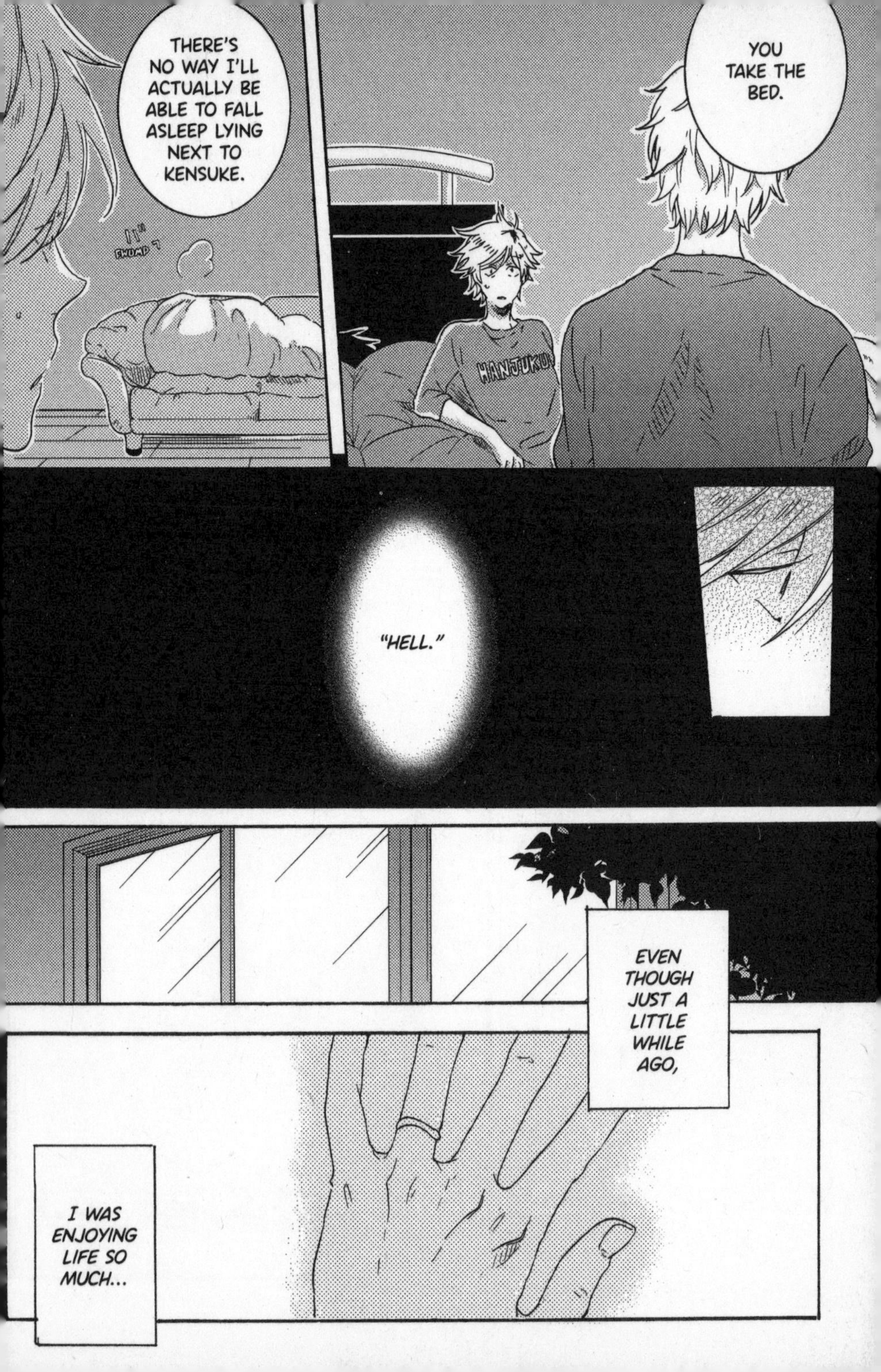
YOU TAKE THE BED.
HANJUKU
THERE'S NO WAY I'LL ACTUALLY BE ABLE TO FALL ASLEEP LYING NEXT TO KENSUKE.
FWUMP
"HELL."
EVEN THOUGH JUST A LITTLE WHILE AGO,
I WAS ENJOYING LIFE SO MUCH...

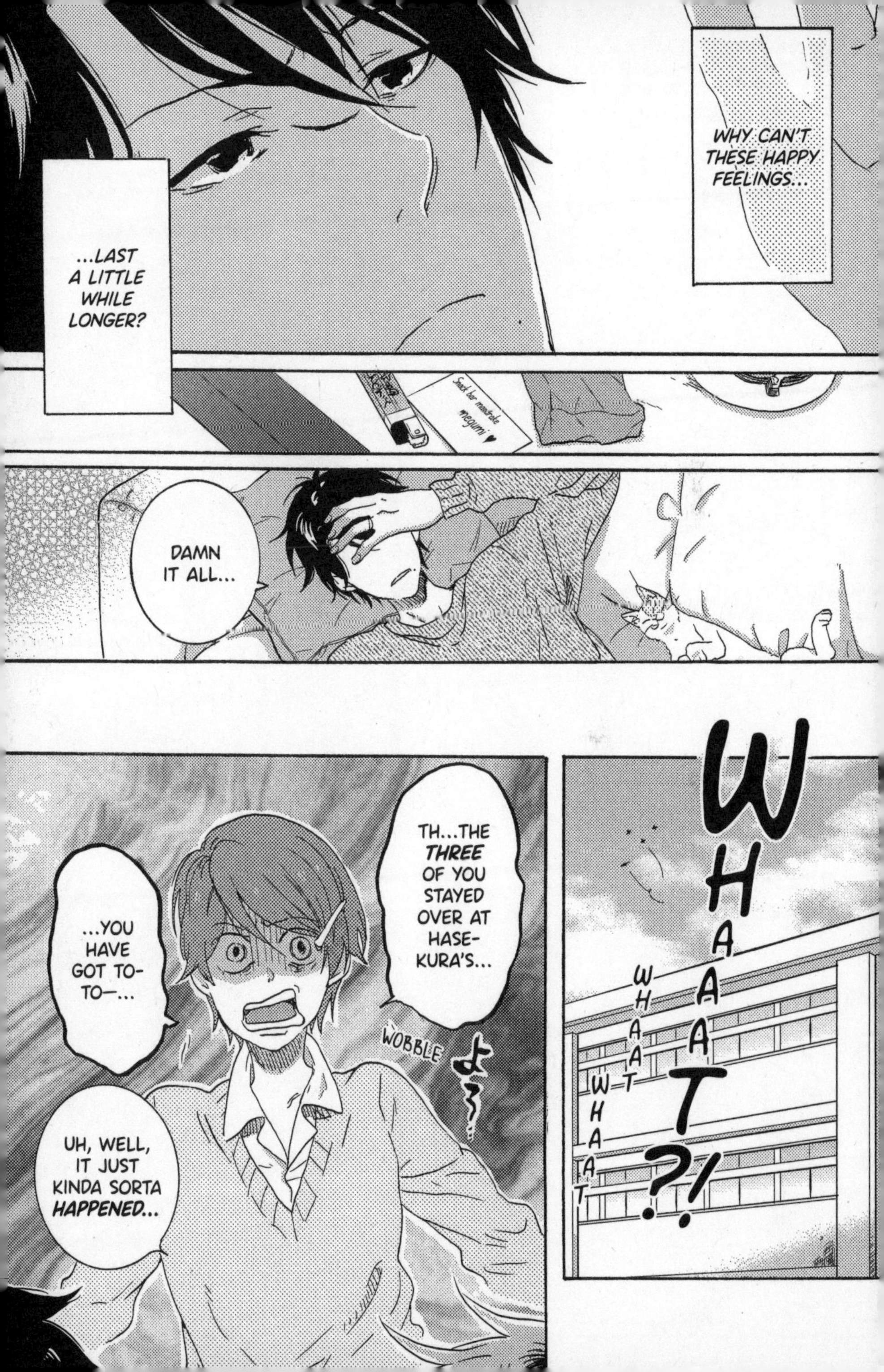
WHY CAN'T THESE HAPPY FEELINGS...
...LAST A LITTLE WHILE LONGER?
DAMN IT ALL...
WHAAAT?!
WHAAT
WHAAT
TH...THE ***THREE*** OF YOU STAYED OVER AT HASE-KURA'S...
WOBBLE
...YOU HAVE GOT TO-TO—...
UH, WELL, IT JUST KINDA SORTA ***HAPPENED...***

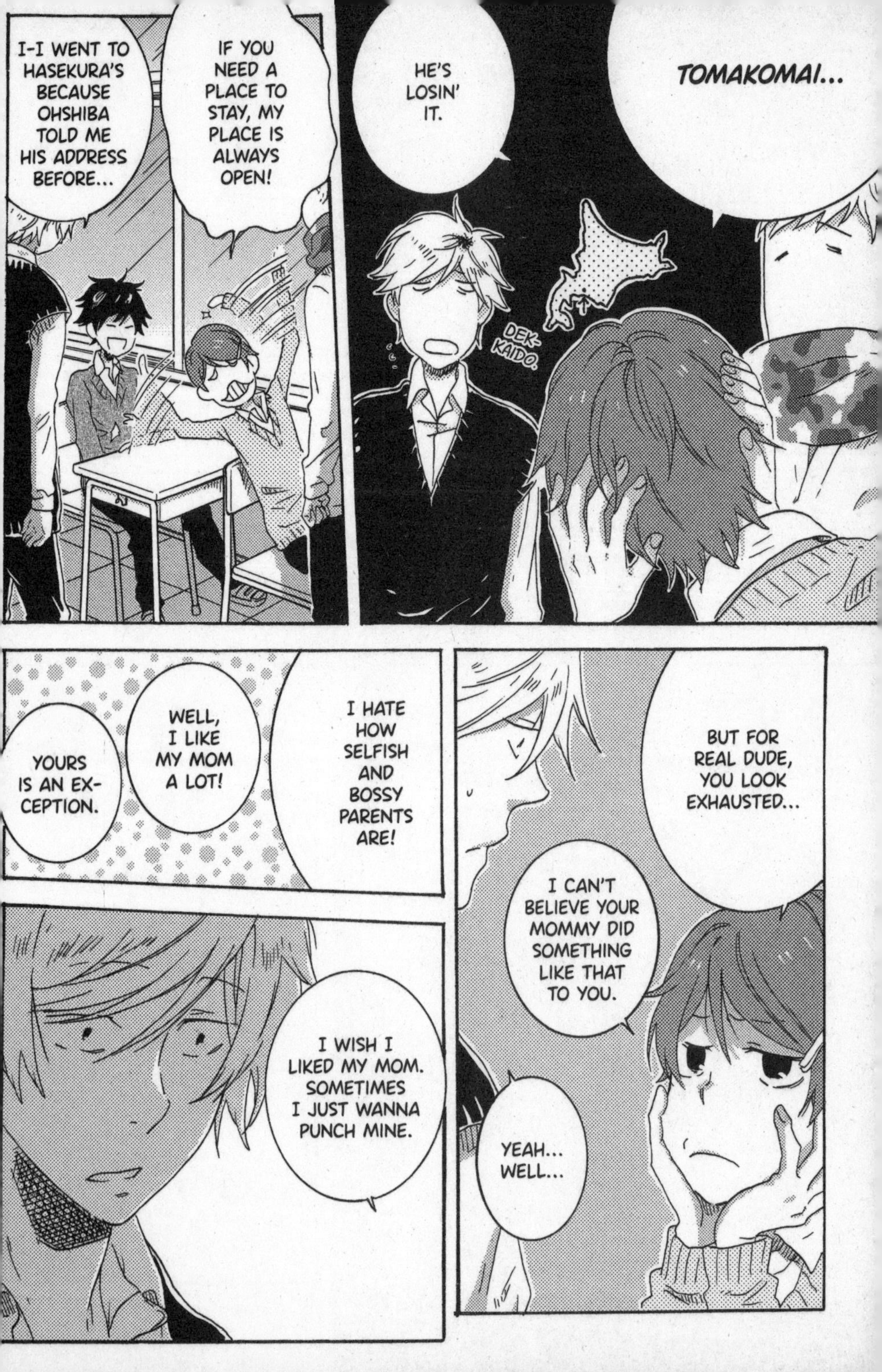
TOMAKOMAI...
HE'S LOSIN' IT.
DEK-KAIDO.
IF YOU NEED A PLACE TO STAY, MY PLACE IS ALWAYS OPEN!
I-I WENT TO HASEKURA'S BECAUSE OHSHIBA TOLD ME HIS ADDRESS BEFORE...
BUT FOR REAL DUDE, YOU LOOK EXHAUSTED...
I CAN'T BELIEVE YOUR MOMMY DID SOMETHING LIKE THAT TO YOU.
YEAH... WELL...
I HATE HOW SELFISH AND BOSSY PARENTS ARE!
WELL, I LIKE MY MOM A LOT!
YOURS IS AN EXCEPTION.
I WISH I LIKED MY MOM. SOMETIMES I JUST WANNA PUNCH MINE.

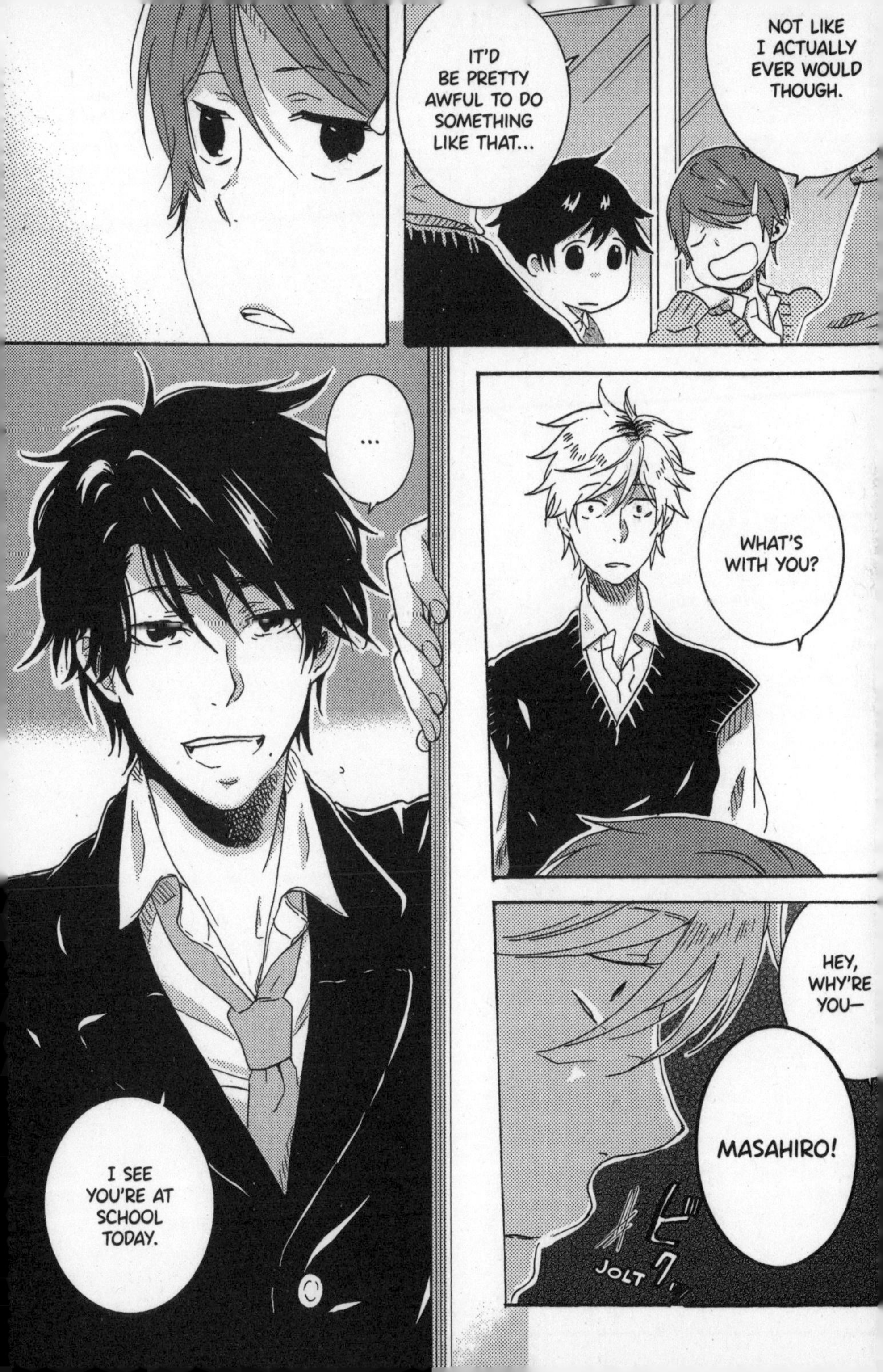
NOT LIKE I ACTUALLY EVER WOULD THOUGH.
IT'D BE PRETTY AWFUL TO DO SOMETHING LIKE THAT...
WHAT'S WITH YOU?
HEY, WHY'RE YOU—
MASAHIRO!
JOLT
...
I SEE YOU'RE AT SCHOOL TODAY.

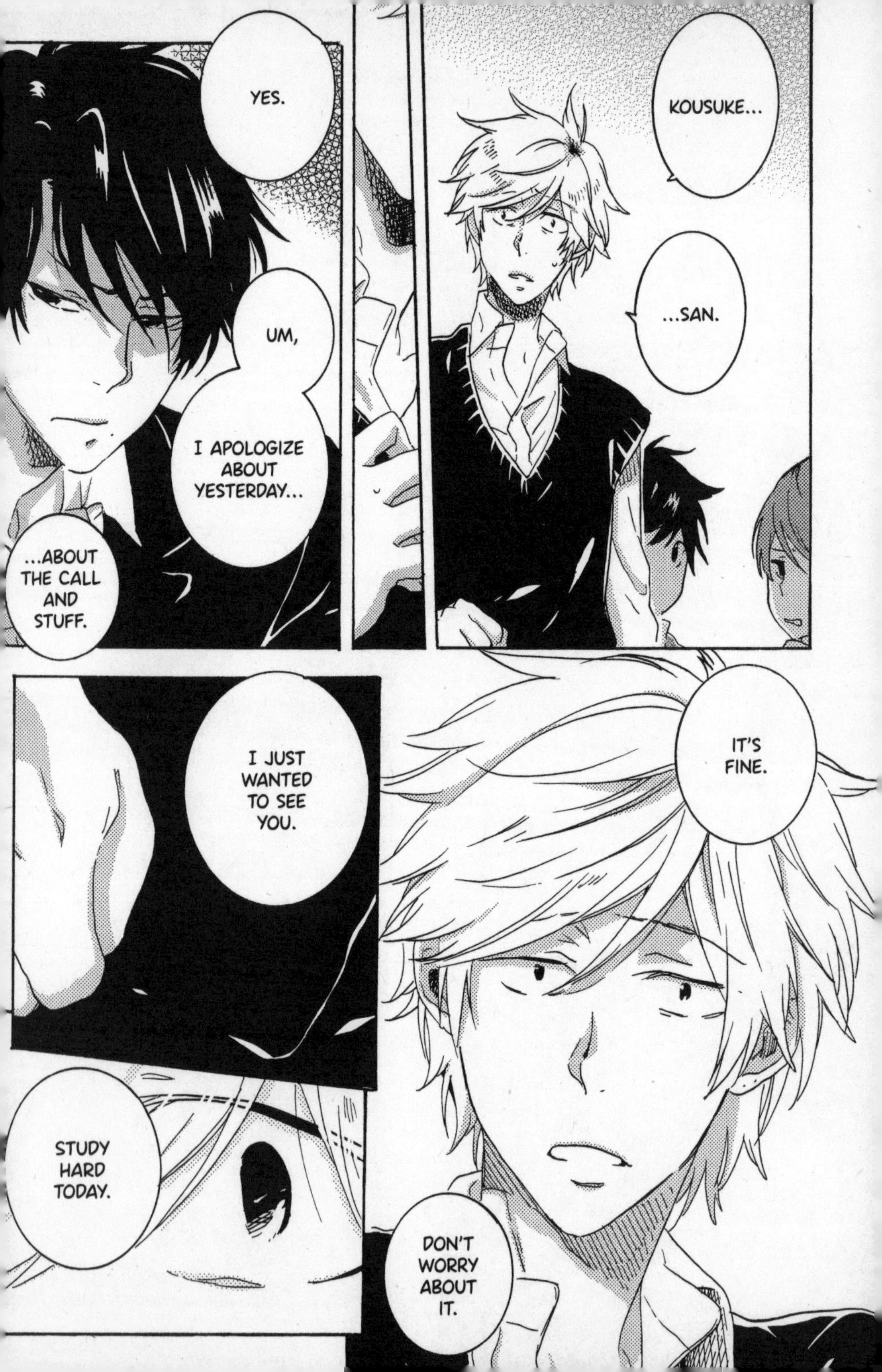
KOUSUKE...
...SAN.
YES.
UM,
I APOLOGIZE ABOUT YESTERDAY...
...ABOUT THE CALL AND STUFF.
IT'S FINE.
DON'T WORRY ABOUT IT.
I JUST WANTED TO SEE YOU.
STUDY HARD TODAY.

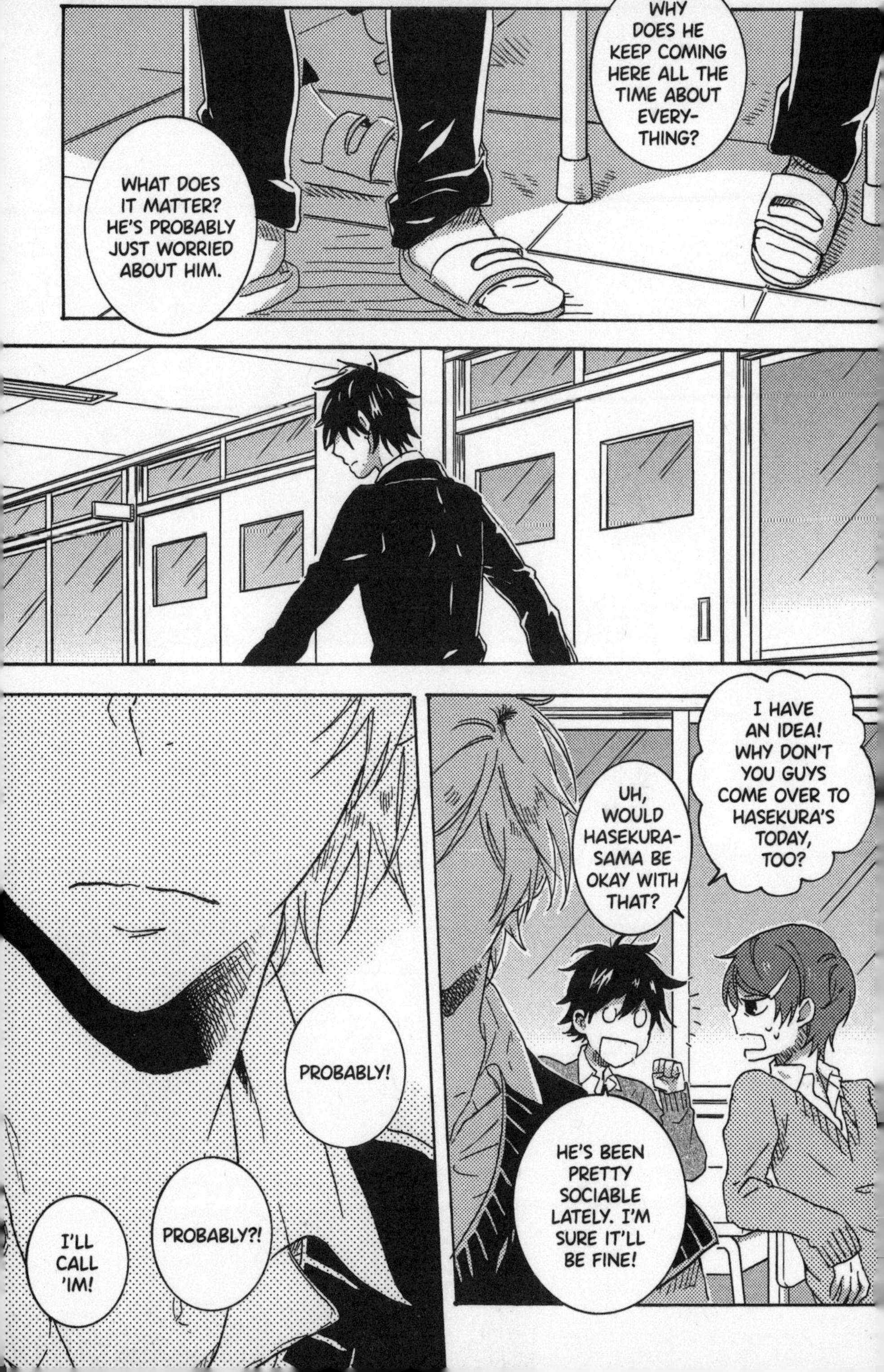
WHY DOES HE KEEP COMING HERE ALL THE TIME ABOUT EVERY-THING?
WHAT DOES IT MATTER? HE'S PROBABLY JUST WORRIED ABOUT HIM.
I HAVE AN IDEA! WHY DON'T YOU GUYS COME OVER TO HASEKURA'S TODAY, TOO?
UH, WOULD HASEKURA-SAMA BE OKAY WITH THAT?
HE'S BEEN PRETTY SOCIABLE LATELY. I'M SURE IT'LL BE FINE!
PROBABLY!
PROBABLY?!
I'LL CALL 'IM!

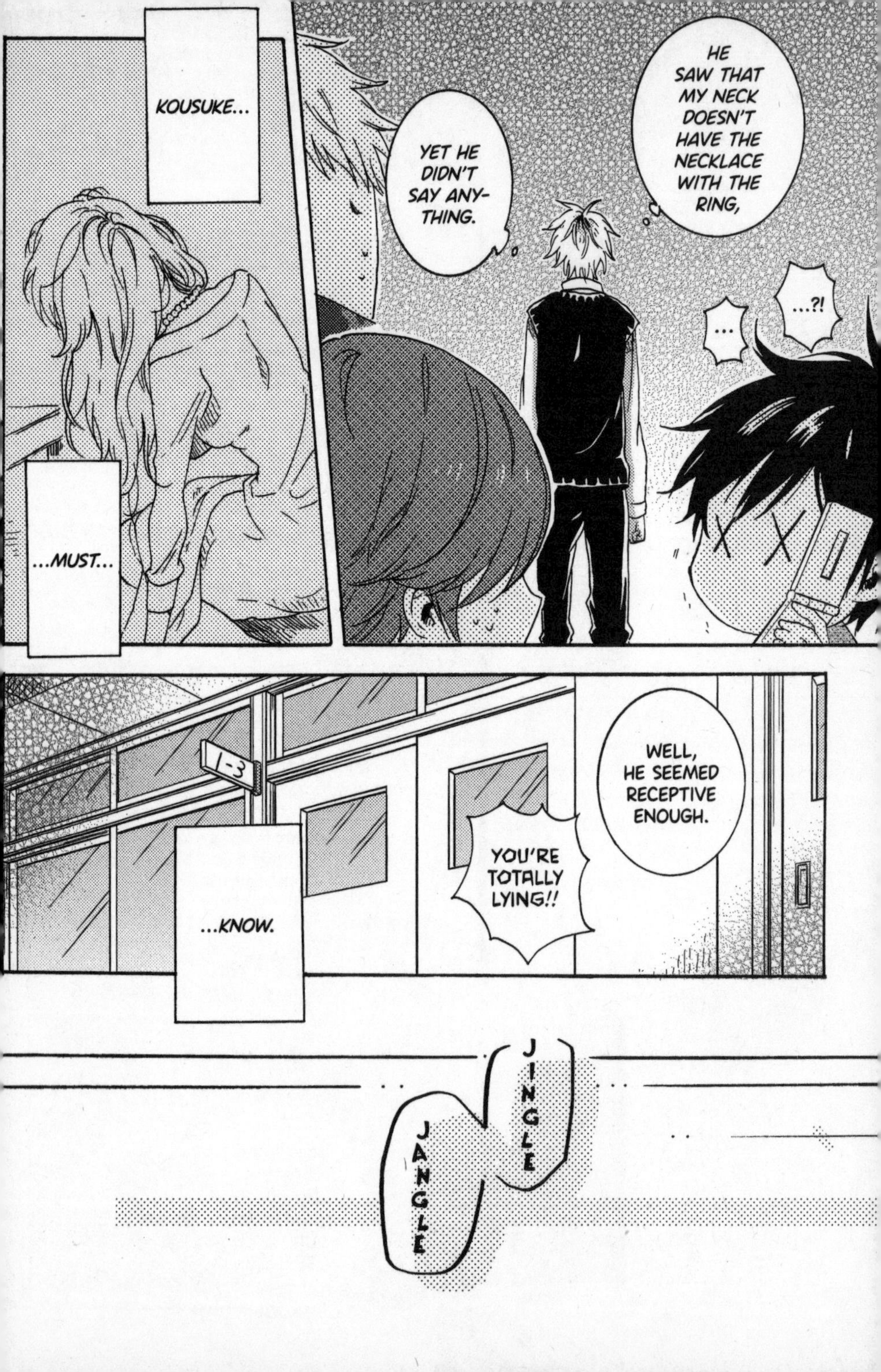
HE SAW THAT MY NECK DOESN'T HAVE THE NECKLACE WITH THE RING,
YET HE DIDN'T SAY ANY-THING.
...?!
...
KOUSUKE...
...MUST...
WELL, HE SEEMED RECEPTIVE ENOUGH.
YOU'RE TOTALLY LYING!!
...KNOW.
JINGLE
JANGLE

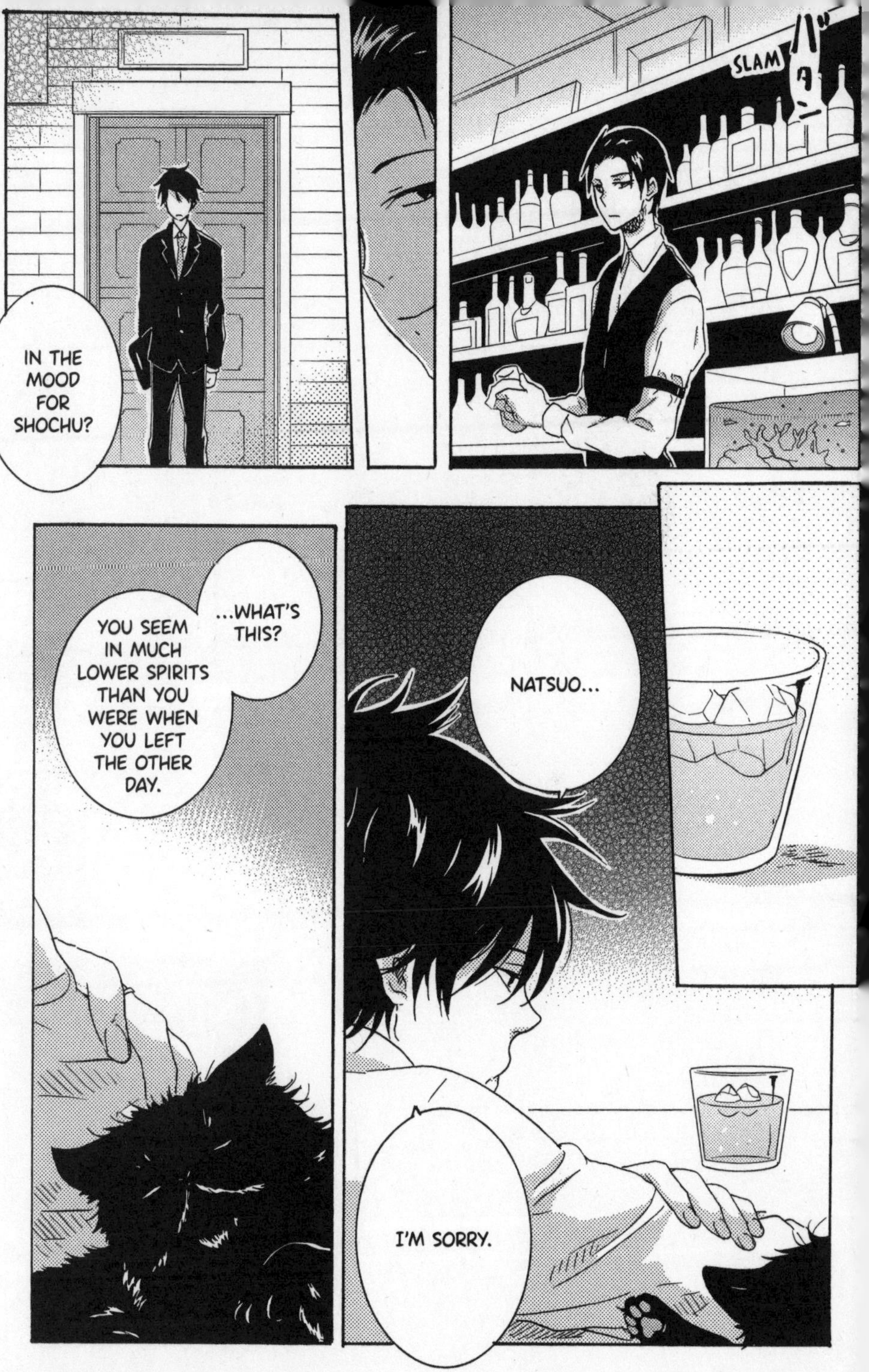
SLAM
IN THE MOOD FOR SHOCHU?
NATSUO...
I'M SORRY.
...WHAT'S THIS?
YOU SEEM IN MUCH LOWER SPIRITS THAN YOU WERE WHEN YOU LEFT THE OTHER DAY.

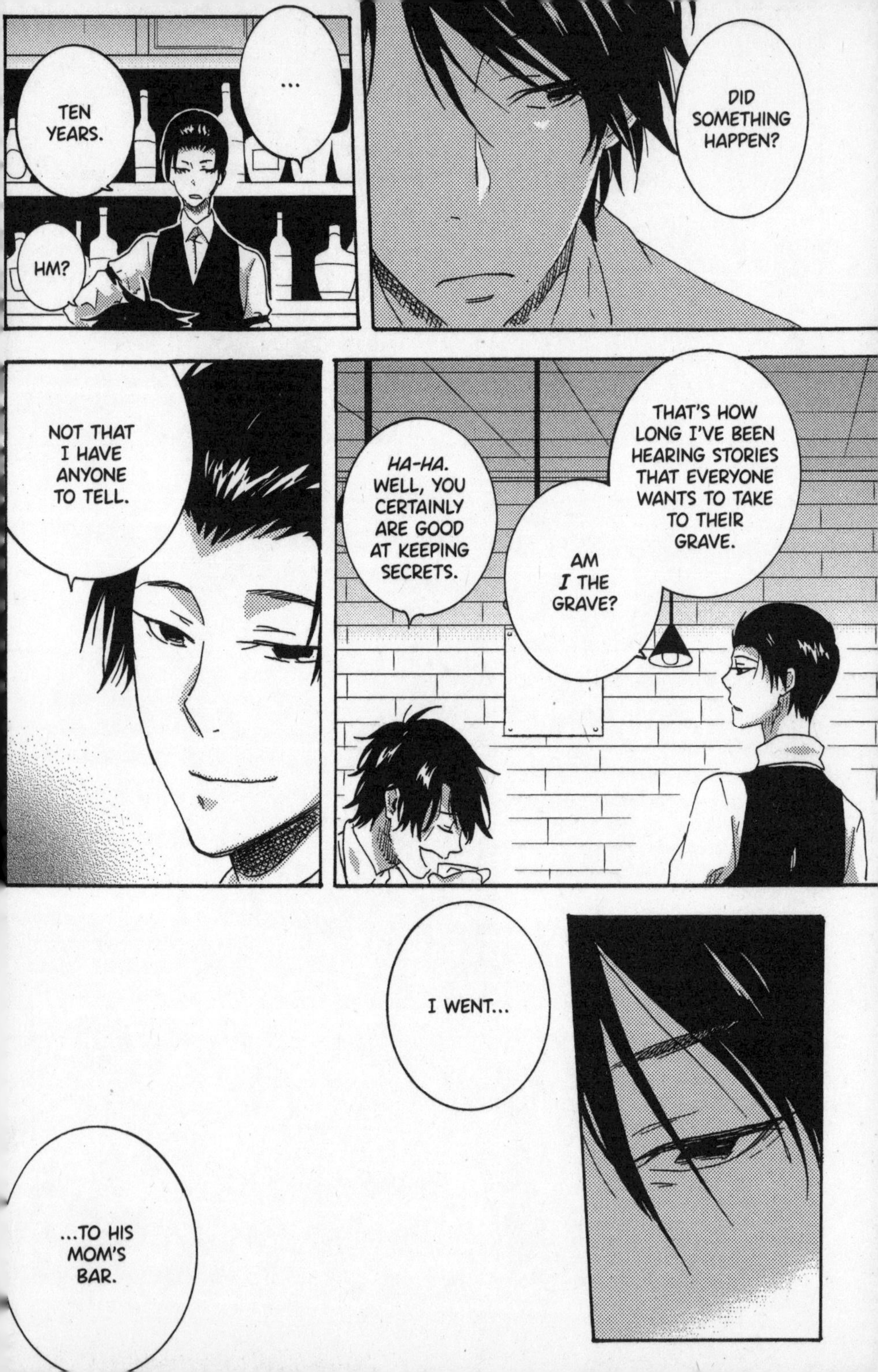
DID SOMETHING HAPPEN?
...
TEN YEARS.
HM?
THAT'S HOW LONG I'VE BEEN HEARING STORIES THAT EVERYONE WANTS TO TAKE TO THEIR GRAVE.
AM *I* THE GRAVE?
HA-HA. WELL, YOU CERTAINLY ARE GOOD AT KEEPING SECRETS.
NOT THAT I HAVE ANYONE TO TELL.
I WENT...
...TO HIS MOM'S BAR.

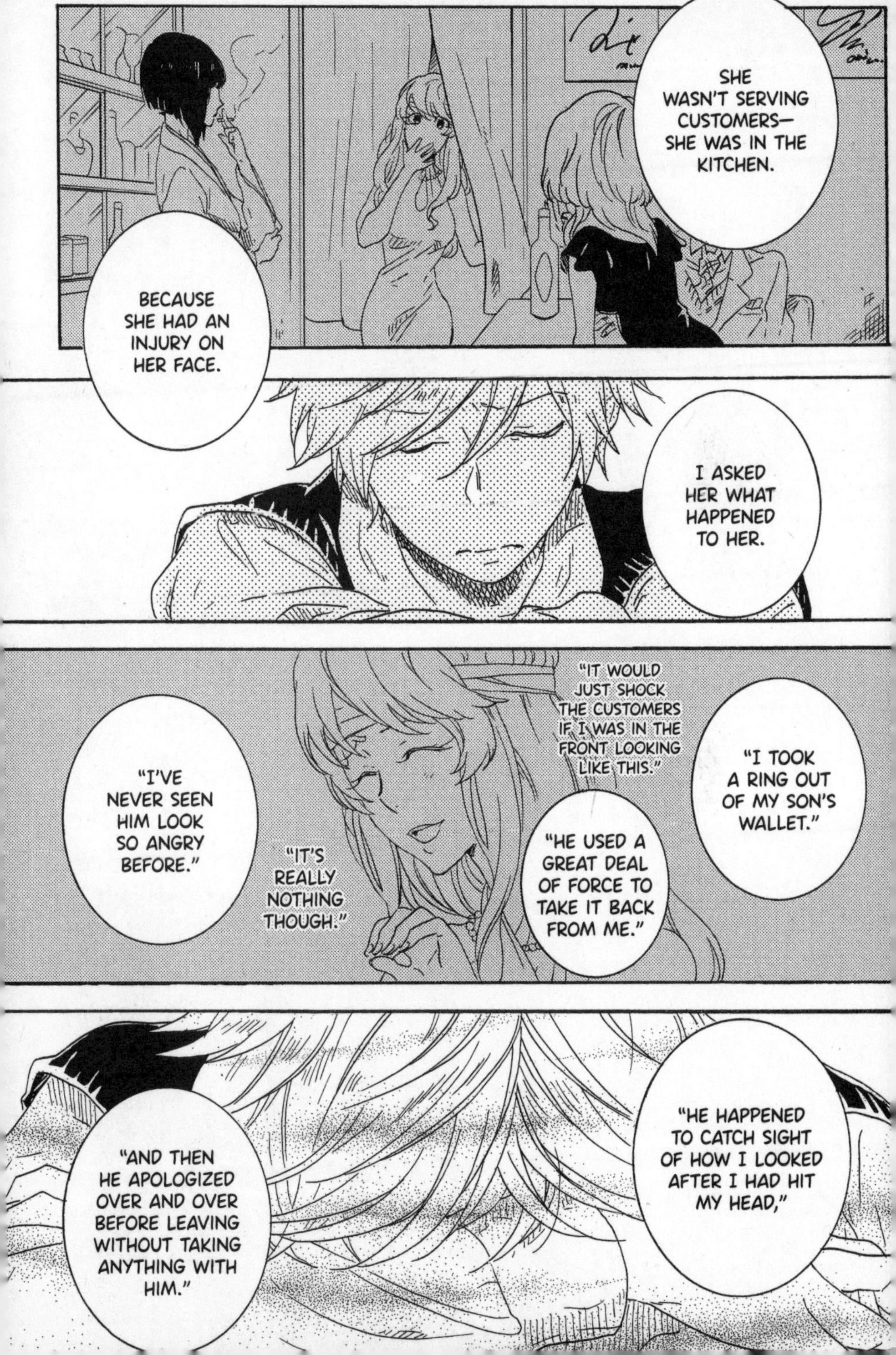
SHE WASN'T SERVING CUSTOMERS—SHE WAS IN THE KITCHEN.
BECAUSE SHE HAD AN INJURY ON HER FACE.
I ASKED HER WHAT HAPPENED TO HER.
"IT WOULD JUST SHOCK THE CUSTOMERS IF I WAS IN THE FRONT LOOKING LIKE THIS."
"IT'S REALLY NOTHING THOUGH."
"I TOOK A RING OUT OF MY SON'S WALLET."
"HE USED A GREAT DEAL OF FORCE TO TAKE IT BACK FROM ME."
"I'VE NEVER SEEN HIM LOOK SO ANGRY BEFORE."
"HE HAPPENED TO CATCH SIGHT OF HOW I LOOKED AFTER I HAD HIT MY HEAD,"
"AND THEN HE APOLOGIZED OVER AND OVER BEFORE LEAVING WITHOUT TAKING ANYTHING WITH HIM."

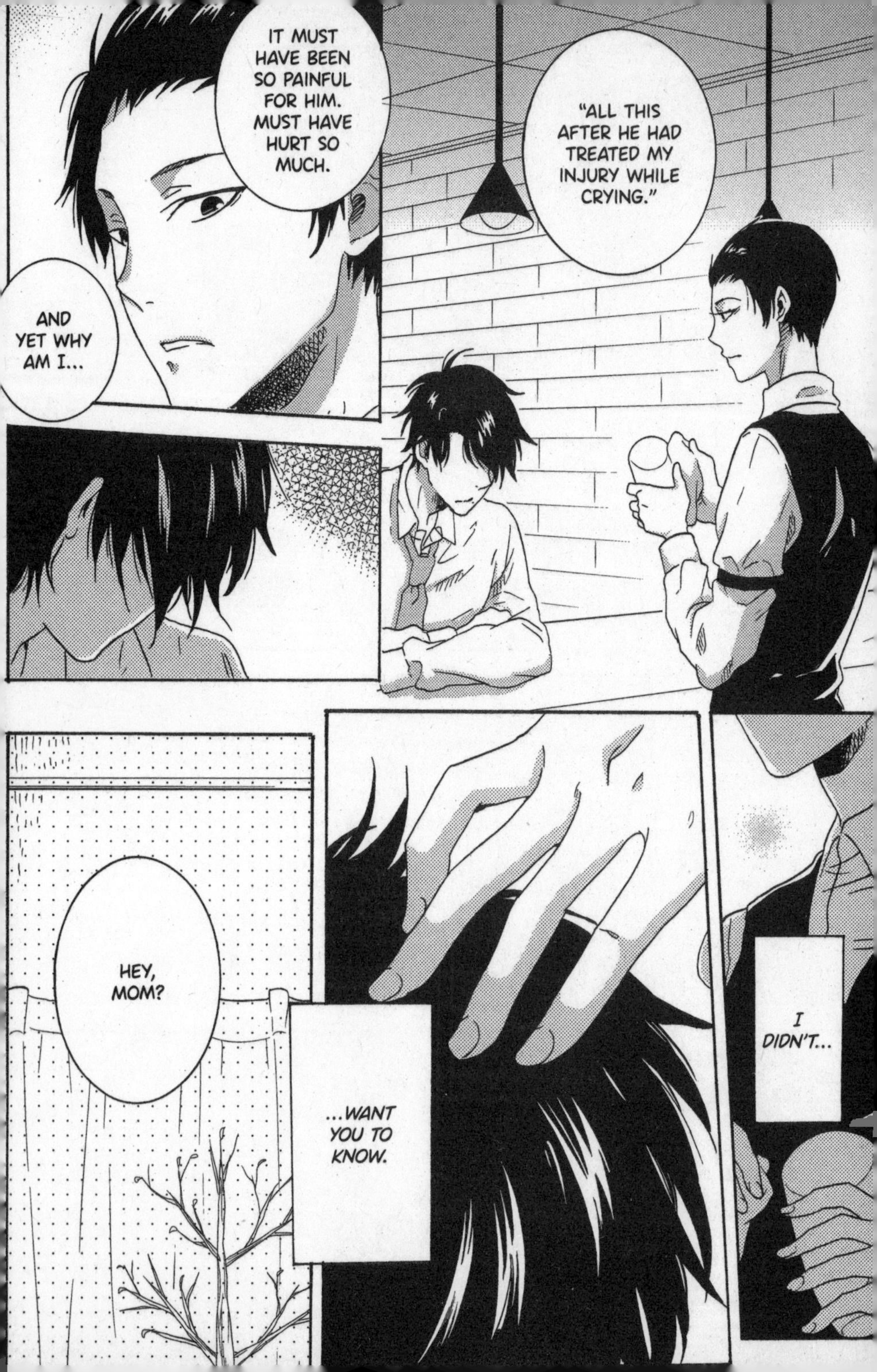
"ALL THIS AFTER HE HAD TREATED MY INJURY WHILE CRYING."
IT MUST HAVE BEEN SO PAINFUL FOR HIM. MUST HAVE HURT SO MUCH.
AND YET WHY AM I...
I DIDN'T...
...WANT YOU TO KNOW.
HEY, MOM?

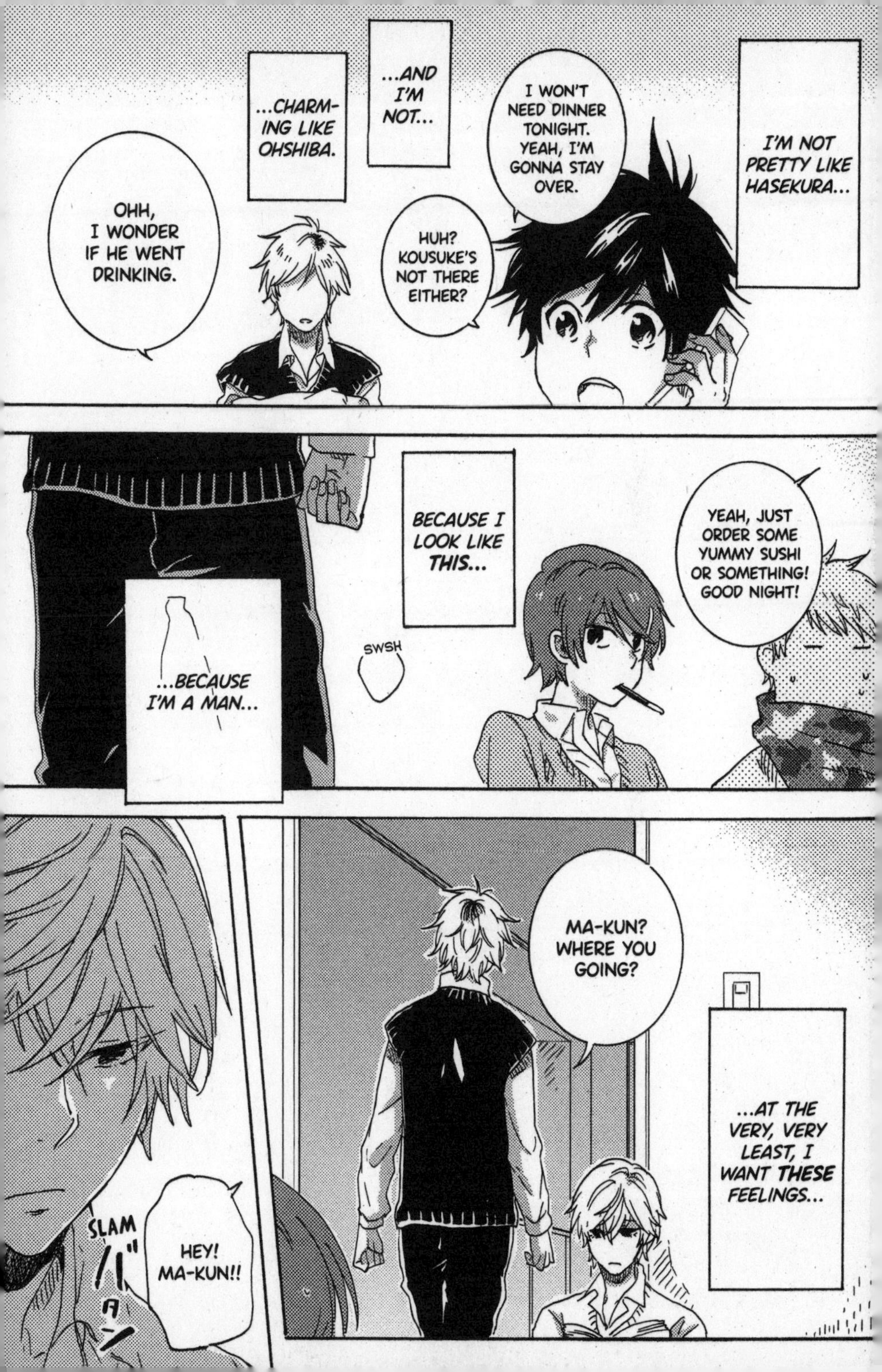
I'M NOT PRETTY LIKE HASEKURA...
I WON'T NEED DINNER TONIGHT. YEAH, I'M GONNA STAY OVER.
...AND I'M NOT...
HUH? KOUSUKE'S NOT THERE EITHER?
...CHARMING LIKE OHSHIBA.
OHH, I WONDER IF HE WENT DRINKING.
YEAH, JUST ORDER SOME YUMMY SUSHI OR SOMETHING! GOOD NIGHT!
BECAUSE I LOOK LIKE THIS...
SWSH
...BECAUSE I'M A MAN...
...AT THE VERY, VERY LEAST, I WANT THESE FEELINGS...
MA-KUN? WHERE YOU GOING?
HEY! MA-KUN!!
SLAM

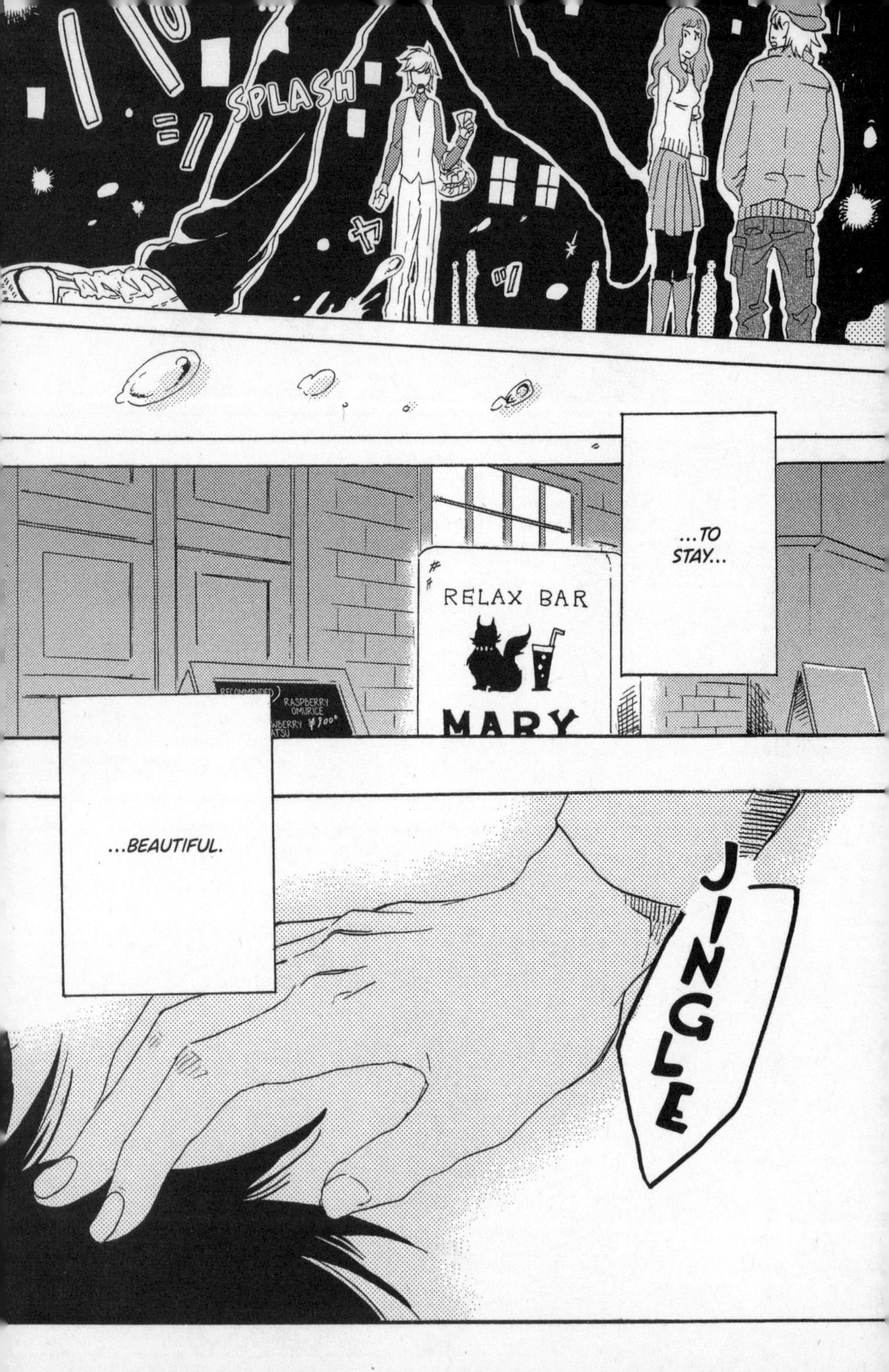
SPLASH
...TO STAY...
RELAX BAR
MARY
RECOMMENDED
RASPBERRY OMURICE
...BEAUTIFUL.
JINGLE

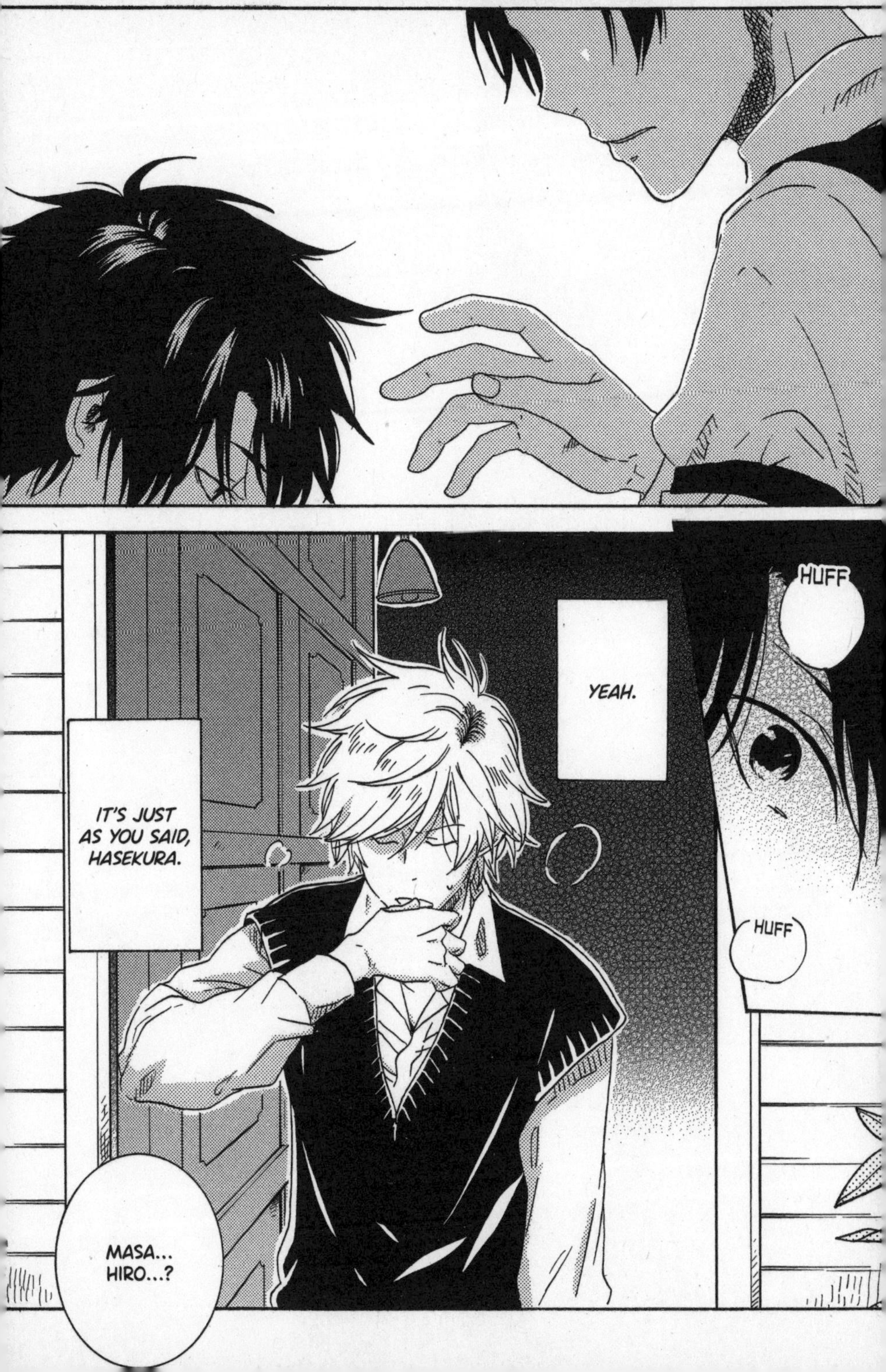
HUFF
HUFF
YEAH.
IT'S JUST AS YOU SAID, HASEKURA.
MASA... HIRO...?

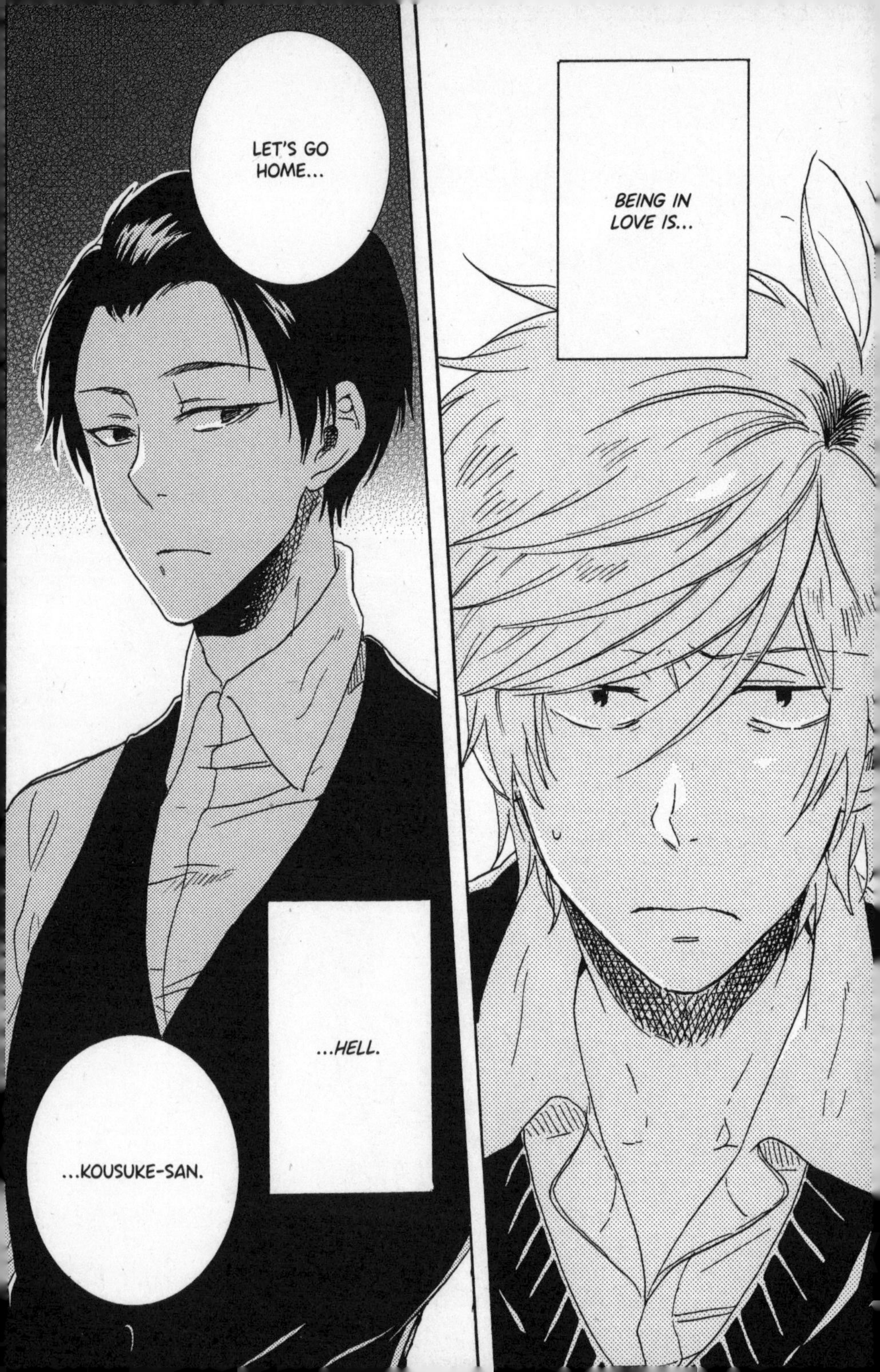
BEING IN LOVE IS...
LET'S GO HOME...
...HELL.
...KOUSUKE-SAN.

Hitorijime
My Hero

Mary-san (male)

The once-feral cat
that's the namesake and
logo of the bar.

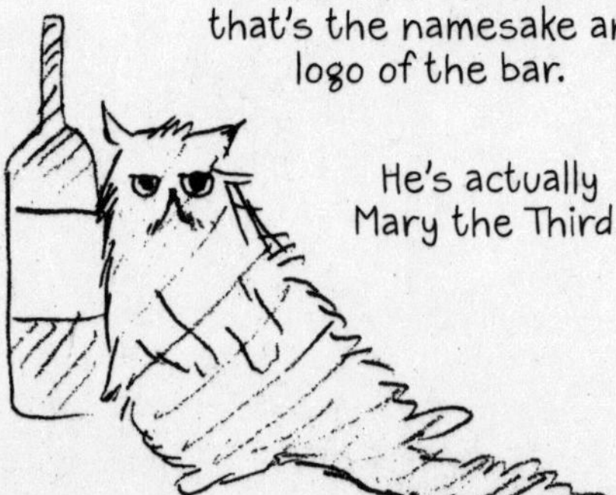

He's actually
Mary the Third.

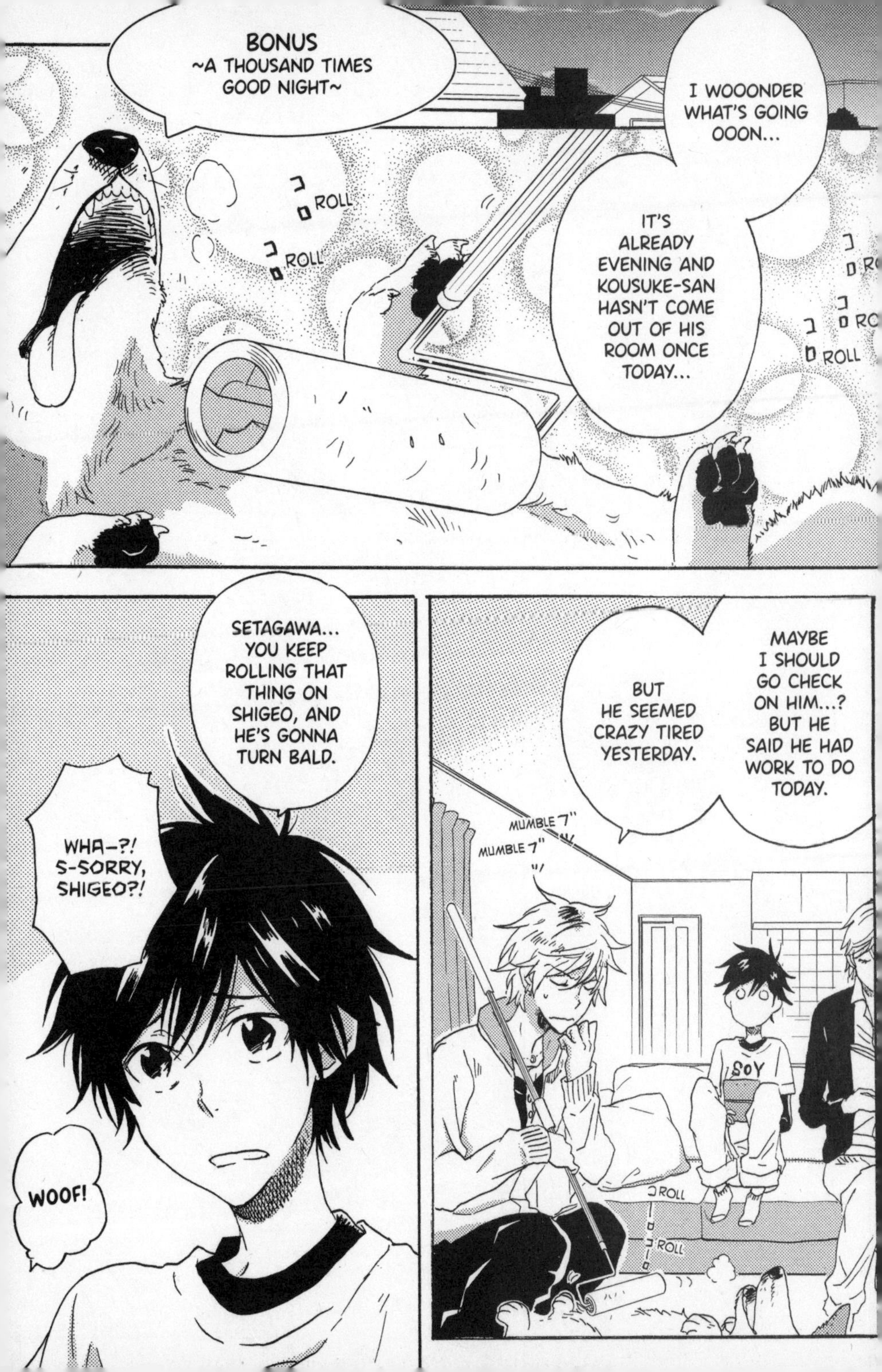
I WOOONDER WHAT'S GOING OOON...
IT'S ALREADY EVENING AND KOUSUKE-SAN HASN'T COME OUT OF HIS ROOM ONCE TODAY...
ROLL
BONUS
~A THOUSAND TIMES GOOD NIGHT~
ROLL
ROLL
MAYBE I SHOULD GO CHECK ON HIM...? BUT HE SAID HE HAD WORK TO DO TODAY.
BUT HE SEEMED CRAZY TIRED YESTERDAY.
MUMBLE
MUMBLE
SOY
ROLL
ROLL
SETAGAWA... YOU KEEP ROLLING THAT THING ON SHIGEO, AND HE'S GONNA TURN BALD.
WHA-?! S-SORRY, SHIGEO?!
WOOF!

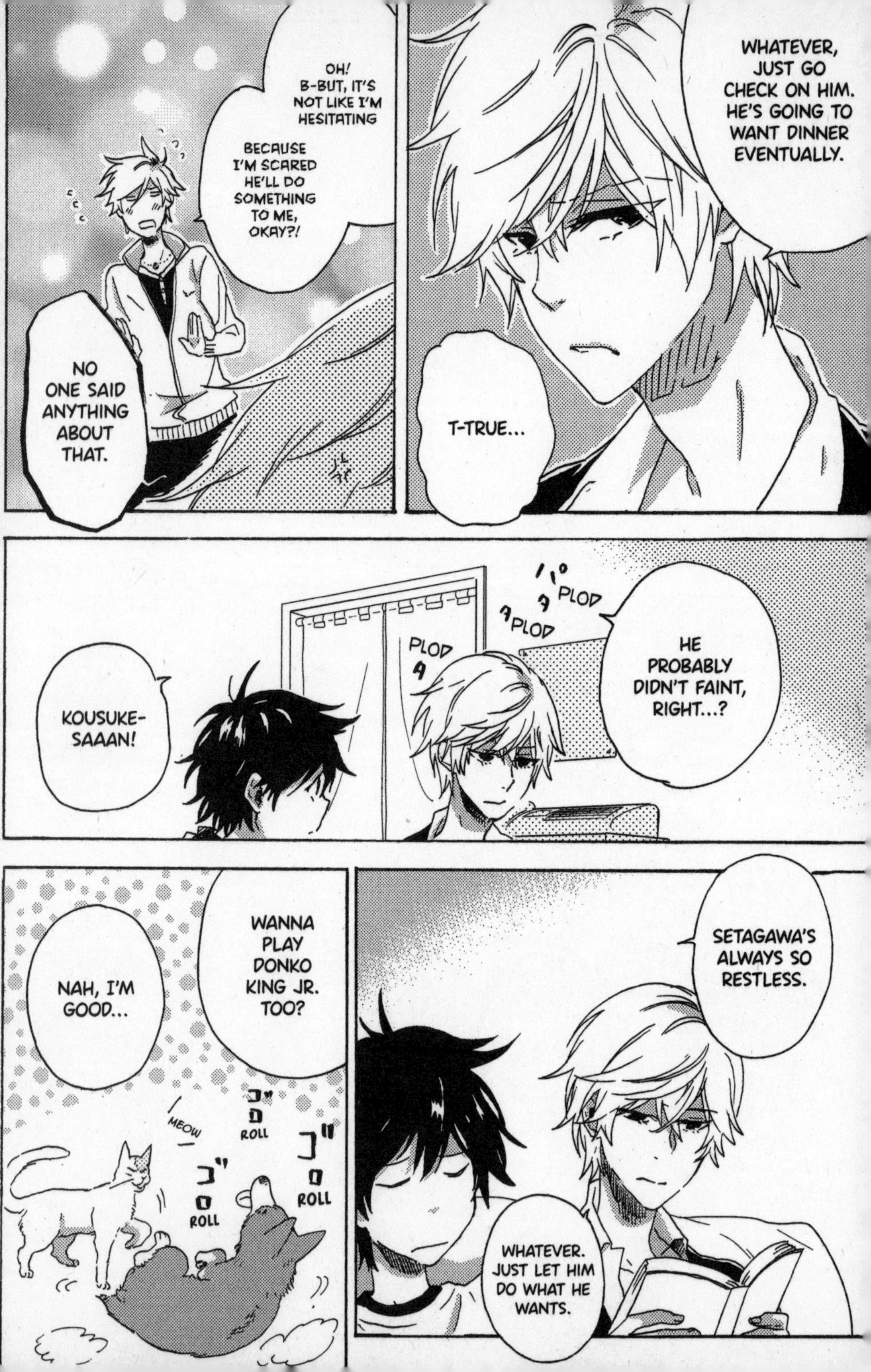
WHATEVER, JUST GO CHECK ON HIM. HE'S GOING TO WANT DINNER EVENTUALLY.
T-TRUE...
OH! B-BUT, IT'S NOT LIKE I'M HESITATING
BECAUSE I'M SCARED HE'LL DO SOMETHING TO ME, OKAY?!
NO ONE SAID ANYTHING ABOUT THAT.
PLOD
PLOD
HE PROBABLY DIDN'T FAINT, RIGHT...?
PLOD
KOUSUKE-SAAAN!
SETAGAWA'S ALWAYS SO RESTLESS.
WHATEVER. JUST LET HIM DO WHAT HE WANTS.
WANNA PLAY DONKO KING JR. TOO?
NAH, I'M GOOD...
ROLL
MEOW
ROLL
ROLL

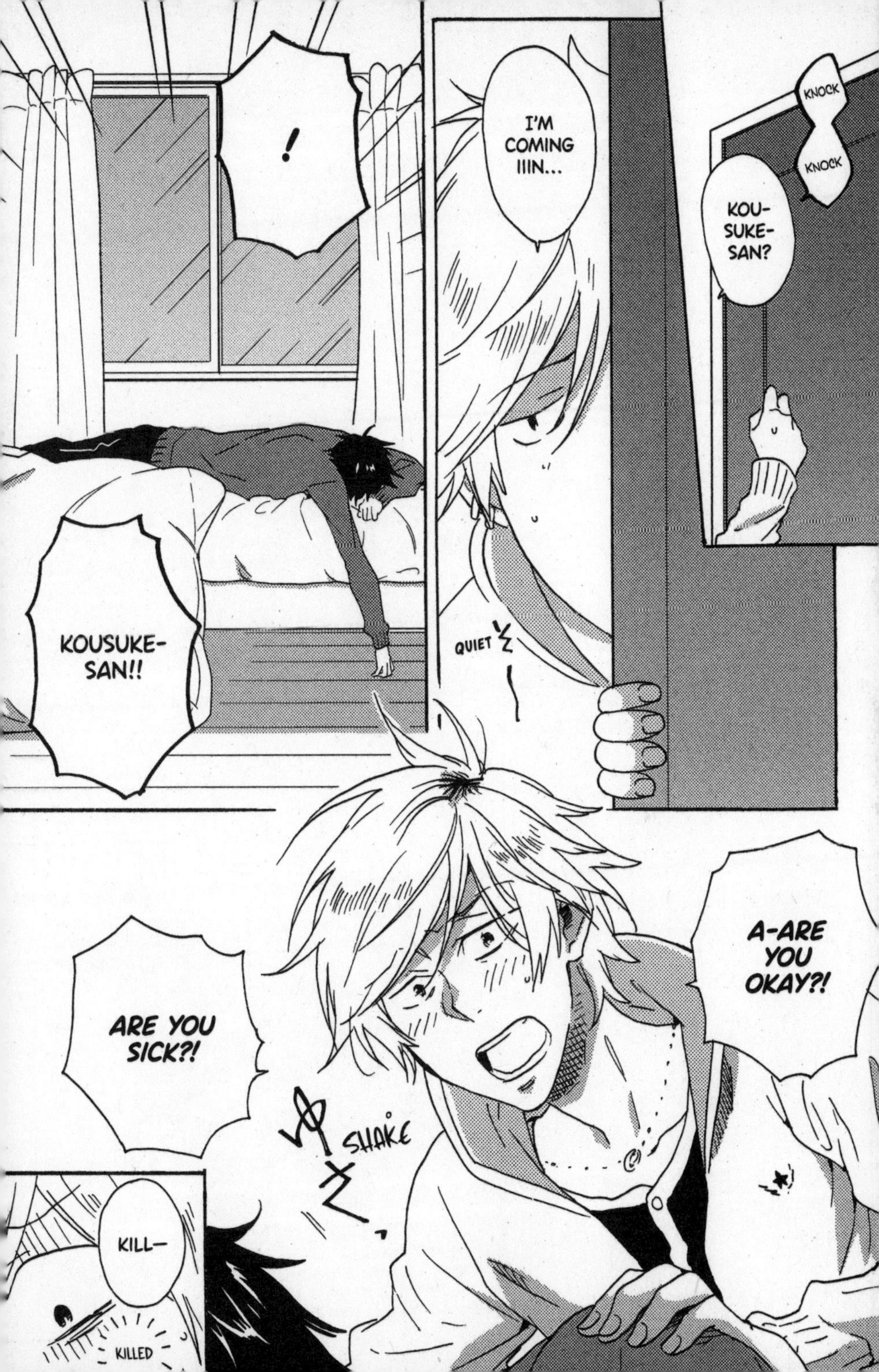
KNOCK
KNOCK
KOU-SUKE-SAN?
I'M COMING IIIN...
QUIET
!
KOUSUKE-SAN!!
A-ARE YOU OKAY?!
ARE YOU SICK?!
SHAKE
KILL—
KILLED

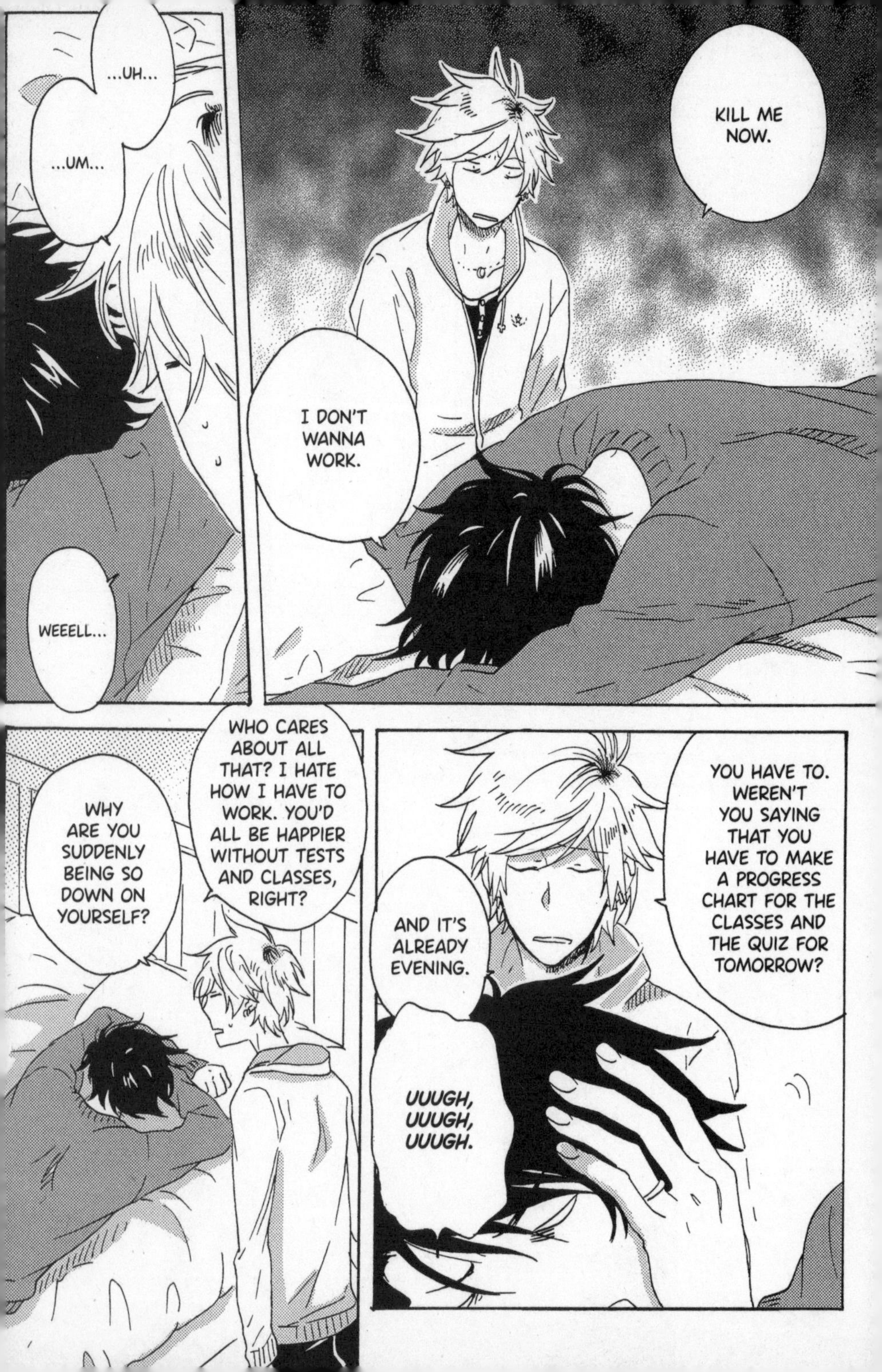
KILL ME NOW.
I DON'T WANNA WORK.
...UH...
...UM...
WEEELL...
YOU HAVE TO. WEREN'T YOU SAYING THAT YOU HAVE TO MAKE A PROGRESS CHART FOR THE CLASSES AND THE QUIZ FOR TOMORROW?
AND IT'S ALREADY EVENING.
UUUGH, UUUGH, UUUGH.
WHO CARES ABOUT ALL THAT? I HATE HOW I HAVE TO WORK. YOU'D ALL BE HAPPIER WITHOUT TESTS AND CLASSES, RIGHT?
WHY ARE YOU SUDDENLY BEING SO DOWN ON YOURSELF?

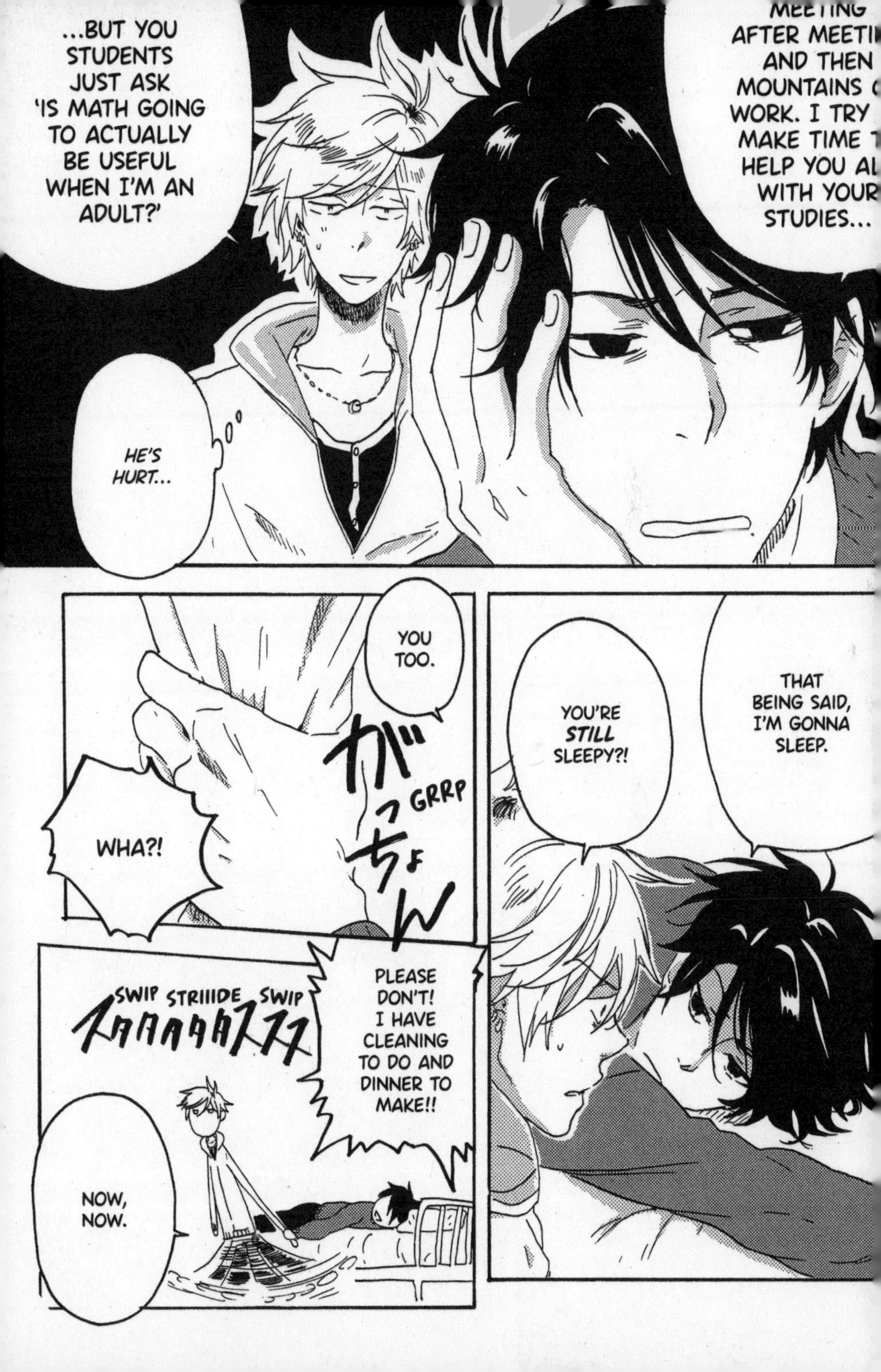
MEETING
AFTER MEETI
AND THEN
MOUNTAINS
WORK. I TRY
MAKE TIME
HELP YOU A
WITH YOUR
STUDIES...
...BUT YOU STUDENTS JUST ASK 'IS MATH GOING TO ACTUALLY BE USEFUL WHEN I'M AN ADULT?'
HE'S HURT...
THAT BEING SAID, I'M GONNA SLEEP.
YOU'RE STILL SLEEPY?!
YOU TOO.
GRRP
WHA?!
PLEASE DON'T! I HAVE CLEANING TO DO AND DINNER TO MAKE!!
SWIP STRIIIDE SWIP
NOW, NOW.

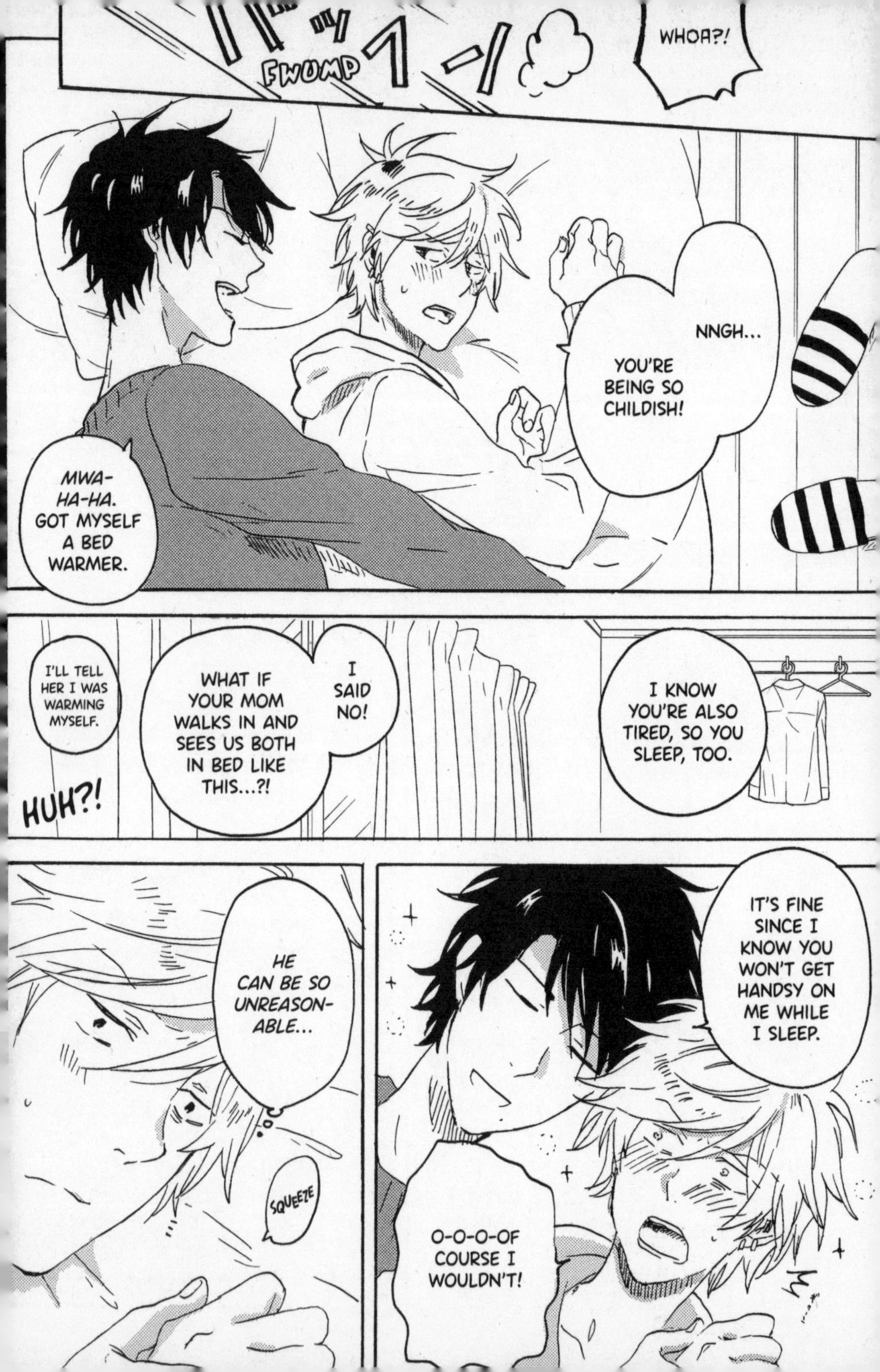
WHOA?!
FWUMP
NNGH...
YOU'RE BEING SO CHILDISH!
MWA-HA-HA. GOT MYSELF A BED WARMER.
I KNOW YOU'RE ALSO TIRED, SO YOU SLEEP, TOO.
I SAID NO!
WHAT IF YOUR MOM WALKS IN AND SEES US BOTH IN BED LIKE THIS...?!
I'LL TELL HER I WAS WARMING MYSELF.
HUH?!
IT'S FINE SINCE I KNOW YOU WON'T GET HANDSY ON ME WHILE I SLEEP.
O-O-O-OF COURSE I WOULDN'T!
HE CAN BE SO UNREASONABLE...
SQUEEZE

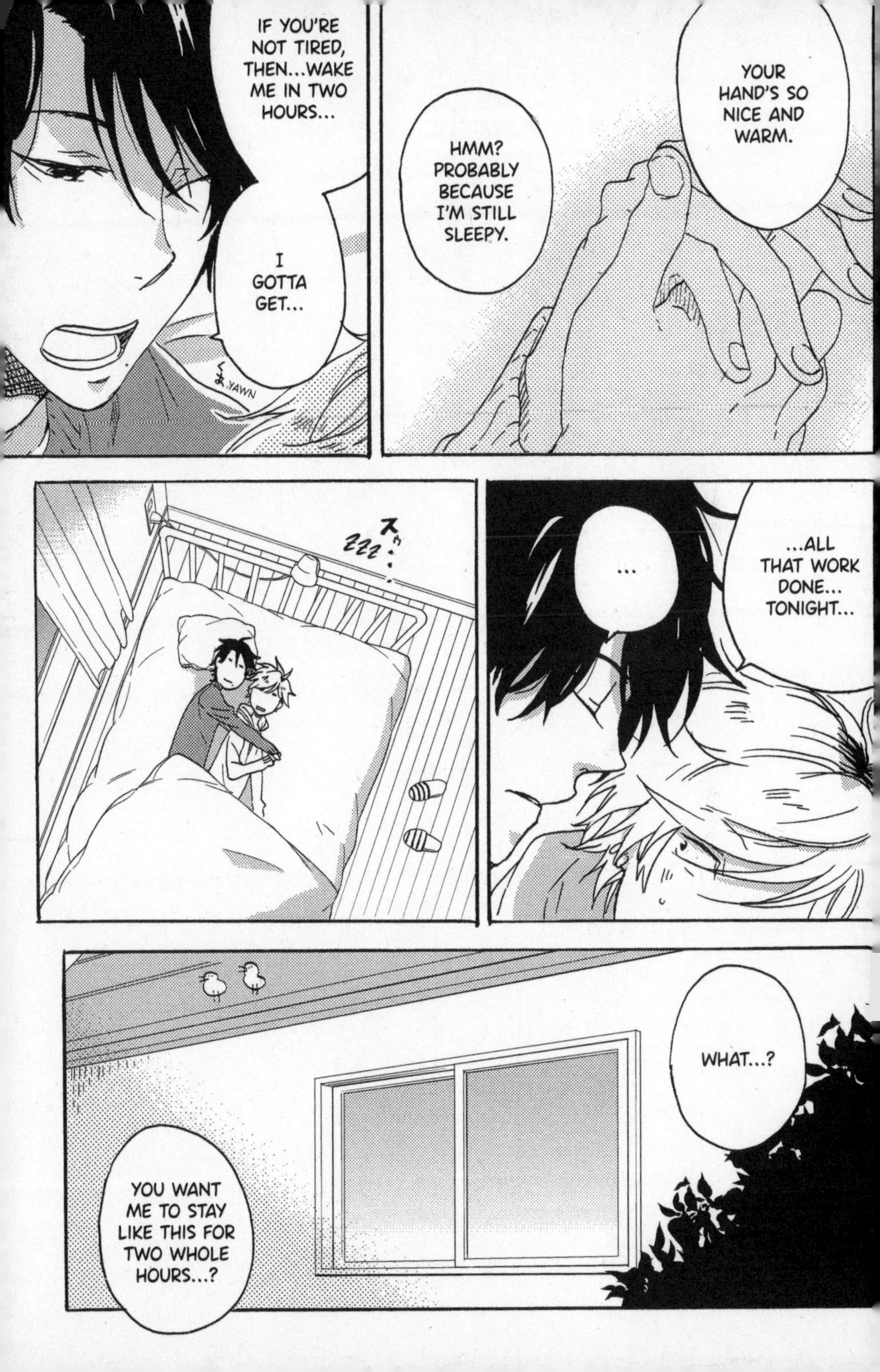
YOUR HAND'S SO NICE AND WARM.
HMM? PROBABLY BECAUSE I'M STILL SLEEPY.
IF YOU'RE NOT TIRED, THEN...WAKE ME IN TWO HOURS...
I GOTTA GET...
YAWN
...ALL THAT WORK DONE... TONIGHT...
...
ZZZ
WHAT...?
YOU WANT ME TO STAY LIKE THIS FOR TWO WHOLE HOURS...?

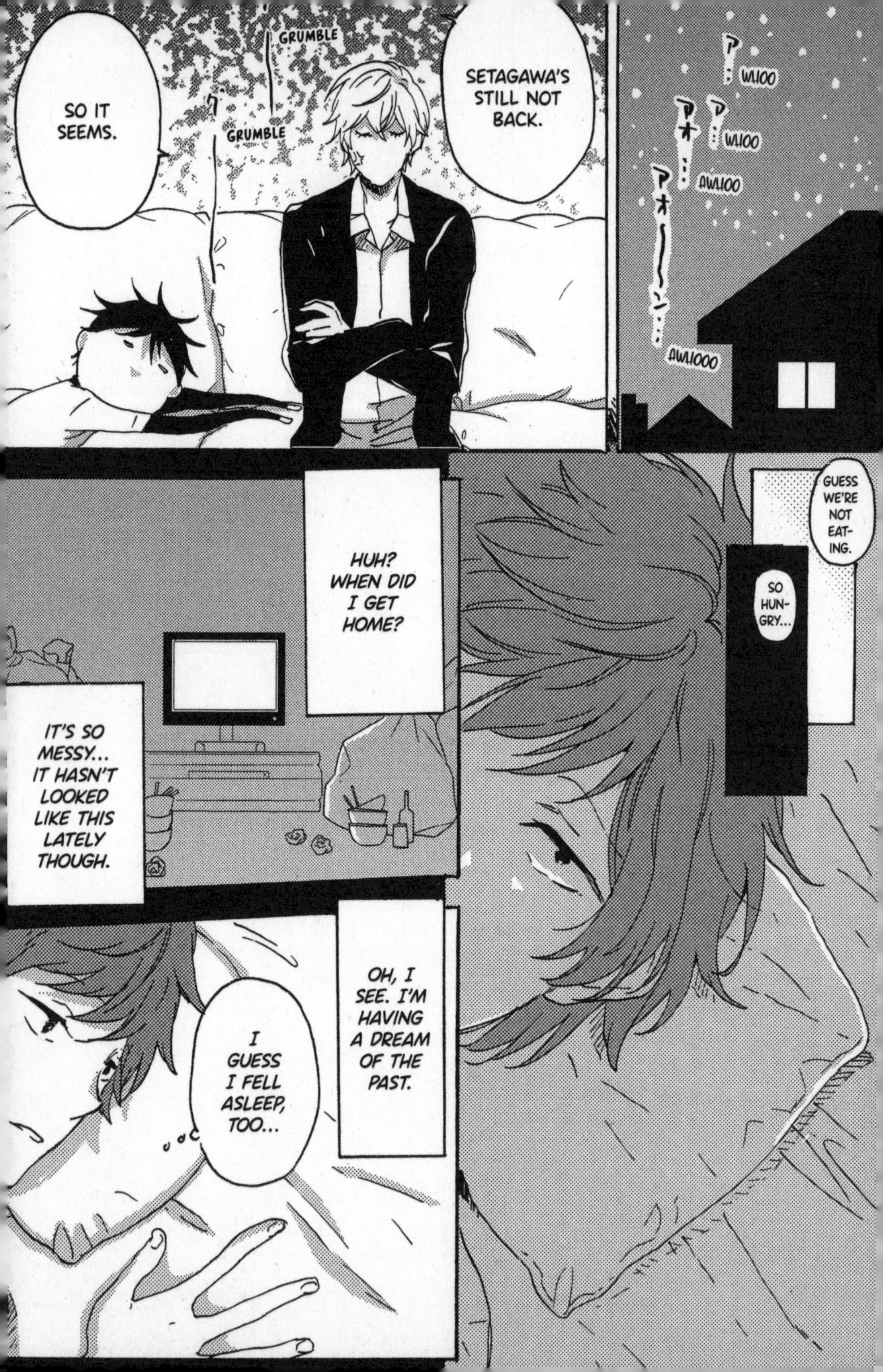
WHOO
WHOO
AWHOO
AWHOOO
SETAGAWA'S STILL NOT BACK.
GRUMBLE
GRUMBLE
SO IT SEEMS.
GUESS WE'RE NOT EAT-ING.
SO HUN-GRY...
HUH? WHEN DID I GET HOME?
IT'S SO MESSY... IT HASN'T LOOKED LIKE THIS LATELY THOUGH.
OH, I SEE. I'M HAVING A DREAM OF THE PAST.
I GUESS I FELL ASLEEP, TOO...

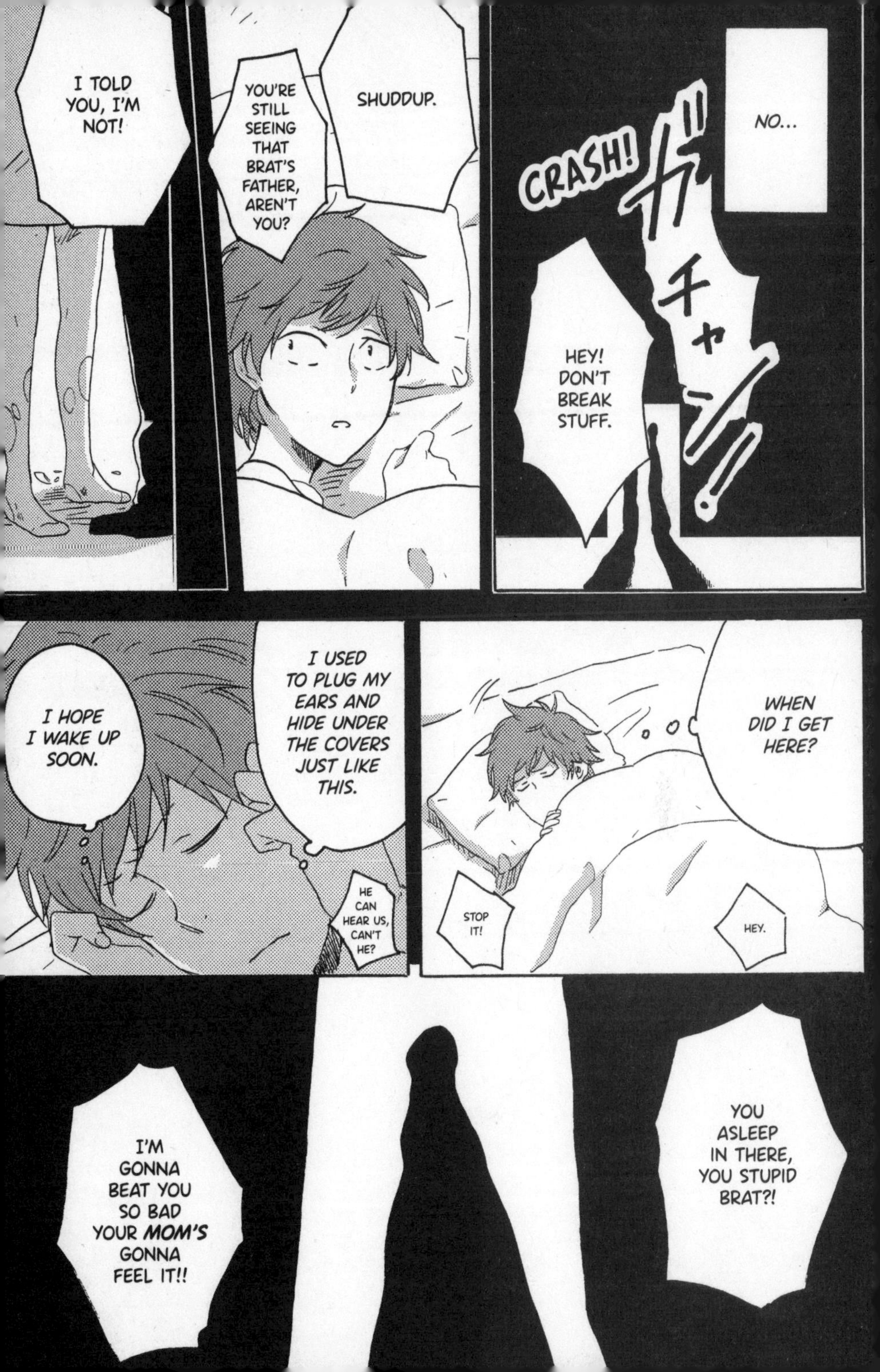
NO...
CRASH!
ガチャーン!!
HEY! DON'T BREAK STUFF.
SHUDDUP.
YOU'RE STILL SEEING THAT BRAT'S FATHER, AREN'T YOU?
I TOLD YOU, I'M NOT!
WHEN DID I GET HERE?
HEY.
STOP IT!
I USED TO PLUG MY EARS AND HIDE UNDER THE COVERS JUST LIKE THIS.
I HOPE I WAKE UP SOON.
HE CAN HEAR US, CAN'T HE?
YOU ASLEEP IN THERE, YOU STUPID BRAT?!
I'M GONNA BEAT YOU SO BAD YOUR *MOM'S* GONNA FEEL IT!!

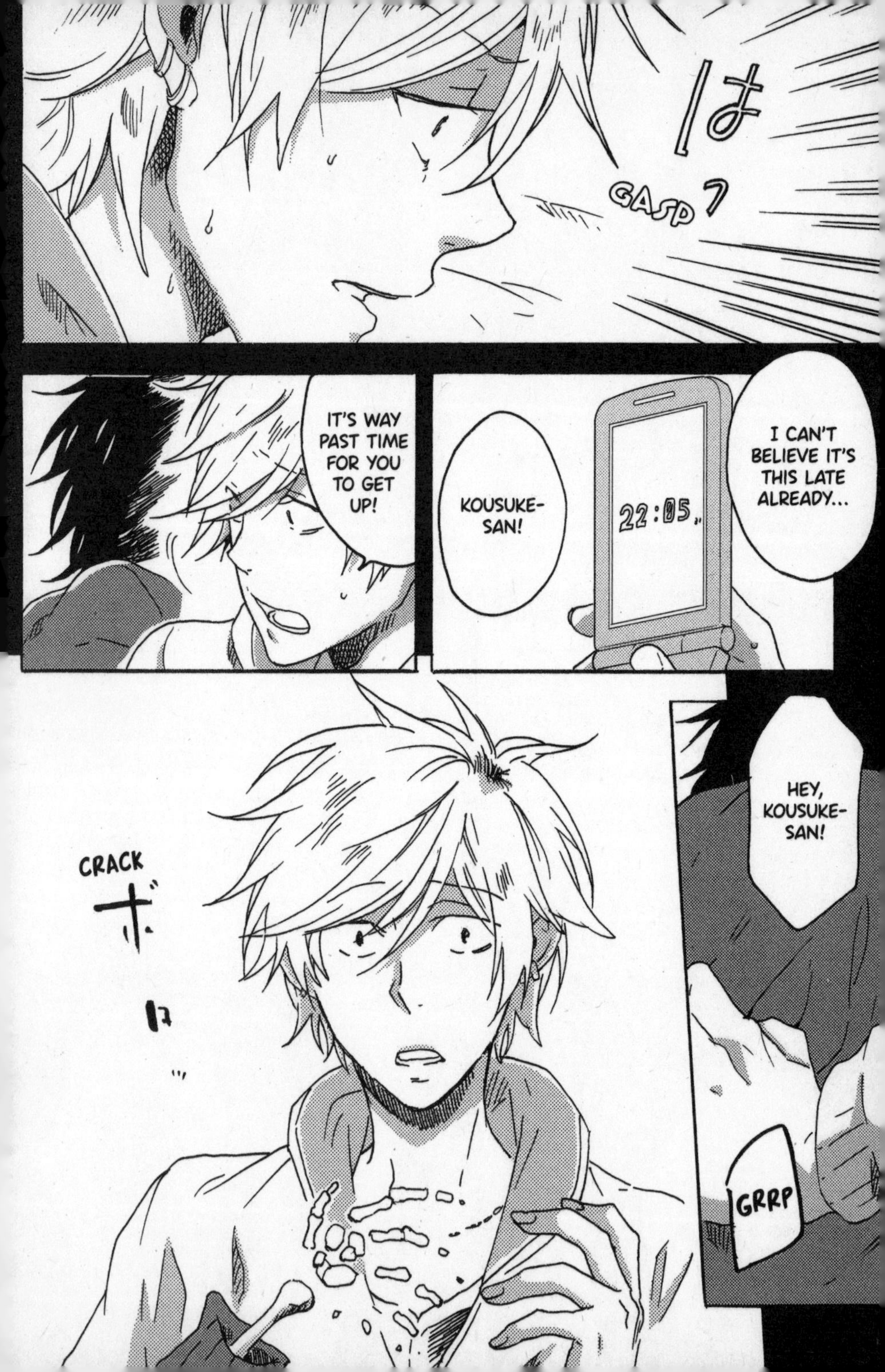
は
GASP
I CAN'T BELIEVE IT'S THIS LATE ALREADY...
22:05
KOUSUKE-SAN!
IT'S WAY PAST TIME FOR YOU TO GET UP!
HEY, KOUSUKE-SAN!
GRRP
CRACK

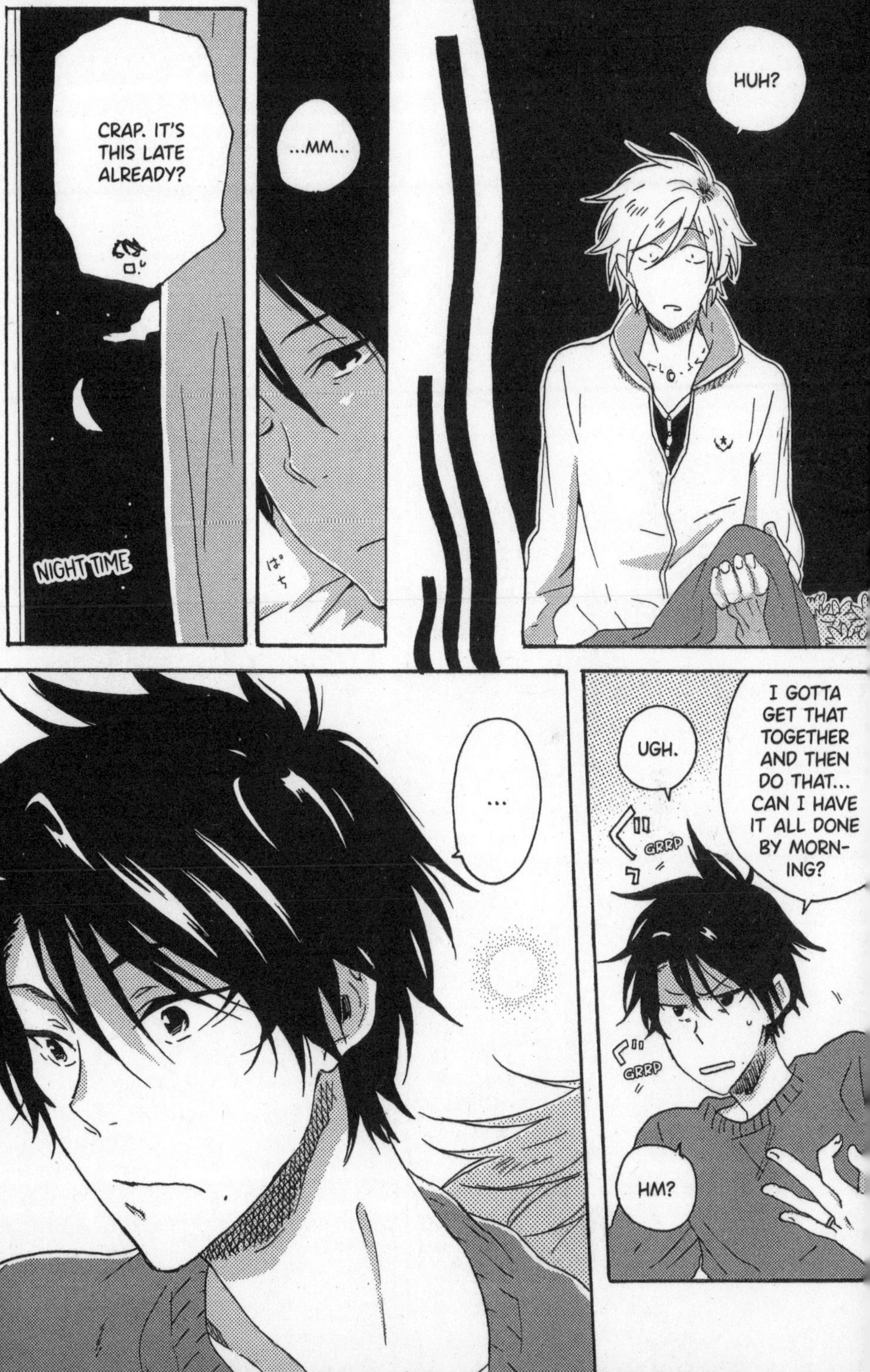
HUH?
...MM...
ぱち
CRAP. IT'S THIS LATE ALREADY?
NIGHT TIME
I GOTTA GET THAT TOGETHER AND THEN DO THAT... CAN I HAVE IT ALL DONE BY MORNING?
UGH.
GRRP
GRRP
HM?
...

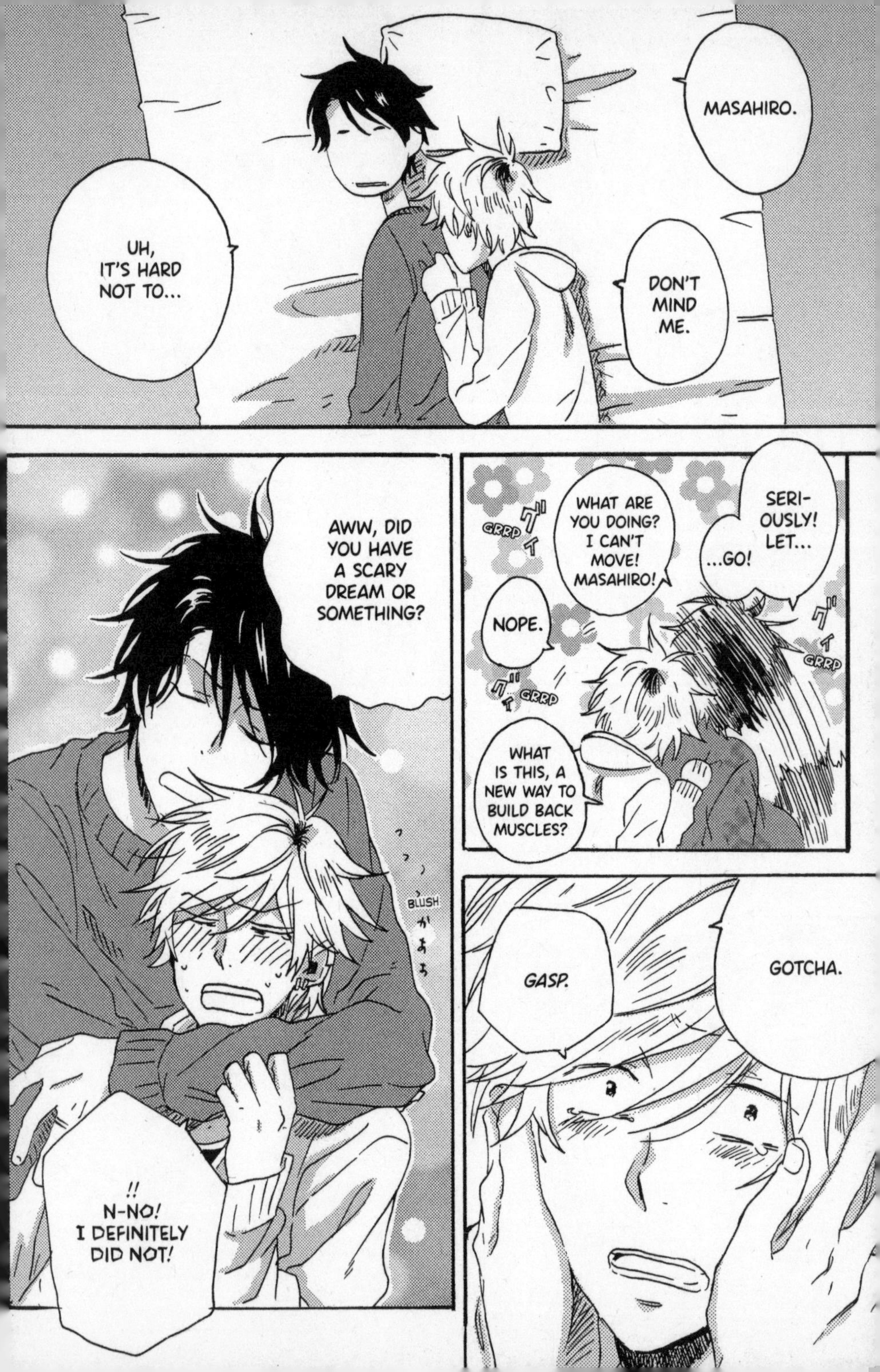
MASAHIRO.
DON'T MIND ME.
UH, IT'S HARD NOT TO...
SERI-OUSLY! LET...
...GO!
GRRP
WHAT ARE YOU DOING? I CAN'T MOVE! MASAHIRO!
GRRP
NOPE.
GRRP
WHAT IS THIS, A NEW WAY TO BUILD BACK MUSCLES?
GOTCHA.
GASP.
AWW, DID YOU HAVE A SCARY DREAM OR SOMETHING?
BLUSH
!! N-NO! I DEFINITELY DID NOT!

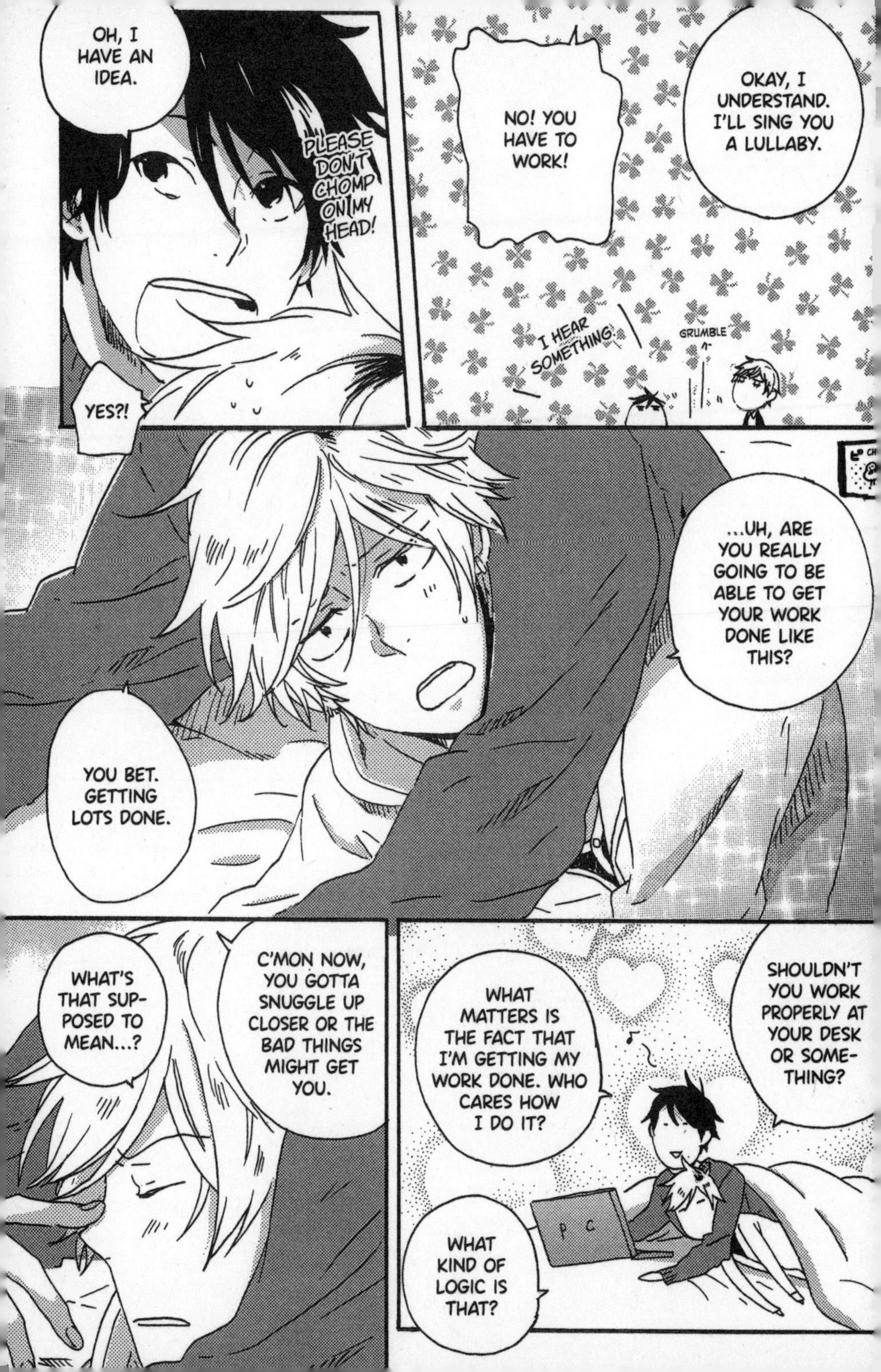
OKAY, I UNDERSTAND. I'LL SING YOU A LULLABY.
NO! YOU HAVE TO WORK!
I HEAR SOMETHING.
GRUMBLE
OH, I HAVE AN IDEA.
PLEASE DON'T CHOMP ON MY HEAD!
YES?!
...UH, ARE YOU REALLY GOING TO BE ABLE TO GET YOUR WORK DONE LIKE THIS?
YOU BET. GETTING LOTS DONE.
SHOULDN'T YOU WORK PROPERLY AT YOUR DESK OR SOMETHING?
WHAT MATTERS IS THE FACT THAT I'M GETTING MY WORK DONE. WHO CARES HOW I DO IT?
WHAT KIND OF LOGIC IS THAT?
C'MON NOW, YOU GOTTA SNUGGLE UP CLOSER OR THE BAD THINGS MIGHT GET YOU.
WHAT'S THAT SUP-POSED TO MEAN...?

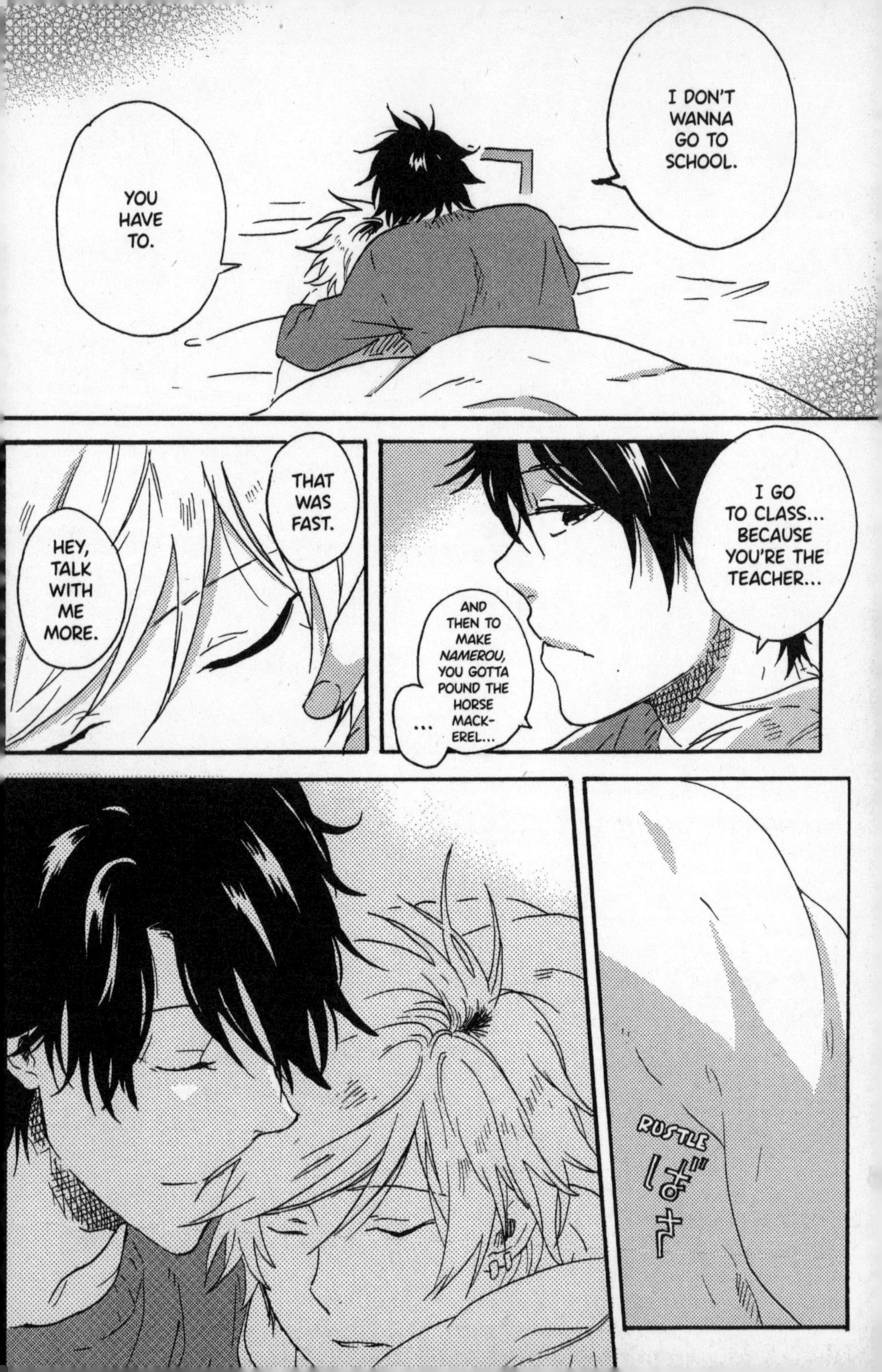
I DON'T WANNA GO TO SCHOOL.
YOU HAVE TO.
I GO TO CLASS... BECAUSE YOU'RE THE TEACHER...
AND THEN TO MAKE *NAMEROU*, YOU GOTTA POUND THE HORSE MACK-EREL...
...
THAT WAS FAST.
HEY, TALK WITH ME MORE.
RUSTLE

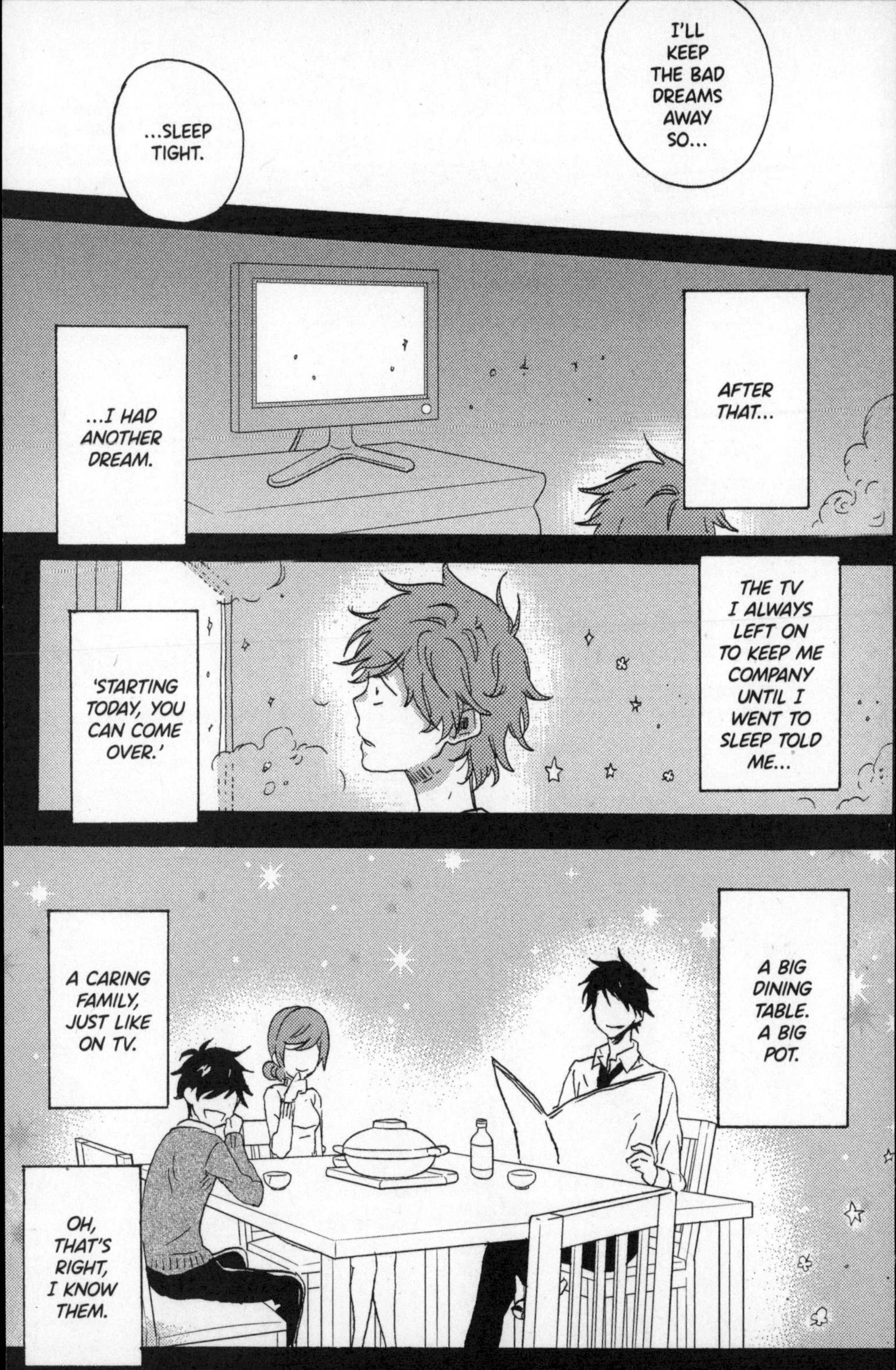
I'LL KEEP THE BAD DREAMS AWAY SO...
...SLEEP TIGHT.
AFTER THAT...
...I HAD ANOTHER DREAM.
THE TV I ALWAYS LEFT ON TO KEEP ME COMPANY UNTIL I WENT TO SLEEP TOLD ME...
'STARTING TODAY, YOU CAN COME OVER.'
A BIG DINING TABLE. A BIG POT.
A CARING FAMILY, JUST LIKE ON TV.
OH, THAT'S RIGHT, I KNOW THEM.

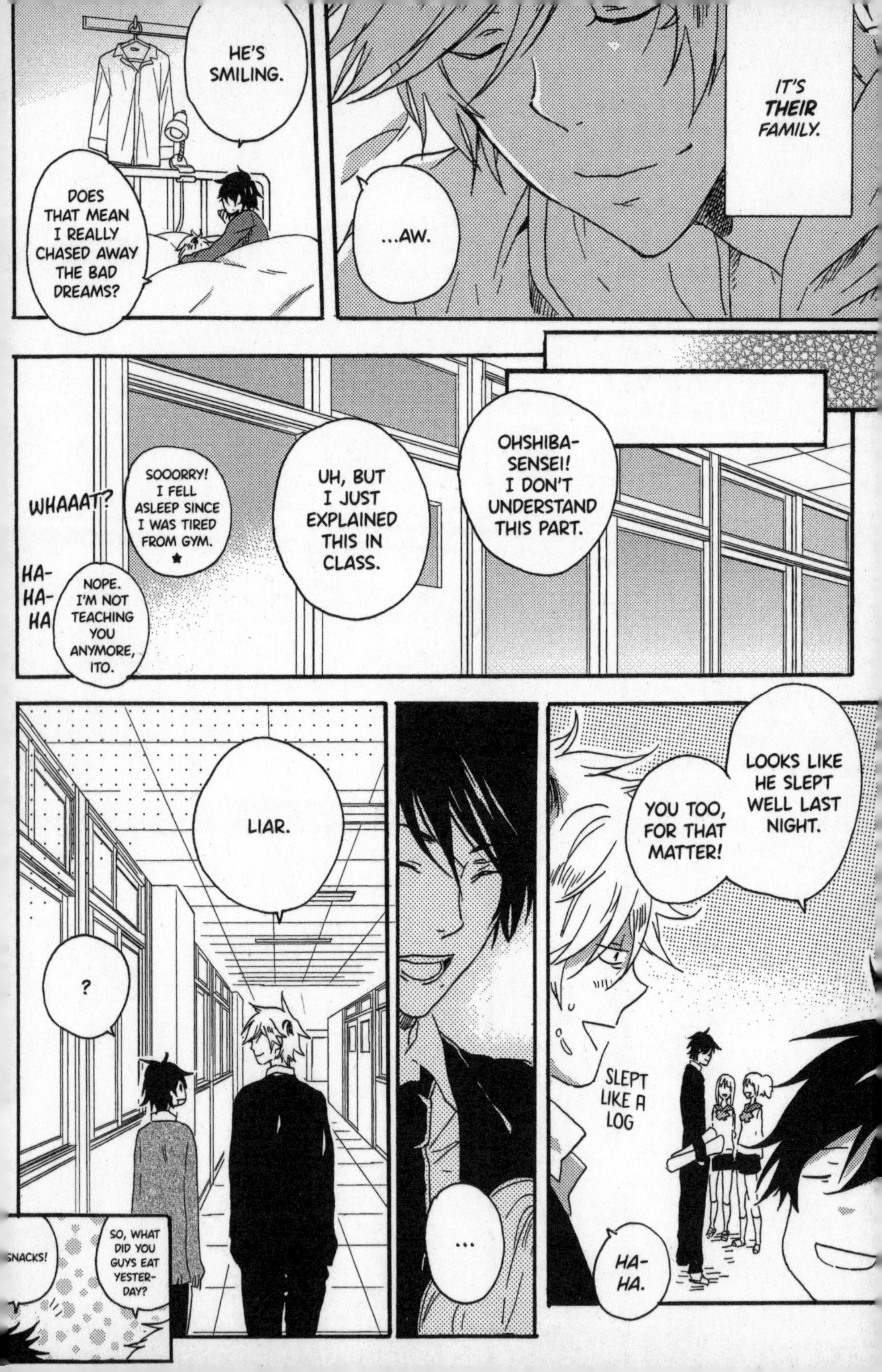
IT'S THEIR FAMILY.
...AW.
HE'S SMILING.
DOES THAT MEAN I REALLY CHASED AWAY THE BAD DREAMS?
OHSHIBA-SENSEI! I DON'T UNDERSTAND THIS PART.
UH, BUT I JUST EXPLAINED THIS IN CLASS.
SOOORRY! I FELL ASLEEP SINCE I WAS TIRED FROM GYM. ★
WHAAAT?
NOPE. I'M NOT TEACHING YOU ANYMORE, ITO.
HA-HA-HA
LOOKS LIKE HE SLEPT WELL LAST NIGHT.
YOU TOO, FOR THAT MATTER!
SLEPT LIKE A LOG
HA-HA.
...
LIAR.
?
SO, WHAT DID YOU GUYS EAT YESTER-DAY?
SNACKS!

Hitorijime My Hero

Starting on the following
page is a story I wrote for
Yuri Hime Magazine about Matsuzawa-san
and Hasekura-san's older sister,
Ayaka. It started as a doodle and
boy was I surprised when it
turned into an actual manga...

Thankfully, a lot of people
requested this get put
into the book, so it was
added into this volume.

Enjoy!

Do
not look
at this
volume's
bonus
pages!!

Ayaka

Huh...?

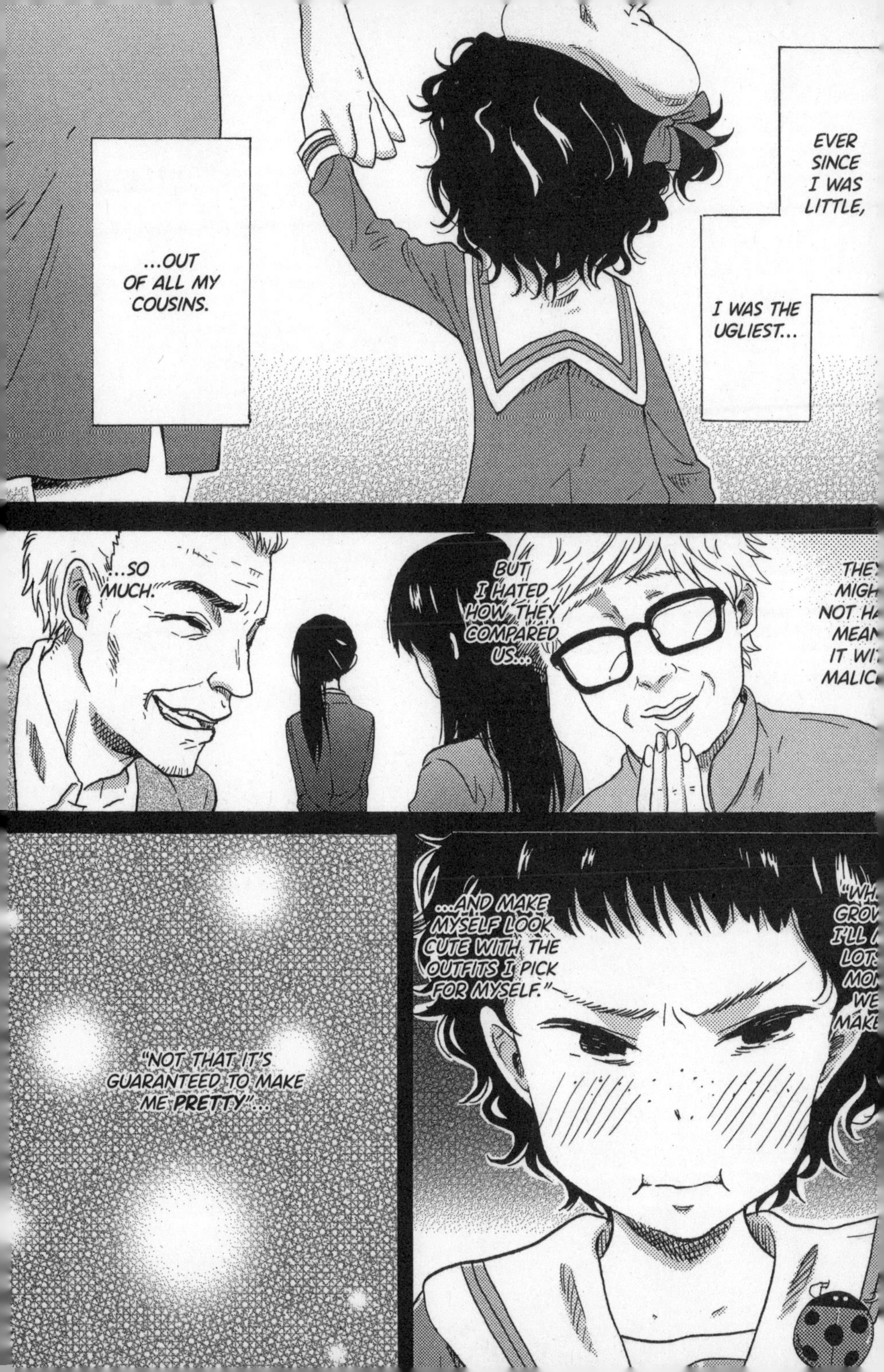
EVER SINCE I WAS LITTLE,
I WAS THE UGLIEST...
...OUT OF ALL MY COUSINS.
THEY MIGH NOT HA MEAN IT WI MALIC
BUT I HATED HOW THEY COMPARED US...
...SO MUCH.
“WH GROW I'LL A LOTS MON WE MAKE
...AND MAKE MYSELF LOOK CUTE WITH THE OUTFITS I PICK FOR MYSELF.”
“NOT THAT IT'S GUARANTEED TO MAKE ME PRETTY”...

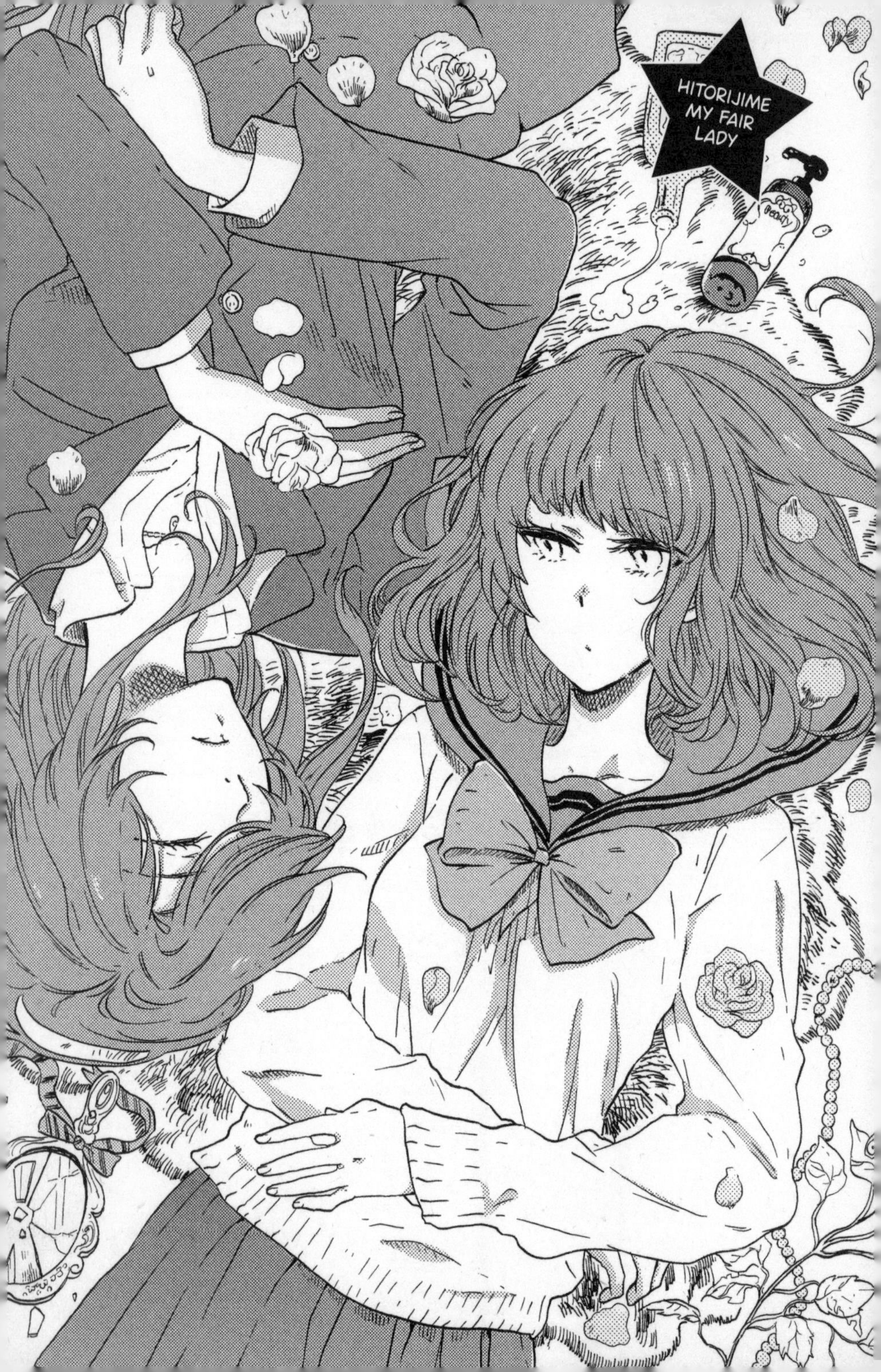
HITORIJIME
MY FAIR
LADY

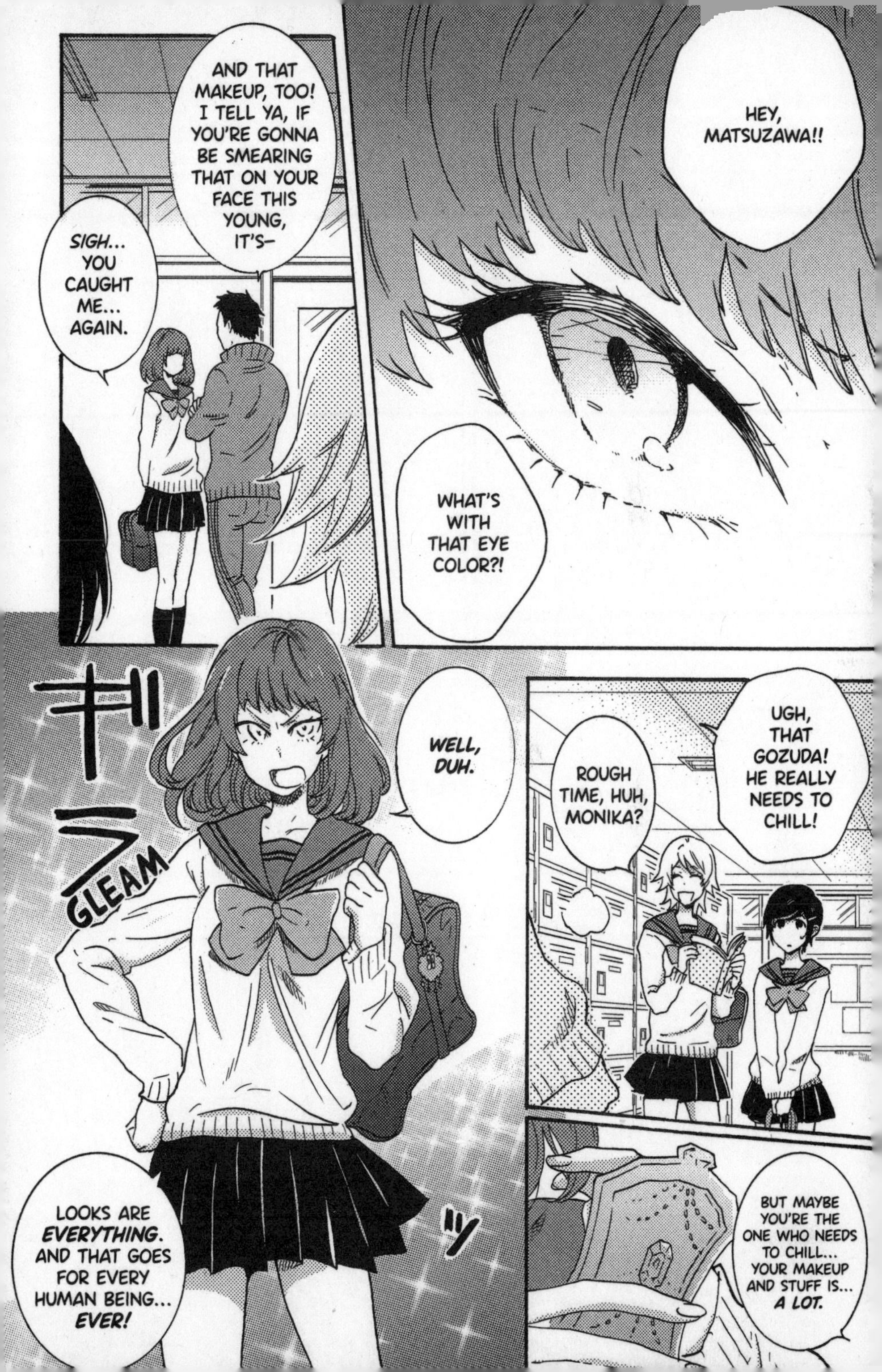
HEY, MATSUZAWA!!
WHAT'S WITH THAT EYE COLOR?!
AND THAT MAKEUP, TOO! I TELL YA, IF YOU'RE GONNA BE SMEARING THAT ON YOUR FACE THIS YOUNG, IT'S—
SIGH... YOU CAUGHT ME... AGAIN.
UGH, THAT GOZUDA! HE REALLY NEEDS TO CHILL!
ROUGH TIME, HUH, MONIKA?
BUT MAYBE YOU'RE THE ONE WHO NEEDS TO CHILL... YOUR MAKEUP AND STUFF IS... *A LOT.*
WELL, DUH.
ギラ
GLEAM
LOOKS ARE *EVERYTHING.* AND THAT GOES FOR EVERY HUMAN BEING... *EVER!*

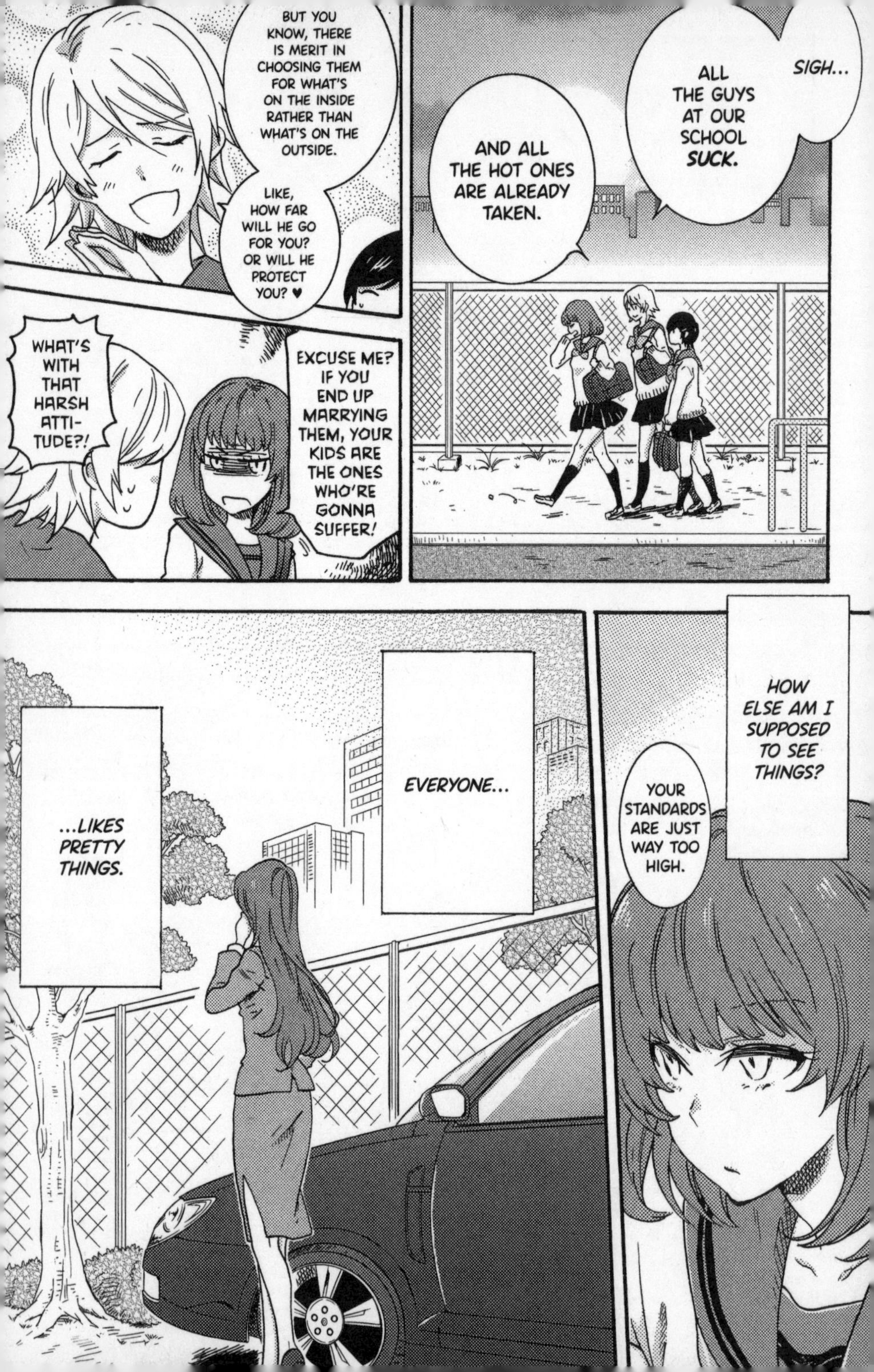
SIGH...
ALL THE GUYS AT OUR SCHOOL **SUCK.**
AND ALL THE HOT ONES ARE ALREADY TAKEN.
BUT YOU KNOW, THERE IS MERIT IN CHOOSING THEM FOR WHAT'S ON THE INSIDE RATHER THAN WHAT'S ON THE OUTSIDE.
LIKE, HOW FAR WILL HE GO FOR YOU? OR WILL HE PROTECT YOU? ♥
EXCUSE ME? IF YOU END UP MARRYING THEM, YOUR KIDS ARE THE ONES WHO'RE GONNA SUFFER!
WHAT'S WITH THAT HARSH ATTI-TUDE?!
HOW ELSE AM I SUPPOSED TO SEE THINGS?
YOUR STANDARDS ARE JUST WAY TOO HIGH.
EVERYONE...
...LIKES PRETTY THINGS.

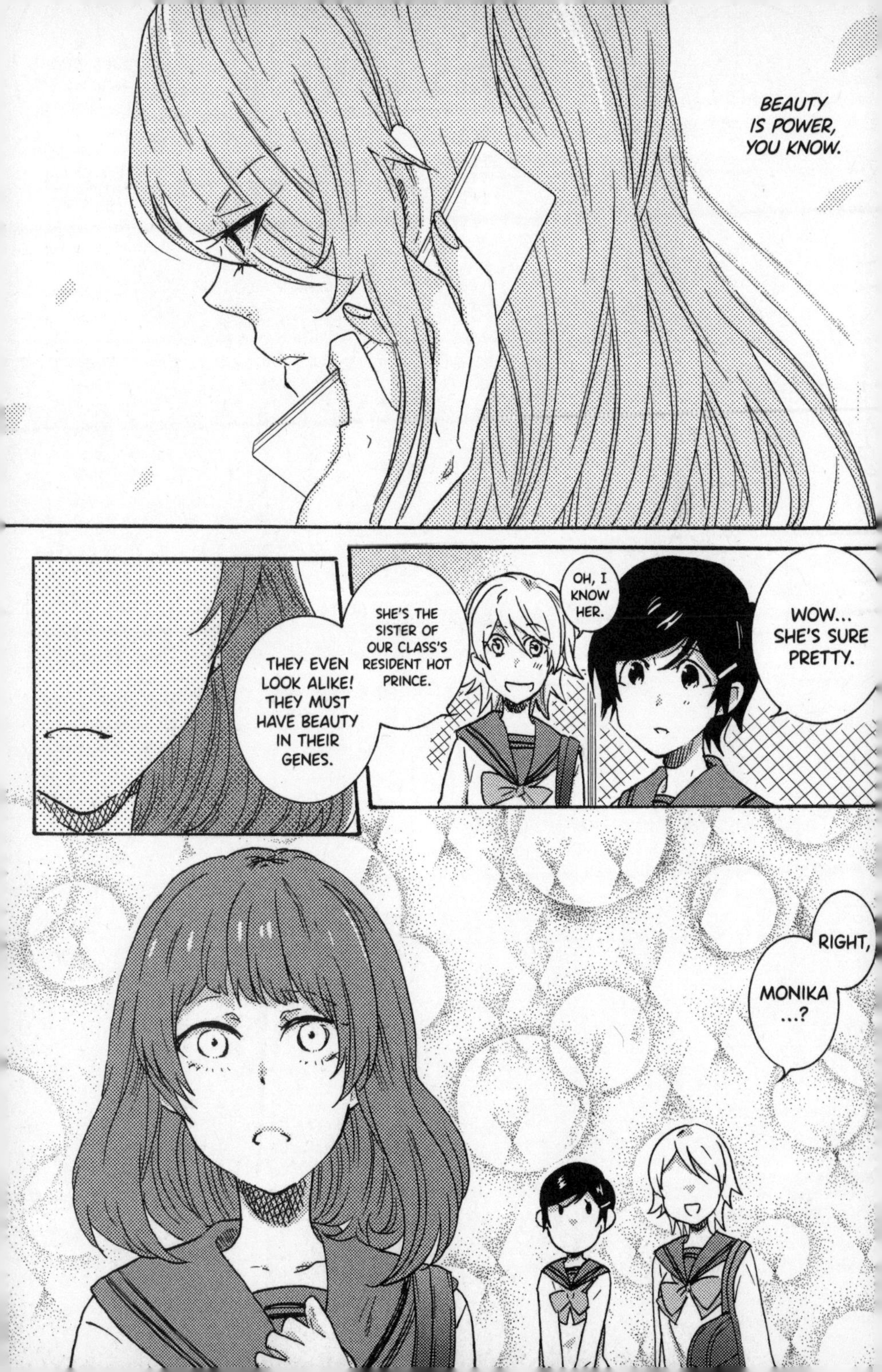
BEAUTY IS POWER, YOU KNOW.
WOW... SHE'S SURE PRETTY.
OH, I KNOW HER.
SHE'S THE SISTER OF OUR CLASS'S RESIDENT HOT PRINCE.
THEY EVEN LOOK ALIKE! THEY MUST HAVE BEAUTY IN THEIR GENES.
RIGHT, MONIKA ...?

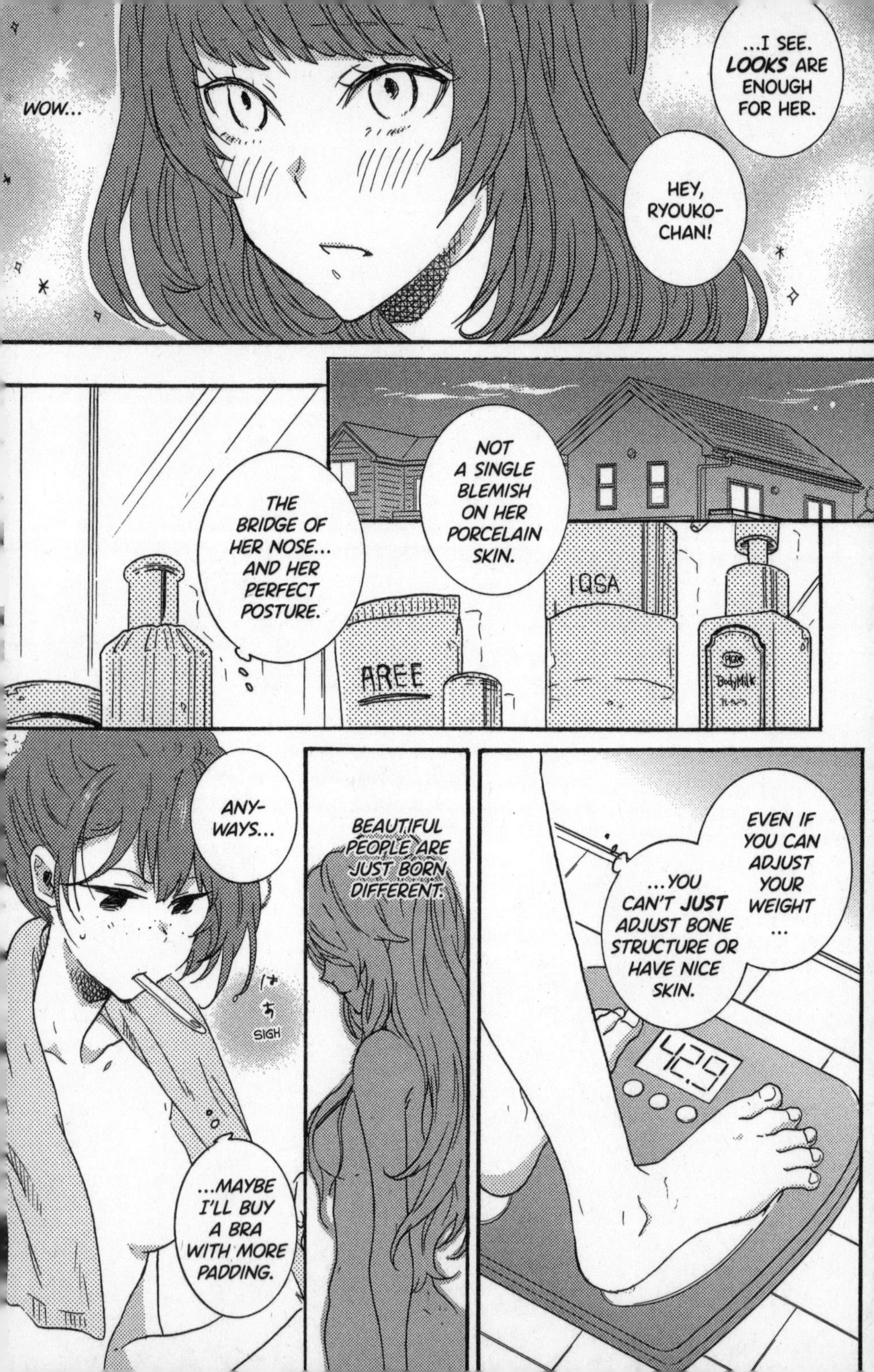
...I SEE. **LOOKS** ARE ENOUGH FOR HER.
HEY, RYOUKO-CHAN!
WOW...
NOT A SINGLE BLEMISH ON HER PORCELAIN SKIN.
THE BRIDGE OF HER NOSE... AND HER PERFECT POSTURE.
IQSA
AREE
BodyMilk
EVEN IF YOU CAN ADJUST YOUR WEIGHT ...
...YOU CAN'T **JUST** ADJUST BONE STRUCTURE OR HAVE NICE SKIN.
42.9
BEAUTIFUL PEOPLE ARE JUST BORN DIFFERENT.
ANY-WAYS...
はぁ
SIGH
...MAYBE I'LL BUY A BRA WITH MORE PADDING.

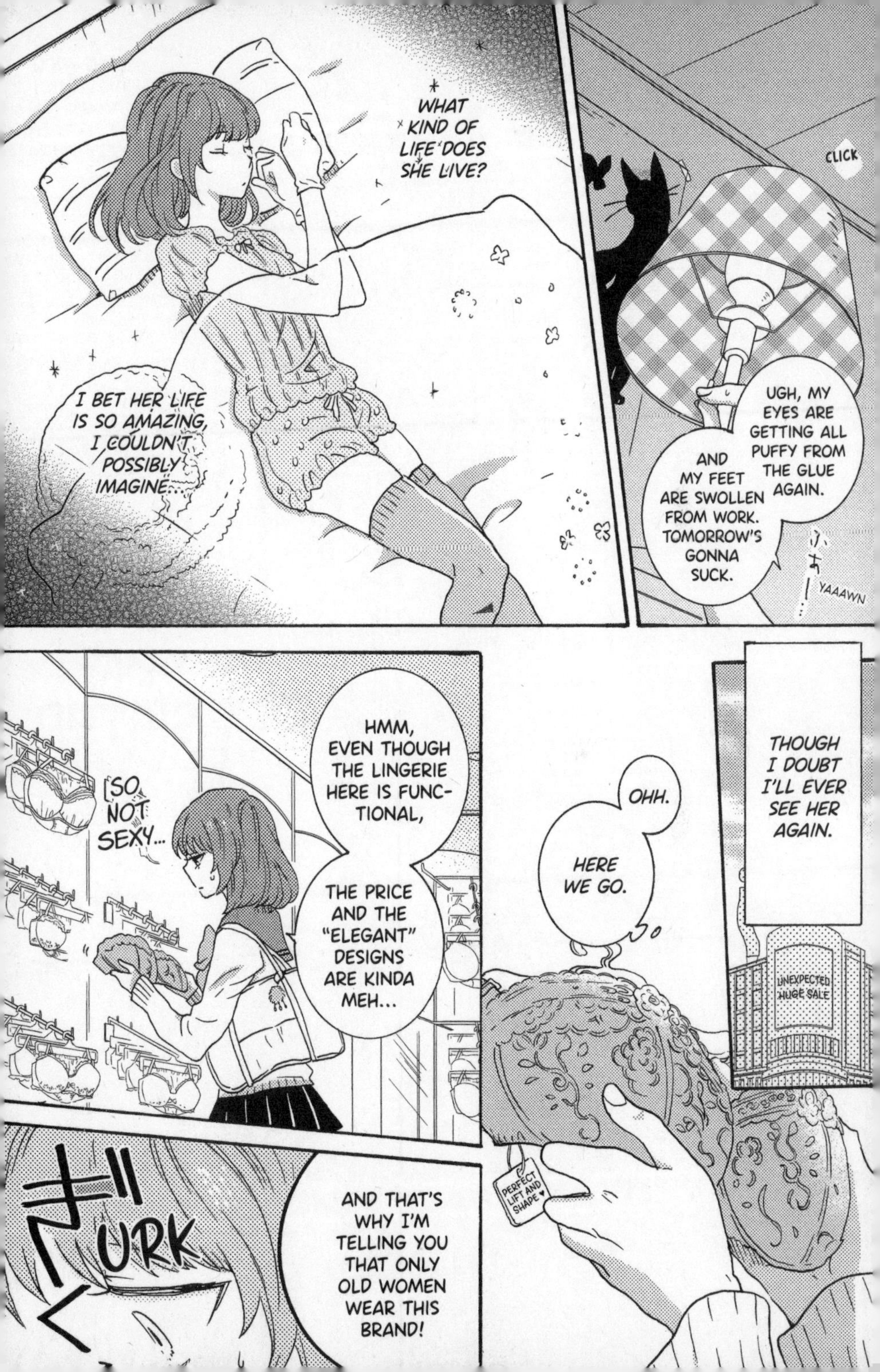
CLICK
UGH, MY EYES ARE GETTING ALL PUFFY FROM THE GLUE AGAIN.
AND MY FEET ARE SWOLLEN FROM WORK. TOMORROW'S GONNA SUCK.
YAAAWN
WHAT KIND OF LIFE DOES SHE LIVE?
I BET HER LIFE IS SO AMAZING, I COULDN'T POSSIBLY IMAGINE...
THOUGH I DOUBT I'LL EVER SEE HER AGAIN.
UNEXPECTED HUGE SALE
OHH.
HERE WE GO.
PERFECT LIFT AND SHAPE♥
HMM, EVEN THOUGH THE LINGERIE HERE IS FUNCTIONAL,
THE PRICE AND THE "ELEGANT" DESIGNS ARE KINDA MEH...
SO NOT SEXY...
AND THAT'S WHY I'M TELLING YOU THAT ONLY OLD WOMEN WEAR THIS BRAND!
URK

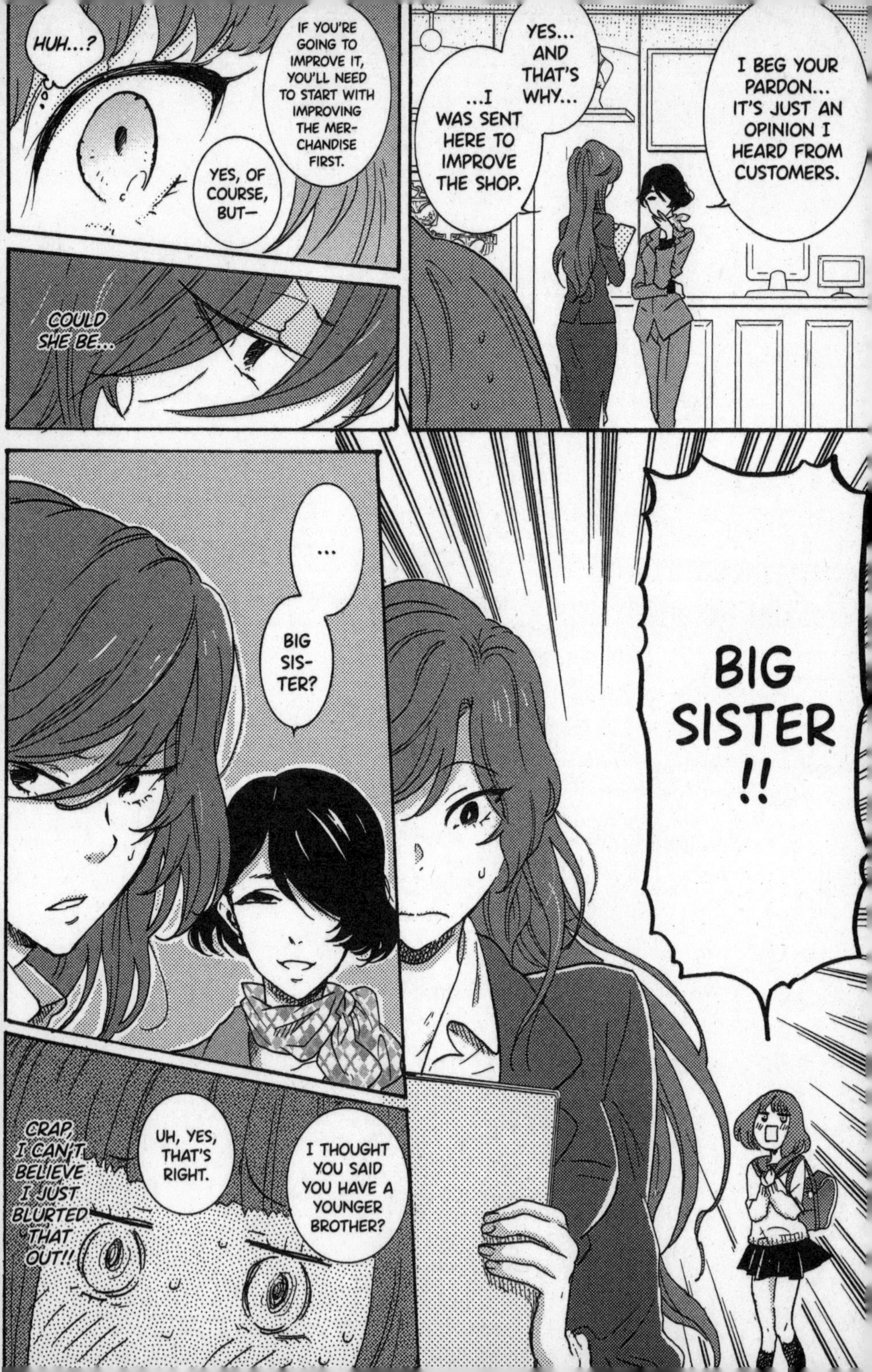

I BEG YOUR PARDON... IT'S JUST AN OPINION I HEARD FROM CUSTOMERS.
YES... AND THAT'S WHY...
...I WAS SENT HERE TO IMPROVE THE SHOP.
IF YOU'RE GOING TO IMPROVE IT, YOU'LL NEED TO START WITH IMPROVING THE MER-CHANDISE FIRST.
YES, OF COURSE, BUT—
HUH...?
COULD SHE BE...
BIG SISTER !!
...
BIG SIS-TER?
I THOUGHT YOU SAID YOU HAVE A YOUNGER BROTHER?
UH, YES, THAT'S RIGHT.
CRAP, I CAN'T BELIEVE I JUST BLURTED THAT OUT!!

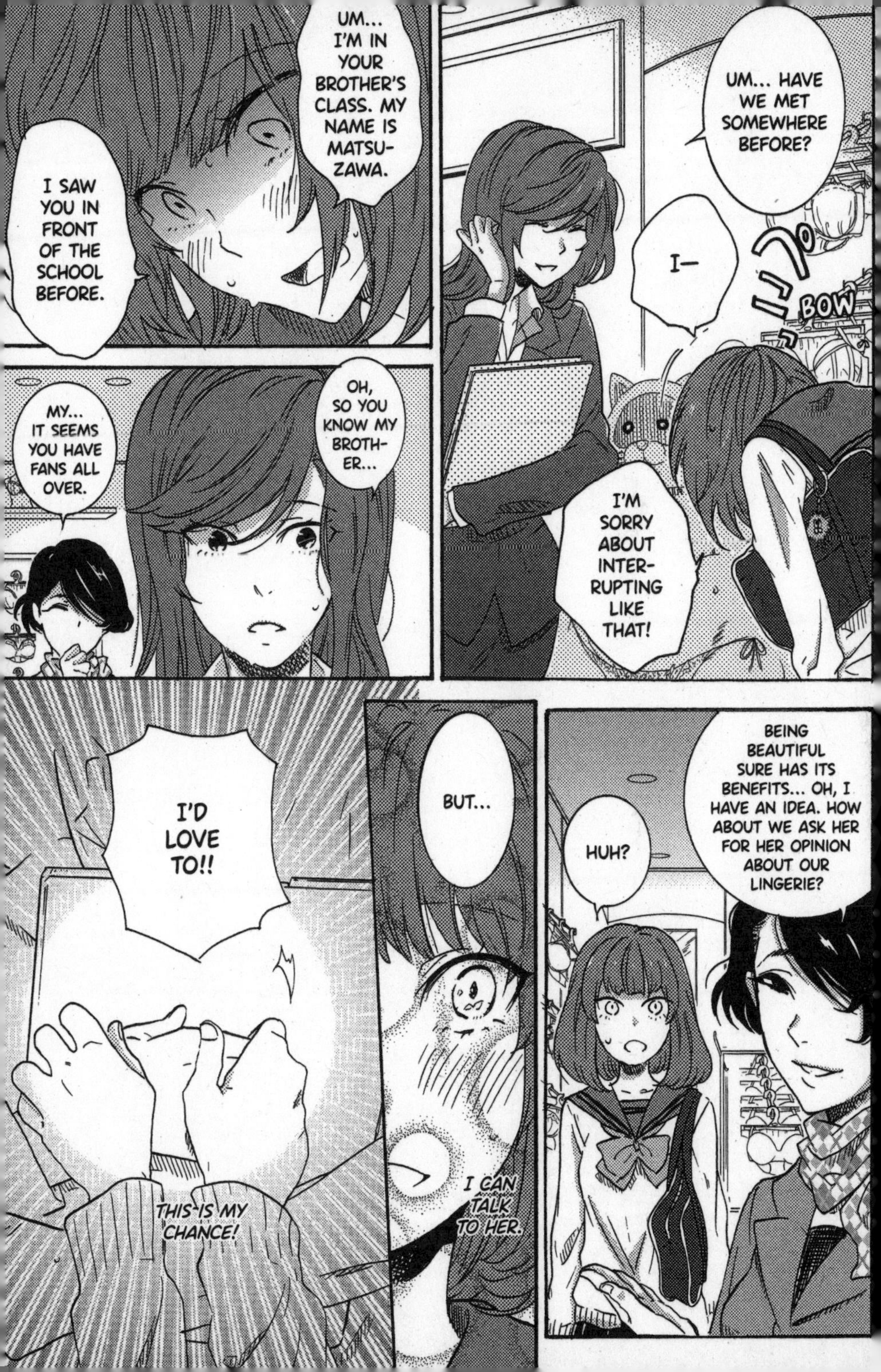
UM... HAVE WE MET SOMEWHERE BEFORE?
I—
BOW
I'M SORRY ABOUT INTER-RUPTING LIKE THAT!
UM... I'M IN YOUR BROTHER'S CLASS. MY NAME IS MATSU-ZAWA.
I SAW YOU IN FRONT OF THE SCHOOL BEFORE.
OH, SO YOU KNOW MY BROTH-ER...
MY... IT SEEMS YOU HAVE FANS ALL OVER.
BEING BEAUTIFUL SURE HAS ITS BENEFITS... OH, I HAVE AN IDEA. HOW ABOUT WE ASK HER FOR HER OPINION ABOUT OUR LINGERIE?
HUH?
BUT...
I CAN TALK TO HER.
I'D LOVE TO!!
THIS IS MY CHANCE!

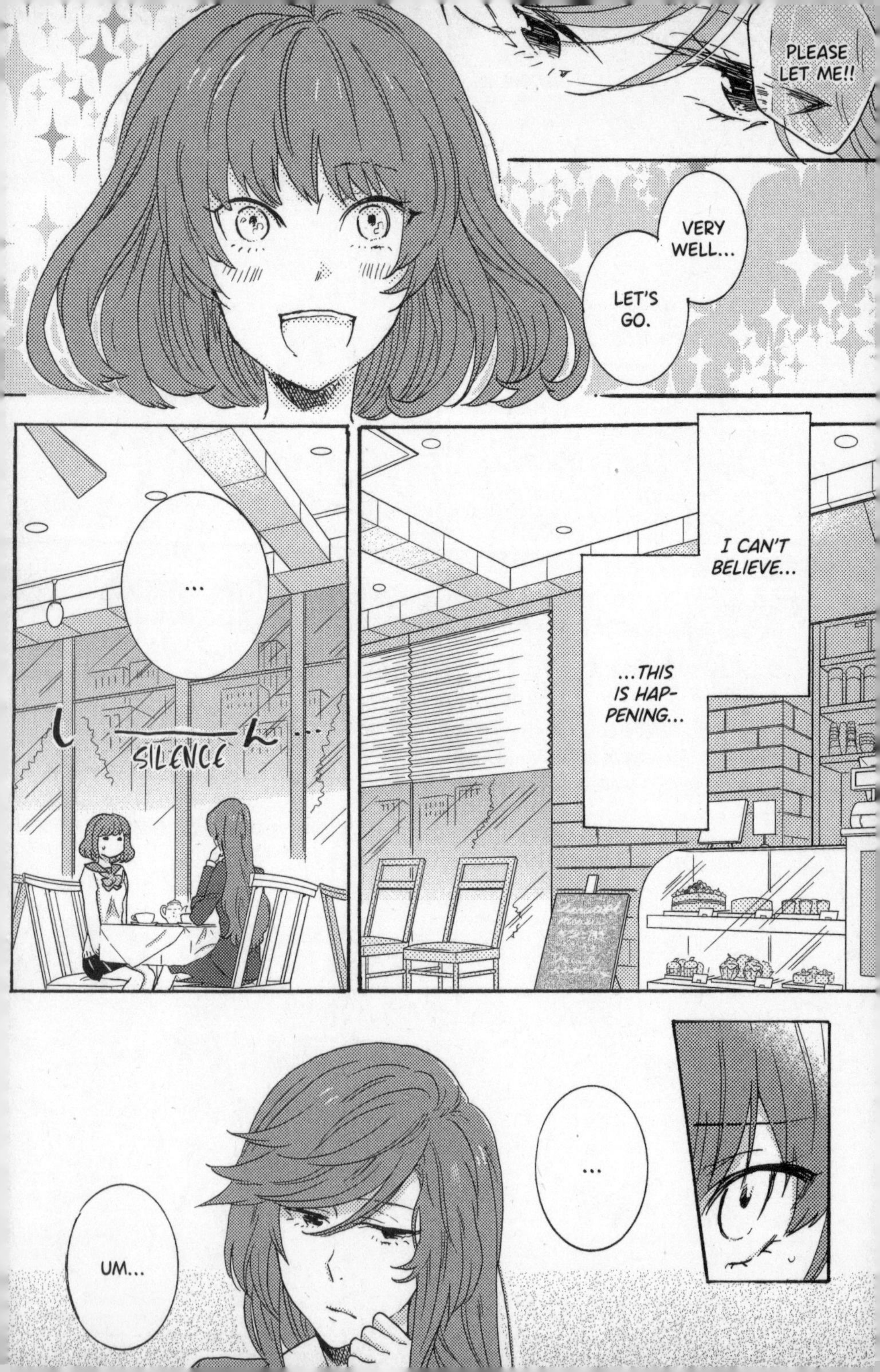
PLEASE LET ME!!
VERY WELL...
LET'S GO.
I CAN'T BELIEVE...
...THIS IS HAP-PENING...
...
SILENCE
...
UM...

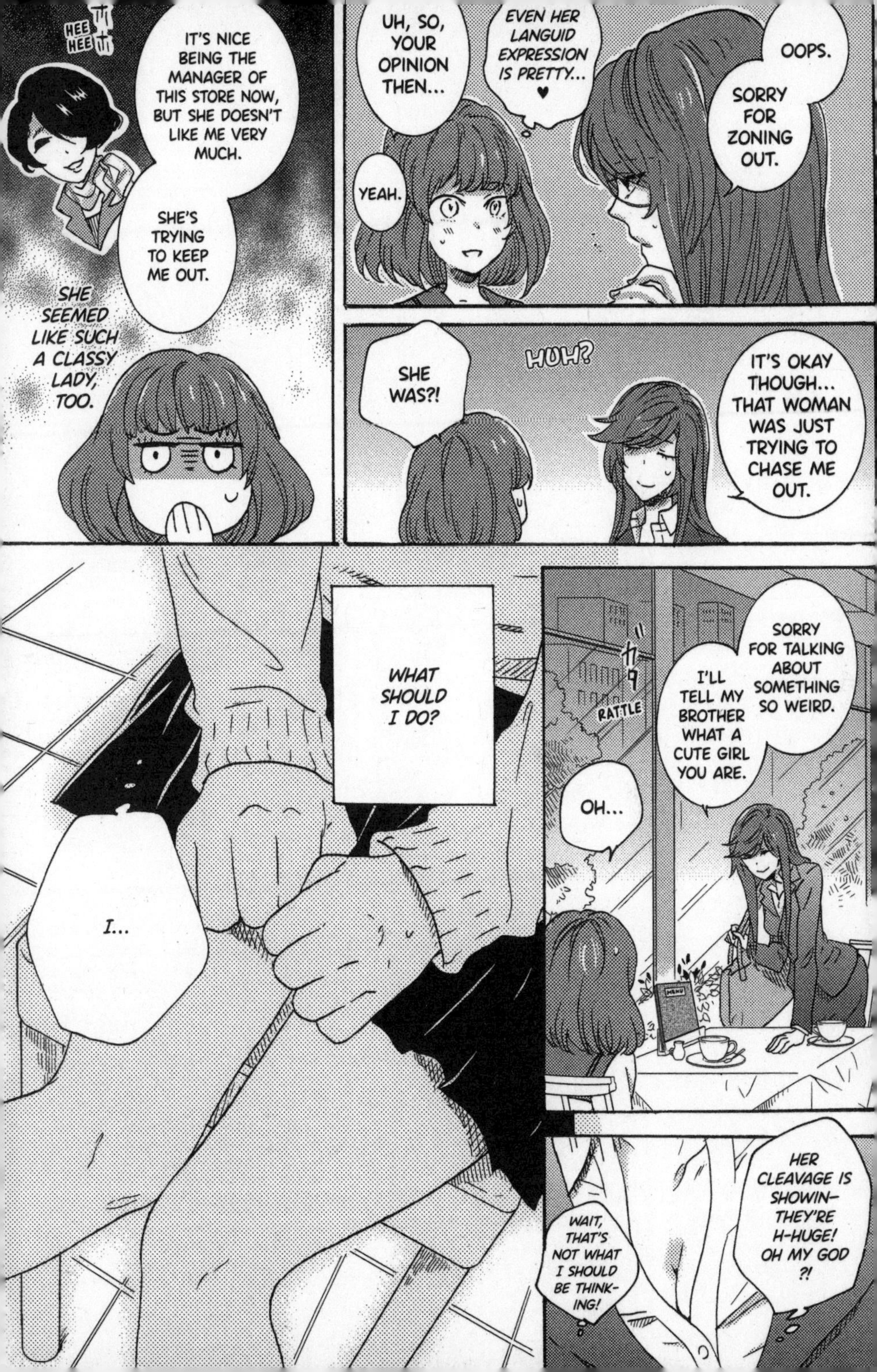
OOPS.
SORRY FOR ZONING OUT.
EVEN HER LANGUID EXPRESSION IS PRETTY... ♥
UH, SO, YOUR OPINION THEN...
YEAH.
IT'S OKAY THOUGH... THAT WOMAN WAS JUST TRYING TO CHASE ME OUT.
HUH?
SHE WAS?!
HEE HEE
IT'S NICE BEING THE MANAGER OF THIS STORE NOW, BUT SHE DOESN'T LIKE ME VERY MUCH.
SHE'S TRYING TO KEEP ME OUT.
SHE SEEMED LIKE SUCH A CLASSY LADY, TOO.
RATTLE
SORRY FOR TALKING ABOUT SOMETHING SO WEIRD.
I'LL TELL MY BROTHER WHAT A CUTE GIRL YOU ARE.
OH...
HER CLEAVAGE IS SHOWIN— THEY'RE H-HUGE! OH MY GOD ?!
WAIT, THAT'S NOT WHAT I SHOULD BE THINK-ING!
WHAT SHOULD I DO?
I...

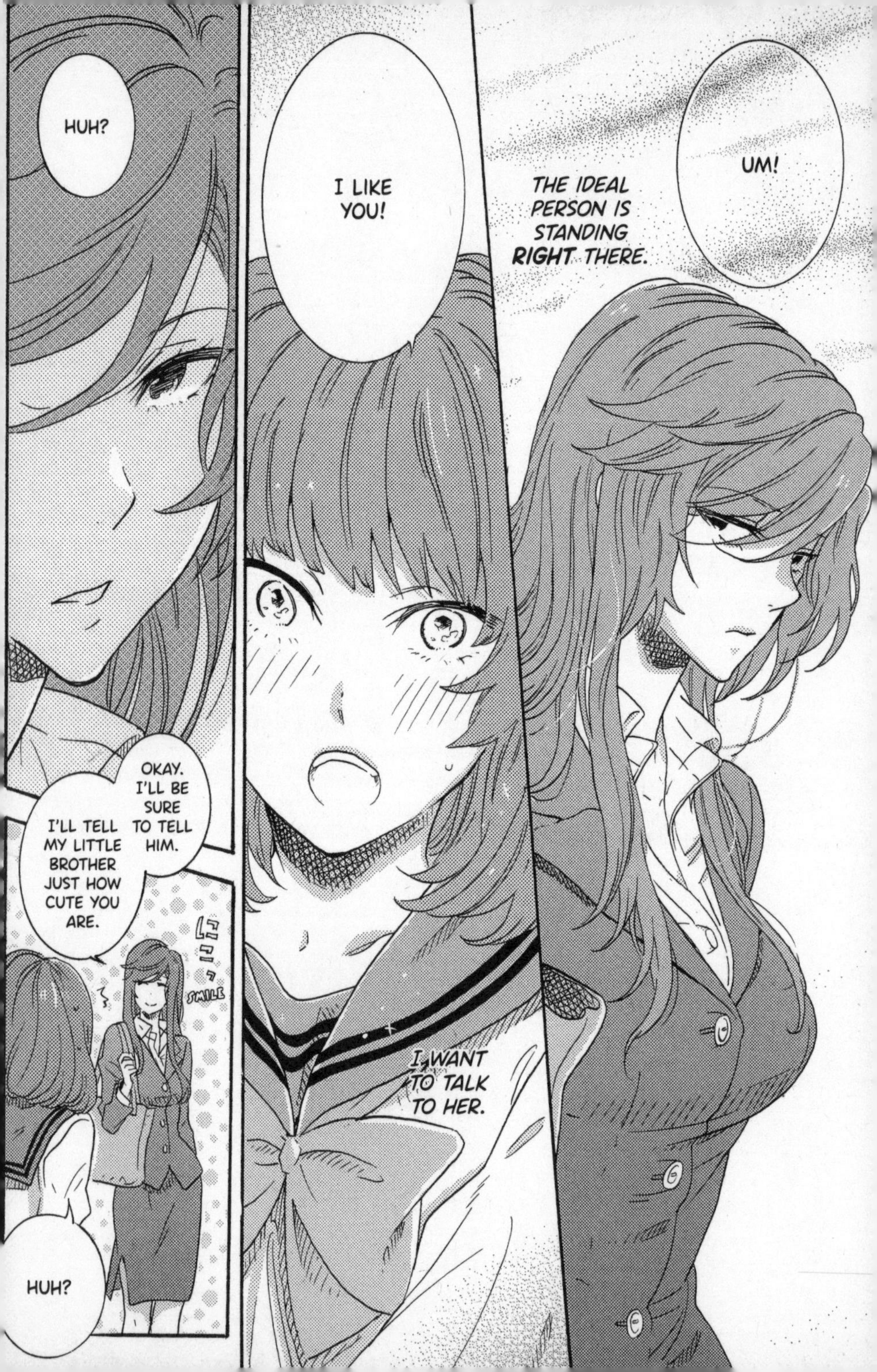
UM!
THE IDEAL PERSON IS STANDING RIGHT THERE.
I LIKE YOU!
I WANT TO TALK TO HER.
HUH?
OKAY. I'LL BE SURE TO TELL HIM.
I'LL TELL MY LITTLE BROTHER JUST HOW CUTE YOU ARE.
SMILE
HUH?

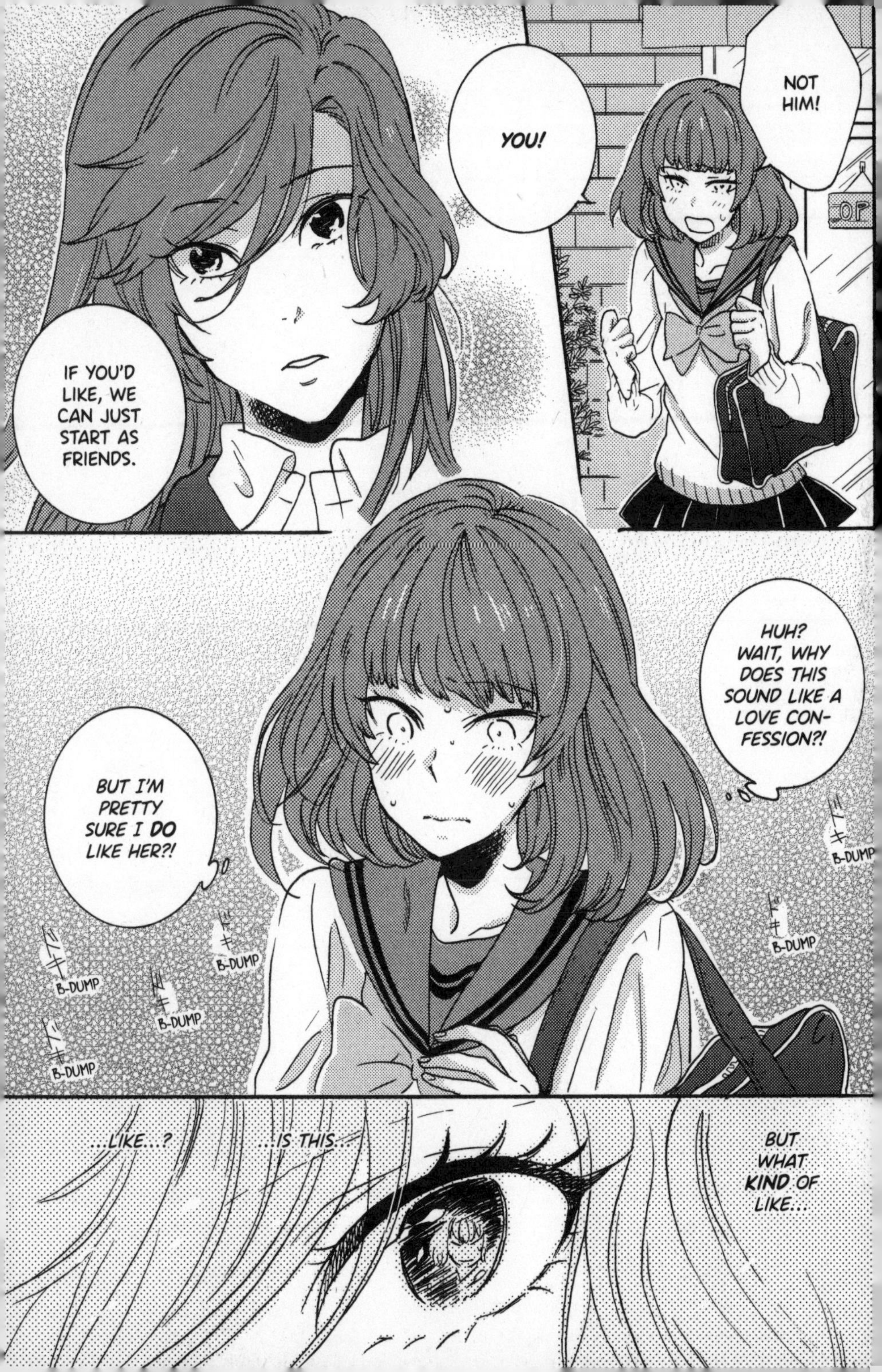
NOT HIM!
YOU!
IF YOU'D LIKE, WE CAN JUST START AS FRIENDS.
HUH? WAIT, WHY DOES THIS SOUND LIKE A LOVE CON-FESSION?!
B-DUMP
B-DUMP
BUT I'M PRETTY SURE I DO LIKE HER?!
B-DUMP
B-DUMP
B-DUMP
B-DUMP
BUT WHAT KIND OF LIKE...
...IS THIS...
...LIKE...?

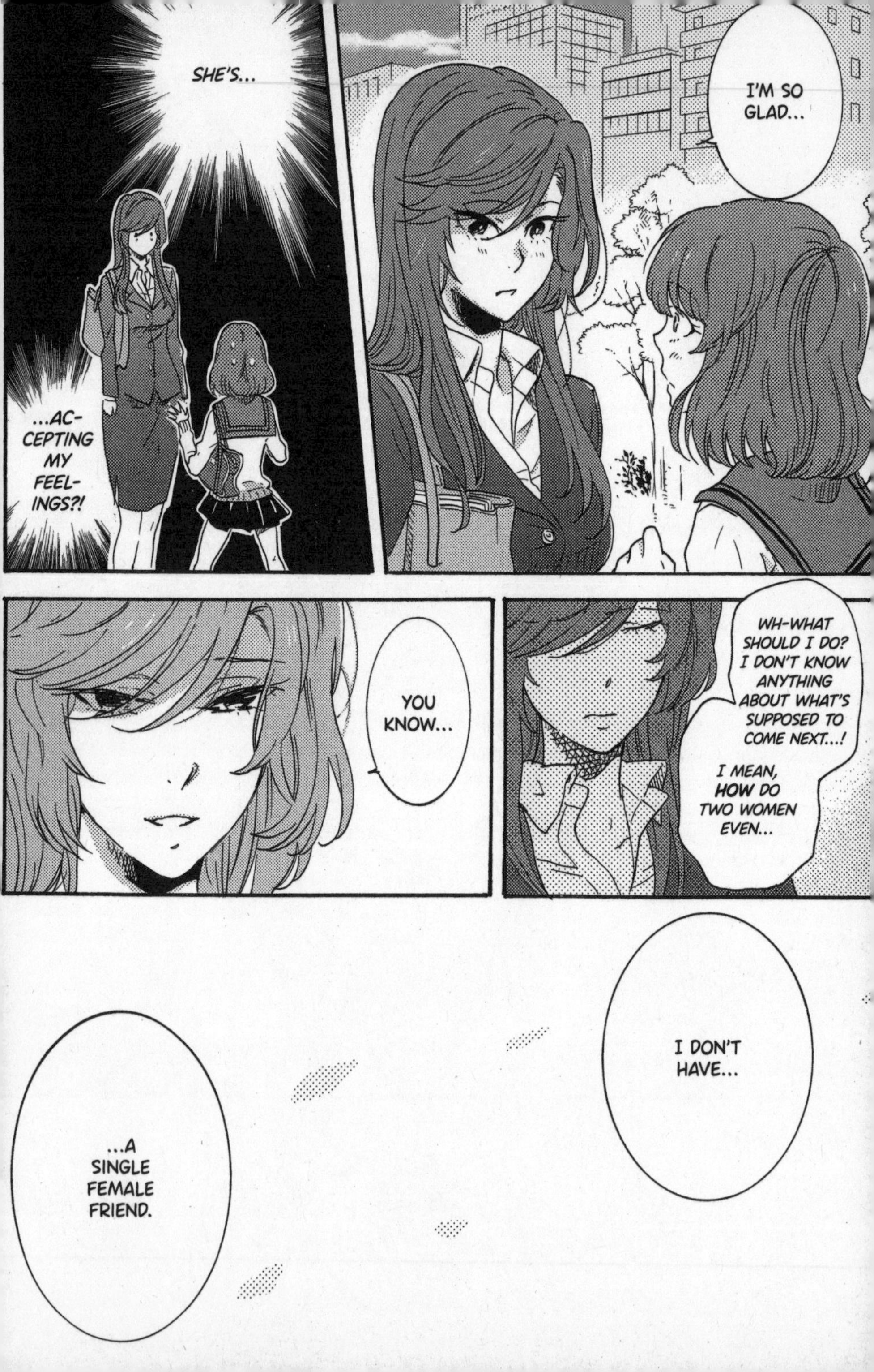
I'M SO GLAD...
SHE'S...
...AC-CEPTING MY FEEL-INGS?!
WH-WHAT SHOULD I DO? I DON'T KNOW ANYTHING ABOUT WHAT'S SUPPOSED TO COME NEXT...!
I MEAN, HOW DO TWO WOMEN EVEN...
YOU KNOW...
I DON'T HAVE...
...A SINGLE FEMALE FRIEND.

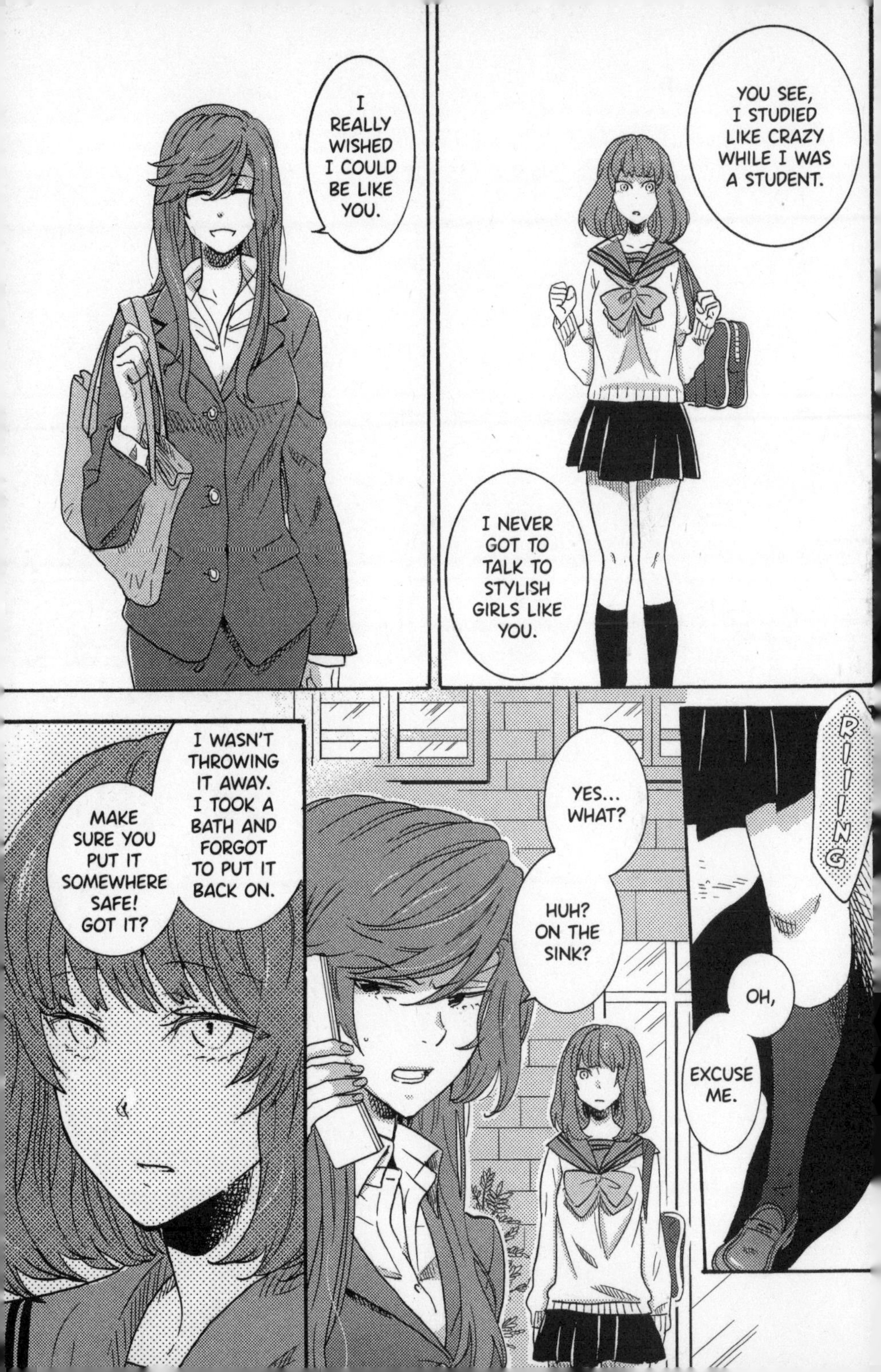
YOU SEE, I STUDIED LIKE CRAZY WHILE I WAS A STUDENT.
I NEVER GOT TO TALK TO STYLISH GIRLS LIKE YOU.
I REALLY WISHED I COULD BE LIKE YOU.
RIIING
OH,
EXCUSE ME.
YES... WHAT?
HUH? ON THE SINK?
I WASN'T THROWING IT AWAY. I TOOK A BATH AND FORGOT TO PUT IT BACK ON.
MAKE SURE YOU PUT IT SOMEWHERE SAFE! GOT IT?

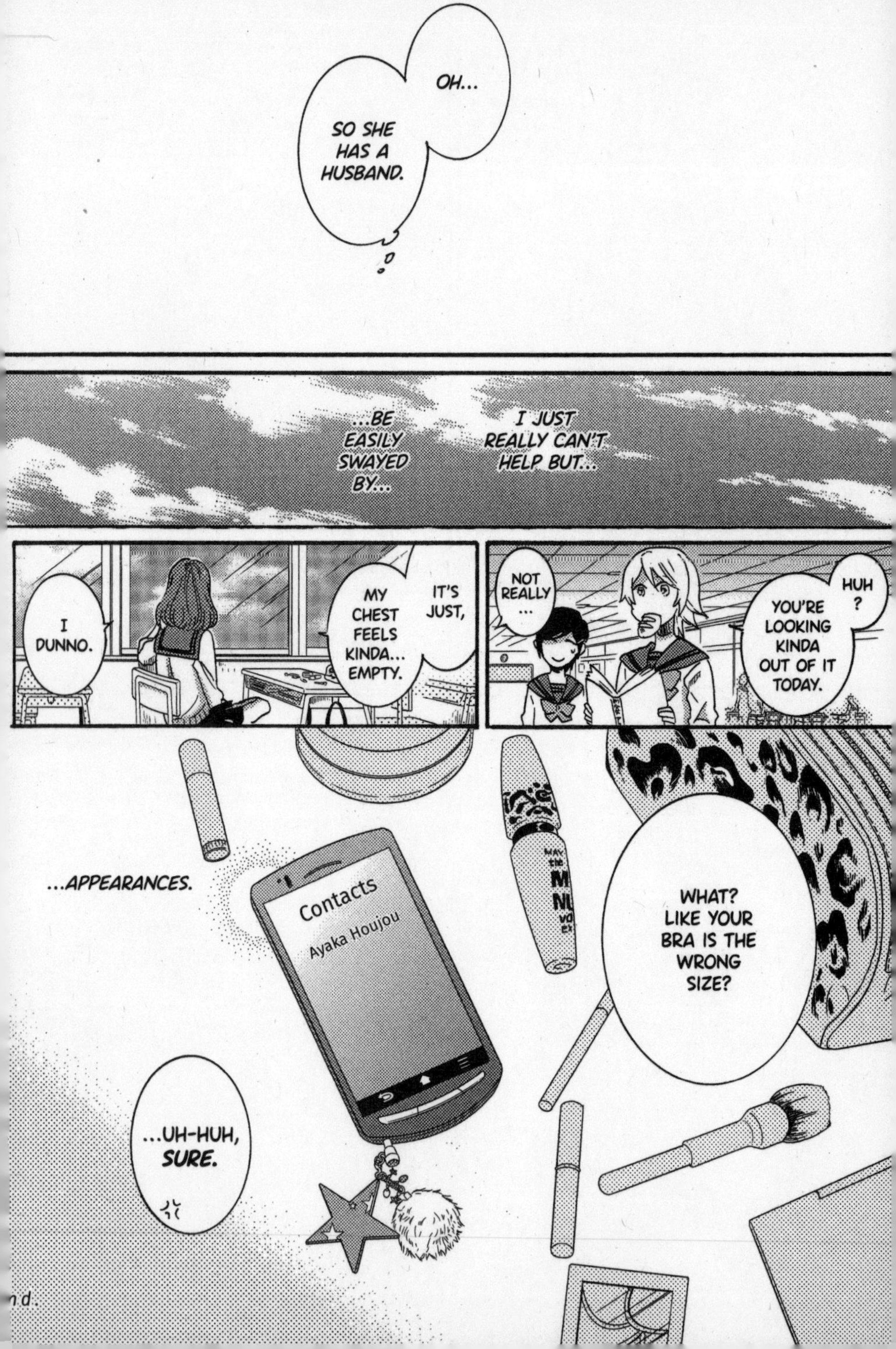

OH...
SO SHE HAS A HUSBAND.
I JUST REALLY CAN'T HELP BUT...
...BE EASILY SWAYED BY...
HUH?
YOU'RE LOOKING KINDA OUT OF IT TODAY.
NOT REALLY...
IT'S JUST,
MY CHEST FEELS KINDA... EMPTY.
I DUNNO.
WHAT? LIKE YOUR BRA IS THE WRONG SIZE?
...APPEARANCES.
Contacts
Ayaka Houjou
...UH-HUH, **SURE.**

{FIRST RUN}

Hitorijime My Hero #16   gateau magazine December 2014 issue
Hitorijime My Hero #16.5   gateau magazine January 2015 issue
Hitorijime My Hero #17   gateau magazine March 2015 issue
Hitorijime My Hero #18   gateau magazine April 2015 issue
Hitorijime My Hero #19   gateau magazine May 2015 issue
Hitorijime My Fairy Lady   Comic Yuri Hime magazine November 2013 issue

Hitorijime My Hero

Primitive Afterword

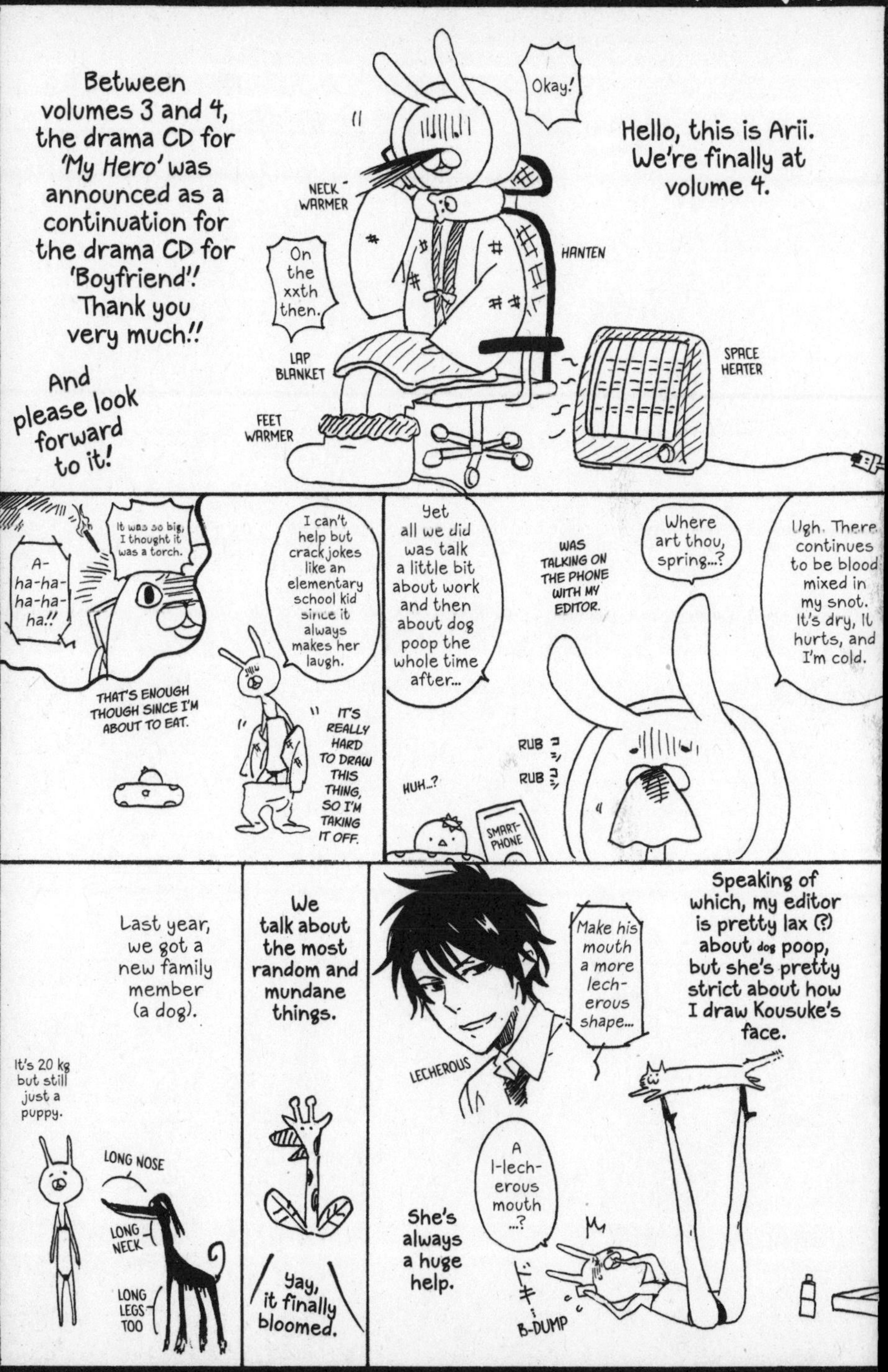
Hello, this is Arii. We're finally at volume 4.
Okay!
NECK WARMER
HANTEN
On the xxth then.
LAP BLANKET
SPACE HEATER
FEET WARMER
Between volumes 3 and 4, the drama CD for 'My Hero' was announced as a continuation for the drama CD for 'Boyfriend'! Thank you very much!!
And please look forward to it!
Ugh. There continues to be blood mixed in my snot. It's dry, it hurts, and I'm cold.
Where art thou, spring...?
WAS TALKING ON THE PHONE WITH MY EDITOR.
Yet all we did was talk a little bit about work and then about dog poop the whole time after...
RUB RUB
HUH...?
SMART-PHONE
I can't help but crack jokes like an elementary school kid since it always makes her laugh.
It was so big, I thought it was a torch.
A-ha-ha-ha-ha!!
IT'S REALLY HARD TO DRAW THIS THING, SO I'M TAKING IT OFF.
THAT'S ENOUGH THOUGH SINCE I'M ABOUT TO EAT.
Speaking of which, my editor is pretty lax (?) about dog poop, but she's pretty strict about how I draw Kousuke's face.
Make his mouth a more lech-erous shape...
LECHEROUS
A l-lech-erous mouth ...?
She's always a huge help.
B-DUMP
We talk about the most random and mundane things.
Yay, it finally bloomed.
Last year, we got a new family member (a dog).
It's 20 kg but still just a puppy.
LONG NOSE
LONG NECK
LONG LEGS TOO

*About 44 lbs.

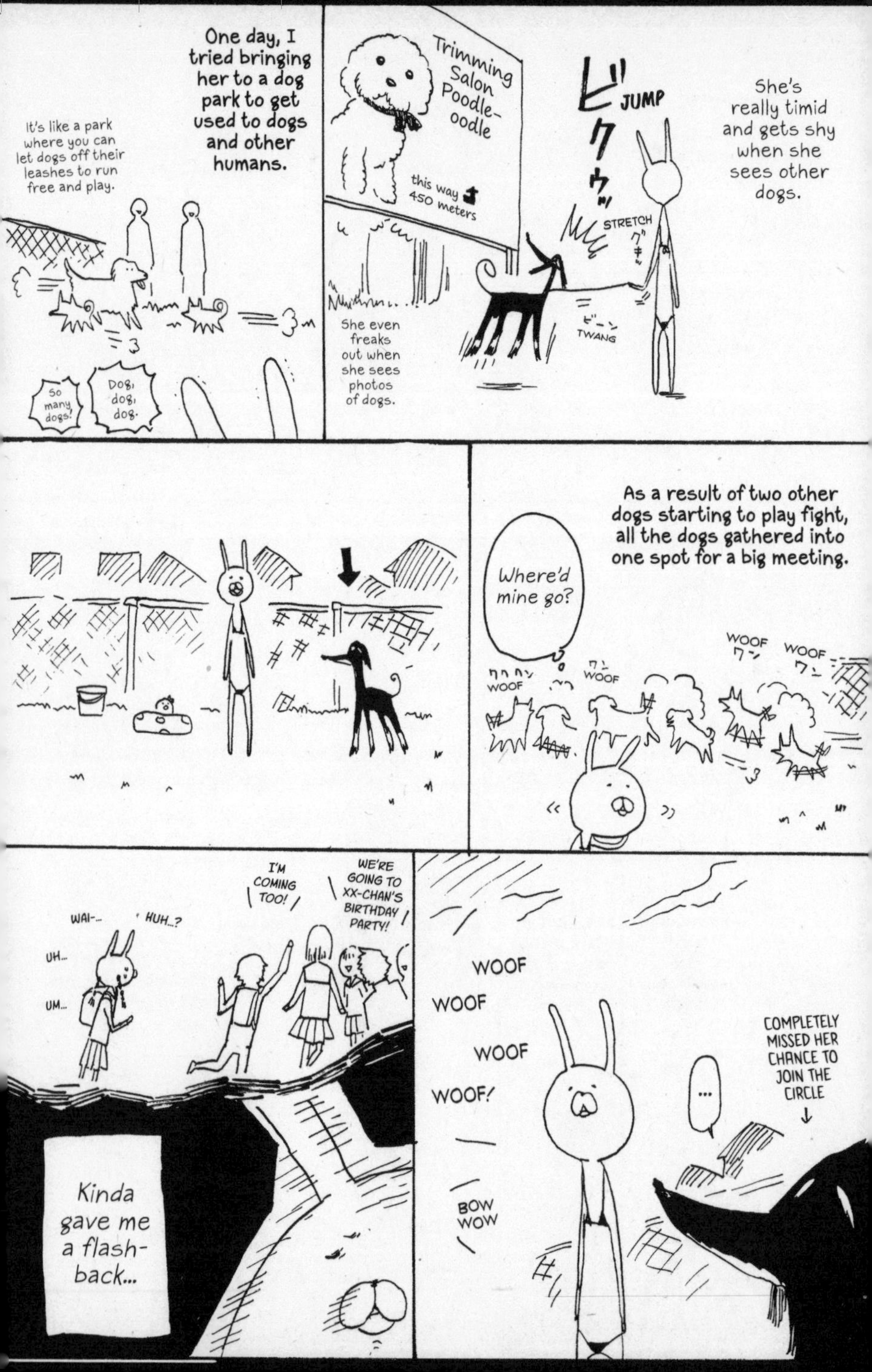
She's really timid and gets shy when she sees other dogs.
Trimming Salon Poodle-oodle
this way 450 meters
ビクゥ JUMP
グギ STRETCH
ビーン TWANG
She even freaks out when she sees photos of dogs.
One day, I tried bringing her to a dog park to get used to dogs and other humans.
It's like a park where you can let dogs off their leashes to run free and play.
Dog, dog, dog.
So many dogs!
As a result of two other dogs starting to play fight, all the dogs gathered into one spot for a big meeting.
WOOF
WOOF
WOOF
Where'd mine go?
WOOF
COMPLETELY MISSED HER CHANCE TO JOIN THE CIRCLE
...
WOOF
WOOF
WOOF
WOOF!
BOW WOW
WE'RE GOING TO XX-CHAN'S BIRTHDAY PARTY!
I'M COMING TOO!
HUH...?
WAI-...
UH...
UM...
Kinda gave me a flash-back...

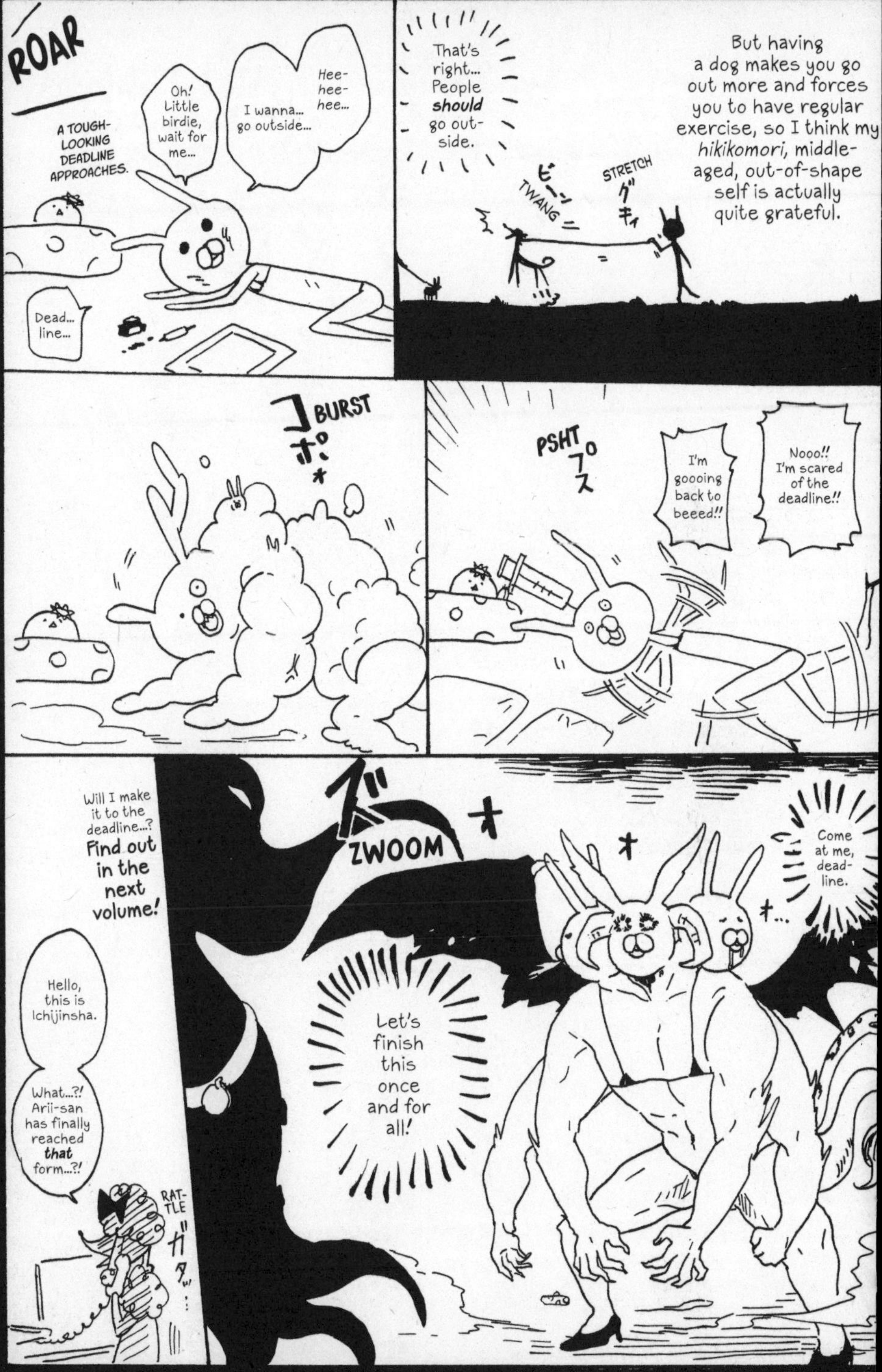
That's right... People **should** go outside.
TWANG
STRETCH
But having a dog makes you go out more and forces you to have regular exercise, so I think my *hikikomori*, middle-aged, out-of-shape self is actually quite grateful.
ROAR
A TOUGH-LOOKING DEADLINE APPROACHES.
Hee-hee-hee...
I wanna... go outside...
Oh! Little birdie, wait for me...
Dead... line...
Nooo!! I'm scared of the deadline!!
I'm goooing back to beeed!!
PSHT
BURST
Come at me, deadline.
ZWOOM
Let's finish this once and for all!
Will I make it to the deadline...? **Find out in the next volume!**
Hello, this is Ichijinsha.
What...?! Arii-san has finally reached **that** form...?!
RATTLE

Acknowledgements → My editor, the book designers, additional thanks for design assistance: K-san, little sister K-san, and my readers. Thank

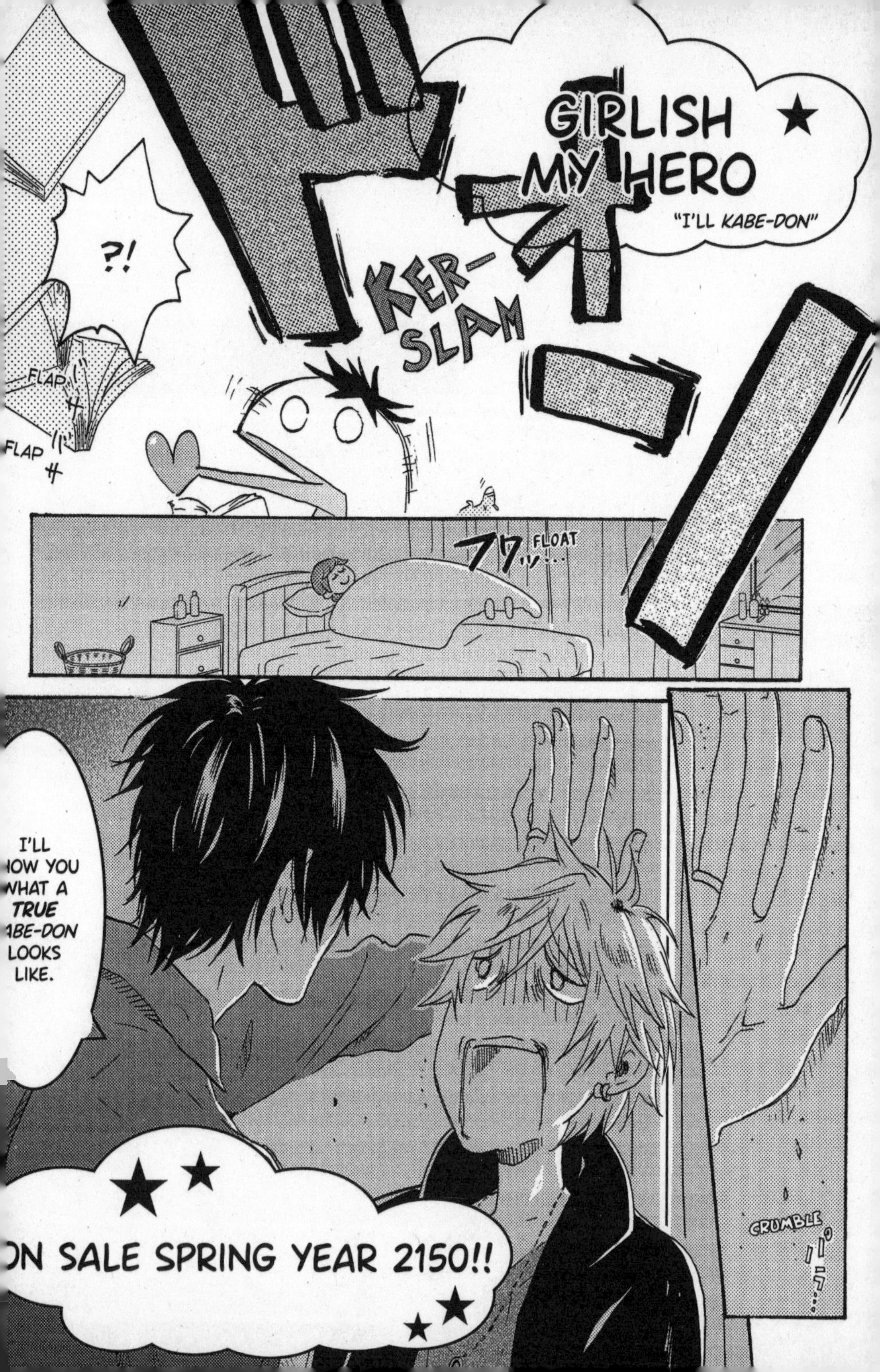
GIRLISH ★ MY HERO
"I'LL KABE-DON"
KER-SLAM
?!
FLAP
FLAP
FLOAT...
I'LL HOW YOU WHAT A TRUE ABE-DON LOOKS LIKE.
CRUMBLE...
ON SALE SPRING YEAR 2150!!

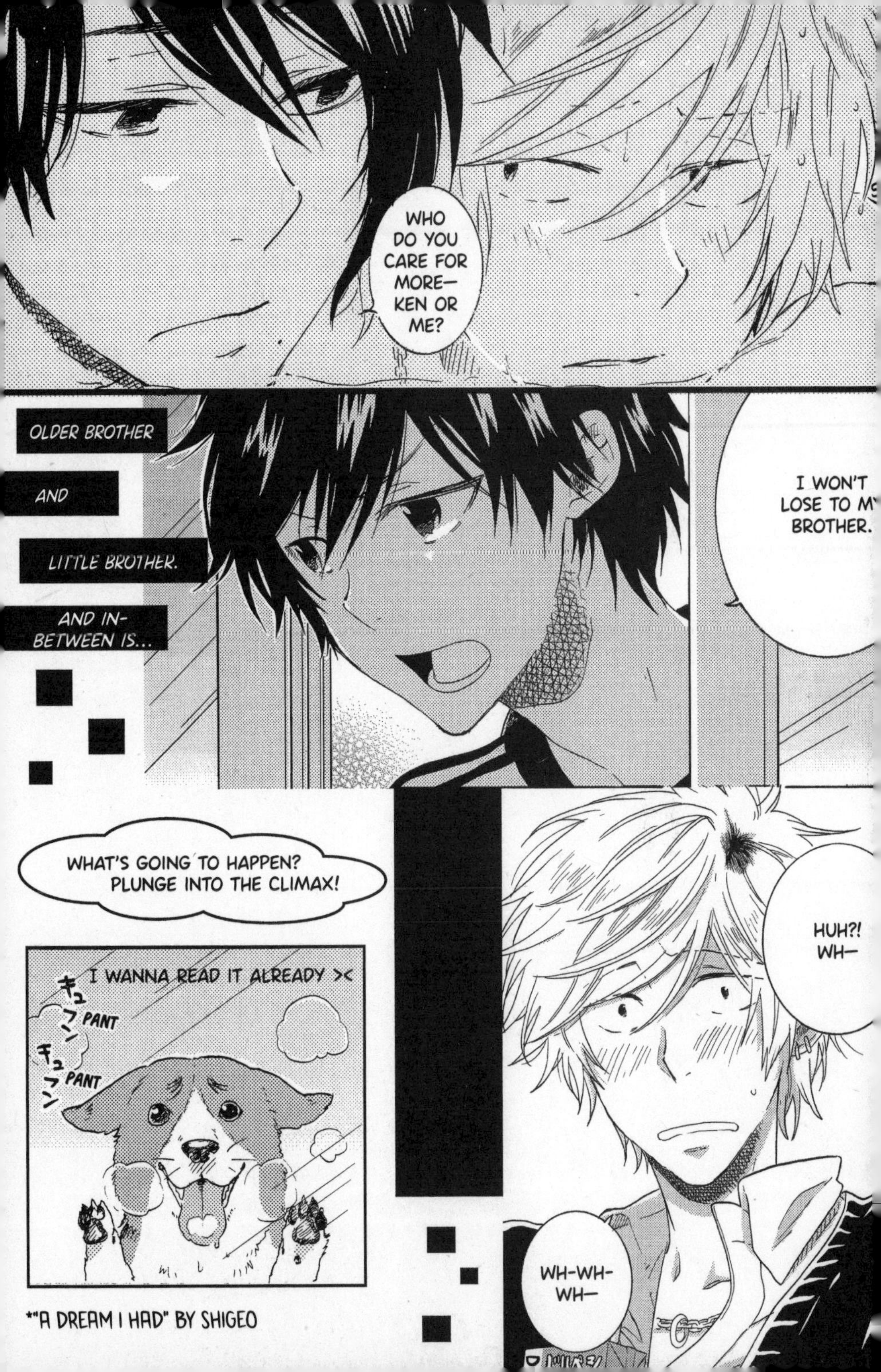
WHO DO YOU CARE FOR MORE— KEN OR ME?
I WON'T LOSE TO MY BROTHER.
OLDER BROTHER
AND
LITTLE BROTHER.
AND IN-BETWEEN IS...
HUH?! WH—
WH-WH-WH—
WHAT'S GOING TO HAPPEN? PLUNGE INTO THE CLIMAX!
I WANNA READ IT ALREADY ><
キュフン PANT
キュフン PANT
*"A DREAM I HAD" BY SHIGEO

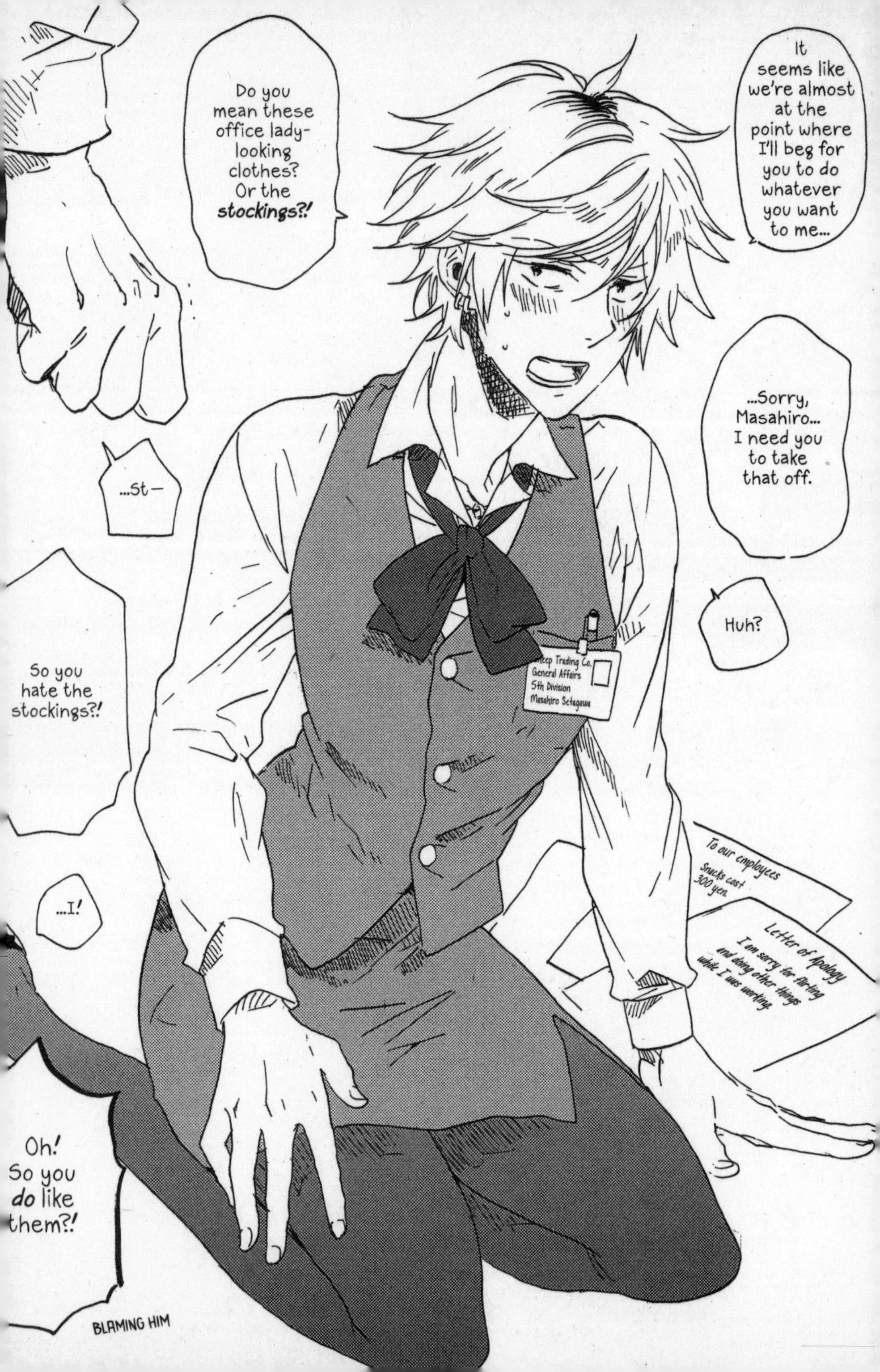

It seems like we're almost at the point where I'll beg for you to do whatever you want to me...
Do you mean these office lady-looking clothes? Or the **stockings?!**
...Sorry, Masahiro... I need you to take that off.
...St—
Huh?
eep Trading Co. General Affairs 5th Division Masahiro Setagawa
So you hate the stockings?!
To our employees
Snacks cost 300 yen.
Letter of Apology
I am sorry for flirting and doing other things while I was working
...I!
Oh! So you *do* like them?!
BLAMING HIM

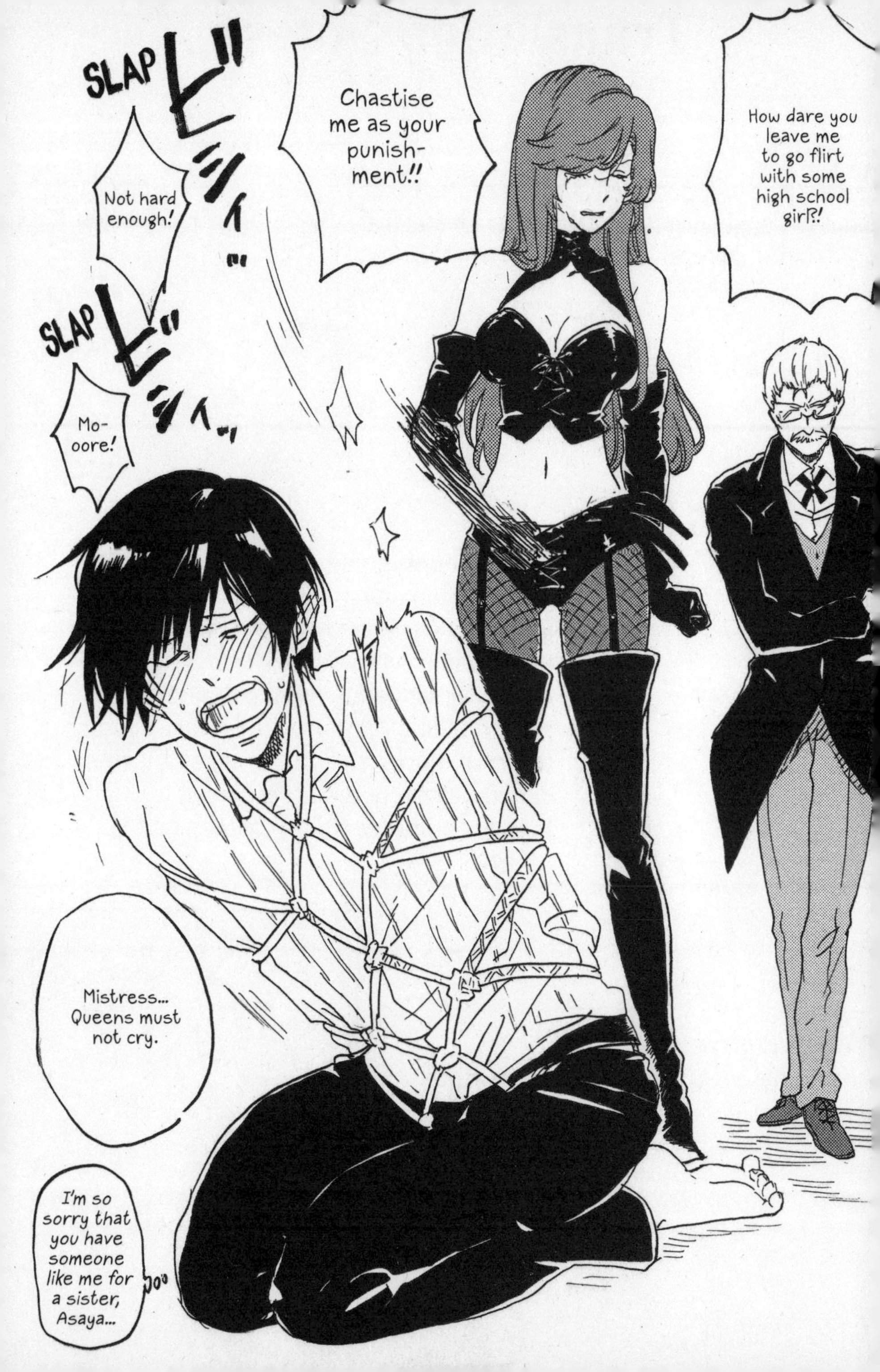
How dare you leave me to go flirt with some high school girl?!
Chastise me as your punish-ment!!
SLAP ビシィ
Not hard enough!
SLAP ビシィ
Mo-oore!
Mistress... Queens must not cry.
I'm so sorry that you have someone like me for a sister, Asaya...

Translation Notes

read in the microwave, page 9

Iicrowaves in Japan have a toaster function, ɔ many people use their microwave instead f a traditional toaster to toast their bread.

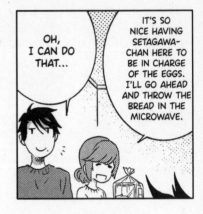

IT'S SO NICE HAVING SETAGAWA-CHAN HERE TO BE IN CHARGE OF THE EGGS. I'LL GO AHEAD AND THROW THE BREAD IN THE MICROWAVE.
OH, I CAN DO THAT...

IF YOU LOVE THE TREE SO MUCH, WHY DON'T YOU ADD MOCHI AND A CLEMENTINE AND LEAVE IT OUT UNTIL NEW YEAR'S?
A KAGAMI-MOMI?
HA-HA-HA!

***Kagami-momi*, page 24**

This is a pun on *momi* (Japanese fir tree) and *kagami-mochi* (mirror rice cakes), a traditional decoration to put on display at New Year's in Japan as an offering to the gods. *Kagami-mochi* is made of two round layers of *mochi* (rice cakes) cakes with a *daidai* (Japanese bitter orange) or a mandarin orange called a *mikan* on top.

I BET THE NEARBY CONVENIENCE STORE SELLS THEM.
ACTUALLY, IT'S A BIT OF A WALK, BUT I THINK I WANT TO GO TO THE 100-YEN SHOP.

00-yen shop, page 25

he Japanese equivalent to a dollar store.

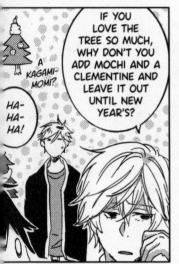

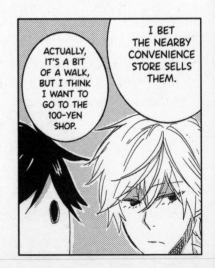

Today of all days, page 30
Masahiro is referring to the fact that it's Christmas day. Christmas in Japan is mostly celebrated by couples, who will often go on romantic dates and exchange gifts. Whether Christmas is on the weekday or the weekend, you can also expect love hotels (short-stay accommodations where people go to engage in sexual activities) throughout the country to be completely booked, so you need to make a reservation far in advance.

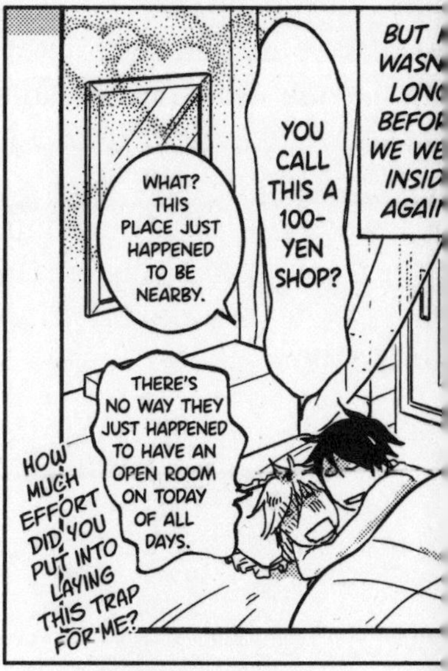
YOU CALL THIS A 100-YEN SHOP?
WHAT? THIS PLACE JUST HAPPENED TO BE NEARBY.
THERE'S NO WAY THEY JUST HAPPENED TO HAVE AN OPEN ROOM ON TODAY OF ALL DAYS.
HOW MUCH EFFORT DID YOU PUT INTO LAYING THIS TRAP FOR ME?

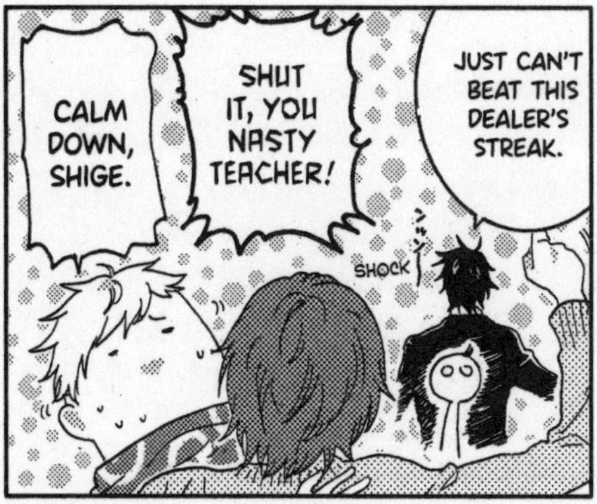
JUST CAN'T BEAT THIS DEALER'S STREAK.
SHUT IT, YOU NASTY TEACHER!
CALM DOWN, SHIGE.
SHOCK

Dealer's streak, page 73
Kousuke uses the term *"renchan"* here which is a Mahjong term for when the dealer wins consecutive hands in a row

Bitter Melon Hill *(gouya no oka)*, page 88
A pun on the Japanese chocolate snacks *"Kinoko no Yama"* (mushroom mountain).

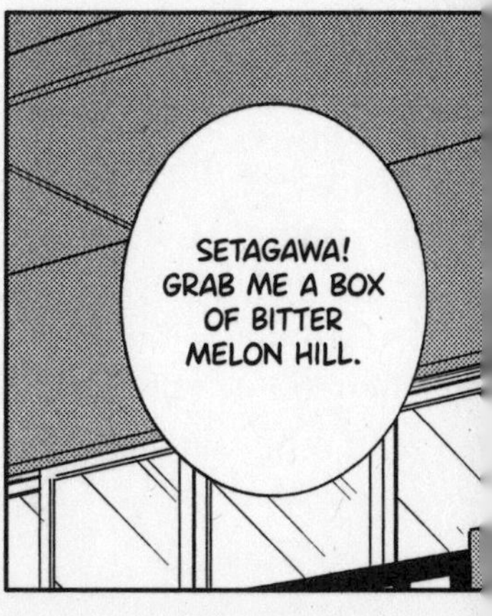
SETAGAWA! GRAB ME A BOX OF BITTER MELON HILL.

nack Bar, page 96
nack Bars are drinking
stablishments run by an older
n older female proprietor who
called a mama-san. They
nostly cater to older men and
iffer from hostess clubs in that
ney are cheaper and offer more
elaxed atmospheres.

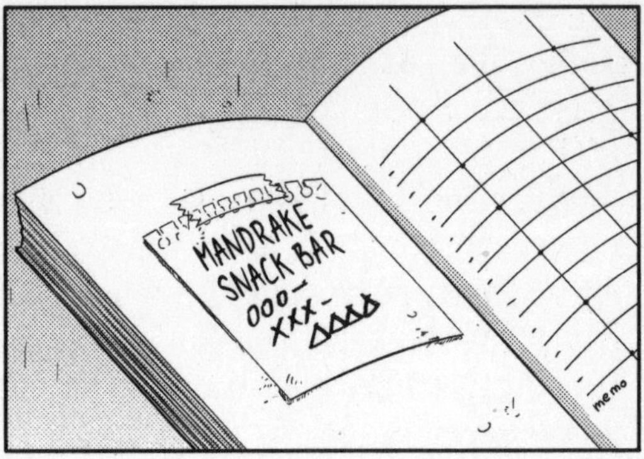
MANDRAKE
SNACK BAR
000-XXX-ΔΔΔΔ
memo

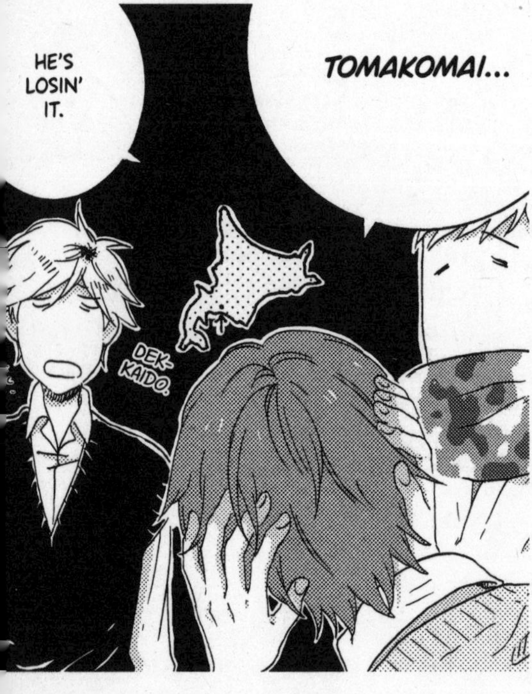
TOMAKOMAI...
HE'S LOSIN' IT.
DEK-KAIDO.

Tomakomai, page 106
Tomakomai is a city in Hokkaido.

Dekkaido, page 106
A pun that combines "Hokkaido" and *"dekai"* (huge) to mean that Hokkaido is big.

***hochu*, page 111**
n alcoholic drink from Japan typically
istilled from rice, sweet potatoes, or other
ngredients. It is quite popular and mixes
vell with other flavors such as tea, juice, etc.

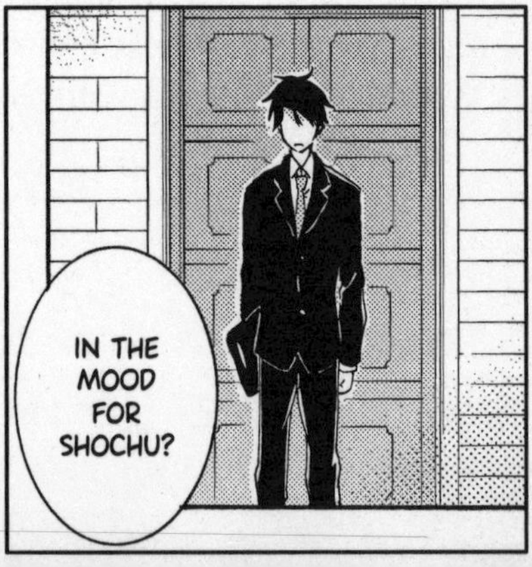
IN THE MOOD FOR SHOCHU?

***Omurice*, page 116**
Omurice is a popular dish made of an omelet with fried rice and usually topped with ketchup.

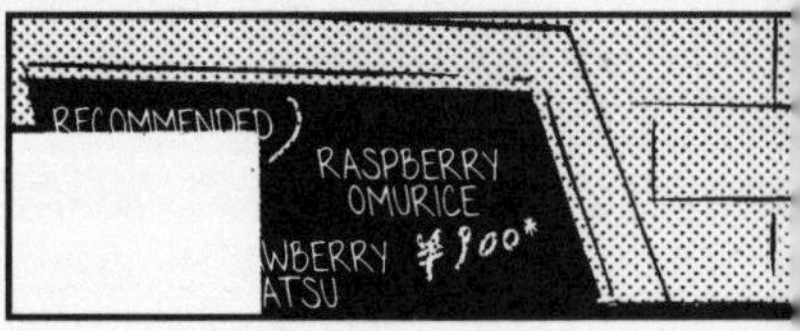
RECOMMENDED
RASPBERRY OMURICE
¥900*

***Namerou*, page 134**
A dish made of fish or other meat finely minced and then mixed with spices and seasonings.

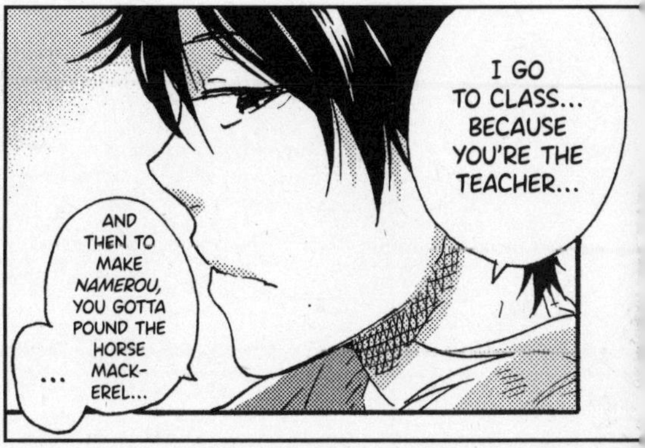
I GO TO CLASS... BECAUSE YOU'RE THE TEACHER...
AND THEN TO MAKE *NAMEROU*, YOU GOTTA POUND THE HORSE MACKEREL...
...

Starting on the following page is a story I wrote for *Yuri Hime* about Matsuzawa-san and Hasekura-san's older sister, Ayaka. it started as a doodle and boy was I surprised when it turned into an actual manga...

Thankfully, a lot of people requested this get put into a *tankobon*, so it was added into this volume.

Feel free to read it if you would like to!

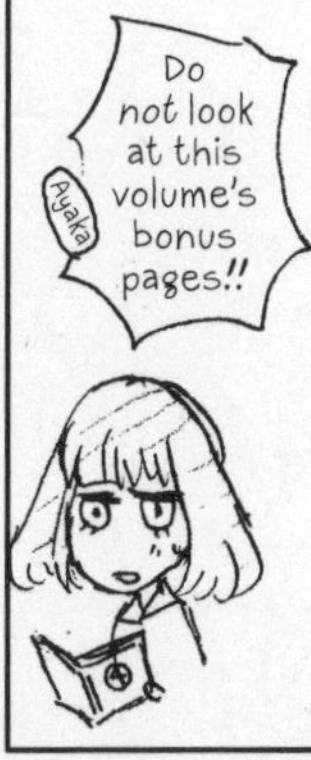
Do not look at this volume's bonus pages!!
Ayaka

***Yuri Hime*, page 138**
Comic Yuri Hime is a monthly magazine for yur manga (such as *Yuri Is My Job!* and *If I Could Reach You*) which is published by the same publisher as *gateau* magazine.

***anten,* page 157**

traditional Japanese short winter coat.

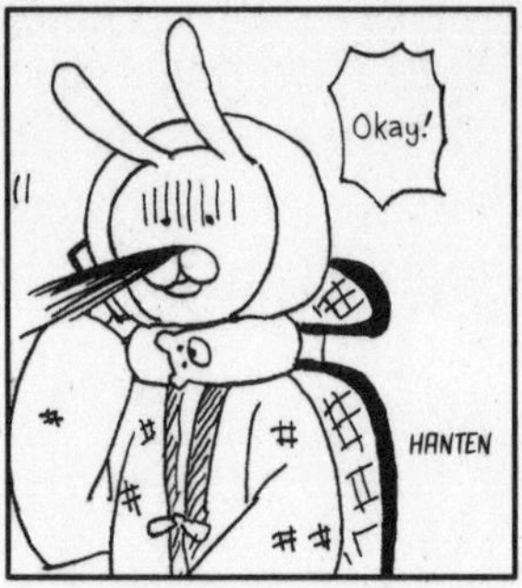
Okay!
HANTEN

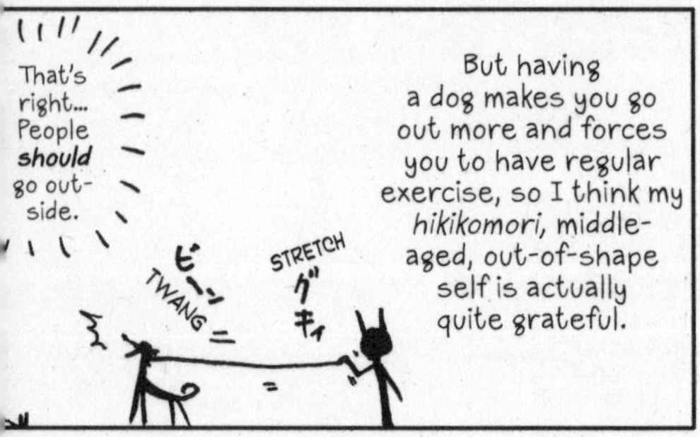
But having a dog makes you go out more and forces you to have regular exercise, so I think my *hikikomori,* middle-aged, out-of-shape self is actually quite grateful.
STRETCH
TWANG
That's right... People ***should*** go out-side.

***Hikikomori,* page 159**

Adolescents and adults who mostly stay alone indoors and don't go outside to socialize much with the outside world, often to extreme degrees.

***abe-don,* page 160**

abe-don refers to the action of slapping the wall hard enough to produce "don" sound. It's often used in romance situations to drive a romantic nterest against the wall and get close enough to whisper in their ear.

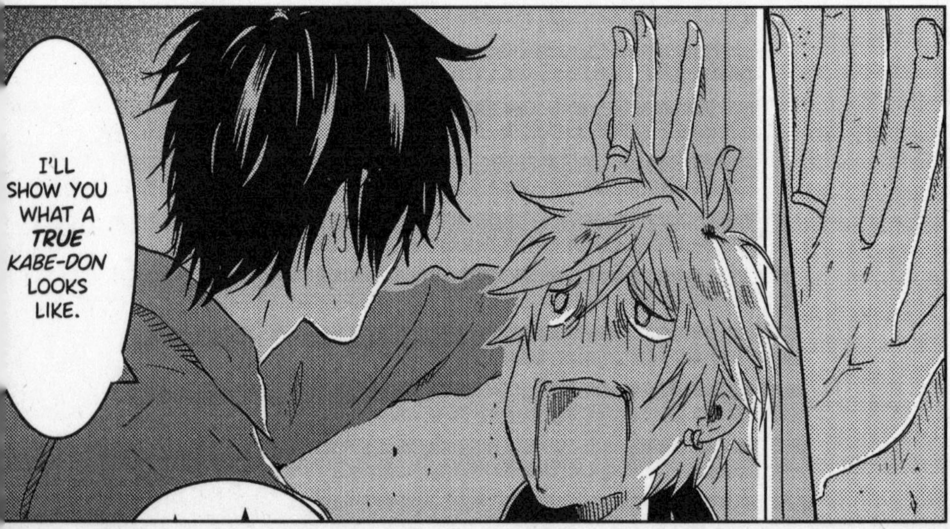
I'LL SHOW YOU WHAT A ***TRUE*** ***KABE-DON*** LOOKS LIKE.

Hitorijime
My Hero

The slow-burn queer romance that'll sweep you off your feet!

10 DANCE

Inouesatoh presents

Shinya Sugiki, the dashing lord of Standard Ballroom, and Shinya Suzuki, passionate king of Latin Dance: The two share more than just a first name and a love of the sport. They each want to become champion of the 10-Dance Competition, which means they'll need to learn the other's specialty dances, and who better to learn from than the best? But old rivalries die hard, and things get further complicated when they realize there might be more between them than an uneasy partnership...

KC
KODANSHA
COMICS

JOIN US FOR AFTERNOON TEA WITH EQUAL PARTS YURI, ROM-COM, AND DRAMA!

Yuri Is My Job!

miman

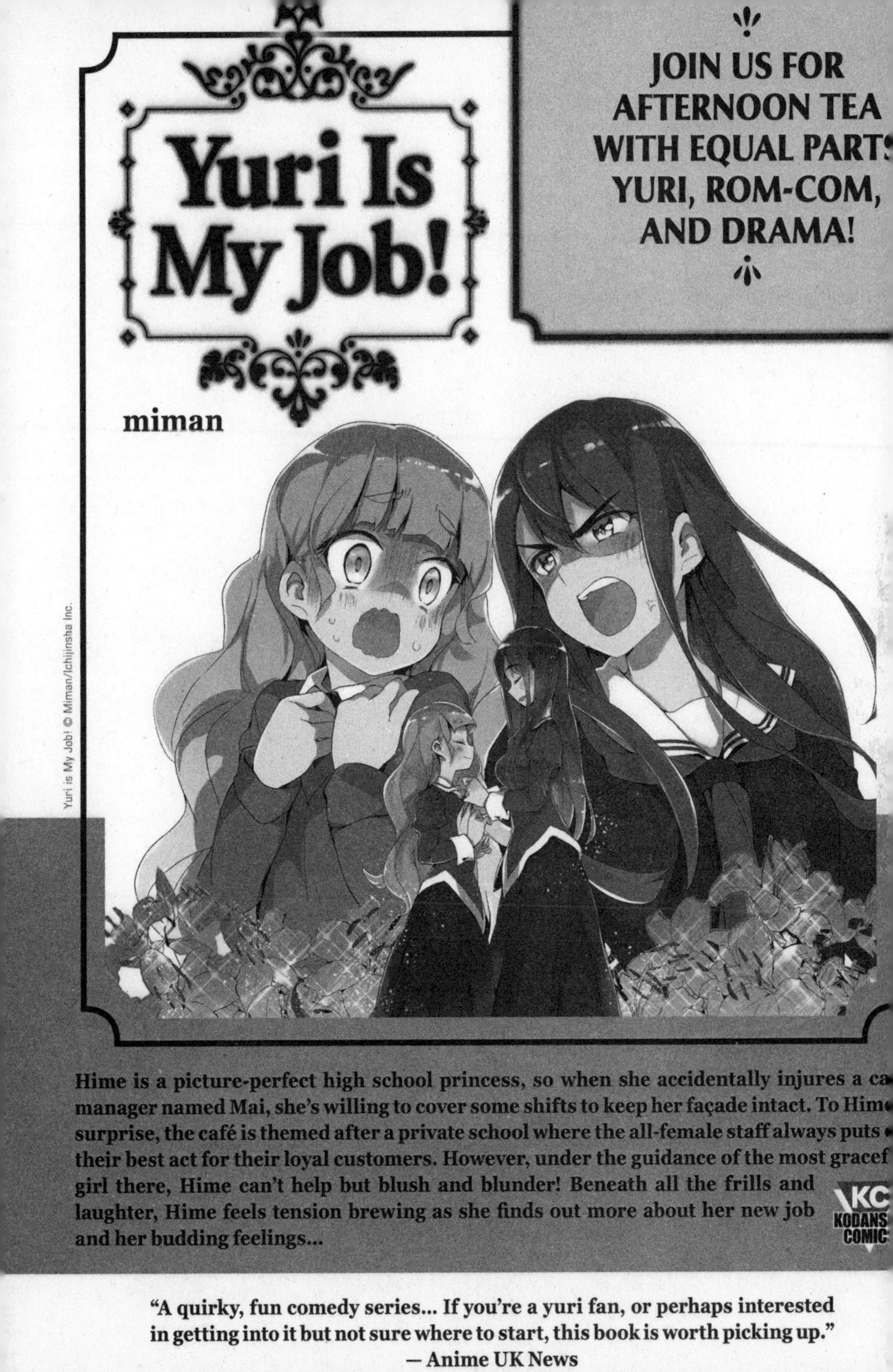

Hime is a picture-perfect high school princess, so when she accidentally injures a ca manager named Mai, she's willing to cover some shifts to keep her façade intact. To Hime surprise, the café is themed after a private school where the all-female staff always puts their best act for their loyal customers. However, under the guidance of the most gracef girl there, Hime can't help but blush and blunder! Beneath all the frills and laughter, Hime feels tension brewing as she finds out more about her new job and her budding feelings...

KC KODANS COMIC

"A quirky, fun comedy series... If you're a yuri fan, or perhaps interested in getting into it but not sure where to start, this book is worth picking up."
— Anime UK News

Acclaimed screenwriter and director Mari Okada (*Maquia*, *anohana*) teams up with manga artist Nao Emoto (*Forget Me Not*) in this moving, funny, so-true-it's-embarrassing coming-of-age series!

When Kazusa enters high school, she joins the Literature Club, and leaps from reading innocent fiction to diving into the literary classics. But these novels are a bit more...*adult* than she was prepared for. Between euphemisms like fresh dewy grass and pork stew, crushing on the boy next door, and knowing you want to do that *one thing* before you die—discovering your budding sexuality is no easy feat! As if puberty wasn't awkward enough, the club consists of a brooding writer, the prettiest girl in school, an agreeable comrade, and an outspoken prude. Fumbling over their own discomforts, these five teens get thrown into chaos over three little letters: S...E...X...!

Anime coming soon!

O Maidens in your Savage Season

Mari Okada   Nao Emoto

KC KODANSHA COMICS

Anime now streaming on Amazon Prime!

The prestigious Dahlia Academy educates the elite of society from two countries; To the East is the Nation of Touwa; across the sea the other way, the Principality of West. The nations, though, are fierce rivals, and their students are constantly feuding—which means Romio Inuzuka, head of Touwa's first-year students, has a problem. He's fallen for his counterpart from West, Juliet Persia, and when he can't take it any more, he confesses his feelings.

Now Romio has two problems: A girlfriend, and a secret…

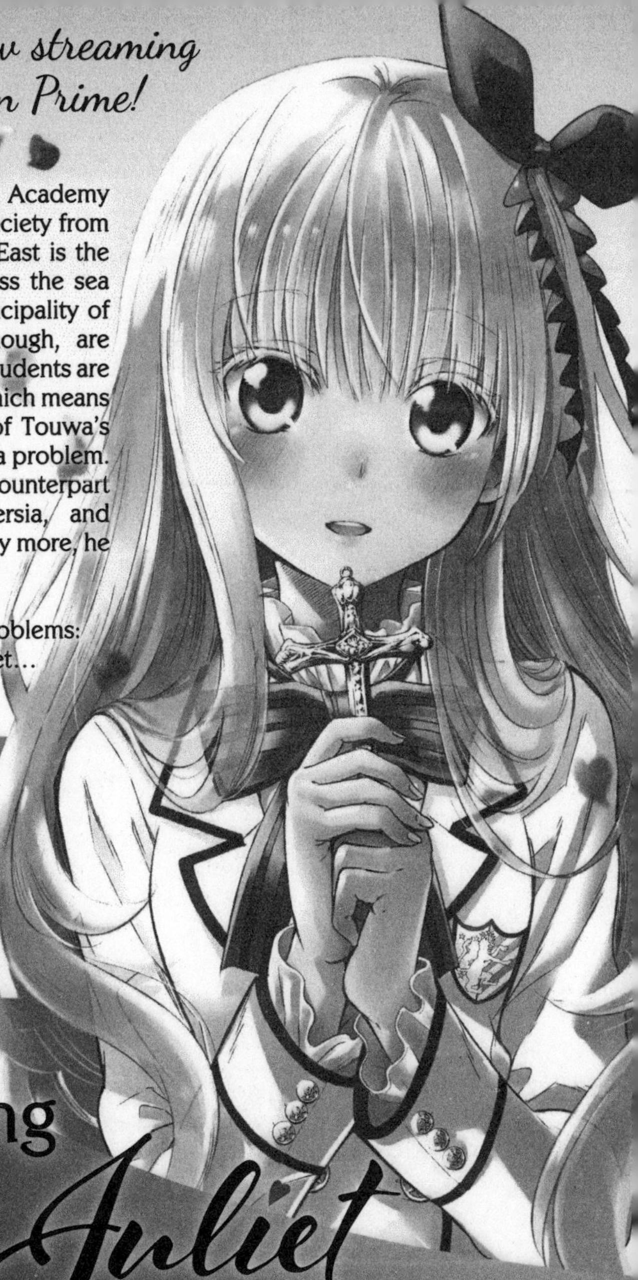

Boarding School Juliet

By Yousuke Kaneda

"A fine romantic comedy... The chemistry betwe the two main characters is excellent and the hum is great, backed up by a fun enough supporting c and a different twist on the genre." –AiPT

KC KODANSHA COMICS

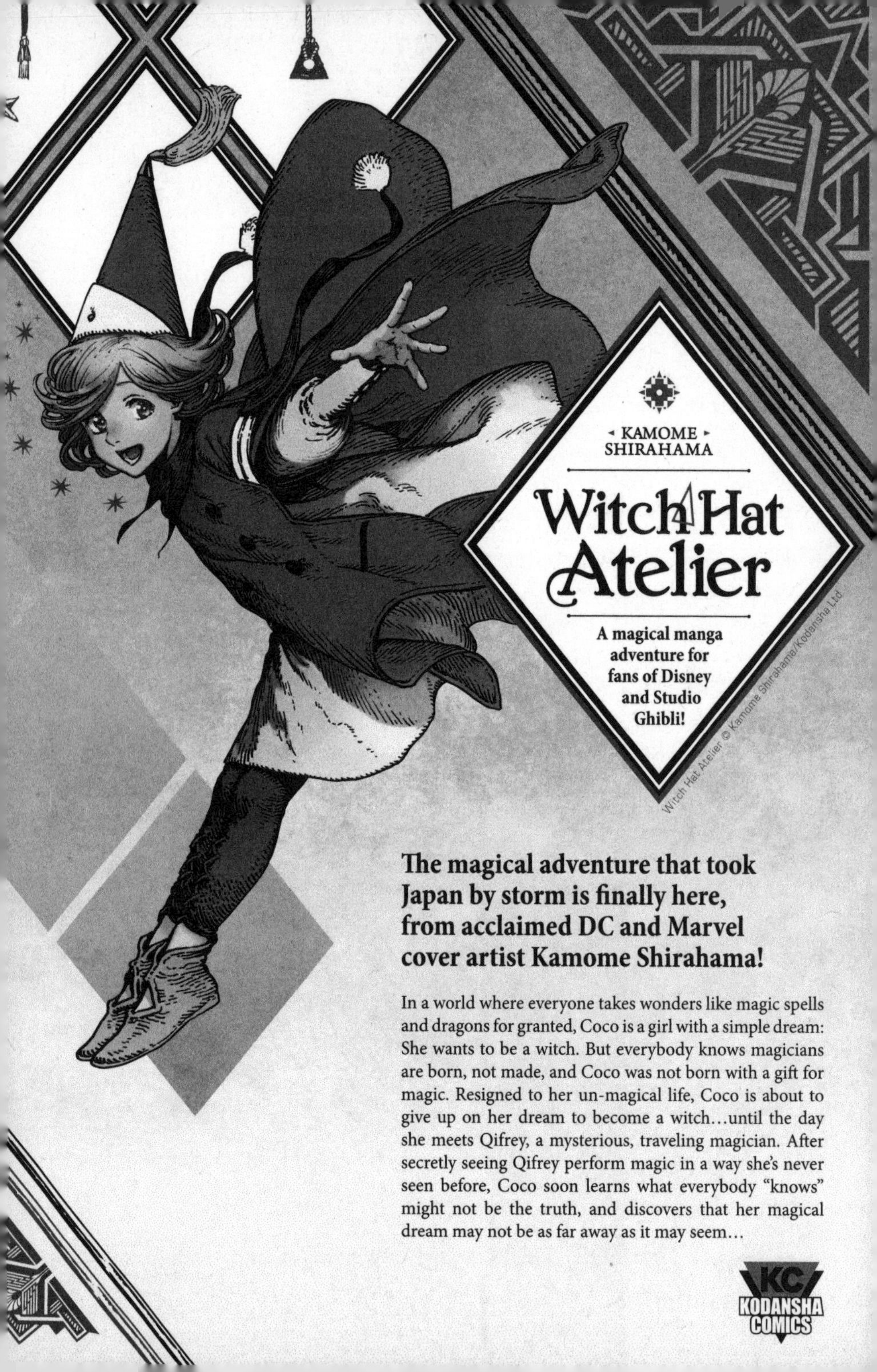
KAMOME SHIRAHAMA
Witch Hat Atelier
A magical manga adventure for fans of Disney and Studio Ghibli!
Witch Hat Atelier © Kamome Shirahama/Kodansha Ltd.

Magus of the Library

Mitsu Izumi

MITSU IZUMI'S STUNNING ARTWORK BRINGS A FANTASTICA LITERARY ADVENTURE TO LUSH, THRILLING LIFE!

Young Theo adores books, but prejudice and hatred of his vill keeps them ever out of his rea Then one day, he chances to m Sedona, a traveling librarian w works for the great library of Aftzaak, City of Books, and his life changes forever...

Futaro Uesugi is a second-year in high school, scraping to get by and pay off his family's debt. The only thing he can do is study, so when Futaro receives a part-time job offer to tutor the five daughters of a wealthy businessman, he can't pass it up. Little does he know, these five beautiful sisters are quintuplets, but the only thing they have in common...is that they're all terrible at studying!

THE QUINTESSENTIAL QUINTUPLETS

negi haruba

ANIME
JT NOW!

KC/
KODANSHA
COMICS

Hitorijime My Hero volume 4 is a work of fiction. Names, characters, places, and incidents are the products of the author's imagination or are used fictitiously. Any resemblance to actual events, locales, or persons, living or dead, is entirely coincidental.

A Kodansha Comics Trade Paperback Original.

Published in the United States by Kodansha Comics, an imprint of Kodansha USA Publishing, LLC, New York.

Publication rights for this English edition arranged through Kodansha Ltd., Tokyo.

First published in Japan in 2015 by Ichijinsha Inc., Tokyo.

ISBN 978-1-63236-795-2

Printed in the United States of America.

www.kodanshacomics.com

9 8 7 6 5 4 3 2 1

Translation: Julie Goniwich
Lettering: Michael Martin
Editing: Haruko Hashimoto
Kodansha Comics Edition Cover Design: Phil Balsman